Investment
Analysis

Investment
Analysis

Edward E. Williams
Vice President/Economist
Service Corporation International

M. Chapman Findlay III
Visiting Associate Professor of Finance
University of Southern California

Prentice-Hall, Inc., Englewood Cliffs, N.J.

Library of Congress Cataloging in Publication Data

Williams, Edward E.
    Investment analysis.

    Includes bibliographies.
        1. Investments.   2. Securities.   3. Corporations —
Valuation.   I. Findlay, M. Chapman, joint author.
II. Title.
HG4521.W478   332.6   73-8815
ISBN   0-13-502633-4

© 1974, by PRENTICE-HALL, INC.,
ENGLEWOOD CLIFFS, N.J.

10 9 8 7 6 5 4 3 2

Printed in the United States of America

Prentice-Hall International, Inc., *London*
Prentice-Hall of Australia, Pty., Ltd., *Sydney*
Prentice-Hall of Canada, Ltd., *Toronto*
Prentice-Hall of India Private Ltd., *New Delhi*
Prentice-Hall of Japan, Inc., *Tokyo*

To our parents

Contents

Preface

Investment Analysis is written to provide a comprehensive treatment of the important aspects of security analysis and portfolio theory. Students and practitioners will find that the volume contains a clearly detailed explanation of many recent developments in portfolio and capital market theory as well as a thorough procedural discussion of security analysis. Professionals preparing for the C.F.A. examinations will benefit from a close scrutiny of the many problems following each chapter. Of course, a mastery of the knowledge presented in the pages to follow is no guarantee of achieving a C.F.A. designation.

The explication progresses from reasonably simple institutional description to somewhat more complicated analytical material. This book should be comprehensible even to the financially uninitiated, but it will prove most beneficial to readers with some financial background, either academic or professional. It is constructed so that the more difficult material is presented in chapter appendices and footnotes, which may be ignored without any loss of continuity. The level of difficulty progresses with more advanced treatment appearing in the latter sections of each chapter, the final chapters of each part, and the last parts of the volume.

Concise English prose is the major vehicle for communicating, and only simple algebra is used in the main body of the text. An understanding of financial mathematics (compound interest, present values, and so on) and statistics is assumed, although two lengthy appendices are provided at the end of the book for those weak in these subjects. Readers lacking any mathematical or statistical background should begin with Appendix A (Financial Mathematics) and Appendix B (Financial Statistics).

The volume is divided into four distinct chapter groupings. Part I (The Investment Environment) considers the scope of investment management, financial information sources, the organized securities markets, and the instruments of the money and capital markets. These chapters summarize the basic institutional framework with which every investor must be familiar and are roughly similar to the treatments provided in the traditional books of a bygone era. Part I also contains a somewhat more rigorous (although not difficult) chapter on the macroeconomic influences on the money and capital markets. This chapter should prove to be unique even for a modern investments book. The analysis is not confined to vague generalities about the exogenous variables that affect security prices, but rather explores the financial aspects of the simplified Keynesian system. Chapter Four concludes this part with an appendix on the term structure of interest rates that will be useful to the seasoned reader.

Part II (Security Analysis) develops, in a workman-like fashion, analytical procedures for appraising securities. Chapter Five begins the process of evaluation with classical ratio analysis and complements the material that follows in Chapter Six (Forecasting Techniques). These two chapters provide the essential tools used later in the book. The specific appraisal of fixed income securities is demonstrated in Chapters Seven and Eight, while a comprehensive scheme for analyzing equities is constructed in Chapters Nine through Twelve. Convertible securities are considered in Chapter Thirteen by combining the fixed income and equity appraisal techniques. The particular characteristics of speculative securities (warrants, rights, and options) are detailed in Chapter Fourteen.

Part III (Portfolio Analysis) describes the process of optimal security selection using the input data generated in Part II. Initially, the unique risk-bearing characteristics of the investor are assessed (Chapter Fifteen). Then, the elements of portfolio theory are constructed in a Markowitz-Sharpe framework (Chapter Sixteen). These constructs are extended into capital market theory (Chapter Seventeen), and more advanced topics in portfolio management (Chapter Eighteen). The material in Part III is considerably more advanced (and theoretical) than that appearing in Parts I and II.

Finally, in Part IV, capital market efficiency is assessed. The efficient capital markets hypothesis is examined (Chapter Nineteen), and conclusions are drawn about real world portfolio management in a constrained environment that is not in equilibrium (Chapter Twenty). This final part is an area where some authorities will dispute the views of the authors. Strong capital market efficiency proponents will disagree with several of the positions taken, but these chapters (Nineteen and Twenty) may be ignored without damaging the preceding analysis. Those who agree with the authors will (hopefully) find their opinions a refreshing statement of the traditional view of investment analysis.

The authors are indebted to a number of people for their help in the preparation of the volume. Professors Michael Keenan (N.Y.U.), Richard McEnally (Univ. of Texas at Austin), Ronald Melicher (Univ. of Colorado), Jack

Clark Francis (Univ. of Pennsylvania), Steven Bolten (Univ. of Houston), Frederick Amling (Geo. Wash. U.), and David West (Univ. of Missouri) read the entire manuscript and made numerous helpful comments. Mr. Devendra Chopra tended to the onerous chore of solving many of the problems that appear in the text and solutions manual. Miss Hilda Gossack, our secretary, typed and proofed the manuscript several times with her usual efficiency. Finally, a special note of appreciation is expressed to Professors James Longstreet, who was the first mentor to half of the authorship, and James C. Dolley who provided us both with many of the skills and much of the philosophy found in these pages.

Montreal   EDWARD E. WILLIAMS

December, 1973   M. CHAPMAM FINDLAY III

Investment
Analysis

I

The Investment
Environment

1

The Scope of Investment Management

THE OBJECTIVES OF INVESTMENT MANAGEMENT

Every individual who has more money than he needs for current consumption is potentially an investor. Whether he places his surplus funds in the bank at a guaranteed rate of interest or speculates by purchasing raw land near a growing metropolis, he has made an investment decision. These decisions may be made wisely or foolishly, but the intelligent investor will seek a rational, consistent approach to managing his money. The best method for many is simply to turn their funds over to someone else for management. A significant number of investors do indeed follow this policy, and it is quite likely the correct decision for them. Others, however, manage their own money or even become professionals who manage other people's funds. The latter groups are the audience for whom this book was written.

In the discussion that follows, we shall not unveil any mysteries about getting rich quickly. Indeed, if such secrets existed, it is doubtful that the authors would be willing to reveal them (nor would they need the income derived from book royalties). Nevertheless, there are systematic procedures for making investment decisions that can enable the rational investor to maximize his economic position given whatever constraints he wishes to impose. Economic position is tacitly assumed to be the primary goal of the investor, although there may well be those who have other central goals. The purchaser of an art collection, for example, may be more interested in the aesthetic aspects of his investment than the money he will make on it. There is nothing irrational about this, and it is not difficult to construct optimal decision models for such an individual. Similarly, another person may be strongly concerned about pollution, or about race relations in South Africa. Such a person may refuse to buy shares in companies that pollute or that do business in segregated countries. Again, this can be perfectly reasonable behavior, but these investors should at least be aware of the opportunity costs of their decisions. That is, they should realize that such an investment policy may have economic costs. The polluter may be a very profitable company whose stock could produce exceptional returns for its holders.

Maximizing economic position cannot usually be taken as the only objective of the investor. There is some correlation between the returns one expects from an investment and the amount of risk that must be borne. Thus, decisions must be made that reflect the ability and desire of the individual to assume risk. In the final portions of this volume, we shall be very specific in both theoretical and practical terms about risk bearing and the optimal portfolio for the investor.

PREREQUISITES FOR INVESTMENT
DECISION MAKERS

Although intelligence is about the only important requisite for any kind of decision making, there are other traits that may be helpful to the money manager. In particular, a certain amount of scientific curiosity may be very important to successful investors. By scientific curiosity we do not mean knowledge or even interest in disciplines generally considered "science," such as biology or chemistry, although the scientifically trained analyst may have an advantage in scrutinizing the stocks of high-technology companies. Rather, scientific curiosity refers to the systematic pursuit of understanding. An investor should be willing to take the time and spend the energy to know himself and his environment. It is unfortunately true that many otherwise successful people make poor investors simply because they do not have a logical investment policy. They have only vague objectives about what they want (such as "capital appreciation" or "safety of principal"), and they often substitute general impressions for solid fact gathering. How many highly competent doctors, for example, go beyond the recommendations of their brokers (friends, relatives, or patients) when selecting a security? How many businessmen take the time to familiarize themselves with the income statements and balance sheets of the firms in which they hold stock? How many portfolio managers make purchases based on a well-researched, documented effort to uncover those securities that others have passed over? Even in the case of portfolio managers, the number is surprisingly small. Of course, it could be reasoned that the doctor may not have the time or knowledge to make a thorough investigation of his investments and that the businessman is too occupied with his own company to do a systematic search for information. If this is the case, then both doctor and businessman should seek expert counsel. To do otherwise would prove foolish and, eventually, costly. The professional manager who bases his decisions on what the boys at Oscar's[1] are saying or what he "feels" the market will do is being negligent. Although knowledge of what other managers are doing is important and an experienced man's market "feel" may be superior to any professor's theoretical model, too often even the professional tends to substitute rumor and hunch for sound analysis and thorough investigation.

In addition to intelligence and scientific curiosity, the modern money manager needs to be reasonably versed in mathematics and statistics. High school algebra supplemented by an elementary knowledge of probability (also now taught in high school) is sufficient. In this book, we provide two appendices for review by those who are somewhat hazy on these subjects. Appendix A discusses financial mathematics, compound interest, present values, and yield calculations. Appendix B examines financial statistics, basic probability theory, variance analysis, and correlation. These appendices are not intended as introductory expositions to the investor who has never heard of compound interest or a standard deviation, but they should serve as an adequate review and handy reference for those who have a basic knowledge of mathematics and statistics. For the reader who is totally unfamiliar with these subjects, this book will be somewhat less useful.

INVESTMENTS MEDIA AND THE ENVIRONMENT

There are any number of investment possibilities that the money manager may consider. The simplest is the insured commercial bank or savings and loan account. These media provide safety of principal, liquidity, and yields that are not unattractive by historical standards. Nevertheless, the savings account requires no analysis as an investment vehicle, and any discussion of it must perforce be brief. There is a place for the savings account in the portfolio of most investors, however, and the role of liquidity in investment strategy will be a focal point in the portfolio chapters of this book.

At the other end of the investments spectrum are such highly illiquid assets as real estate, oil well interests, paintings, coins, stamps, antiques, and even ownership of business enterprises. These investments require a very specialized analysis, and anyone who is contemplating the purchase of such assets should be

---

[1]For the uninitiated, Oscar's is a restaurant (and bar) off Wall Street that is heavily patronized by the investment "crowd."

even more careful than the investor in securities. The unique nature of the aforementioned investment possibilities precludes them from extensive discussion in this book, although many of the techniques that are described in the pages that follow could be equally well applied to these investments.

In between the savings account and the illiquid assets mentioned above are a host of investments that can generally be described as securities. A *security* is an instrument signifying either ownership or indebtedness that is negotiable and that may or may not be marketable. Securities are by far the most popular form of semiliquid investment (that is, investment that is marketable but that may not be salable near the price at which the asset was purchased), and they can be analyzed in a systematic, consistent fashion. For this reason, the focus of this volume will be on securities.

It was mentioned before that the investor should be well aware of the investment environment before he makes a decision. The environment for securities includes such important variables as the general state of the economy, the expected risk and return levels from purchasing a specific security, and the economic position of the investor. It also includes the more specific aspects of securities regulations, financial information flows, the securities markets, and general measures of security price performance (such as the Dow Jones averages). There are entire books devoted to each of these topics, and we will not purport to examine any of them in much detail. Nevertheless, the more important elements of these subjects will be discussed in Chapter 2 of this book.

CAN YOU MAKE MONEY IN THE STOCK MARKET?

Of all the forms of securities (which we shall outline and discuss in Chapter 3), common stocks are the most romantic. Although the bond markets are more important to both issuing corporations and many investors (pension fund money, life insurance reserves, bank portfolio funds, and so on are far more heavily invested in bonds than equities), it is the stock market that engenders the interest of most investors. This is undoubtedly true because the rewards (and penalties) of stock market investment well exceed those obtainable in the bond market.[2] Furthermore, equity analysis is more complicated than bond appraisal, and greater skill is required in selecting common stocks than fixed income securities. This is not to say that bond analysis is simple or even uninteresting. Indeed, some of the most sophisticated minds in the investments business are engaged in the bond market. We shall devote two chapters of this book to bond analysis, and the reader will be convinced that bonds have their own rewards

[2]Speculators can make even the stodgy government bond market exciting, however, because of the low margin required for bond purchases. On 10 percent margin, a speculator can double (or lose) his money from a small change in the price of a bond (see Chapter 2).

(and difficulties). Nevertheless, few people spend their lunch hours talking about the bond market (except bond men), and the future performance of a bond rarely comes up in bridge table or golf course discussions. It is common stocks that entice most investors, and some investors have been known to feel a greater empathy for their stocks than their wives (or husbands). Thus, common stocks will correctly occupy a significant portion of our discussion.

There is a school of thought that maintains that only insiders and those privileged to have information not known to the rest of us can make large profits in the stock market. These people subscribe to a theory of stock prices called the *efficient market hypothesis* (EMH). EMH believers argue that the current price of a stock contains all available information possessed by investors and only new information can change equity returns. Because new information becomes available randomly, there should be no reason to expect any systematic movements in stock returns. Advocates of the strong form of the EMH feel that the stock market is perfectly efficient and the cost of research and investigation would not be justified by any "bargains" (that is, undervalued stocks) found. The efficient market hypothesis has been tested by a number of scholars.[3] These researchers have considered various hypotheses about the behavior of the stock market, from notions that past stock prices can be used to forecast future prices (the belief held by stock market chartists or "technicians") to reasoned opinions that there are stocks that are undervalued by the market and that these stocks can be uncovered by a thorough investigation of such fundamental variables as reported earnings, sales, price-earnings multiples, and other pieces of economic or accounting data. The latter view of the market has long been held by most investors, and the whole profession of security analysis depends upon it. From the early days of the first edition of Graham and Dodd (1934)[4] down to the present, analysts have been taught that there are overpriced stocks and underpriced stocks and it is the job of the analyst to determine which are which. The EMH advocates have found, however, that the presence of so many individuals trying to find bargains (and overpriced stocks to sell short) makes it impossible for any one of them to outperform the general market consistently. Thus, as the economy grows and earnings increase, it is possible to make money in the stock market, but it is impossible to expect more than "average" returns. This is true because there are many buyers and many sellers in the market who have a great deal of similar information about stocks. If any one stock were "worth" more than the price for which it was currently selling, sharp analysts would recommend buying until its price rose to the point at which it was no longer a bargain. Similarly, if a stock were selling for more than its intrinsic

[3]A summary of the findings of many EMH researchers is found in E. F. Fama, "Efficient Capital Markets: A Review of Theory and Empirical Work," *Journal of Finance,* May 1970, pp. 383–417. A more rigorous treatment of efficient market theory is presented in Chapter 19 of this text.

[4]B. Graham and D. Dodd. *Security Analysis,* 1st ed. (New York: McGraw-Hill, 1934).

value, analysts would recommend selling. The price of the security would fall until it was no longer overpriced.

The efficient market hypothesis has gained great currency in many quarters, particularly among academic economists. Nevertheless, it has not convinced too many practitioners. This may be for two reasons. In the first place, if the EMH were believed, it would be hard for professionals to justify the salaries that they are paid to find better-than-average performers. Second, many analysts have suggested that their very presence is required for the EMH to work. If they could not find undervalued stocks, they would not come to their desks each day; and if they did not appear, there would no longer be that vast army of competitors to make the stock market efficient and competitive! Moreover, many analysts point out that there are substantial differences of opinion over the same information. Thus, although every investor has available to him similar information, some see favorable signs where others see unfavorable ones. Furthermore, various analysts can do different things with the same data. Some may be able to forecast future earnings, for example, far more accurately than others simply because they employ a better analytical and more systematic approach. It is these differences of opinion and analytical abilities that make a horse race, and most practitioners believe that this is what the market is all about.

THE STOCK MARKET AS A SPECULATIVE INSTITUTION

The efficient-market school is matched by an equally vociferous group that maintains that the stock market is neither competitive nor efficient. These individuals see the market historically as an expression of the whim and fancy of the select few, a large gambling casino for the rich, so to speak. It has been observed that securities speculation in the past has been far from scientific and that emotion rather than reason has usually guided the path of stock prices. Inefficiency proponents believe that people are governed principally by their emotions and that bull and bear markets are merely reflections of the optimism or pessimism of the day. Most of us have been tempted by the thought that economics plays an unfortunately slight role in the market and that investor psychology may in fact be more important.

There is good historical reason for one to feel that people are anything but rational when it comes to investing. Charles Mackay, in his *Memoirs of Extraordinary Popular Delusions and the Madness of Crowds,* points out:

> In reading the history of nations, we find that, like individuals, they have their whims and their peculiarities; their seasons of excitement and recklessness, when they care not what they do. We find that whole

communities suddenly fix their minds upon one object, and go mad in its pursuit; that millions of people become simultaneously impressed with one delusion, and run after it, till their attention is caught by some new folly more captivating than the first. We see one nation suddenly seized, from its highest to its lowest members, with a fierce desire of military glory; another as suddenly becoming crazed upon a religious scruple; and neither of them recovering its senses until it has shed rivers of blood and sowed a harvest of groans and tears, to be reaped by its posterity . . . . Money, again, has often been a cause of the delusion of multitudes. Sober nations have all at once become desperate gamblers, and risked almost their existence upon the turn of a piece of paper.[5]

Mackay's fascinating story details some of the most unbelievable financial events in history:[6] (1) John Law's Mississippi scheme, which sold shares, to the French public, in a company that was to have a monopoly of trade in the province of Louisiana. Mississippi shares were eagerly bought up by French investors who knew that this "growth stock" could not help but make them rich. After all, it was common knowledge that Louisiana abounded in precious metals.[7] (2) The South-Sea Bubble, which induced Englishmen to speculate on a trading monopoly in an area (the South Atlantic) owned by a foreign power (Spain) that had no intention of allowing the English into the area for free trading purposes. The fevers produced by the South-Sea spilled over into other "bubbles," one of which proposed to build cannons capable of discharging square and round cannon balls ("guaranteed to revolutionize the art of war") and another that sought share subscribers to "a company for carrying on an undertaking of great advantage, but nobody to know what it is."[8] (3) The Tulipomania, which engulfed seventeenth-century Holland. Fortunes were made (and later lost) on the belief that every rich man would wish to possess a fine tulip garden (and many did, for a while at least). Tulip bulb prices reached astronomical levels, as one speculator bought bulbs to sell at higher prices to a second speculator who purchased to sell at even higher prices to yet another speculator.

As Mackay was writing, Jay Gould and Jim Fisk were busily manipulating the value of the shares of the Erie Railroad in the United States.[9] It was common practice for directors in many companies to issue information causing the price of their firm's stock to rise. They then sold their shares at inflated prices to the unsuspecting public. Some months later, they would release discouraging information about the company's prospects, in the meanwhile selling short the

---

[5]*Memoirs of Extraordinary Popular Delusions and the Madness of Crowds* (London: George Routledge and Sons, 1869), pp. vii–viii.

[6]*Ibid.*, pp. 1–92.

[7]They were correct in the long run. Two hundred fifty years later Louisiana was one of the oil centers of the world!

[8]*Ibid.*, p. 53.

[9]See C. F. Adams and Henry Adams, *Chapters of Erie* (Ithaca: Great Seal Books, 1956).

shares of their company.[10] When the new information drove the price of the shares down, the directors would cover their short positions, again reaping nice profits at the expense of the unaware.

The decade of the 1920s in the United States was characterized by a mythical optimism that has few parallels in history. It was an era when everybody believed that the life style of a J. P. Morgan or a Harvey Firestone could be within his reach. As Frederick Lewis Allen has pointed out in his wonderfully nostalgic yet penetrating *Only Yesterday,* it was a time when "the abounding confidence engendered by Coolidge Prosperity . . . persuaded the four-thousand-dollar-a-year salesman that in some magical way he too might tomorrow be able to buy a fine house and all the good things of earth."[11] The binge started in 1924 with the Florida land boom (where "investors" paid large sums of money for plots that turned out in many cases to be undeveloped swampland) and ended in October 1929, with the stock market crash.[12] It was against the background of these excesses, and the Great Depression that they produced, that John Maynard Keynes wrote *The General Theory.*

Keynes believed that much of man's social activities (including the stock market) were better explained by disciplines other than economics. He felt that "animal spirits" exercised greater influence on many economic decisions than the "invisible hand." His reasoning was based partly on a very acute understanding of human nature. It also depended on Keynes' lack of faith in the credibility of many of the inputs that go into economic decision making. He argued, ". . . our existing knowledge does not provide a sufficient basis for a calculated mathematical expectation. In point of fact, all sorts of considerations enter into the market valuation which are in no way relevant to the prospective yield."[13] He would thus condemn many of the procedures to be outlined in the following pages of this book on the grounds that ". . . the assumption of arithmetically equal probabilities based on a state of ignorance leads to absurdities."[14]

To Keynes, the market was a battle of wits more like a game of Snap, Old Maid, or Musical Chairs than a serious means of resource allocation. One of his favorite metaphors was to compare the "game" to the newspaper competitions in which contestants try to pick the prettiest faces, a prize being given to the person who comes closest to choosing the girls most often selected by the other competitors. In this instance, each competitor is not really interested in selecting the prettiest girls. He is, rather, trying to assess which girls *everyone else* will

[10]*Short selling* is discussed in Chapter 2.

[11]*Only Yesterday* (New York: Harper & Row, 1964), p. 227.

[12]See John Kenneth Galbraith, *The Great Crash* (Boston: Houghton-Mifflin Co., 1954), for an exciting discussion of the events that led up to the crash and the depression that followed.

[13]J. M. Keynes, *The General Theory of Employment, Interest, and Money* (New York: Harcourt, Brace, and World, 1936), p. 152.

[14]*Ibid.,* p. 152.

think are the prettiest. In the stock exchange, pretty girls are replaced by equities that one speculator believes will appeal to other speculators. Thus,

> A conventional valuation which is established as the outcome of the mass psychology of a large number of ignorant individuals is liable to change violently as the result of a sudden fluctuation of opinion due to factors which do not really make much difference to the prospective yield; since there will be no strong roots of conviction to hold it steady.[15]

Many modern-day practitioners agree with Keynes' arguments. They feel that the lessons of history reveal economic analysis to be a bankrupt approach to making an investment decision. It is suggested that esoteric discussions of whether or not the stock market is efficient are meaningless because whim and fancy are more important than yield calculations in setting the prices of securities. Stock prices move up or down depending on the mood of the public. Frenzy and unbridled optimism make for bull markets, and gloom and severe pessimism produce bear markets. The states of optimism and pessimism often have little basis in economic fact.

A restatement of Keynes' view was recently made in a book that was religiously read by nearly every Wall Street participant. This volume goes so far as to call Keynes the "Master" and credits him with insights that are still quite applicable. George Goodman, in his pseudonymously written *The Money Game,* pokes a bit of fun at his own profession and suggests that we have not really come terribly far in making the investments business a rational activity.[16] A sequel to this volume, entitled *Supermoney,* argues that the 1970 bust resulted from eager traders trying to find the new Xeroxes and Polaroids.[17] Unfortunately, they all too often found National Student Marketing and Four Seasons Nursing Homes (which subsequently collapsed). The mistakes were not only made by foolish individuals trying to get rich quickly; many of the more prestigious American financial institutions participated in running the prices of these securities to totally unrealistic levels.

Although much of what has been said above would seem to possess a great deal of merit, the reader would be ill-advised to throw his hands up in despair at the impossibility of making rational investment choices. We believe that he still can learn more about investments from an analytical study of the subject than he would if he became a psychologist or metaphysician. The very presence of Keynes and others like him has forced a reexamination of many of the assumptions underlying the investment process. Keynes' contribution in aggregate economic policy has led to a far less volatile business cycle than in the past, and this has made it easier for those who do attempt to make superior long-run forecasts to at least influence (if not govern) the market. The advent of the

[15]*Ibid.,* p. 154.
[16] "Adam Smith," *The Money Game* (New York: Random House, 1967).
[17] "Adam Smith," *Supermoney* (New York: Random House, 1972).

computer has made it less difficult for analysts to engage themselves in the task of interpreting large quantities of data. Although it is doubtful that we have entered the world of perfectly efficient capital markets, it is likely that the very chaotic world that Keynes described has passed. In some respects, we live in ideal times for the modern, well-versed analyst. Markets are not so perfect that all opportunities for better-than-average returns are eliminated, and they are not so imperfect as to render impossible the task of making rational choices.

REFERENCES

Adams, C. F., and Henry Adams, *Chapters of Erie.* Ithaca: Great Seal Books, 1956.

Allen, F. L., *Only Yesterday.* New York: Harper & Row, 1964.

Cootner, P. H., ed., *The Random Character of Stock Market Prices.* Cambridge: The M.I.T. Press, 1964.

Fama, E. F., "Efficient Capital Markets: A Review of Theory and Empirical Work," *Journal of Finance* (May 1970), pp. 383–423.

———, "Random Walks in Stock Market Prices," *Financial Analysts Journal* (Sept.–Oct. 1965), pp. 55–59.

Galbraith, J. K., *The Great Crash.* Boston: Houghton-Mifflin Co., 1954.

Graham, B., and D. Dodd, *Security Analysis,* 1st ed. New York: McGraw-Hill, 1934.

Keynes, J. M., *The General Theory of Employment, Interest, and Money.* New York: Harcourt, Brace, and World, 1936.

Mackay, Charles, *Memoirs of Extraordinary Popular Delusions and the Madness of Crowds.* London: George Routledge and Sons, 1869.

"Smith, Adam," *The Money Game.* New York: Random House, 1967.

———, *Supermoney.* New York: Random House, 1972.

2

Financial Information, Securities Markets, and Market Indicators

FINANCIAL INFORMATION

A fundamental postulation of the efficient market hypothesis is that investors (except insiders) have similar information with which to work. Indeed, the entire foundation of the EMH is based upon the presumption that all data have been digested by the market and that the current price of a security reflects all available information. Opponents of the EMH believe that information is not perfectly disseminated among investors and that investors may tend to interpret information differently. Because the ability to make above-average returns in the market depends upon differences in the flow and understanding of information, it is very important that the purchaser of securities appreciate all the possible sources of financial data.

Data Supplied by Research Agencies and Services

A large quantity of information is generated by agencies and services that put together reports for the investing public (institutional and personal). These reports vary from general economic prognostications to very concrete analyses of industry and corporate prospects. Moody and Standard & Poor both supply numerous bulletins and reports on a daily, weekly, and monthly basis. They prepare substantial reference volumes including Moody's *Manuals* and Standard & Poor's *Corporation Records.* These volumes are updated regularly to include the most recent financial information about several thousand companies. Standard & Poor issues a *Stock Guide* that provides pertinent facts about some five thousand common and preferred stocks. This *Guide* is widely distributed by most brokers to their customers, and it is regarded by many small investors as the best single summary source of data for all major listed securities in the United States.

Moody and S&P also publish detailed reports on individual corporations. Standard & Poor's *Encyclopedia* and Moody's *Handbook* cover about one thousand stocks in detail and include charts of price performance over time, a history of important financial statistics, and an analysis of the firm's background and current prospects. Separate reports from the S&P *Encyclopedia* are updated regularly (about once every three months as new quarterly reports are published by companies) and are available from most stockbrokers. In Canada, a similar service covering individual Canadian corporations is offered by the *Financial Post*.

The Value Line Investment Survey publishes *Ratings and Reports* on over fourteen hundred companies. The Value Line Survey is somewhat more specific than either Moody or S&P in that it ranks stocks in terms of quality, potential short-term and long-term price performance, and yield. Securities included in the *Survey* are appraised by Value Line analysts and are given a normative market value.

Brokerage and investment banking houses also publish numerous reports that analyze and evaluate individual companies and securities. These services are normally provided to customers at no specific charge (the cost is actually included in the commissions that the firms generate from their customers). The bigger firms maintain substantial staffs of analysts, and it is not unusual that an extremely large concern have analysts who cover the securities in only one industry.

In addition to the services listed above, there are a number of private investment letters that are distributed to a clientele of paid subscribers. These letters cost varying amounts from one or two dollars per year to over one thousand dollars, depending on the nature of the information provided and the previous track record of the publishers of the letter. Some investment letters, such as Babson's Reports, Inc., *Investment and Barometer Letter* and American Investors Corporation's *Stock Market Survey,* have been prepared for years and are widely respected.

Reports in the Financial Press

An unfortunate feature of the established service and agency reports is that the information that they contain is available to a large audience. Thus, if one of the leading brokerage houses recommends a particular stock, that knowledge is immediately transmitted to all participants in the market. There would appear to be a strong tendency for information of this sort to be rapidly incorporated into stock prices, and if only these data existed there would be good reason to accept the efficient market hypothesis on *a priori* grounds. There are other pieces of information, however, that may not be easily transmitted or understood. Important data are not always available to the general public, and even when widely disseminated some information is not easily interpreted.

Data in the latter category often appear in the financial press and require specialized knowledge for proper understanding. Although many of the articles that are found in such publications as *The Wall Street Journal, Barron's, Forbes, Commercial and Financial Chronicle, Financial World,* and the *Financial Post* (Canada) are very specific and provide obvious inputs for the appraisal of a firm, frequently it is not easy to make sense of an isolated fact that may be reported about a particular company. For example, suppose a firm reports its third quarter earnings and the statement is immediately carried by *The Wall Street Journal.* Suppose further that reported earnings are up significantly from the previous quarter and from the same period (quarter) in the previous year. What does this mean? The average reader might assume that the report is bullish and that the firm has done well. However, he looks at the price of the firm's stock and finds that it went *down* with the publication of the information. How can this be explained? One possibility is that professional analysts who had been scrutinizing the company very carefully for years had expected the firm to do *even better* than the reported figures and were disappointed by the result. Another possibility is that the market had discounted the good news (that is, the improvement was expected and the price of the stock had been previously bid up accordingly). When the news was not quite as good as expected, the market realized that it had *over-*anticipated the result, and the price thus had to fall.

Information of this sort can often bewilder the "little" investor, and even the seasoned analyst is sometimes surprised by the way the market reacts to certain new inputs. Nevertheless, it is situations such as these that make possible above-average stock market performance. The investor who went against the crowd with the belief that the firm was not going to do as well as others expected and sold his shares (or took a short position) would have profited. Here, of course, superior forecasting or a better understanding of the situation would have enabled the shrewd investor to realize better-than-average returns.

Analysis and Interpretation of Financial Information

The appropriate evaluation of financial information is clearly the key to long-run investment success, and the trained analyst will have a decided advantage. It is for this reason that substantial space is devoted below to discussions of financial analysis and forecasting. Virtually all of Part II is written to provide a clearer understanding of the variables pertinent to a firm's success, and a mastery of the material that follows in Chapters 5 through 14 is imperative for the analyst *who makes his own appraisal.* Because the published investigations of others will very likely be generally available, and hence already included in the current price of a security, it should be obvious that the portfolio manager or private investor who really desires above-normal profits will have to make independent evaluations.

The inputs that go into independent appraisals may include publicly available information, such as a corporation's annual report, but these data will be uniquely interpreted. Moreover, the professional analyst may have access to certain inputs that are not generally known to the public. Competent securities analysts spend many hours each week interviewing corporate officers and employees of the firms that they follow. The capable analyst learns how to take clues from what managers say and use these clues to good advantage. This is not quite as good as inside information, but the really top analysts can sometimes deduce facts from evidence garnered that equals that possessed by management. These fellows are rare, however, and they are very highly paid.

Because there are so many pieces of information available, it is fortunate that slide rules and hand calculators are no longer the only tools available to the investment decision maker. Large electronic computers that have substantial memory banks and can perform tedious calculations rapidly and without error are becoming a necessity for the professional investor. These machines are being used by an increasing number of Wall Street firms to perform tasks that previously required thousands of man-hours but that can be done by the computer in a matter of seconds. Services have been established based on the improved technology offered by the computer. Perhaps the most significant of these services is Compustat, which has been supplied by an S&P subsidiary (Investors Management Sciences) since 1964. Compustat is a punched-card and magnetic-tape library that contains numerous inputs from financial statements plus other pertinent information such as share prices. The Compustat file covers over three thousand U.S. corporations and some four hundred Canadian concerns. The tapes are updated on a daily basis, and subscribers can access data on many companies for as far back as twenty years.

THE SECURITIES MARKETS

There is another prerequisite even more important than widely available information to the efficient market hypothesis: the existence of large, well-behaved securities markets. From economics, it will be recalled that a perfectly competitive market is one in which: (1) there are many buyers and sellers, no one of which can influence price; (2) there exists perfect information that is equally available to all participants in the market; (3) there is a homogeneous commodity traded in the market; and (4) there is free entry of sellers and buyers into the market. The second of these conditions has figured most prominently in discussions of the EMH thus far, but a perfectly efficient market depends upon all four.

A market exists whenever there is an exchange of goods, services, or other property. For a market to be competitive, it usually must be sufficiently large so that any buyer (or seller) can purchase (sell) whatever quantity he wishes at the "going" price (that is, the price set through the negotiations of all buyers and sellers together). The securities markets generally satisfy the size requirement in that literally billions of dollars worth of stocks and bonds are traded weekly just in the United States. This does not mean that there is a good market for every single stock or bond in the hands of the public, however. If there is sufficient trading depth in a particular security, it will be possible to trade at a price very near the most-recent past transaction price. As many investors can testify, there are numerous stocks (and many more bonds) that trade in very *thin* markets. That is, the number of participants in the market is so small that one may have to bid well above the last price to buy or ask well under that price to sell. Such a market is clearly neither perfect nor efficient.

The Organized Exchanges

To a large extent, whether or not a particular stock or bond is traded in an efficient market depends on the "floating supply" of the issue outstanding. A stock with only 100,000 shares in the hands of the public that "turns over" only 10 percent of the supply annually (that is, 10,000 shares) will probably not trade often enough to have market depth. Such a security may show rather substantial price volatility from one transaction to the next, because the time span between transactions may be several days. Thus, no one buyer could accumulate more than a few shares at any one time without driving the price higher. Similarly, no seller could liquidate much of his position without pushing the price down.

One way to be sure that a stock (or bond) does have a reasonably large floating supply and regular transaction patterns is to make certain that it is traded on some organized exchange. Although the total dollar volume of securities transactions on exchanges is less than in the *over-the-counter* market (the unorganized markets), it is generally the case that the dollar volume *per security* is greater for listed securities.[1] Furthermore, most exchanges have listing requirements that are designed to guarantee market depth. The New York Stock Exchange, for example, requires that a firm have at least 700,000 shares

---

[1]This will not always be true. The government bond market is conducted almost exclusively over-the-counter, and the dollar volume of specific government issues can be quite large. Furthermore, some stocks that are widely held and actively traded are not listed on any exchange.

outstanding in the hands of a minimum of 2,000 shareholders.[2] Additionally, a stock which trades only infrequently would not usually be a candidate for listing.

Organized securities markets have existed for some time. Records show that securities were trading as early as 1602 in Antwerp and that an organized exchange existed in Amsterdam by 1611.[3] Today, most of the leading capitalist countries have at least one major exchange, and the United States boasts sixteen. In North America, the New York Stock Exchange (NYSE) is by far the most important exchange. Over sixteen hundred stocks and nearly twelve hundred bonds are traded on the NYSE, and 1,375 brokers, specialists, and registered traders are members entitled to the privilege of buying and selling on the Exchange's floor.[4] The American Stock Exchange and a number of U.S. regional exchanges list some two thousand other securities that do not generally have the market depth (or the earnings and assets) of stocks listed on the NYSE. In Canada, the Toronto Stock Exchange lists most leading Canadian industrial securities and a large number of mining and oil and gas securities as well.

Many securities are traded on more than one exchange. An advantage of *dual* listing is that extra trading hours may be secured for a firm's stock. Thus, a company's shares listed on both the NYSE and the Pacific Coast Stock Exchange would be traded from 10:00 a.m. Eastern Standard Time until 6:30 p.m. EST. The NYSE closes at 3:30 p.m. EST, but the Pacific Coast Exchange (in California) closes at 3:30 PST. Hence, a stockholder would have three extra hours for exchanging shares. Some securities also trade in the *third market,* which is the over-the-counter market for stocks that are also listed on an exchange.[5] Both dual listing and third market trading tend to increase the depth of the market for a stock and hence contribute to greater market efficiency.

The development of several trading areas (the exchanges, third market, and so on) has focused attention on the necessity of developing a centralized data source where the price and trading volume on all transactions could be reported on a consolidated basis. Recently (March 1973), the Chairman of the Securities & Exchange Commission (S.E.C.) proposed establishment of an automated quotation system and a computerized specialists' book. (The current role of the specialist is discussed later in this chapter.) Under this system, all brokers could trade listed stocks whether or not they were members of an exchange. Price and volume data would be transmitted on a consolidated ticker for all exchanges and off-the-floor trading. Thus, every broker would have the best quotations available.

Needless to say, the exchanges, particularly the NYSE, are not terribly

---

[2] See Gilbert W. Cooke, *The Stock Markets* (Cambridge, Mass.: Schenkman Publishing Company, 1969), p. 337.

[3] *Ibid.,* p. 305.

[4] *Ibid.,* p. 323.

[5] In this parlance, the "first market" is composed of the organized exchanges and the "second market" is over-the-counter. A "fourth market" has also been identified as that in which investing institutions trade securities directly with each other.

enthusiastic about this proposal. The Big Board (NYSE) has an alternative plan which would centralize all trading in listed NYSE stocks on the exchange. In effect, this would eliminate dual listing and third market trading for all NYSE listed securities. At the time of this writing, it is unclear which plan(s) will be adopted. One thing is certain, however, and that is dramatic changes are going to occur. By making information more perfect, these changes should contribute to a more efficient market.

The Over-the-Counter Market

Any securities transaction that does not take place on an exchange is said to be an *over-the-counter* (OTC) trade. The OTC market consists of numerous brokers, traders, and dealers who "make a market" in bonds and shares and stand ready to buy or sell to each other and the investing public. Business is done via telephone or teletype, and there may be no formal signal to other investors when a transaction has taken place.[6] On an exchange, there is a record of each transaction, and an investor can observe the last price at which the security was traded. He may call his broker and find out at what price a particular stock *opened* (its first price for the day) and obtain the current quotation. In the OTC market, there may be no information available about the most recent transaction, and one's broker can only secure *bid* and *ask* prices on a security. A *bid* price is the amount that is offered for the purchase of a security; an *ask* price is the amount demanded by a seller. There will customarily be a "spread" between the bid and ask prices that serves to compensate those who make a market in the security. Depending upon the depth of the market, spreads may vary from 1 or 2 percent to as large as 5 percent.

Most transactions in the *primary* market are OTC trades. The primary market is the first sale or new issue market. When a firm (or government) sells its securities to the public, it is a primary transaction. After a bond or share is in the hands of the public, any trading in the security is said to be in the *secondary* market. Both exchange and OTC transactions can be secondary trades.

Purchases of securities in the primary markets are usually made through *investment bankers* who originate, underwrite, and sell new issues to the public. In the usual case, a firm will arrange to "float" an issue through its bankers. The firm will be given a price for its securities that reflects market conditions, yields

[6] A computer-based, automatic quotation service for over-the-counter stocks, known as NASDAQ, has begun operation recently. Dealers can "punch in" quotations for securities in which they make a market; securities salesmen can then input the symbol for a stock and obtain a read-out of the best bid and asked prices. Investors are thus assured of obtaining execution of orders at the best available prices. Some listed securities have also been carried by NASDAQ on an experimental basis. Because this system has the potential for eliminating organized exchanges, opposition has developed that will undoubtedly slow its expansion into listed securities.

on equivalent securities (either the company's or those of similar concerns), and the costs involved to the investment bankers to distribute the stocks or bonds. Title to the securities is customarily taken by the underwriting syndicate (several banking houses), although small corporations usually have to settle for a *best-efforts* distribution in which the bankers merely act as selling agents for the company.

The primary (new issue) market has been quite popular in recent years for speculative investors. The reason for this popularity is the fantastic price movements experienced by many stocks after initial sale. One of the more spectacular performances of a new issue was experienced by the Communications Satellite Corporation (Comsat), which was originally sold in 1964 at twenty dollars per share. Within months after the underwriting, the stock had zoomed up to seventy dollars, even though the company had just started business, had no prospects for earning any money for several years, and was a regulated public utility as well! Other examples have been equally spectacular, and at the crest of the market in the mid-1960s just the mention of a new issue was enough to get investors clamoring for "a piece of the action." Of course, many of the more startling performers fell almost as fast as they rose when more sober market conditions reappeared (as they always must), and Comsat has only recently returned to the peak that it reached during the initial speculative orgy.

The primary markets, particularly for unseasoned firms, are clearly affected by investment banking practices that do not encourage market efficiency. Nevertheless, it is very difficult to price an issue that has never before traded. Behavior such as that witnessed in the 1965–1970 period (boom and then bust) could hardly be described in any terms other than excess speculation, although there is some evidence that the new-issue after-market even during this period conforms to efficiency standards. In a recent study of 142 unseasoned new issues of common stock issued in the first quarter of 1969, two researchers found that initial subscribers could indeed earn significantly large returns in the first week following the offering.[7] Nevertheless, their evidence suggests that subsequent returns from the first week until the end of the year "were not different for issues with large initial price increases as compared with returns on new issues as a whole."[8] They conclude that "short-term holdings were highly profitable to initial subscribers, but that initial price behavior did not have significant predictive value to investors making purchase decisions at the market price *a short time after the offering*" (emphasis added).[9]

Trading Securities

Technically speaking, a securities *dealer* maintains an inventory of securities in which he makes a market by purchasing and selling from his own

[7]See J. G. McDonald and A. K. Fisher, "New-Issue Stock Price Behavior," *The Journal of Finance* (March 1972), pp. 97–102.

[8]*Ibid.,* p. 102.

[9]*Ibid.*

account as a principal; thus, the OTC market is maintained by dealers. A *broker* acts as an agent for his customer in purchasing or selling securities on the floor of the exchange or from a dealer in the OTC market; as an agent, the broker is expected to obtain the best available price for his customer and is paid a commission for his services. The investment banker advises issuers of securities and purchases such issues for resale to syndicates of dealers (the banker is generally prominent in such a syndicate) and ultimate resale to the public (with a commission allowance for brokers and dealers which are not members of the syndicate).

The simplest order to a broker to buy or sell a security at the best available price is a *market order.* In the OTC market, the broker would check dealer quotes and execute the order at the best available price. On the floor of the NYSE, the floor broker for the customer's firm would walk to the post where the security is traded. From the assembled group of other floor brokers, floor traders (who trade for their own account), and the *specialist* (a floor broker charged by the exchange with maintaining a market in the stock), he would determine the best available price and execute the order. There are, however, other types of orders; we shall be concerned with two: limit and stop. A *limit* order includes a maximum (minimum) price that the customer is willing to pay (receive) to buy (sell) the stock. A *stop* order contains a price above (below) the current market price of the stock that, if reached by the market, the customer desires to trigger a buy (sell) market order; for example, a stop-buy order might be entered at a price a few points above the market at the same time the stock was sold short to limit the risk exposure of the investor if the price moved the wrong way. Since it is quite likely that neither stop nor limit orders could be executed immediately, the floor broker would instruct the specialist to enter them in his "book" for execution when their terms were met.

The major functions of the specialist are to execute the orders in his book and to buy and sell for his own account in order to maintain an orderly market. To limit possible abuses, the specialist is required to give the orders in his book priority over trades for his own account and to engage in the latter in a stabilizing manner. The larger blocks of stock being traded on the exchanges have caused the capital requirements for specialists to be increased, and rule violations (such as destabilizing trading) are investigated. Even the EMH advocates, however, grant that the specialist's book constitutes "inside information" and this group can earn above-normal profits. For this reason, many reform proposals (such as those recently made by the SEC) seek to reduce or eliminate the role of the specialist. Specialists do not exist on Canadian exchanges; the equivalent of the "book" is maintained on a computer.

The impact of reform proposals on trading securities goes well beyond a modification of the function of the specialist, however. Aside from consolidating trading and price information, the centralized market plan discussed previously could allow for the elimination of duplicate facilities and provide for a central depository of shares (bonds) whereby ownership could pass by means of a computer entry validated by a simple print-out. Such uses of a centralized market computer could resolve many of the difficulties that brokers have recently encountered.

As a result of large increases in trading volume on the organized exchanges, the ability of brokers to consummate transactions has been impaired. Significant problems have developed in the timely delivery of security certificates (called "fails"); theft of certificates has become widespread; and transferral procedures have clogged the clerical departments of many firms. All of these difficulties have raised the costs of a brokerage business and have severely reduced the profitability of the industry.

Also contributing to the profit squeeze is a reduction in revenues produced by recent changes in commission structures. In the past, NYSE designated commissions were charged by member firms on a 100 share (*round lot*) basis. No discounts were given to large purchasers, although until recently "give-ups" were allowed on regional exchanges and OTC transactions. A *give-up* is the practice of permitting the customer to direct his broker that part of the required commission be paid to another broker for services rendered (such as research work, etc.). For large transactions, as much as 75 percent of a commission might have been so directed; and, when give-ups were banned, there was considerable pressure on the part of large institutional purchasers either to be allowed NYSE membership or to negotiate commissions with their brokers. For the most part, the latter path has been followed, and at this writing all commissions on that part of every transaction above $300,000 (scheduled to be reduced to $100,000) must be negotiated.

Reduced revenues resulting from negotiated commissions coupled with the higher costs of doing business have altered the structure of the brokerage industry. A number of less efficient houses have collapsed, been merged with stronger concerns, or undertaken voluntary liquidation. During 1970, several large houses failed and millions of dollars in customer accounts were jeopardized. In order to prevent loss of investor confidence, the NYSE assessed its members to establish a fund to protect the customers of member firms. This arrangement has been formalized with standby borrowing power at the U.S. Treasury in case of short run difficulties in liquidity. In addition, the capital requirement for firms has been increased. Thus, a more concentrated, and hopefully stronger, brokerage community has emerged.

The impetus toward negotiated commissions has focused increasing attention upon cost-based pricing policies. Commissions on smaller trades have thus risen appreciably, speeding the process of institutionalization of small investor savings. There is also growing pressure for the "unbundling" of (or extracting a separate charge for) such services as research and share-certificate custody. Thus, the investment community is confronted with: (1) a small investor who is leaving the market and, if he trades at all, increasingly does so through mutual funds or third market houses that charge reduced rates; (2) large institutional investors that are demanding reduced commissions or exchange membership and, at the same time, are trading enormous blocks of stock; and

(3) a broker-specialist system that is inadequately capitalized to handle enormous transactions and lacks the profit potential to attract the capital required on a permanent basis. In recent years, there has almost been a "crisis cycle" in the brokerage business; too little volume hurts profits and too much volume buries the houses in paperwork backlogs. Reform is needed and will certainly be initiated; the exact direction, however, cannot be predicted at this writing.

REGULATION OF SECURITIES MARKETS

A major element contributing to the efficiency of the U.S. securities markets is the regulation of those markets by the federal government. Before 1933, there were no laws governing stock-exchange or investment-house activities, and widespread manipulation and questionable practices abounded. Corporations were not required to provide information to investors, and fraudulent statements (or no statements at all) were issued by any number of companies. The excesses of the 1920s were traced in part to the lack of comprehensive legislation regulating the securities industry, and with the coming of the New Deal a number of laws were passed to prevent a recurrence of the events that led to the 1929 crash.

Major Legislation

The Securities Act of 1933 requires full and complete disclosure of all important information about a firm that plans to sell securities in interstate commerce. Issues of securities exceeding $300,000 in value, and all issues sold in more than one state, must be registered with the S.E.C. A *prospectus* must be prepared by the issuing company and distributed to anyone who is solicited to buy the securities in question. The prospectus must include all pertinent facts about the company, such as recent financial reports, current position, a statement about what will be done with the funds raised, and a history of the company. Details about the officers and directors of the company are also required.

The Securities Exchange Act of 1934 serves to regulate the securities markets and institutional participants in the market, such as brokers and dealers. All exchanges are required to register with the S.E.C., although much of the supervision of individual exchanges is left up to the governing bodies of each exchange. Amendments to the act now also include the OTC markets, although broker-dealer associations are accorded the same self-regulatory authority as the exchanges enjoy. (See discussion under "Self-regulation" below.)

The Investment Company Act of 1940 regulates the management and disclosure policies of companies that invest in the securities of other firms. Under the act, investment companies may be organized as *unit trusts, face-amount certificate companies,* or *management investment companies.* Only the last classification is currently significant, and it is further subdivided into open-end and closed-end management investment companies. *Closed-end* companies sell their shares and conduct their operations much the same way as an industrial corporation. *Open-end* companies are better known as *mutual funds* and are required to redeem their shares at net asset value upon demand; because of this requirement, they may not issue long-term debt or preferred stock. If a mutual fund registers with the S.E.C., agrees to abide by the above rules, invests no more than 5 percent of its assets in the securities of any one issuer, holds no more than 10 percent of the securities of any issuer, pays at least 90 percent of its income out to fund shareholders, and meets other rules, it may pay taxes only on earnings retained.

Other acts that are important include the Public Utility Holding Company Act of 1935, which regulates the operations and financial structure of gas and electric holding companies; the Trust Indenture Act of 1939, which requires that bonds (and similar forms of indebtedness) be issued under an *indenture* that specifies the obligations of the issuer to the lender and that names an independent trustee to look after the interests of lenders; and the Investment Advisors Act of 1940, which requires the registration of investment counselors and others who propose to advise the public on securities investment.

Margin Purchases

One of the major excesses of the pre-1933 era was the practice of buying stocks on low *margin.* Margin purchases are those for which the investor does not advance the full value of the securities that he buys. Thus, if an investor bought one hundred shares of General Motors at 80 on 60 percent margin, he would only put up $4,800. The remaining $3,200 would be borrowed either from his broker or a bank. Margin purchases may increase the rate of return earned by an investor. If General Motors went up 10 percent to 88, the investor in the above example would have made $800/$4,800 = 16.7 percent. They also increase his risk exposure. If GM went down 10 percent, the *loss* would be 16.7 percent. During the late 1920s, investors were buying stocks on less than 10 percent margin. Large rates of return were earned by everyone so long as stock prices were advancing. When prices began to skid in late 1929, however, many people were wiped out in a matter of days. Investors tended to build their margin positions as prices rose by buying more shares with the profits earned. Thus, a man might have put $1,000 into stock worth $10,000 in January 1929. As prices advanced by 10 percent, say, in February, he might have used his profit to buy another $9,000 worth of stock. His commitment was still $1,000, but he controlled $20,000 in stock. As prices rose further, he might have increased his position to $25,000. But suppose prices fell just a little, say 4 percent. This decline would be enough to wipe out his investment completely! Such a decline began during October 1929, and many investors were sold out of their stocks as prices fell. The process of liquidating shares as prices went below margin levels caused further price deterioration that, in turn, forced more liquidations. The snowballing effects of this phenomenon produced the major crash of October 29, 1929 and contributed to the subsequent collapse of both the stock market and the American economy.[10]

Because of the problems directly traceable to margin purchases, the Securities Exchange Act of 1934 gave the Board of Governors of the Federal Reserve System the power to set margin requirements for all stocks and bonds. Since 1934, margins have been allowed as low as 40 percent but have also been as high as 100 percent (no borrowing permitted). To some extent, the sobering experiences of 1929 caused a natural reaction against margin purchases in subsequent years. Nevertheless, there are those in the market today who have only read about 1929 and would, if given the chance, follow their fathers and grandfathers down the same speculative path. To protect them and society from such excesses, extremely low margins are no longer permitted.[11]

Short Selling

Another practice that caused problems prior to 1933 was the *short sale.* When one sells a security he does not own but borrows from someone else to make delivery, he is said to sell that security short. The device has been used for years and can be defended on economic grounds even though it does sound a bit immoral to be selling something one does not own. In practice, the short sale is consummated by specialists (who have responsibility for maintaining an orderly market on the NYSE) and dealers far more frequently than by the investing public. The average investor might consider selling short a security if he believed its price were going to decline. He would simply call his broker and ask to sell so many shares of such and such company short at a given price. If the broker could find the shares for the customer to borrow (usually from securities held by the broker in his own account or securities margined with the broker), the transaction could be effected.

Because short selling can tend to exacerbate downward movements in stock prices, it is easy to see how speculative excesses could occur through unregulated use of the device. Thus, the Securities Exchange Act of 1934 allows the S.E.C. to set rules for short selling. There are several regulations in effect now governing the practice, the most important being the "up-tick" requirement. This rule prevents a short sale while a stock is falling in price. Thus, if a

---

[10]See J. K. Galbraith, *The Great Crash* (Boston: Houghton-Mifflin Co., 1954).

[11]It is possible to buy government bonds on 10 percent margin on occasion. Because bond prices on long-term maturities may rise (or fall) by more than 10 percent within a period of a year or less, one can still speculate in this market. Nevertheless, it takes a bond quite some time (weeks at least) to fall by 10 percent, whereas stocks in the 1920s would fluctuate by that amount sometimes in a single trading session. Furthermore, the number of bond speculators is so small that they do not cause major disruptions to the market or to the economy.

stock sells at 40, then 39½, then 39, no short sale could be effected until there is an advance. If the stock rose to 39¼, it could be sold short.[12]

Section 77 of the Companies Act in Canada provides many of the same regulations for Canadian companies that the Securities Act of 1933 and the Securities Exchange Act of 1934 provide in the United States. In general, however, the respective provinces in Canada exercise the authority possessed by the federal government in the United States. Each province has its own securities laws and most have Securities Commissions. As a result, regulation in Canada tends to be somewhat less effective than in the United States. There is a tendency for the provinces to compete among themselves to gain corporate citizens, and strict regulation is sometimes lost in the process.[13]

Self-regulation

Since the average securities firm functions as investment banker (representing the issuing firm), broker (representing the customer), and dealer (representing itself) simultaneously, the potential for conflict of interest is great. Many of the laws previously discussed were passed to protect the general public when such conflicts arise. These laws, in turn, provide for substantial *self-regulation.* This is manifested by exchange regulations for member firms and NASD (National Association of Securities Dealers) rules for most others, who subject themselves to such rules in order to obtain securities from other NASD firms at less than the price to the general public.

NYSE members must restrict all transactions in listed stocks to the floor of the exchange, even though the larger firms could merely match buy and sell orders in their own offices. NASD firms may only trade with their customers if their price is the best obtainable and must reveal if they acted as principal on the other side of the transaction. Any research recommendations by broker-dealers must indicate if the firm holds a position in the stock. Other regulations call for ethical behavior on the part of members by prohibiting such practices as: (1) the spreading of rumors; (2) the recommending of securities clearly inappropriate for a given customer; and (3) the encouraging of excessive numbers of transactions (called "churning") in a given account. Although many of these rules have protected the public, others are clearly designed to protect the monopoly position of the broker-dealer community itself.

---

[12]The regulation is actually somewhat more complicated than the explanation given in that it applies to shares traded "the regular way," that is, for delivery five business days after the sale.

[13]State regulation of the securities business also exists in the United States. Most states have boards or commissions to regulate intrastate practices, and various "blue sky" laws in each state require registration of securities before they may be sold within the boundaries of the state.

Insider Information

The Securities Exchange Act of 1934 defines officers, directors, and holders of more than 10 percent of the shares of a firm as *insiders*. Such persons are required to file a statement of their holdings of the firm's stock and any changes in such holdings (within a month) with the S.E.C. Profits made by insiders on shares held less than six months must also be reported and may be legally recovered by the firm (through a shareholders' derivative suit if necessary); in addition, malfeasance suits could be filed for other injuries to shareholder interests. Over the years, holdings of related persons have come to be included in the determination of whether the 10 percent rule were met and persons related to insiders were also considered to be insiders for the purpose of the law. In general, the principle was established that insiders and their relatives should not gain a special benefit over other shareholders by virtue of the information about the firm they possess. The Texas Gulf Sulphur case of the mid-1960s, in which corporate insiders withheld information about a minerals discovery until they could obtain stock, clearly reestablished this point through both civil and criminal action.

Several recent cases, however, promise to greatly expand the concept of insider information. In the cases of Douglas Aircraft and Penn-Central, brokerage houses obtained insider information (of bad earnings and impending bankruptcy, respectively) and informed selected institutional investors before the general public. Subsequent suits and exchange disciplinary actions against the brokerage houses involved, and suits against the institutions, would indicate that second- and third-hand possessors of inside information are increasingly being classed as insiders. As this is written, an analyst has been charged in the Equity Funding case for providing information to selected investors that did not even originate from the company itself but rather from the charges of former employees. We seem to be moving in the direction of classifying insiders more on the basis of the information they possess than the position they hold in regard to the firm. Although such a situation would validate the EMH by default, its long-run implications for investigative research analysis and individualistic portfolio management are not encouraging.

STOCK MARKET INDICATORS

When the EMH postulates that only "normal" returns can be earned in the stock market, an implicit assumption is made that there is some sort of average that summarizes stock market performance in general. In fact, it is extremely difficult to calculate measures of this sort.

Perhaps the most widely used average is the Dow-Jones Industrial (DJI) stock price average that appears in *The Wall Street Journal* each day. The DJI is computed by taking the price of each of thirty selected blue-chip stocks, adding them, and dividing by a divisor. The divisor initially was the number of stocks in the average (originally twelve), but because of the obvious biases of stock splits (a two-for-one split would tend to cause the price of a share to fall by one half), the divisor was adjusted downward for each split. The divisor now is just over 1.5.

In addition to the DJI, there is a Dow-Jones Transportation (formerly rail) average of twenty stocks, a Dow-Jones Utility average of fifteen stocks, and a composite average of all sixty-five stocks. Each is computed in the same manner as the DJI.

For many investors, the Dow-Jones averages *are* the market. When an investor calls his broker to ask what the market is doing, he is very likely to get a response such as "down 7.34." The broker means, of course, that the DJI is down 7.34 points. This information may have very little to do with what the investor really wants to know (that is, how are *my* stocks doing?). The DJI is not an overall indicator of market performance, although many use it as if it were. In fact, only blue-chip stocks are included in the average. The thousands of other stocks that are not blue chips are not represented. Moreover, the DJI has been criticized by many even as a measure of blue-chip performance. Because the DJI merely adds the prices of all included stocks before applying the divisor, a stock that sells for a higher price receives a larger weight in the measurement. Thus, if General Motors sells at 80 and DuPont sells for 160, DuPont is given *twice* the weight of General Motors, even though the aggregate market value of GM (the price per share times the number of shares) is much greater than for DuPont.

The difficulties associated with the Dow-Jones averages have led to the development of other stock price averages and indexes. Standard & Poor computes an industrial index (425 stocks), a transportation index (25 stocks), a utility index (50 stocks), and a composite index (all 500 stocks) that include both the price per share of each security *and* the number of shares outstanding. These figures thus reflect the total market value of all the stocks in each index. The aggregate number is expressed as a percentage of the average value existing during 1941–1943, and the percentage is divided by ten. The S&P indexes are better overall measures of stock market performance than the Dow-Jones averages because more securities are included. Furthermore, the statistical computation of the S&P indexes is superior to the Dow-Jones method.

There are a number of other indexes and averages that are also prepared. *The New York Times* publishes an average that is computed in virtually the same manner as the DJI, except that splits are accounted for by multiplication of the numerator rather than reduction of the divisor. Moody computes a weighted arithmetic average that is much like the S&P index, but there is no base year in the computation (hence, it is an average rather than an index). United Press

International prepares an indicator to measure the performance of an equal dollar portfolio composed of all NYSE stocks. Finally, both the New York and American stock exchanges compute measures that include all their respective stocks. The NYSE Common Stock Index multiplies the market value of each NYSE common stock by the number of shares listed in that issue. The summation of this computation is indexed, given the summation value as of December 31, 1965. The American Stock Exchange average simply adds all positive and negative changes of all shares and divides by the number of shares listed. The result is added to or subtracted from the previous close.

Although there is no single perfect indicator of average performance, many analysts are tending to favor the NYSE and AMEX indexes, which have only been computed since the mid-1960s. Most observers do not ignore the Dow-Jones averages, however, because so many investors are influenced by them. Fortunately (at least for measurement purposes), there is a high covariance between the price movements of all stocks. Thus, if most stocks are going up (or down), almost any measure will indicate this.

SUMMARY

A crucial assumption of the efficient market hypothesis is that investors have similar information with which to make investment decisions. A major form of such information is that supplied by research agencies and services. A number of reports are periodically prepared by investment advisory companies. These are designed to aid the investing public in making decisions. An important feature of the established service and agency reports is that they are available to large audiences. Thus, the data that are contained in them could be expected to be incorporated in stock prices just as soon as the information is published.

Other information that is not so easily transmitted or interpreted appears in the financial press. Much of this information requires special expertise or training for proper understanding, and one of the goals of this book is to provide the tools and understanding required for the investor or analyst who must appraise these data. Because of the large quantity of information currently available to the investment decision maker, large electronic computers are being employed to store, sort, and compare pieces of data.

The efficient market hypothesis postulates the existence of large, well-behaved securities markets. For a market to be competitive (or efficient), it must be sufficiently large so that any buyer (or seller) can purchase (sell) whatever quantity he wishes without affecting the market price. The securities markets satisfy this requirement for some securities but not for others. In general, stocks and bonds traded on an organized exchange will have a more efficient market than those that are traded over-the-counter, because exchanges have listing requirements designed to guarantee market depth. Many securities are dually listed, and some are traded in the third market. The development of several trading areas has focused attention on the need for a centralized data bank for price and volume statistics. The Securities and Exchange Commission has proposed such a plan, but the NYSE would prefer to centralize all trading on the Exchange.

Security trading in the over-the-counter market may be a primary or a secondary transaction. The primary market exists for the distribution of new securities; the secondary markets include both listed and OTC securities that are in the hands of the public. New-issue securities (primary market) are sold by investment bankers to investors, and the new-issue market has been very popular among speculators in recent years.

The functioning of the securities markets depends upon dealers, brokers, and specialists. Dealers maintain an inventory of securities and trade from their own accounts. Brokers act as agents for customers and accept market, stop, limit, as well as other, orders to buy and sell securities. The specialist is charged by the exchange with maintaining a market for particular stocks. His role has become more controversial recently, and many reform proposals have been made to alter or eliminate the specialist function.

Recent problems in the securities industry have prompted new ideas for restructuring the trading mechanism. A central depository of securities would improve the efficiency of transactions and reduce the number of fails. Altering commission structures to reflect economies of scale in transactions should focus attention on cost-based pricing policies. Unbundling services should improve brokerage profitability and allow customers to pay only for services used.

A major element contributing to the efficiency of the American securities markets is the regulation provided by the United States government. After the 1929 crash, a number of laws were passed that were designed to correct some of the abuses that existed in the past. Disclosure requirements were established, and the Securities and Exchange Commission was created to supervise the invest-ments business. One of the excesses of the pre-1933 era was the practice of buying stocks on margin. Use of this device is now regulated by the Board of Governors of the Federal Reserve System. Another practice that caused problems prior to 1933 was the short sale. This process is still permitted, although the S.E.C. may make rules governing its use. In Canada, regulatory legislation exists at the federal level, although the respective provinces have a greater role in prescribing activities in the securities business.

Much of the securities business is self-regulated. The exchanges and the National Association of Securities Dealers provide rules for members to promote ethical conduct, although many also tend to protect the monopoly position of the broker-dealer community as well. Regulation of insider information is designed to insure that corporate insiders and their relatives do not gain a special advantage over other shareholders. Recent cases have greatly expanded the scope of this regulation.

In order to determine whether one has earned above (or below) market returns, one must have a good measure of the average performance of stocks in general. No perfect indicator exists. The most widely used average is the Dow-Jones Industrial. The DJI is primarily a blue-chip measure, although many investors use it for overall market activity. Standard & Poor computes indexes that have a larger base than the DJI. The S&P measures are also statistically superior to the Dow calculation. There are a number of other indexes and averages that are also figured. Many analysts are tending to favor those computed by the New York Stock Exchange and the American Exchange, which include all common stocks traded on those exchanges.

REFERENCES

Ashley, C. A., and J. E. Smyth, *Corporation Finance in Canada,* Chaps. 4-7. Toronto: Macmillan Canada, Ltd., 1956.

Cohen, Jerome B., and Edward D. Zinbarg, *Investment Analysis and Portfolio Management,* Chaps. 2 and 3. Homewood, Ill.: Richard D. Irwin, Inc., 1967.

Cooke, Gilbert W., *The Stock Markets,* rev. ed., Chaps. 2, 3, 4, 7, 14, 15, 16, 20, 21, and 23. Cambridge, Mass.: Schenkman Publishing Company, 1969.

Eiteman, W. J. and S. C. Eiteman, *Nine Leading Stock Exchanges.* Ann Arbor: University of Michigan Press, 1968.

Findlay, M. Chapman, and Edward E. Williams, *An Integrated Analysis for Managerial Finance,* Chap. 11. Englewood Cliffs, N.J.: Prentice-Hall Inc., 1970.

Francis, J.C., *Investments: Analysis and Management,* Chaps. 3, 4, 7. New York: McGraw-Hill Book Company, 1972.

Galbraith, J. K., *The Great Crash.* Boston: Houghton Mifflin Co., 1954.

Latané, Henry, and Donald Tuttle, *Security Analysis and Portfolio Management,* Chap. 7. New York: The Ronald Press, 1970.

Leffler, G., and L. Farwell, *The Stock Market,* 3rd ed. New York: The Ronald Press, 1963.

McDonald, J. G. and A. K. Fisher, "New-Issue Stock Price Behavior," *The Journal of Finance* (March 1972), pp. 97-102.

Robbins, S., *The Securities Markets.* New York: Free Press, 1961.

3

The Money and Capital Markets

THE MONEY MARKET

Negotiable financial assets are traded in the money and capital markets. The distinction between the two is based upon the maturity of the financial asset under consideration. The money market is generally defined to consist of negotiable securities with a maturity of one year or less; the capital market is composed of the longer-term securities (including equities, which have a theoretically perpetual life). The distinction, however, is generally more significant than the mere artificial division at the one-year maturity level. The instruments of the money market, aside from being less than a year in maturity, are also generally of high investment quality and are purchased as a means of obtaining some return on temporarily idle funds; in other words, the money market is a market in near-money instruments where safety of principal and liquidity are the primary considerations. The capital market, on the other hand, not only includes securities of all degrees of risk but also tends to be utilized by investors with funds to be committed for substantial periods. Finally, long-term debt securities constitute a portion of the capital market at the time of their issuance, but as they approach maturity they become money-market instruments. We shall begin the discussion with the more traditional money-market instruments, which, in the context of this book, may be viewed as possible interest-earning cash substitutes in the investment portfolio.

Securities of the U.S. Government

The *treasury bill* is one of the most significant money-market instruments. This short-term government obligation is generally sold at weekly offerings in 91- and 182-day maturities. Bills do not carry an interest coupon but are auctioned (actually, by sealed bid) at less than their face value. The auction is held on Monday for delivery and payment the following Thursday; there will, of course, be a prior issue of bills maturing on Thursday that may be used to pay for new subscriptions (an effort by the government to encourage roll-overs). The winning bidders, mostly composed of banks and bond dealers, will then add a small markup and try to resell the bills to investors, corporations with idle balances, and so on. Because of the large amount of bills outstanding, the narrow spreads between bid and asked prices, and the lack of credit risk,[1] treasury bills are viewed as very desirable liquidity instruments.

In addition to the competitive auction, treasury bills may also be purchased in amounts up to $200,000 at the average competitive rate through the submission of a *noncompetitive bid.* Prior to 1970, the minimum noncompetitive bid had been $1000, but the high yields of the late 1960s attracted small investors away from banks and savings and loan associations. Thus, the government raised the minimum to $10,000. Investors of moderate wealth may still find this mechanism useful.

Bills of nine- and twelve-month maturity are also offered, generally monthly. The *certificate of indebtedness*, an interest-bearing treasury security of six- or twelve-month maturity, has been offered in the past but has been of little importance in recent years. Some of the government agencies discussed below also issue short-term debt that would qualify as money-market instruments. Finally, as mentioned before, the longer-term government and agency securities become money-market instruments when they approach maturity.

Suppose that an investor desired to find the price and yield on a treasury bill due in 300 days on a 6 percent basis. It must be noted first that treasury bills are quoted on a "discount" basis. The price would therefore be:

$$6\% \times (300/360) = 5\% \text{ "discount"}$$

Price = $95 per $100 face value of bill, and the approximate

true rate would be:

$$(5/95) \times (365/300) = 6.55\%$$

[1]Because we shall continually refer to federal government securities as devoid of credit (default) risk, we shall explain this point. It does not mean that we feel an entity over $300 billion in debt with additional unfunded liabilities (for example, Social Security) is a great credit risk by normal standards of evaluation. What it does mean is that, because the government has the power of money creation, it would undoubtedly create enough new money to repay any bondholder who demanded redemption. Only events like war, revolution, or, by some definitions, hyperinflation, could prevent this and would cause all other dollar-denominated obligations to become worthless anyway.

The latter is an approximation because it assumes annual compounding. The government has devised a more complicated computation for equivalent bond yield assuming semiannual compounding.[2]

Securities of States and Municipalities

Securities of states and their political subdivisions are usually known by the broad term *municipals* and are distinguished by the fact that their interest is in most cases exempt from federal income taxes. Although municipals are generally long term and are considered later in the chapter, certain situations give rise to short-term obligations. A city or state may borrow in anticipation of tax receipts or the proceeds of a bond issue. A municipal bond issue itself may have a portion that matures rather quickly and thus might qualify as a money-market instrument. The quality of these issues can vary widely, and, although the rating agencies will not evaluate these short-term issues, the ratings on the bonds of the entity will give some indication of credit-worthiness. Only the issues of bodies having one of the top two or three bond ratings would be of sufficiently high quality to be considered a true money-market instrument.

The short-term municipal market is also fed by the interim financing needs of housing and renewal authorities. The notes of state and local housing authorities are generally treated as obligations of the appropriate government body, and their quality is judged accordingly. The project notes of the Housing Assistance Administration and the Renewal Assistance Administration (both part of The Department of Housing and Urban Development) are backed by the federal government yet are still tax exempt. An additional advantage of municipals is that they are also usually exempt from state taxes in the state of issuance. A disadvantage is that the issues may be small, thus the secondary markets are often rather illiquid.

To illustrate the tax effect of municipals, consider the treasury bill analyzed above. If an investor were in the 40 percent marginal tax bracket, 2.62 percent (that is, .4 $\times$ 6.55%) of the yield would be taxed away, leaving a net return of 3.93 percent. Thus, if an otherwise similar municipal security offered a return in excess of 3.93 percent, the after-tax return to the holder would be more attractive.

Bankers' Acceptances

A *bankers' acceptance* arises from a commercial transaction, often involving international trade. An American importer may send a letter of credit with an order for goods to a foreign exporter. The exporter may then draw a

[2]For this and other points see *Handbook of Securities of the United States Government and Federal Agencies* (New York: First Boston Corp., biennial), and *Money Market Investments* (New York: Morgan Guaranty Trust Co., 1970).

time draft (an order to pay in the future) against the importer and sell it to his local bank at a discount in order to receive immediate payment. The foreign bank will then send the draft and title to the goods to the importer's bank. The importer's bank accepts the draft by indicating that it will guarantee payment. The time draft is now a bankers' acceptance that is sold in the money market to pay the foreign bank. Because the bank is obligated on the instrument, acceptances tend to trade on the basis of the bank's credit rather than that of the company primarily obligated. In a very crude sense, an acceptance may be viewed as a postdated certified check sold at a discount. Most large banks and bond dealers carry a wide range of sizes and maturities in acceptances, although it may not be possible to match desires exactly. A fairly strong point is made by the First Boston Corporation:

> In its more than fifty years of usage in the United States, the bankers' acceptance has come through the trials of war and economic depression with no known principal loss to the investor. Courts have held that the letter of credit agreement, from inception to conclusion, is based on the principle that the acceptor bank holds the agreement not for its own benefit or the benefit of its general creditors but in trust for the holder of the acceptance.[3]

Negotiable Certificates of Deposit

Negotiable CD's are claims upon time deposits at banks that may be sold prior to the maturity of the deposit. The deposit itself is made for a specified period (at a rate tied to the maturity) and may not be withdrawn early. The ability to negotiate the ownership of the deposit, however, provides essentially the same liquidity benefits as withdrawal to the owner and allows the higher rates associated with longer-term deposits to be earned. These deposits are backed by the Federal Deposit Insurance Corporation (FDIC) to $20,000; but because negotiable CD's are rarely smaller than $100,000 (and generally in multiples of $1 million), this is little comfort. Beyond FDIC insurance, the only security is the size and quality of the issuing bank. As a result, only the CD's of the larger money-market banks really qualify as money-market instruments.

The market for negotiable CD's is generally regarded as good, but it can be erratic. The rates banks may pay on time deposits are subject to ceilings set by the Federal Reserve. At times, the returns on other money-market instruments may go through these ceilings, causing the deposit to be withdrawn at maturity; the volume of outstanding CD's contracted from $24 billion in late 1968 to $10 billion in early 1970 because of this effect. Such sharp expansions and contractions can obviously be disruptive.

[3] *Handbook, op. cit.*, p. 110.

Commercial Paper

The *commercial paper* market consists of the short-term, unsecured promissory notes of industrial and financial companies. *Directly placed paper* is that sold directly by the borrower to the lender. Sales finance and consumer finance companies are the major sellers of directly placed paper, using the proceeds to carry the inventory of dealer and consumer loans they hold. Directly placed paper is generally sold to mature on any day desired by the lender from 3 to 270 days hence (an obvious advantage if the lender knows exactly when he wants his money back). A disadvantage of directly placed paper is that there is no secondary market, although in cases of hardship the issuer may buy it back early.

Dealer placed commercial paper is sold in the form of a one-time issue through a bond dealer. Finance companies also use this approach, and industrial companies employ it for seasonal working capital needs or as an alternative to bank borrowing. In all cases, and especially with dealer placed paper, the issuer will be required to keep open bank lines of credit to secure the retirement of the issue.

Industrial paper was rated exclusively by Dun and Bradstreet prior to 1970; if the paper was not rated "prime," it could not be sold through regular channels. Unfortunately, the Penn Central paper carried a "prime" rating at the time that the railroad filed bankruptcy. As a result, D&B has reassessed its criteria, and the bond rating houses have entered the field. The result will be, hopefully, a better refinement of the risks and return on commercial paper. Table 3-1 provides a review of the major points covered thus far.

Eurodollar Market

From the lender's point of view, the *Eurodollar market* merely presents the opportunity to buy negotiable CD's, expressed in dollars, from non-U.S. banks (either foreign banks or foreign branches of U.S. banks). American industrial and financial corporations are effectively precluded from this market by the American exchange control laws. Others, at this writing, may still participate, although U.S. banks are ordered by the Federal Reserve to avoid providing information or assistance.

The advantages to the investor are that the rates are not regulated and it may be possible to earn a higher return. A major disadvantage is that the regulation, disclosure, and deposit insurance in this market leave much to be desired, so the possibility of a panic or default cannot be ignored. This possibility is enhanced by the fact that the bank of deposit is creating a liability in a currency (the dollar) that its own government is under no obligation to provide in times of crisis.

TABLE 3-1
Money-Market Investments (United States)

	Obligation	Denominations	Maturities	Marketability	Basis
United States Treasury bills	U.S. Government obligation. U.S. Treasury auctions 3 and 6 month bills weekly, 9 month and 1 year bills monthly. Also offers tax anticipation bills through special auctions.	$10,000 to $1 million	Up to 1 year.	Excellent secondary market.	Discounted. Actual days on a 360-day year.
Prime sales finance paper	Promissory notes of finance companies placed directly with the investor.	$1,000 to $5 million ($25,000 minimum order)	Issued to mature on any day from 3 to 270 days.	No secondary market. Under certain conditions companies will buy back paper prior to maturity. Most companies will adjust rate.	Discounted or interest-bearing. Actual days on a 360-day year.
Dealer paper I. Finance	Promissory notes of finance companies sold through commercial paper dealers.	$100,000 to $5 million	Issued to mature on any day from 15 to 270 days.	Limited secondary market. Buy-back arrangement usually can be negotiated through the dealer.	Discounted or interest-bearing. Actual days on a 360-day year.
Dealer paper II. Industrial	Promissory notes of leading industrial firms sold through commercial paper dealers.	$500,000 to $5 million	Usually available on certain dates between 30 and and 180 days.	Limited secondary market.	Discounted. Actual days on a 360-day year.

38

	Description	Denominations	Maturity	Marketability	Basis
Prime bankers' acceptances	Time drafts drawn on and accepted by a banking institution, which in effect substitutes its credit for that of the importer or holder of merchandise.	$25,000 to $1 million	Up to 6 months.	Good secondary market. Bid usually 1/8 of 1% higher than offered side of market.	Discounted. Actual days on a 360-day year.
Negotiable time certificates of deposit	Certificates of time deposit at a commercial bank.	$500,000 to $1 million	Unlimited.	Good secondary market.	Yield basis. Actual days on a 360-day year. Interest at maturity.
Short-term tax-exempts I. Project Notes of local public housing agencies	Notes of local agencies secured by a contract with Federal agencies and by pledge of "full faith and credit" of U.S.	$1,000 to $1 million	Up to 1 year.	Good secondary market.	Yield basis. 30-day month on a 360-day year. Interest at maturity.
Short-term tax-exempts II. Tax & bond anticipation notes	Notes of states, municipalities, or political subdivisions.	$1,000 to $1 million	Various, usually 3 months to 1 year from issue	Good secondary market.	Yield basis. Usually 30 days on a 360-day year. Interest at maturity.

Source: *Money Market Investments, op. cit.,* front cover.

TABLE 3-2

Money-Market Investments (Foreign)

	Obligation	Denominations	Maturities	Marketability	Basis
Canadian Treasury bills	Canadian Government obligation. Offered by Canadian Treasury through weekly auctions on Thursday for settlement the next day. Subject to Canadian withholding tax.	$1,000 to $1 million	Normally up to 180 days.	Good secondary market.	Discounted. Actual days on a 365-day year.
United Kingdom Treasury bills	British Government obligation. Offered by British Treasury through weekly auctions on Friday for settlement any day the following week. Not subject to U.K. withholding tax.	$5,000 to $100,000	Normally 91 days. Occasional 63-day maturity offered.	Good secondary market.	Discounted. Actual days on a 365-day year.
Canadian commercial paper	1. Finance Promissory notes of finance companies sold through commercial paper dealers and in some cases placed directly with the investor. Subject to Canadian withholding tax.	$5,000 to $5 million	3 days to 1 year.	No secondary market. Sale of paper before maturity is subject to negotiation with issuer in each case.	Discounted or interest-bearing. Actual days on 365-day year.

Canadian commercial paper	II. Industrial	Promissory notes of industrial companies sold through commercial paper dealers. Subject to Canadian withholding tax.	$50,000 to $5 million	Demand to 1 year.	No secondary market. Sale of paper before maturity is subject to negotiation with issuer in each case.	Normally interest-bearing. Actual days on 365-day year.
British hire purchase paper		Deposit receipts of finance companies placed directly with investors. Not subject to U.K. withholding tax.	Open	30 days to 364 days.	No secondary market. Sale of deposit receipt before maturity subject to negotiation.	Interest-bearing. Actual days on 365-day year.
British local authority paper		Deposit receipts of British municipalities arranged through brokers in London. Not subject to U.K. withholding tax.	Open	2-day notice to 20 years.	No secondary market. Sale of deposit receipt before maturity subject to negotiation.	Interest-bearing. Actual days on 365-day year.

Source: *Ibid.*, back cover.

Money-Market Instruments of Other Countries

Table 3-2 provides the major characteristics of Canadian and British money-market instruments. In theory, there is no reason why an American investor should not consider the liquidity instruments of any major foreign country if the credit standing is adequate. To minimize the risk of the transaction, however, it is necessary to "cover" it in the forward exchange market (which merely involves reaching an agreement in the present as to the price at which one will buy or sell an amount of foreign money at some point in the future).

To illustrate covered arbitrage, suppose that the NKV Trust wished to buy $1 million of 10 percent, 180-day securities of the Dak government. The Dak currency is currently exchanging at 30 to the dollar. The 180-day forward Dak is quoted at 31 to the dollar (the rate at which it would be possible to contract now for delivery in six months). The return to be earned by NKV on a covered transaction would be determined as follows:

Now: (a) Sell 1\overline{m}$ to obtain Dak (@ 30:1) = 30$\overline{m}$ Dak

          (b) Buy 30$\overline{m}$ Dak securities

                (will earn interest of 1.5$\overline{m}$ Dak)

          (c) Sell 31.5$\overline{m}$ Dak for delivery in 180

                days against the dollar (@ 31:1)

In six months: (a) Redeem bonds = 31.5$\overline{m}$ Dak

             (b) Deliver on forward contract

                    (31.5$\overline{m}$/31) = \$1,016,130.

$$\text{Return} = \frac{\$16,130}{\$1,000,000} \times \frac{360}{180} \approx \underline{\underline{3.2\%}}$$

THE CAPITAL MARKET

The major distinction between the money and capital markets is the maturity of the instruments. Because capital-market instruments have maturities beyond one year, the measurement of yield on these securities depends upon time value of money calculations.[4] The basic equation for the yield on any asset is:

$$P_0 = \frac{A_1}{(1+i)^1} + \frac{A_2}{(1+i)^2} + \cdots + \frac{A_n}{(1+i)^n} \tag{3.1}$$

[4]A comprehensive review of time value of money and financial mathematics is presented in Appendix A.

Where: P_0 is the current price of the asset

A_1 is the dollar return from the asset one period (year) from now

A_2 is the dollar return two periods from now, and so on

n is the number of periods the asset will generate payments

i is the yield on the asset

This equation may be rewritten as:

$$P_0 = \sum_{t=1}^{n} \frac{A_t}{(1+i)^t} \qquad (3.2)$$

The computation of a rate of return is easy if the dollar payments in the future are constant. All one need do is divide the dollar payments into its current value. This quotient is the factor that appears in Appendix C.4. For example, if a mortgage obligates the borrower to pay a sum of $1,000 per year for eighteen years, and the face value of the mortgage is $10,000, the factor is:

$$\$10,000/\$1,000 = 10$$

Checking Appendix C.4, we find that a factor 10.059 exists for an eighteen year present value if the rate of return is 7 percent. Thus, the mortgage has a yield of about 7 percent. In many cases, the solution for a rate of return will not be found directly from the tables but will require interpolation.

When the future payment stream is not constant but differs from year to year, the solution is more tedious and requires a trial and error approach. Bonds pay an annual (or more frequently, semiannual) coupon. At the date of maturity of the bond, the principal sum (par value) of the bond is repaid to the holder. Thus, equation 3.1 could be rewritten in this case as:

$$P_0 = \sum_{t=1}^{n} \frac{C_t}{(1+i)^t} + \frac{P_n}{(1+i)^n} \qquad (3.3)$$

Where: P_0 is the current market price of the bond

C_t is the annual dollar coupon payment on the bond

P_n is the par value of the bond

n is the number of years until the bond matures

i is the yield to maturity on the bond

Suppose a bond will mature in five years. The bond will pay $1,000 upon maturity and pays $70.00 per year each year for the five-year period. What is its yield to maturity? To find the answer, we must know the current price of the bond, which we shall assume is 95. Since bond prices are quoted in percentages of par, this means that for a $1,000 par bond one pays $950.00 for a stream of payments of $70.00 for five years plus $1,000 at the end of the fifth year. Because the bond is selling at a discount, we know that its yield must be greater than its coupon yield of 7 percent (that is, $70.00 on a par of $1,000). From Appendix C.3 we find that at 8 percent, the present value of this stream is:

$$3.993 \times \$70.00 = \$279.51$$

$$.681 \times \$1000.00 = \underline{\ \ 681.00\ }$$

$$\$960.51$$

This present value is too high. Hence, the yield must be greater than 8 percent. Let us try 9 percent:

$$3.890 \times \$70.00 = \$272.30$$

$$.650 \times \$1000 = \underline{\ \ 650.00\ }$$

$$\$922.30$$

The value of $950.00 is between $960.51 and $922.30. Thus, by interpolation we may find the yield to maturity:

$$8.0 \text{ percent} = \$960.51$$

$$9.0 \text{ percent} = \$922.30$$

$$8.3 \text{ percent} = \$950.00$$

For a bond, there is a shortcut formula that will give the yield to maturity rather closely if the bond is selling reasonably near par and if there are only a few years before it matures. This equation is:

$$i = \frac{C + (P_n - P_0)/n}{(P_n + P_0)/2} \tag{3.4}$$

We may use equation (3.4) to solve for the yield in the previous example:

$$i = \frac{70 + (1000 - 950)/5}{(1000 + 950)/2}$$

$$= \frac{80}{975} = 8.2 \text{ percent}$$

Thus, the shortcut formula comes close to the actual yield to maturity of 8.3 percent.

LONG-TERM DEBT INSTRUMENTS

The capital market may be distinguished from the money market in several ways other than maturity. The securities involved are far more numerous and varied. The markets themselves generally lack the breadth and depth of the money market in the technical sense that the spread between bid and asked prices is greater and the change in price on consecutive transactions is also generally greater. Finally, the capital market is regulated by the government (primarily through the Securities and Exchange Commission and its various self-regulatory arms) in many more specific ways than the money market.

Federal Government and Agency Securities

The long-term marketable debt of the federal government consists of *treasury notes* and *treasury bonds*, both of which usually pay interest semiannually. The notes are issued with an original maturity of one to seven years and are generally sold quarterly. Although the bonds have no maturity restrictions, they have mostly been issued for periods in excess of five years. For more than one hundred years, a law has existed prohibiting the payment of interest in excess of 4 1/4 percent on treasury bonds. As a result, sales ground to a halt in the mid-1960s; in 1971, however, Congress gave the Treasury limited power to sell bonds at rates in excess of this ceiling. Certain treasury bonds may be used to pay estate taxes at par. Because many of the issues that qualify for paying estate taxes at par were sold long ago at low coupons, they are now priced at substantial discounts from par and are therefore attractive to aged tax-payers. The result of this purchasing pressure causes the pattern of bond yields to be distorted, as by no means are all treasury bonds qualified.

To illustrate the effect of the estate tax qualification, consider the case of Mr. Aged who has a five-year life expectancy. Assume he can purchase a 2 percent qualified bond at 80 or a five-year, 8 percent treasury security at par. If Mr. Aged is in the 50 percent marginal tax bracket, his decision might appear as follows:

Year	Non-Qual.	Qual.	Difference
0	−100	− 80	−20
1–5	+ 4	+ 1	+ 3
5	+100	+100	−

At no positive rate of discount will five annual after-tax flows of $3 recover the initial $20 difference. Therefore, the qualified bond should be purchased.

Government agencies and sponsored corporations also issue short- and long-term debt in their own names. This group includes the Federal National Mortgage Association ("Fanny Mae"), the Government National Mortgage Association ("Ginny Mae"), Tennessee Valley Authority (TVA), the Federal Land Banks, Banks for Cooperatives, the Export-Import Bank, and other agencies constantly being established by the government. None of the debts of these agencies is a direct obligation of the government, although it has been assumed by the investment community that none of them would be allowed to default. As a result, *agency issues* command a rate only slightly higher than treasury securities. The securities are generally issued originally following an announcement by the fiscal agent and trade in a reasonably active secondary market.[5]

Finally, bonds are also offered by international institutions of which the United States is a member. Included in this group are the International Bank for Reconstruction and Development (IBRD or simply, World Bank) and the Inter-American Development Bank. These issues are secured by the assets of the banks and, beyond that, by the right of the banks to call upon their members for additional contributions to meet debt requirements. The investment community has viewed this "back door" guarantee as only slightly weaker than the implicit guarantee of the agency issues and has priced the securities accordingly.

State and Local Government Securities

Municipals were introduced earlier in this chapter, and the point was made that they are currently exempt from federal income taxes. These bonds are often in *serial* form, meaning that a specified portion of an issue matures each year. They may also be identified as either *general obligations* or *revenue bonds.* General obligation bonds (GO's) pledge the "full faith and credit" of the government entity to the payment of the bonds. In analyzing such bonds (discussed in detail in Chapter 8), aside from the ratings given by the bond agencies and the default record of the community, one often looks at the value of property, the tax rate, debt per capita, debt service as a proportion of the

[5]One aid in market efficiency is size of issue. Even with the best of intentions, it is very difficult to maintain an active secondary market in a security of which there is little outstanding. This is one reason that treasury bills are such good liquidity instruments; every weekly offering is for several billion dollars, and therefore a transaction involving several million dollars' worth of bills should not upset the market greatly. The longer-term issues, however, are much smaller, raising the possibility of a large transaction upsetting the price. For example, if an investor wished to acquire in the market 1\overline{m}$ of a 20\overline{m}$ corporate bond issue, he would undoubtedly need to bid the price up significantly. Fortunately, ratings come to his rescue. Instead of seeking a particular issue, the investor might simply specify that he wished 1\overline{m}$ of Aa-rated industrials maturing in the next ten to fifteen years. His broker could then obtain whichever bonds of this type were offered, and the investor would receive several different bonds at a far more reasonable price. Thus, ratings help make "thin" markets more efficient.

operating budget, and various demographic factors (is the community growing? is it dependent upon one industry? and so on).

Revenue bonds, on the other hand, do not pledge the credit of the community but only the proceeds from the project being financed by the bonds (everything from toll roads to college dormitories). In this case, therefore, the investor looks at the need for the project, the adequacy of the expected usage and charges, and so on. Confusion can arise because there have been cases of quite credit-worthy communities defaulting upon revenue bonds when proceeds were inadequate because they were not obligated to pay the bonds; the Calumet Skyway bonds issued by Chicago are a case in point.[6]

Foreign Securities

Several factors are currently in operation to frustrate the efforts of American investors to purchase foreign stocks and bonds. First, of course, is the currency risk — the possibility that the currency in which the foreign security is denominated will change its parity vis-a-vis the dollar. In the short-term area, it was suggested that a covering transaction in the forward exchange market could eliminate this risk. Unfortunately, however, the forward market in most currencies becomes quite thin beyond six months, and even in the most active currencies it is difficult to obtain a commitment beyond a few years.

The Interest Equalization Tax (IET), in effect in the United States as a "temporary" measure since 1963, places a tax on the purchase of most foreign securities (with the major exception of certain Canadian securities). The tax on stock was originally 15 percent of the price, has been as high as 22 1/2 percent, and is 11 1/4 percent at this writing. The tax on bonds is scaled up by maturity, with the longest-term bonds bearing the same tax as stock.

Taxes in foreign countries present an additional burden. Most long-term foreign securities are subject to withholding tax on interest and dividends paid (most of the short-term foreign instruments are exempted). Depending upon the tax treaty between the United States and the foreign country involved, taxes withheld abroad may serve as either a credit or deduction on American tax returns. If only a deduction is allowed, a greater total tax is paid. Even if a full tax credit is allowed, a loss may occur if the foreign withholding rate is greater than the American rate paid (often the case for financial institutions and obviously so for tax-exempt organizations).

It has therefore become extremely difficult for American citizens or residents to invest in foreign securities. Except for Canadian securities, which

---

[6]This also illustrates some additional protection offered by the bond market. It is almost an unwritten rule that an issuer who has defaulted will find it virtually impossible to raise new funds until settlement is made with the old holders. Even though Chicago was not legally obligated on the Calumet bonds, it found the reception for its other bonds after the default sufficiently cold that officials for some years seriously considered paying them off and recently have begun doing so.

remain popular and are generally exempt from the IET, it appears that the only major purchases are foreign stocks that are expected to appreciate rapidly. One unfortunate aspect of this regulatory position is that foreign securities provide an entire dimension of portfolio diversification that is currently denied to the American investor.[7]

To illustrate the international tax effects, consider the case of Mr. Ronson, who is contemplating the purchase of a British consol (a perpetual bond). The bond pays interest of £10 per year and is currently selling for £100, at which it is expected to remain. The pound is currently selling at $2.40, although there is a 10 percent chance that at the end of ten years, when he plans to sell the bond, it will be $2.00. The purchase is subject to an 11 percent IET and taxes are withheld by the British at 30 percent, which is only allowed as a deduction by the U.S. Mr. Ronson's American tax rate (adjusted for the British tax deduction) is 40 percent.

Initial Cost	Annual Income	Final Proceeds	
£100	£10	$240	$200
X 2.40 $/£	X .7 Br. Tax	X .9	X .1
$240	£ 7	$216	$ 20
X 1.11 IET	X 2.40 $/£		
$264	$16.80	$216	
	X .6 US Tax	+20	
	$10	μ = $236	

Year	Cash Flow	@3%	Present Value
0	−$264	1.000	−$264.00
1–10	+ 10	8.53	+ 85.30
10	+236	.744	+ 175.58
			−$ 3.12

Thus, an apparent 10 percent return is reduced to just under 3 percent.

Corporate Debt

Corporate debt may take the form of either a publicly offered bond issue or a privately placed note. The private placement is generally made with one or a few large institutional investors and is, as a rule, held until maturity by the original purchasers. In return for this lack of marketability, the lenders generally receive a slightly higher coupon and are able to obtain a larger portion of the

[7]For the potential of this area of portfolio diversification if and when capital controls are dismantled, see H. G. Grubel, "Internationally Diversified Portfolios," *American Economic Review*, (December 1968), pp. 1299–314. For the EMH view that there is only one world capital market, see T. Agmon, "The Relations Among Equity Markets," *Journal of Finance* (September 1972), pp. 839–55.

issue (an advantage to institutions such as insurance companies that have small staffs and much money to invest).

Bonds are sold to the public through an underwriting, by which an investment banker buys the bonds from the issuer, marks them up, and attempts to sell them to the general public. The bonds can be bought from the issuer by the investment banker either at a price negotiated by the parties involved or by competitive bid. Most companies regulated by agencies of the government (power companies, railroads, and so on) are required to sell their securities by competitive bid; most others negotiate. The bonds are issued and sold under an *indenture*, which is a statement of rights and obligations negotiated between the issuing company and the trustee (often the trust department of a bank) as representative of the lenders. The importance of the indenture, and its salient features printed in the prospectus, cannot be overstated; it is the final arbiter of the rights and duties of borrower and lender, as many bond buyers have subsequently discovered to their sorrow.

Among the facts to be found in the indenture are the provisions for retirement and refunding of the issue. The former are called the *sinking fund* provisions. As a rule, a portion of the bond issue will be retired each year prior to maturity. This may be done by having the company pay the trustee, who, in turn, determines by lot which bonds will be called for redemption or by merely having the company enter the market to buy the required number of bonds. These two methods may usually be employed at the company's option, which is a disadvantage to the bondholder. If rates rise and the bonds go to a discount, the company can buy them in the market; if rates fall, the company can have the trustee call the bonds at or about par. In like manner, the refunding (or *call*) provisions also work to the disadvantage of the lender.[8] If interest rates decline, the issuer invariably has the right to call the bond issue and refund it at the lower rate. The only protection to the bondholder is that such a call must generally be made at a slight premium over par and that there may be an interval of five or ten years after the bonds are issued (the *no-call period*) during which a call is not allowed. Finally, the company may be allowed to call the issue at a very small premium if the funds do not come from a cheaper bond issue (for example, if the company sells assets), and it may also be allowed to double the sinking fund payments at its option. The issuer can generally be expected to undertake its most advantageous option, which is also generally the least advantageous for the holder.

The indenture will also indicate the security of the issue. *Mortgage bonds* are secured by a lien on all or part of the property of the issuer. In bankruptcy, the mortgage bondholders have first claim upon the proceeds of the property against which they hold a lien; to the extent that these proceeds are inadequate, the bondholders become general creditors for the rest. It is also possible to issue

[8] In a reasonably efficient market, of course, the bondholder would receive a higher return in compensation for these disadvantages.

second (and even lower priority) mortgage bonds; these holders have a claim on any proceeds from the mortgaged property after the prior mortgage holders are satisfied (and become general creditors for any of the remainder). A very strong mortgage bond would include an *after-acquired clause,* indicating that not only is all current property of the company subject to the mortgage but all new property acquired later is also encumbered; this provision is so strong that it would require the company to make any new debt second mortgage or lower in priority. The *open-end* indenture is less rigid in that the company is allowed to issue additional debt on the same mortgage; to protect the old holders, however, the new debt is generally limited to some fraction (often 50-66 percent) of the net increase in property subject to the mortgage. Two other types of secured bonds are the *collateral trust bond* and the *equipment trust certificate.* For the first type, the borrower places the securities of other companies into a trust and then issues securities against the trust. For the second type, used extensively by railroads and airlines, title to the equipment is held by a trustee for the benefit of the lenders until the company has redeemed the debt; thus, the lenders can obtain immediate possession of the equipment and resell it if the borrower goes into bankruptcy.

Debentures are not secured by any particular piece of property and are only covered by the general credit of the borrowing corporation. In bankruptcy, the debenture holder ranks as a general creditor of the corporation. *Subordinated debentures* are of even lower priority, in that the proceeds that the holders would receive as general creditors in bankruptcy must go to satisfy the claims of the issues to which they are subordinated. Even junior subordinated debentures have been issued. *Income bonds* obligate the issuer to pay interest only if the firm's earnings are sufficient to make payment. The income bond has been used by trustees in many railroad reorganizations. As a result, these bonds have achieved a relatively poor reputation. It might also be noted that, in the purchase of most bonds, the investor pays the price quoted plus accrued interest on the bond; in the case of income bonds and bonds in default, no accrued interest is included (the bonds are said to trade "flat"). Finally, *convertible bonds,* which grant the holder the option to exchange the bond for stock at a specified ratio, are also issued in debenture form; these are discussed in greater detail in Chapter 13. In conclusion, it must be stressed that only an examination of the indenture will reveal the attributes of any given issue.

EQUITY SECURITIES

Equity instruments are also a part of the capital market. *Preferred stock* represents a curious combination of various features of debt and common stock.

It is like common stock in that the instrument is called stock and included in the equity section of the balance sheet; payments are called dividends and are not deductible for tax purposes; the payment of dividends is not legally required; and the issue has no fixed maturity. Preferred stock is like debt in that the dividends have a fixed maximum rate;[9] preferred holders generally have no vote (unless a specified number – often four to six quarterly – of dividends are passed, in which case they may elect a minority of the board); holders are entitled to no more than the amount paid in to the firm in case of liquidation; and preferred stock may contain the same call, sinking fund, or conversion features as any debenture.

Cumulative preferred requires that all past, unpaid dividends be paid (although not with interest) before any common dividend may be paid; *noncumulative preferred* only requires that the current year's dividend be paid before a common dividend is paid. Companies with either large arrearages on their preferred stock or high-dividend noncallable preferred are often forced to make an exchange offer for cash or other securities in order to retire the preferred. The yield on preferred is simply dividend/price; the computation is meaningless for preferred in arrears. The tax law allows corporations that hold stock (either preferred or common) of other corporations to exclude 85 percent of any dividends received from taxes. Because this causes preferreds to be almost tax exempt to a corporate holder, it may appear in some cases that a company's preferreds yield less in the market than its bonds.

The residual owners of the firm are the *common stockholders*. As such, they have claim on the earnings of the firm after all creditors are paid. In case of the dissolution or liquidation of the firm, the common stockholders are entitled to the net assets remaining after the claims of creditors are satisfied. They have the right to examine the books of the company (usually deemed satisfied by having the company send out the annual report containing audited statements) and may have the right to maintain their proportionate ownership (the "preemptive" right to be discussed in Chapter 12). They also have the right to elect a board of directors to act as their agent in running the firm.

Two voting systems are possible in the election of a board of directors. Under the majority voting system, a shareholder votes for each place on the board according to the number of shares he owns. If he owns one hundred shares, the holder casts one hundred votes for each director position to be filled. A candidate must obtain votes representing a majority of the shares to win. Under the cumulative voting system, a shareholder has votes equal to the number of shares owned times the number of directors to be elected. These may be cast in any manner, including all for one director (because this method allows

---

[9]A rare type, called *participating preferred*, provides that after preferred dividends have been paid and common shareholders have received a like return, both classes may participate by some formula in any additional dividends to be paid.

minority shareholders to elect a director it is opposed by most companies). The minimum number of shares required to elect a specific number of directors under cumulative voting is given as follows:

$$\frac{S \times N}{D + 1} + 1 \tag{3.5}$$

Where: S = total number of shares outstanding

N = number of directors desired to elect

D = total number of directors to be elected

Significant statistics regarding common stock are *earnings per share* (net income available to common/number of shares), *dividends per share* (dividends paid to common/number of shares), *book value per share* (assets − liabilities − preferred/number of shares), *current yield* (dividends per share/price per share), and *price-earnings ratio* (price per share/earnings per share). These are very important measures that will be examined in much greater detail in several chapters to follow.

PROBLEMS

1. Find the price and yield on a treasury bill:
   a. due in 30 days on a 4 percent basis.
   b. due in 180 days on a 5 percent basis.
   c. due in 150 days on a 6 percent basis.
2. Refer to 1, above:
   a. Suppose you bought the bill in 1b and were selling it 30 days later as per 1c. What return did you earn?
   b. Would you have been wiser to elect 1a?
   c. Would your answer to 1a change depending upon whether the bill were originally a 91- or 182-day bill? Why?
   d. What return on a tax-exempt security would be equivalent to 1a, b, and c if the investor's tax rate were 30 percent? Sixty percent?
3. In the example on page 42, suppose that the NKV Trust decided not to cover their transaction and instead to sell the Dak at the end of six months for whatever the going rate was at the time. What would their return have been if the exchange rate at the time were 30:1? 35:1? 50:1? Why is an uncovered transaction inconsistent with the basic function of the money market?
4. Compute the annual return, on both a covered and uncovered basis, of the purchase of $10m̄, ninety-day U.K. Treasury bills at 9 percent if the spot

pound is $2.40 = £1, and the ninety-day forward pound is $2.35, if the actual spot rate in ninety days is:

    a. $2.40 = £1

    b. $2.30 = £1

    c. $2.50 = £1

5. A bond has a coupon yield of 5 percent (that is, pays $50.00 per year on a par of $1,000), matures in twenty years, and sells for 80. Compute the yield to maturity of the bond using the discount tables and the shortcut formula. Compare your results.

6. Mr. Elgar has bought stock in the Pomp and Circumstance Corp. The firm pays a dividend of $1.00 per share per year. Elgar feels that this dividend will be maintained over the ten years he plans to hold the stock. If Elgar paid $25.00 per share and sold his stock for $30.00 per share in ten years what is his expected yield from holding the stock?

7. Suppose Mr. Aged (see the example on page 45) is expected to live ten years and ten-year securities yield 8 percent. Would this change the solution?

8. Mr. Ronson (see example on page 48) is also contemplating the purchase of a ten-year security of the Ziff government. The Ziff trades at 50 to the dollar and could trade at 40 to the dollar at the end of ten years with a probability of 0.2. Gross yield is 12 percent, with 30 percent withholding treated as a credit on U.S. taxes. The IET is 5 percent. Determine Mr. Ronson's expected return.

9. The Lafarge Corporation has a 40 percent tax rate and is contemplating the purchase of securities of the Camus Corporation. Camus twenty-year, 7 percent debentures are selling at 95, while the preferred (6 percent) is selling at par. What is the return on each security? Which should be purchased? Why? Would your answer change if Lafarge were a tax-exempt institution?

10. D. Sent wishes to elect himself to the board of the Webster Corporation. There are 1 million Webster shares outstanding and ten directors to be elected.

    a. How many shares must D. Sent control to elect himself under a majority voting system?

    b. How many under a cumulative system?

    c. How would the answers to a and b change if the company reduced the board to six?

REFERENCES

Dougall, Herbert E., *Capital Markets and Institutions,* 2nd ed., Chaps. 1 and 7–11. Englewood Cliffs, N.J.: Prentice-Hall, Inc., 1970.

Handbook of Securities of the United States Government and Federal Agencies. New York: First Boston Corp., biennial.

Money Market Investments. New York: Morgan Guaranty Trust Co., 1970.

Monhollon, Jimmie R., ed., *Instruments of the Money Market.* Richmond: Federal Reserve Bank of Richmond, 1970.

Robinson, Roland I., *Money and Capital Markets,* Parts II and III. New York: McGraw-Hill Book Co., 1964.

"The Row Over Commercial Paper Ratings," *Fortune,* May 1971, p. 274.

Woodworth, C. Walter, *The Money Market and Monetary Management,* Chaps. 5–9. New York: Harper and Row, 1965.

4

Macroeconomic Influences Upon the Money and Capital Markets[1]

INFLUENCE OF SAVINGS AND INVESTMENT

The return that can be expected from securities depends upon the financial condition of the issuer. This condition, in turn, is influenced by the economic condition of the nation. Thus, it may be said that the benefit stream to be received by a security holder is, to a degree, dependent upon the prospective state of the economy. Furthermore, the magnitude of changes in the condition of the economy will affect the issuer and hence the risk of the security. Finally, economic conditions will affect the supply of and demand for securities and hence the return that may be earned.

One of the major developments of Keynesian and neo-Keynesian economic theory has been an increased awareness of the impacts of real investment and, especially, government spending upon the level of aggregate economic activity. Because the return to be earned on securities in the long run and the level of their market prices in the short run are related to the level of economic activity, the latter must be a matter of continuing interest to the security analyst and portfolio manager. This chapter considers some of the major macroeconomic factors that influence the securities markets and the probable direction and magnitude of their impacts.

[1] This chapter does not presume to take the place of an adequate grounding in macroeconomics and monetary economics. The reader is referred to any number of standard texts in the area, some of which are cited at the end of this chapter.

The Basic Keynesian Model

The basic Keynesian model postulates that the level of aggregate economic activity (Y) is the sum of all consumer spending (C), business investment (I), and government spending (G) that takes place in any single year. Symbolically,

$$Y = C + I + G \tag{4.1}$$

Consumer spending is related to the overall level of income, however. If we assume that consumers pay T dollars per year in total taxes, that they receive T_r dollars from the government in transfer payments (for example, social security, unemployment compensation, and so on), and that they spend a constant proportion (b) of each extra dollar of disposable income $[b = \Delta C/\Delta(Y-T+T_r)]$, then changes in consumption spending may be viewed as:

$$\Delta C = b(\Delta Y - \Delta T + \Delta T_r) \tag{4.2}$$

Furthermore, if we postulate a world in which taxes and transfer payments are not a function of the level of income, it is possible to derive the *simple investment multiplier:*

$$\Delta Y = \Delta C + \Delta I + \Delta G$$

$$\Delta Y = b(\Delta Y - \Delta T + \Delta T_r) + \Delta I + \Delta G$$

Let $\Delta T = \Delta T_r = \Delta G = 0$, then:

$$\Delta Y = b\Delta Y + \Delta I$$

$$\Delta Y(1-b) = \Delta I$$

$$\Delta Y = \frac{1}{1-b} \Delta I \tag{4.3}$$

The quantity $[1/(1-b)]$ is the simple investment multiplier. It indicates the amount by which the total level of income would rise (fall) if there were an exogenous increase (decrease) in business investment for plant and equipment. Thus, if we considered a simplified economy without income taxes in which consumers had a *marginal propensity to consume* (b) of 0.8, autonomous investment would increase income not just by ΔI but rather by $[1/(1-b)]\Delta I$, or $[1/(1-.8) = 5]\Delta I$. A $10 billion increase in business investment would not only add this amount to total aggregate income, but because such spending would induce further spending in the consumer sector, the total increase to income would be:

$$\Delta Y = \frac{1}{(1-b)} \Delta I = (5)\,(\$10 \text{ billion}) = \$50 \text{ billion}$$

The reader will note that an exogenous increase in government spending (or consumption for that matter) would produce the same result. If $\Delta I = 0$ but $\Delta G = \$10$ billion, the same $50 billion increase in aggregate income would be effected.

Admittedly, the economy postulated above is greatly simplified. In the first place, it is very likely that higher levels of income may not only stimulate consumers to spend more but may also encourage businessmen to invest extra amounts. Hence, we may conceive of a *marginal propensity to invest* $Z(Z = \Delta I / \Delta Y)$. The presence of this factor may add an "accelerator" effect to economic activity such that:

$$\Delta Y = \Delta C + \Delta I + \Delta G$$

Let $\Delta T = \Delta T_r = 0$, then:

$$\Delta Y = b\Delta Y + Z\Delta Y + \Delta G$$

$$\Delta Y(1 - b - Z) = \Delta G$$

$$\Delta Y = \frac{1}{1 - b - Z} \Delta G$$

Suppose in the previous example $Z = 0.1$. The change in national income, given an increase in government spending (or investment) of $10 billion, would be:

$$\Delta Y = \left(\frac{1}{1 - .8 - .1} \right)(\$10 \text{ billion}) = \$100 \text{ billion.}$$

In a world of proportional income taxes, total taxes (T) could be expressed as (tY), where t is the rate of taxation. If we assume that transfer payments are inversely proportional to income, changes in total payments (ΔT_r) may be expressed as $-t_r\Delta Y$, where $t_r = -(\Delta T_r / \Delta Y)$. The government expenditure multiplier (in the absence of induced investment) then becomes:

$$\Delta Y = \Delta C + \Delta I + \Delta G$$

$$\Delta Y = b(\Delta Y - \Delta T + \Delta T_r) + 0 + \Delta G$$

$$\Delta Y = b[(\Delta Y) - (t\Delta Y) + (-t_r\Delta Y)] + \Delta G$$

$$\Delta Y = b\Delta Y - bt\Delta Y - bt_r\Delta Y + \Delta G$$

$$\Delta Y(1 - b + bt + bt_r) = \Delta G$$

$$\Delta Y = \left(\frac{1}{1 - b(1 - t - t_r)} \right) \Delta G \tag{4.4}$$

For the society discussed above, let the rate of taxation (t) be 30 percent and the marginal rate of transfer payments (t_r) be 0.1. Then,

$$\Delta Y = \left(\frac{1}{1-b(1-t-t_r)} \right) \Delta G$$

$$\Delta Y = \left(\frac{1}{1-.8(1-.3-.1)} \right) (\$10 \text{ billion})$$

$$\Delta Y = \left(\frac{1}{1-.48} \right) (\$10 \text{ billion}) = \$19.2 \text{ billion}$$

Notice that the multiplier effect is greatly reduced because added taxes and lower transfer payments tend to dampen the stimulating aspects of the increase in government spending.

Investment-Savings Equilibrium

Now that some of the implications of the income-constrained multiplier process have been demonstrated, let us consider more concretely the equilibrium conditions that the economy will reach. The Keynesian system specifies not only that $Y = C + I + G$ but also that $Y = C + S + T$ (where S = savings). For the two definitions to be the same, and thus for equilibrium conditions to exist, it is necessary that $I + G = S + T$.[2]

Let:

A = amount of consumption if $Y = 0$

S = saving

i = interest rate

B = level of investment if $i = 0$

g = interest elasticity of investment $\left(-\frac{\Delta I}{\Delta i} \right)$

Then:

$$S = -A + (1-b)(Y - T + T_r)$$

$$S = -A + (1-b-t+bt-t_r+bt_r)Y, \text{ and}$$

$$T = tY \tag{4.5}$$

It follows, therefore, that:

$$S + T = -A + (1-b+bt-t_r+bt_r)Y \tag{4.6}$$

[2] A more detailed discussion may be found in David E. W. Laidler, *The Demand for Money: Theories and Evidence* (Scranton, Pa.: International Textbook Company, 1969).

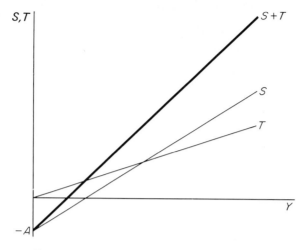

Figure 4-1   Savings and Taxes as a Function of Income

This relationship is graphed as Figure 4-1. It shows that as the level of income rises, the volume of saving generated and taxes paid in the economy also increases. To add further realism to the model, we may postulate that the level of investment is inversely related to the rate of interest. Hence:

$$I = B - gi \qquad (4.7)$$

If G is exogenously determined by the government, then:

$$G + I = \bar{G} + B - gi \qquad (4.8)$$

This relationship is graphed in Figure 4-2 with the axes reversed (to correspond to Figure 4-3).

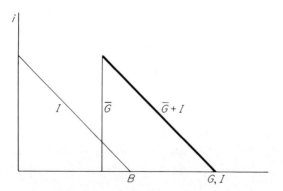

Figure 4-2   Investment and Government Spending as a Function of the Interest Rate

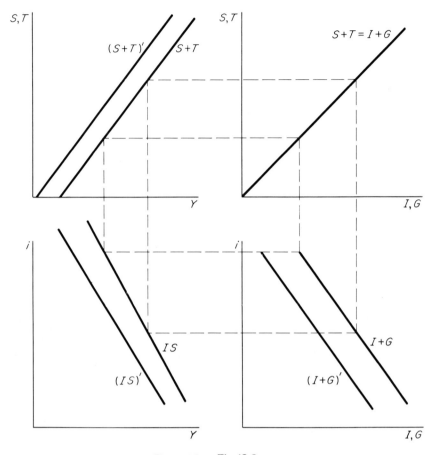

Figure 4-3   The IS Curve

By equating equations 4.6 and 4.8, it is possible to determine the equilibrium conditions.

$$-A + (1 - b + bt - t_r + bt_r)Y = \bar{G} + B - gi$$

$$i = \frac{1}{g}(A + B + \bar{G}) - \frac{(1 - b + bt - t_r + bt_r)}{g}\, Y \qquad (4.9)$$

These conditions are also graphed in Figure 4-3. It will be observed that no unique solution exists, but rather a set of income and interest rate levels at which $S + T = I + G$; this is called an *IS* curve. A second equilibrium condition, introduced in the next section, is required before a specific solution may be obtained. It will be noted, however, both from the graph and equation 4.9 that an upshift in the *S+T* function *(S+T)'* or a downshift in the *I+G* function *(I+G)'* will cause a downshift in the *IS* function *(IS)'* and vice versa. The implication is that as the rate of saving or taxation rises or the level of government spending or the efficiency of investment falls, the equilibrium level of the interest rate and/or the income level tends to fall; the reverse is also true.

In light of the above, it should be anticipated that an increase in government spending, a reduction in taxes, an increased propensity to consume, or improved expectations for investment should cause national income to rise. Assuming that industry sales keep pace and a company can maintain its market share, the increase in national income should be reflected in larger company cash flows. Larger company flows, in turn, cause its bonds to be more secure and the dividend-paying potential of its stock to be enhanced. Thus, an initial impact (subject to qualification below) of such changes should be upward pressure on the prices of both shares and bonds, especially in the case of companies that would benefit the most from the increase in aggregate demand. The use of aggregate data to predict company flows is considered in more detail in Chapter 6.

INFLUENCE OF MONEY SUPPLY AND DEMAND

In addition to the requirement that $S + T = I + G$, equilibrium in the Keynesian system also requires that the supply of money equal the demand for money. The supply of money $(\bar{M})$, which consists of all currency and demand deposits held by the public, is essentially fixed by policy actions of the Federal Reserve and is therefore treated as an exogenous variable in the analysis. The demand for money (L) has historically been divided into two parts. The combined Keynesian transactions and precautionary demand for money (L_1) is generally assumed to be a direct function of income $(L_1 = lY)$; this demand constitutes the need for money to purchase goods in the normal course of events and to hold against a "rainy day." The Keynesian asset or speculative demand for money (L_2) is generally assumed to be an inverse function of the rate of interest $(L_2 = J - mi)$; this demand *for* money can most easily be viewed as a *lack* of demand for long-term bonds when interest rates are low (bond prices high) and there is a high probability that rates will rise (prices fall). Therefore:

$$L_1 = lY$$

$$L_2 = J - mi$$

$$L = L_1 + L_2 = lY + J - mi \qquad (4.10)$$

In equilibrium, $L = \bar{M}$.

$$\bar{M} = J + lY - mi$$

$$i = \frac{J - \bar{M}}{m} + \frac{l}{m} Y$$

(4.11)

These relationships are graphed in Figure 4-4.[3] It will again be noted that no single answer emerges but rather a set of Y,i combinations at which $L=M$. It will also be noted that an increase in the money supply (to $M'M'$) causes an outshift in the LM curve (to LM').

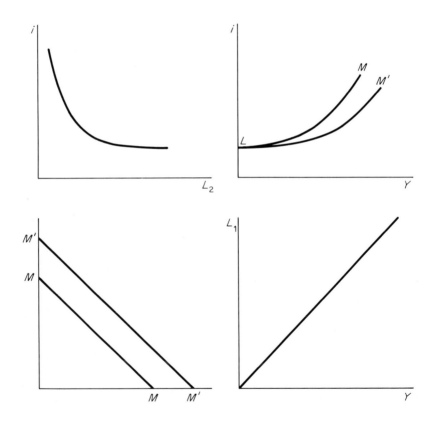

Figure 4-4   The LM Curve

[3] It will be noted that the L_2 function is graphed as curvilinear even though it is expressed in the formula as linear. This is done to allow for the possible existence (empirically challenged) of the "liquidity trap" discussed later in this chapter.

It is now possible, at a given price level, to equate equation 4.11 with equation 4.9 in order to obtain a unique equilibrium level of i and Y. This level corresponds to the point of intersection of the IS and LM curves, as shown in Figure 4-5 as Y_0, i_0. From this initial equilibrium position, an increase in the money supply $(L'M')$ will shift the new equilibrium position to Y_1, i_1 with higher income (which will be a real gain to the extent unemployment existed) and lower interest rates. An increase in government spending or investment $(I'S')$ will also raise income (Y_2) but at the expense of higher interest rates (i_2); the higher income will raise L_1, but, because $\bar{M}$ is held constant, L_2 must be reduced (which requires the higher rates of interest). Finally, the simultaneous application of an easier monetary policy $(L'M')$ and an expansionary fiscal policy $(I'S')$ should definitely raise dollar income (Y_3) – and will raise real income to the extent Y_3 lies below the full employment level of output – but the effect upon the interest rate (i_3) cannot be foretold by Keynesian analysis (whether $i_3 \gtrless i_0$); this will depend upon the relative magnitude of the two effects.

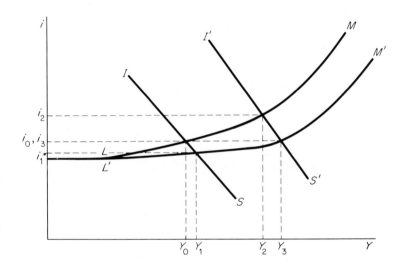

Figure 4-5   Equilibrium in IS-LM Analysis

A secondary effect upon security markets resulting from increased spending can now be seen with the addition of the LM curve. To the extent that the money supply remains constant, the securities sold to finance government and business spending must put upward pressure on the general level of interest rates. Such an increase in the required return upon securities puts downward pressure on their prices. As indicated above, this effect can be mitigated if the money supply is also increased (subject to the qualification on inflation discussed later in this chapter).

NEO-CLASSICAL MONETARIST VIEW

The Keynesian model developed thus far makes some rather specific assumptions about the chain of events following an increase in the money supply. It is posited that investors, finding themselves with more money in relation to bonds than they want at the going rate of interest, will attempt to use the extra money to buy bonds, thus bidding up the price of bonds (reducing the rate of interest). Because the investors as a group must hold the new money supply, the above process will continue until the rate of interest is reduced to the point that they are willing to hold the total money supply (remember that the asset demand for money increases as the rate of interest declines). The lower rate of interest will cause increased investment, which through the multiplier process will cause increased income and consumption. Keynesians suggested that this process could break down if either (1) interest rates were already so low (bond prices so high) that nobody would want to risk a capital loss when bond prices came down and would thus not buy more bonds (the so-called "liquidity trap"), or (2) investment spending was insensitive to changes in the interest rate. Indeed, it was on the basis of these limitations that neo-Keynesians were more enthusiastic about fiscal than monetary policy for a quick recovery from depression.

The Quantity Theory of Money

A different school of thought (the so-called monetarists — traceable from Irving Fisher through Milton Friedman) takes exception to the above chain of causation and some of the major conclusions of the Keynesian school. Much of their argument is based upon the *equation of exchange*:
Let:

M = money supply

V_o = output velocity of money (number of times the money supply "turns over" in purchase of final output)

P = price level

O = output of final goods and services

$P \cdot O$ = surrogate for GNP

Then:[4]

$$MV_o \equiv PO \quad \text{or} \quad MV_o = PO \tag{4.12}$$

[4]The equation can also be expressed for all transactions where V_t = transactions velocity and T = transactions, then $MV_t = PT$.

The equation of exchange as expressed above is simply definitional. It can be used, however, to illustrate several forms of the quantity theory of money. In its crudest form, the quantity theory assumes that V_O is determined by institutional means of payment and thus is constant. Under the assumption of full employment, O is at a maximum and constant in the short run. It follows that any changes in the money supply will have direct and proportional effects upon the price level. In such a world, monetary policy is not only ineffective, but positively harmful. More modern versions of the quantity theory allow V_O to vary inversely with M (but not by so much as to cancel the net effect) and O to vary as well (depending upon employment levels). A simple statement of the modern quantity theory might be that an increase in the money supply will put pressure on both P and O, the proportions being determined by how near the economy is to full employment.

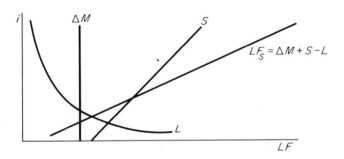

Figure 4-6   Supply of Loanable Funds

A model of interest rate determination consistent with this view that takes explicit account of flow variables is the *loanable funds* theory.[5] In this model, the supply of loanable funds over a period consists of (1) changes in the money supply, (ΔM), plus (2) saving (here considered a function of both income and interest, or $S = S(Y,i)$), less (3) changes in the demand for money (L) or, as it is sometimes called in this literature, the demand for hoards. The supply schedule of loanable funds is illustrated in Figure 4-6. The demand for loanable funds consists of (1) investment ($I = I(i)$), plus (2) net federal government borrowing ($B_f = G + T_r - T = B_f(Y)$ because it is assumed that the federal government is not interest sensitive), plus (3) net borrowings by state and local governments ($B_{SL} = B_{SL}(Y,i)$). The demand for loanable funds is graphed in Figure 4-7. The intersection of the supply and demand curves provides the equilibrium rate of interest (i_0) in the loanable funds market, as shown in Figure 4-8.

[5]See Murray E. Polakoff, "Loanable Funds Theory and Interest Rate Determination" in Polakoff et al., *Financial Institutions and Markets* (Boston: Houghton Mifflin Co., 1970), pp. 37–61.

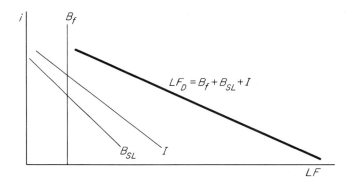

Figure 4-7   Demand for Loanable Funds

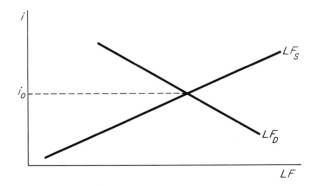

Figure 4-8   Loanable Funds Equilibrium

It should be noted that the monetarists assume that changes in the money supply operate directly upon the demand for output (rather than indirectly through the interest rate and investment as posited by the Keynesians). They contend that an increase in the money supply makes money less desirable in relation to all goods and services, not just bonds. The monetarists would agree that the first observable effects might be an increase in bond prices (and lower interest rates), as suggested by the Keynesians. But, the monetarists claim, a much more important secondary effect then occurs. Not only will the public increase consumption because of their greater liquidity with the additional money[6] but also the higher prices for financial assets will cause the public to feel wealthier and also increase consumption. The increased consumption will induce additional investment, and all these factors will increase the demand for loanable funds and put upward pressure on interest rates. Should this process be

[6]These points could be incorporated into the consumption function by including a liquidity-asset effect, such that $C=f[Y,(M^*/P)-(M/P)]$ where M/P represents real money balances and the asterisk indicates the desired level.

continued to the point of full employment and beyond, the effects of inflation cause even more pronounced upward pressure on the interest rate. In an inflationary period, everybody wants to be a borrower so as to pay back "cheaper" dollars out of higher incomes in the future. Because lenders are quite hesitant in such periods, only ever-higher rates of interest will clear the market.

Money and Investments

Because it is not the goal or function of this book to resolve the Keynesian–monetarist controversy, let us merely consider several points raised by the monetarists that are relevant to the field of investments:

(1) *Money-supply increases in excess of real-output increases tend to result in inflation.*

Stated in crude form, the above implies that $\Delta M - \Delta O \cong \Delta P$. A fairly impressive body of evidence from many countries and many periods of history exists to demonstrate this tendency.[7] It also contributes to the reasons for the advocacy by Milton Friedman and others that the money supply be increased automatically in line with productivity and real-output increases.

(2) *Large rates of increase in the money supply tend to be associated with high, not low, rates of interest.*

The theoretical justification for this phenomenon is the increased demand for loanable funds caused by the monetarists' secondary effect discussed above. Empirical evidence of this effect also exists, although it is subject to some dispute.[8]

Another implication of this hypothesis is that much of the change in the interest rate on riskless securities (the *pure rate of interest* – usually approximated by the rate on short-term government securities) can be attributed to inflationary expectations. The monetarists, as well as many other economists, believe that the *real rate of interest* is determined by nonmonetary factors, such as the productivity of capital, and can be altered only by other real factors, such as technological change. This real rate of interest, plus (or minus) a premium for expected inflation (deflation), then becomes the pure rate in reasonably perfect markets. The St. Louis Federal Reserve has computed the implied real rate (the pure rate minus the rate of inflation) for some years, and it has been much more stable (at about 3 percent) than observed market rates.[9] If the full implications of this hypothesis are accepted, it would then appear that lenders are able to

[7]See Beryl W. Sprinkel, *Money and Markets: A Monetarist View* (Homewood, Ill.: Richard D. Irwin, Inc., 1971), Chap. 7.

[8]See Milton Friedman and Anna Schwartz, *A Monetary History of the United States 1867–1960* (Princeton, N.J.: Princeton University Press, 1963).

[9]Technically, this computation is subject to some error, because the expected rate of inflation at the beginning of the period (which cannot be measured) should be used instead of the actual rate experienced.

obtain full compensation for anticipated inflation and that market rates of interest rise accordingly.

Finally, it should be iterated that the required returns on bonds and shares should move together. Cases may arise, however, where it is observed that interest rates rise, bond prices fall, and stock prices rise. The uninitiated might assume that stock and bond returns were moving in opposite directions. A simple monetarist explanation would be, however, that an increase in the money supply generated inflationary expectations and caused the required return on both stocks and bonds to rise. The possibility of inflation, however, also meant that income to stockholders would rise, and, in the case cited, the increased expected income was greater than the increased required return, causing stock prices to rise.

(3) *Changes in the rate of growth of the money supply affect the business cycle and, through it, the securities market.*

As this is primarily Dr. Sprinkel's argument, we cite him:

The empirically observed pattern of economic and financial events over a typical business cycle appears to be consistent with the explanation offered by the modern quantity theory. First we note that all business expansions have been preceded by increased growth in the money supply. If, in fact, expanding growth in the money supply causes subsequent acceleration in income creation, the modern quantity theory explains the ascending phase in a typical business recovery. Also, since income growth slows or actually becomes negative in an economic contraction, the prior reduction in monetary growth is consistent with a monetarist explanation. An acceleration in monetary growth during a recession or depression explains the tendency for income creation to recover beginning at the lower turning point of the economic contraction.

But inflation also has a cyclical characteristic. During the early phase of an economic expansion inflation is usually quite subdued. An increase in income creation is accompanied by an increase in real output, and prices do not rise significantly. So long as sufficient productive capacity is available, more rapid dollar income growth is typically accompanied by more rapid real growth. But after the economy approaches full employment of resources so that higher income creation cannot be accompanied by similar real income growth, expanding demand is accompanied by rising prices. Even after income growth slows near the peak of a business expansion, prices tend to continue rising for a few quarters, but after the first or second quarters of a recession, the rate of price rise typically tapers as excess demand is removed from the economy. Inflation does not again become a serious problem until the subsequent recovery has proceeded to the point where rapid income creation cannot be matched by equal real output gains.

Bond prices or their opposite (interest rates) tend to be at their low (high) near business cycle highs when inflation is near its peak. As inflationary fires cool in the subsequent recession, bond prices (interest rates) typically rise (fall). When inflationary fears are renewed somewhere in the subsequent recovery, bond prices (interest rates) typically go down (up) as the demand for funds rises.

But stock prices typically lead business cycle turning points. In other words, stock prices generally decline prior to the beginning of a recession, just as they usually rise in a recession period well before the trough in the economic contraction has been reached. Therefore, stock prices are a leading indicator of economic activity. Knowing what is happening to business activity and profits is not sufficient for predicting stock prices, since prices move first. [Figure 4-9] presents a schematic view of the usual relations between business peaks and troughs and such related variables as monetary growth, inflation, stock prices, and bond prices.[10]

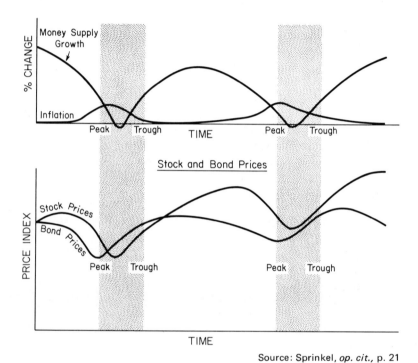

Source: Sprinkel, *op. cit.,* p. 21

Figure 4-9   Monetary Change and Markets

It would thus appear that business cycles, set in motion by monetary policy among other factors, are anticipated and reflected in the securities markets, setting up cycles of their own. Most other models presented in this book, being static equilibrium models by nature, can only hope to suggest the general direction in which securities prices can be expected to move (the secular trend in prices) but cannot deal with the cycles about this trend. But these cycles can be observed to exist and, unfortunately, can wipe out the gains of many years' trend rather quickly. Therefore, cycles can only be ignored at the

[10]Sprinkel, *Money and Markets, loc. cit.,* pp. 19–20.

analysts' peril, and the monetarists seem to have one of the more operational prediction models.

CONCLUSIONS

In this chapter, we have observed the conflicting effects of both monetary and fiscal policy upon the securities markets. Increases in government spending (or business investment), by increasing aggregate demand, tend to put upward pressure on security prices; yet, the increased supply of securities issued to finance such spending exerts downward pressure on prices. Likewise, increases in the money supply, by making money more plentiful in the portfolio relative to securities, tend to push security prices upward (rates downward); yet, constant infusions of money can fuel inflationary expectations and drive rates up. All the above contradictions indicate the difficulty of determining the final effects of changes in macroeconomic variables. Nevertheless, because these variables are essential determinants of the risk and return patterns evidenced by individual securities, the analyst must assess them as best he can.

PROBLEMS

1. Ignoring taxes and transfers, if $b = .9$ and $\Delta I = \$5$ billion, what is ΔY?
2. If $b = .7$, $Z = .1$, and $\Delta G = \$1$ billion, what is ΔY?
3. If $b = .7$, $t = .2$, $t_r = 0$, and $\Delta G = \$5$ billion, what is ΔY?
4. Answer 3 assuming $t_r = .1$.
5. If $A = \$100$ billion, $b = .8$, $t = .2$, and $t_r = 0$, plot the $S + T$ curve.
6. If $\bar{G} = \$50$ billion, $B = \$40$ billion, and $g = \$3$ billion per 1 percent Δi, graph the $G + I$ curve.
7. Given the data in problems 5 and 6, graph the IS curve.
8. What would happen to the IS curve derived in 7 given each of the following:
   a. t becomes .25;
   b. $\bar{G}$ becomes $60 billion;
   c. g becomes $4 billion per 1 percent Δi;
   d. b becomes .85?
9. In a loanable funds framework, determine the effect of each of the following changes upon the equilibrium rate of interest:
   a. an increase in the federal government's deficit
   b. an increase in the marginal propensity to consume

c. an increased aversion on the part of localities to go into debt to pay for "frills" like education

d. a decrease in businessmen's expectations of the future profit to be earned from investment projects

e. a public lack of confidence in the future manifesting itself in the form of an increased asset demand for money

f. a federal deficit partially financed by the sale of bonds to the Federal Reserve, causing an equivalent increase in the money supply

10. Interpret the above events in a Keynesian framework. What differences, if any, do you find? Why?

11. If $l = .2$, $m = \$10$ billion per 1 percent Δi, $J = 170$ billion and $M = \$200$ billion, construct an LM curve.

12. Given the data in problems 5, 6, and 7, and 11, determine the equilibrium level of Y and i.

13. Assume that GNP = \$800 billion, M = \$200 billion, V_O is constant, and the current level of output represents 95 percent of full employment. Give a monetarist explanation of what would happen if M were increased to \$220 billion.

14. Assuming the facts in problem 13:

a. If the long-run real rate of interest is 3 percent and the former pure rate of interest was 5 percent, what should happen as a result of the increase in M?

b. What should happen if a 10 percent increase in M were expected to become an annual event, while the increase in real output at full employment (caused by improved technology and population growth) were estimated at 4 percent?

15. A recent U.S. Secretary of the Treasury analyzed a stock market collapse this way: "The stock-market decline reflects the smart people being convinced they don't need common stocks as a hedge against inflation. Our economic policies have broken the back of the rampant price increases of recent years." Discuss the merits of the secretary's argument.

APPENDIX

Term Structure Theory: Pure Expectations Hypothesis

The material in the body of Chapter 4 deals with the effects of monetary and fiscal policy upon the level of national economic activity and interest rates. With regard to the latter, the nature of monetary policy and governmental finance causes the rate on treasury securities (and especially bills) to be among the first influenced. From the discussion in Chapter 3, it should be obvious that money-market instruments possess a fairly high level of substitutability for each other (on both the supply and demand side of the market), and thus any change in treasury bill rates would be quickly reflected in the rates of the other instruments. The basic topic of this book, however, is long-term securities. Even here, as it was shown in the chapter, actions of the government will affect dividend and interest-paying ability. A question arises, however, as to whether such policy actions have a direct effect upon long-term security prices, and thus, market rates of return. To be specific, is there a mechanism through which changes in short-term rates (or security prices) are also reflected in changes in long-term rates? This appendix is directed to that question.

The theory of the *term structure of interest rates* holds that the observable market yield on otherwise identical securities may be a function of the securities' term to maturity. In other words, market return may be dependent upon maturity as well as all the other factors determining yield. Acceptance of this theory allows a *yield curve* to be drawn as a valid functional relationship. Three hypothetical yield curves are shown in Fig. 4A-1. It must be assumed that the securities depicted on a given curve differ only by maturity, not by other risk factors (U.S. government bonds are often used in the analysis for this reason). Curve *A* is called a flat yield curve, curve *B* is upward sloping, and *C* is downward sloping. The implications of the slope of the curve and the exact relationship of maturity to yield will depend upon which of the several term structure hypotheses one is prepared to accept.[1]

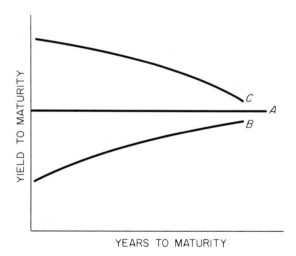

YEARS TO MATURITY

**Figure 4A-1   Three Hypothetical Yield Curves for
Homogeneous Bonds which Differ Only By Maturity**

[1]A more complete discussion of term structure theory in readable form may be found in James C. Van Horne, *Function and Analysis of Capital Market Rates* (Englewood Cliffs, N.J.: Prentice-Hall, Inc., 1970), Chap. 4, and William L. Silber, "The Term Structure of Interest Rates," in Polakoff et al., *Financial Institutions and Markets* (Boston: Houghton Mifflin Co., 1970), Chap. 21. A more technical discussion may be found in Burton G. Malkiel, *The Term Structure of Interest Rates* (Princeton, N.J.: Princeton University Press, 1966), and David Meiselman, *The Term Structure of Interest Rates* (Englewood Cliffs, N.J.: Prentice-Hall, Inc., 1962).

Perhaps the *pure expectations hypothesis* of the term structure is the simplest to understand.[2] Let it be assumed that taxes and transactions costs do not exist, all securities are riskless as to income (the coupon will be paid), and all investors have identical expectations as to future short-term interest rates (the model should also work if enough investors at the margin share common expectations). It should then follow that an individual wishing to invest in bonds for ten years could buy a series of ten one-year issues, two five-year issues, a single ten-year issue, or a twenty-year issue to be sold at the end of ten years. Assuming the individual to be a profit maximizer, he would presumably engage in that series of bond transactions promising the greatest return. Because everyone has been assumed to hold the same expectations, equilibrium would not be established until the returns on all such courses of action were the same. At this point, one would earn the same return for a ten-year investment in bonds whether he bought a ten-year issue, a series of one-year issues, and so on. As the expected short-term rates have been assumed to be agreed upon, the pure expectations hypothesis essentially posits that long-term rates will adjust accordingly to maintain holding-period returns constant. Let:

R_n = Average rate of return, compounded once per period, on a bond maturing at the end of period n if purchased at the beginning of period t

r_j = expectation in period t of the rate of interest on one-period bonds purchased at the beginning of period j (note that if $t = j$, the rate is known)

$\rho_{p,n}$ = expectation in period t of the average rate of return, compounded once per period, on bonds bought at the beginning of period p to mature at the end of period n.

Then, for an investment of n years to have a uniform expected return regardless of maturity purchased:

$$(1 + R_n)^n = (1 + r_t)(1 + r_{t+1}) \ldots (1 + r_n) \qquad (4A.1)$$

Equation 4A.1 merely reaffirms that the value of the investment after n years should be the same whether an n year bond or n one-year bonds were bought; this equation is restated in more general form as equation 4A.2. It illustrates that the average annual return on the long-term bond is the geometric mean of the intervening expected short-term rates:

$$R_n = \left(\prod_{j=1}^{n} (1 + r_j) \right)^{1/n} - 1 \qquad (4A.2)$$

[2] Early writers who employed this concept included Fisher, Keynes, and Lutz.

It should follow for any length of time $n-k$ $(k<n)$:

$$(1 + R_{n-k})^{n-k} = (1 + r_t) (1 + r_{t+1}) \ldots (1 + r_{n-k}) \qquad (4A.3)$$

Dividing equation 4A.1 by equation 4A.3 and rearranging terms, we obtain:

$$(1 + r_{n-k+1}) (1 + r_{n-k+2}) \ldots (1 + r_n) = \frac{(1 + R_n)^n}{(1 + R_{n-k})^{n-k}} \qquad (4A.4)$$

The information in equation 4A.4 tells us that, given the assumptions above, if we can observe the market rate on n-year (say, ten-year) bonds and on $n-k$ (say, seven) -year bonds, then we have also obtained information about the currently expected one-year yields for the intervening period (years eight, nine, and ten). Furthermore, the pure expectations hypothesis would imply that it is currently expected that bonds with a maturity of k (three) years bought at the beginning of year $n-k+1$ (eight) would have an average yield equal to the geometric mean of these expected one-year yields. Therefore:

$$(1 + \rho_{n-k+1,n})^k = (1 + r_{n-k+1}) (1 + r_{n-k+2}) \ldots (1 + r_n) \qquad (4A.5)$$

Substituting equation 4A.4 into equation 4A.5 we obtain:

$$(1 + \rho_{n-k+1,n})^k = \frac{(1 + R_n)^n}{(1 + R_{n-k})^{n-k}} \qquad (4A.6)$$

or

$$\rho_{n-k+1,n} = \sqrt[k]{\frac{(1 + R_n)^n}{(1 + R_{n-k})^{n-k}}} - 1 \qquad (4A.7)$$

Under the assumptions made, the investor could input the current market rate on ten-year and seven-year bonds to the right side of equation 4A.7 and obtain the market's current expectation of the rate on three-year bonds seven years from now. Before the reader becomes unduly excited about the interest rate prediction implications of equation 4A.7, a strong caveat is required. In the first place, it is necessary that the long-term rates be unbiased estimators of the expected intervening short-term rates (for example, equations 4A.1, 2, and 3 must hold); possible causes for this assumption to be unrealistic are considered below. Even if this condition holds however, equation 4A.7 solves only $\rho_{p,n}$ (the rate currently *expected* on bonds sold in p to mature in n), not $R_{p,n}$ (the actual rate in year p on bonds maturing in n). Thus, as a practical matter, expectations may change over time or be wrong in the first place (possibilities assumed away in formulating the model) such that $\rho_{p,n} \neq R_{p,n}$.

EXAMPLE:

Riskless securities are currently available in five-year maturities to yield 6 percent and three-year maturities to yield 5 percent. Under all the assumptions of the pure expectations hypothesis, what is the rate currently expected on two-year bonds three years hence?

$$n = 5; \; n-k = 3; \; k = 2; \; R_n = .06; \; R_{n-k} = .05$$

$$\rho_{n-k+1,n} = \sqrt[k]{\frac{(1 + R_n)^n}{(1 + R_{n-k})^{n-k}}} - 1$$

$$\rho_{4,5} = \sqrt[2]{\frac{(1.06)^5}{(1.05)^3}} - 1 = \sqrt{\frac{1.338}{1.158}} - 1$$

$$= \sqrt{1.1554} - 1 \approx 7.5\%$$

Thus, it is currently expected that two-year bonds will sell at an annual return of about 7.5 percent at the beginning of year four.

Term Structure Theory: Other Hypotheses and Implications

In view of the discussion in Chapter 4, the reader may be wondering what impact inflation would have on the pure expectations model. It should be borne in mind that the theory deals only with nominal (market) rates of interest, not real rates. To the extent that future inflation is anticipated, then, by the monetarist view, the expected one-year rates (r_j) would be adjusted accordingly and, if all the other assumptions held, the model would remain valid. The problem arises, of course, if future inflation is incorrectly estimated. In this case, unexpected inflation merely becomes another factor that can cause expectations to change over time and cause the failure of predictions made with equation 4A.7 to be fulfilled.

Another complication has been raised by a school of thought associated with Sir John Hicks.[3] It can be shown that a given change in the market rate of interest will have a greater effect upon the price of a bond the longer its term to maturity (see the example below). Sir John and his followers contend that the increased capital risk on long-term bonds makes lenders prefer short-term issues and require a liquidity premium in order to lend on a long-term basis.[4] It is also argued that borrowers prefer the security of having money for long periods (thus not being forced into the market at unseemly times) and are willing to pay this premium. The result is the Hicksian *liquidity preference version* of the

---

[3] John Hicks, *Value and Capital*, 2nd ed. (London: Oxford University Press, 1946).

[4] Although short-term lending does reduce principal risk, it increases income risk (the risk of what will be earned in future periods) because the investor is then at the mercy of future short-term rates. Hicks assumes the former is more compelling than the latter.

expectations hypothesis. This version contends that long-term rates reflect expected future short-term rates plus a liquidity premium for lending long and, as such, are biased estimates upward of the expected future short-term rates. Let:

$$L_j = \text{liquidity premium required in period } t \text{ to lend long-}$$
$$\text{term rather than short-term in period } j.$$

Then equation 4A.1 in liquidity preference form becomes:

$$(1 + R_n)^n = (1 + r_t + L_t)(1 + r_{t+1} + L_{t+1}) \ldots (1 + r_n + L_n) \quad (4A.8)$$

The simplest comparison is with bonds maturing in year $n-1$:

$$(1 + R_{n-1})^{n-1} = (1 + r_t + L_t)(1 + r_{t+1} + L_{t+1}) \ldots (1 + r_{n-1} + L_{n-1})$$
$$(4A.9)$$

Dividing equation 4A.8 by equation 4A.9 and simplifying, we obtain:

$$r_n = \rho_{n,n} = \frac{(1 + R_n)^n}{(1 + R_{n-1})^{n-1}} - L_n - 1 \quad (4A.10)$$

It thus becomes obvious that we cannot even predict currently expected rates, much less actual future rates, without a complete schedule of the liquidity premiums embodied in the long-term rates.

It can be shown from equation 4A.1 that, if future short-term rates are expected to be constant ($r_t = r_{t+1} = \ldots = r_n$), then the long-term rate should equal the short-term rate ($R_n = r_t = \ldots r_n$) for any term selected. This implies a flat yield curve for neutral expectations under the pure expectations hypothesis. In like manner, if future short-term rates are expected to rise from the current level ($r_t < r_n$), then the long-term rate, as the geometric mean of the short-term rates, should be greater than the current short-term rate ($R_n > r_t$). This implies an upward sloping yield curve. The liquidity preference version will imply an upward sloping yield curve even under neutral expectations, however. Remember that even if short-term rates are assumed constant in equation 4A.8, the existence of the liquidity premiums (the L terms, assumed to be positive and increasing with n) assures that R_n will rise as n increases. Thus, an upsloping yield curve does not mean that rates must rise in the future or necessarily that people think they will; it may merely represent neutral expectations and liquidity preference.

Note should be taken of the behavior of the yield curve over an interest rate cycle.[5] If there exists some concept of the "normal" level of interest rates,

[5]See Reuben Kessel, *The Cyclical Behavior of the Term Structure of Interest Rates* (New York: National Bureau of Economic Research, 1965).

then it should follow that when rates are "low" relative to the norm the yield curve should be upward sloping. The mere fact that future short-term rates are expected to be higher than current rates would cause the long-term rate to exceed the short-term rate by the analysis given above for the pure expectations case. Under the Hicks' version, the upslope should be greater than that for liquidity preference under neutral expectations.[6] Likewise, at "high" interest-rate levels, the curve would be downward sloping under the pure expectations model and moderately upward sloping, flat, or downward sloping (depending upon how "high" the rates are) under the liquidity preference version.

The null hypothesis with regard to term structure theory is the *market segmentation*, or *institutional pressure*, theory.[7] The advocates of this theory contend that the market at each maturity level (especially long-term versus short-term) is populated by borrowers and lenders who, because of the nature of their operations, legal restrictions, and so on, find it very difficult to operate at any other maturity level. As a result, it is contended, the markets at different maturity levels are segmented from each other. Long and short rates would thus be determined by supply and demand conditions within their respective markets and, at least within broad limits, would have no necessary relationships to each other. A yield curve would represent a specious functional relationship, and no information at all could be derived from its slope.

Now that we have come full circle from establishing the concept of term structure to discrediting it, perhaps it is time to reassess. The yield curve in the United States has been fairly generally upward sloping since the end of World War II. Rates have risen during this period, but not by enough to justify the slope. In addition, the downslope when rates were at cyclical peaks has not been nearly so steep as the upslope when rates were "low." This casual evidence, plus a good bit of empirical work, tends to indicate that the liquidity preference version may be more useful than the unmodified pure expectations hypothesis.

Predictions made on the basis of even the liquidity preference version have turned out badly, however. The fact that the implied rates differ from the actual rate ($\rho_{p,n} \neq R_{p,n}$) does not disprove the theory, of course; people could simply be wrong in their expectations. To assume that they are wrong consistently, however, is not very appealing. Nor is it terribly inviting to, join the market segmentationists; it is difficult to accept that the most fungible of all commodities could be traded in such imperfect markets. Fortunately, Meiselman has come forward with an analysis that allows us to avoid both the choices presented.[8] He developed a model that assumes that people change their expectations of future rates on the basis of errors they make in estimating past rates. His error-learning model is fairly successful in explaining rate changes. Although Meiselman based his model on the pure expectations hypothesis, it has been shown to be consistent with the liquidity preference version as well and has been applied with some success by other researchers. Needless to say, much work in the area of term structure remains to be done.

[6] There seems to be a dispute as to whether the liquidity premium also rises in such a case to cause the slope to be even steeper than the normal premium plus the expected increase in rates would imply. See Van Horne, *op. cit.*, pp. 78ff.

[7] Primarily associated with J. M. Culbertson. See his "The Term Structure of Interest Rates," *Quarterly Journal of Economics*, (November 1957), pp. 489–504.

[8] Meiselman, *op. cit.*

EXAMPLES

1. Assume that a 3 percent bond, paying interest semiannually, is selling at par. If the rate of interest goes to 4 percent, what would happen to the price of the bond if its maturity were:

    a.   one year
    b.   ten years
    c.   never – a perpetual bond

	Period	Payment	@ 2%/period	P. V.
a.	1	$ 15	.980	$ 14.70
	2	1015	.961	975.42
				$990.12
b.	1–19	$ 15	15.678	$235.17
	20	1015	.673	683.10
				$918.27

c. $\dfrac{\$15}{.02} = \$750.00.$

2. Assume that expected one-year rates are: year one – 4 percent; year two – 5 percent; year three – 6 percent. Assume further that lenders require a liquidity premium of 0.2 percent to lend two years instead of one and that this premium grows at a compounded rate of 6 percent as the term of the loan increases.

    a.   What are the market rates on two- and three-year bonds?
    b.   If four-year bonds are yielding 6 percent, what is the implied one-year rate for year four?

a. $(1 + R_n)^n + (1 + r_t + L_t)(1 + r_{t+1} + L_{t+1})$

$(1 + R_2)^2 = (1 + .04 + 0)(1 + .05 + .002)$

$R_2 = \sqrt{1.09408} - 1 = 4.6\%$

$(1 + R_3)^3 = (1 + .04 + 0)(1 + .05 + .002)(1 + .06 + (.002)(1.06))$

$(1 + R_3)^3 = (1.04)(1.052)(1.06212) = 1.162044$

$R_3 = \sqrt[3]{1.162044} - 1 = 5.1\%$

b. $\rho_{4,4} = \dfrac{(1 + R_4)^4}{(1 + R_3)^3} - L_4 - 1$

$\rho_{4,4} = \dfrac{(1.06)^4}{1.1620} - (.002)(1.06)^2 - 1$

$\rho_{4,4} = \dfrac{1.262}{1.162} - (.002)(1.124) - 1$

$\rho_{4,4} = 1.086 - .002 - 1 = 8.4\%$

PROBLEMS

1. Assume that the following one-year interest rates are anticipated:

Year	Rate
1	5%
2	10%
3	5%
4	20%

a. If $100 were invested in one-year bonds at the beginning of year one, to what amount will it grow by the end of year four?

b. What annual rate of interest would a four-year bond need to offer to be competitive?

c. Answer b for a three-year bond sold at the beginning of year two.

d. Answer b for a two-year bond sold at the beginning of year three.

e. Answer b for a three-year bond sold at the beginning of year one.

f. At what price would the bond in b sell at the end of year two? Year three?

g. How would your answer to f change if, during year two, the expected rate in year four declined to 15 percent?

2. Riskless bonds are currently selling as follows:

Yield	Maturity
6%	5 years
7%	6 years
8%	7 years

Employing the pure expectations hypothesis:

a. What is the expected one-year rate five years from now?

b. What is the expected two-year rate five years from now?

c. What is the expected one-year rate six years from now?

3. If twenty-five-year riskless bonds yield 4 percent, and ten-year bonds yield 6 percent, what is the expected fifteen-year rate ten years hence under the pure expectations hypothesis?

4. Suppose that the long-run real rate of interest is expected to be 3 percent. In addition, there is expected to be inflation of 3 percent in year one, 2 percent in year two, 1 percent in year three, and none thereafter. In a monetarist pure expectations framework, what rate of interest should be currently observable in the market on (a) one-year bonds; (b) three-year bonds; (c) ten-year bonds? If, in the next instant, the market also began to expect 2 percent inflation in year four, what would happen to the prices of the three bonds?

5. Suppose that a 6 percent riskless security is currently selling at par and pays interest semiannually. If the interest rate were to drop to 4 percent, what would be the effect upon the price of the bond if its maturity were (a) six

months; (b) one year; (c) five years; (d) ten years; (e) fifteen years; (f) perpetual?

6.

a. Rework problem 5 under the assumption that the interest rate went from 6 percent to 8 percent.

b. Graph both sets of prices obtained against maturity.

c. Suppose that in the next instant there is an 0.5 probability that the rate will stay at 6 percent, a .25 probability that it will go to 8 percent, and a .25 probability that it will go to 4 percent.

(1) What is the expected value of the interest-rate level and the price of the 6 percent bond that corresponds to it?

(2) What is the expected value of the price of the 6 percent bond at each maturity level?

(3) Which maturity would you prefer to hold in this case?

d. Can you now explain what Malkiel and others mean when they discuss how a symmetrical distribution of expected interest rates will result in an asymmetrical distribution of expected bond prices?

e. What slope of the yield curve has been assumed in this problem? Are the assumptions concerning interest rate expectations consistent with this slope? Does it seem likely that this slope could be maintained? Why?

f. May changes in interest rates and inverse changes in bond prices be used interchangeably in capital market analysis as though they were equivalent?

7. Under the liquidity perference version, assume that lenders require a premium of 0.1 percent to lend for two years instead of one ($L_2 = 0.1\%$) and that this premium grows at a compound rate of 10 percent per year for each additional year they must lend long [that is, $L_3 = (0.1\%) \cdot (1.10) = 0.11\%$]. Under this assumption, rework problem 2.

8. In a pure expectations framework, assume that currently expected one-year rates are:

Year	Rate
1	3%
2	4%
3	5%
4	6%
5	7%

a. Graph the yield curve (up to five-year bonds) implied by the data.

b. Rework a assuming the order of the rates is reversed.

c. Assuming that expectations are fulfilled, what will the first four years of the yield curves drawn in a and b look like next year?

9. Rework problem 8 employing the liquidity preference assumptions of problem 7. Compare your results by placing the corresponding curves on the same graph. What is the effect of the presence of liquidity preference?

REFERENCES

Ball, R. J., *Inflation and the Theory of Money.* Chicago: Aldine, 1965.

Chandler, Lester V., *The Economics of Money and Banking,* 5th ed., Part IV. New York: Harper and Row, 1970.

Conard, Joseph W., *Introduction to the Theory of Interest,* Part II. Berkeley: University of California Press, 1959.

Culbertson, J. M., "The Term Structure of Interest Rates," *Quarterly Journal of Economics,* November 1957, pp. 489–504.

Davidson, P. and E. Smolensky, *Aggregate Supply and Demand Analysis.* New York: Harper & Row, Publishers, 1964.

Friedman, Milton, *Dollars and Deficits,* Parts I and II. Englewood Cliffs, N.J.: Prentice-Hall, Inc., 1968.

_____, and Anna Schwartz, *A Monetary History of the United States 1867–1960.* Princeton, N.J.: Princeton University Press, 1963.

Hansen, Alvin, *Monetary Theory and Fiscal Policy.* New York: McGraw-Hill Book Co., 1949.

Hart, Albert, Peter Kenen, and Alan Entine, *Money, Debt and Economic Activity,* 4th ed., Part II. Englewood Cliffs, N.J.: Prentice-Hall, Inc., 1969.

Hicks, John, *Value and Capital,* 2nd ed. London: Oxford University Press, 1946.

Kessel, Reuben, *The Cyclical Behavior of the Term Structure of Interest Rates.* New York: National Bureau of Economic Research, 1965.

Keynes, John Maynard, *The General Theory of Employment, Interest and Money.* New York: Harcourt, Brace, and World, 1964 (first published 1936).

Laidler, David, *The Demand for Money: Theories and Evidence,* Part II. Scranton: International Textbook, 1969.

Malkiel, Burton, *The Term Structure of Interest Rates.* Princeton, N.J.: Princeton University Press, 1966.

Meiselman, David, *The Term Structure of Interest Rates.* Englewood Cliffs, N.J.: Prentice-Hall, Inc., 1967.

Moore, Basil, *An Introduction to the Theory of Finance.* New York: Free Press, 1968.

Patinkin, Don, *Money, Interest, and Prices,* 2nd ed. New York: Harper and Row, 1965.

Polakoff, Murray, et al., *Financial Institutions and Markets,* Parts I, II and III. Boston: Houghton Mifflin Co., 1970.

Silber, William, "The Term Structure of Interest Rates," in Polakoff et al., *Financial Institutions and Markets,* Chap. 21. Boston: Houghton Mifflin Co., 1970.

Smith, W. L., and R. L. Teigen, *Readings in Money, National Income, and Stabilization Policy,* rev. ed., Part I. Homewood, Ill.: Richard D. Irwin, Inc., 1970.

Sprinkel, Beryl W., *Money and Markets: A Monetarist View.* Homewood, Ill.: Richard D. Irwin, Inc., 1971.

Thorn, Richard, ed., *Monetary Theory and Policy.* New York: Random House, 1966.

Van Horne, James, *Function and Analysis of Capital Market Rates,* Chap. 4. Englewood Cliffs, N.J.: Prentice-Hall, Inc., 1970.

Weintraub, Robert, *Introduction to Monetary Economics,* Part III. New York: Ronald Press, 1970.

Weintraub, S., *An Approach to the Theory of Income Distribution.* New York: Chilton, 1958.

II

Security Analysis

5

Financial Statement Analysis

RATIO ANALYSIS[1]

In Part II, we begin the process of analyzing individual securities. The culmination of our efforts will be the estimation of the variables needed to build an optimal portfolio: expected returns, variances, and covariances. In Chapter 5, some useful techniques for obtaining crude measures of these variables will be discussed. More refined procedures will be developed in Chapter 6.

The art of financial analysis has depended for years on the computation of ratios of data secured from the published financial statements of corporations (for example, balance sheets, income statements, cash flow statements, and so on). The earliest attempts at evaluating a firm and its securities were mainly

---

[1]There was a time when searching for data and calculating ratios occupied most of the energies of the financial analyst. Today, computers record vast quantities of information about almost every major company and relay these data to the analyst upon command. Large brokerage houses and investment banking institutions subscribe to such services as those provided by Standard and Poor's Corporation, Ultronic Systems Corporation, and Canada's Financial Research Institute. Programs contained within these systems of financial information take much of the pencil pushing out of financial analysis. A computer, for example, can recall the relevant data, compute all forty-five ratios (and more) given in Table 5-1 for a number of firms over a ten-year period, and print out the results in seconds. Hence, a job that used to take days of unpleasant effort can be done painlessly in virtually no time. The computer thus frees the analyst to spend more time analyzing and less time calculating. Unfortunately, the analyst must conform to the program design and data output generated by the computer. This may limit his discretion in researching particular problem areas.

qualitative assessments and shrewd guesses. These early attempts were succeeded by the computation of a growing battery of comparative financial statistics. These comparisons were of two kinds: comparisons over time and comparisons among different variables. The first form yielded simple but important information. As an example, suppose ABC Corp. earned $125,000 last year and $150,000 this year. The computation of a simple ratio [(This Year Sales − Last Year Sales) / (Last Year Sales)] would show that sales were up by 20 percent [($150,000 − 125,000) / ($125,000)]. Although such a comparison is extremely crude in that it gives no clue as to *why* sales increased or whether such an increase will be sustained in the future, it is nonetheless a very significant first step in analyzing the financial position of the company. The second form of comparison is one among variables. Suppose ABC had sales this year of $150,000 and net income of $15,000. A comparison of these data would show that net income was 10 percent of sales. This information by itself may not be terribly useful, although if it were observed that such a relationship had held fairly steadily over time, perhaps a meaningful conclusion could be drawn.

Ratio comparisons have been made and can be made whenever it makes sense to examine the relationship between two or more financial numbers. There is nothing sacrosanct about any given set of ratios, and different comparisons may be necessary when conditions differ. Nevertheless, there is some advantage in attempting to standardize the computation of ratios whenever possible. Hence, financial analysts have developed a core of ratios that may be used in determining such things as the current financial condition of the firm, the trend in the firm's financial condition, and the financial condition of the firm in relationship to the position of other firms.

The information content of ratios and their use in determining the risk position of the firm and the expected rates of return on the firm's securities will be the focal point of this chapter. Table 5-1 contains most of the basic ratios that the financial analyst may require. Additional ratios for unique industries are given in the section that begins on page 104.

A number of interest groups, including internal management, may find ratios a useful guide for policy making. We shall focus here, however, on the use made of them by investors. Hence, we shall examine each category of ratios as they may apply to the evaluation of the securities of the firm.

Short-term creditors, bondholders, and stockholders are all concerned with the liquidity of the firm (group I ratios). Liquidity is important to short-term creditors because payment of their claims may depend on the cash-conversion ability of the firm. Bondholders are concerned because deteriorating liquidity may impair the security of the firm's debt. If the firm's cashable assets (cash, accounts receivable, and in some cases, inventory) are low in comparison with liabilities soon to come due, then the payment of bond interest may be jeopardized. Even if the firm has adequate fixed assets, the conversion of these assets into cash in order to meet liabilities may be expensive (the assets may have to be liquidated by the firm at prices below their economic values) and time

TABLE 5-1

Core of Financial Ratios

Ratio	Method of Computation	Interpretation
I Liquidity ratios		
a. Current ratio	$\dfrac{\text{Current assets}}{\text{Current liabilities}}$	Ability to meet current debts with current assets
b. Cash ratio	$\dfrac{\text{Cash + Short-term securities}}{\text{Current liabilities}}$	Ability to meet current debts with cash on hand
c. Quick (acid test) ratio	$\dfrac{\text{Cash + Short-term securities + Receivables}}{\text{Current liabilities}}$	Ability to meet current debts with more liquid current assets
d. Basic defensive interval	$\dfrac{\text{Cash + Short-term securities + Receivables}}{\text{Daily operating expenditures}}$	How long the firm could meet cash obligations from liquid assets
e. Working capital to total assets	$\dfrac{\text{Current assets} - \text{Current liabilities}}{\text{Total assets}}$	Liquidity of total assets and working capital position
II Profit ratios		
a. Gross profit margin	$\dfrac{\text{Net sales} - \text{Cost of goods sold}}{\text{Net sales}}$	Gross profit per dollar of sales
b. Operating-income ratio	$\dfrac{\text{Net sales} - \text{CGS} - \text{Selling \& adm. expenses}}{\text{Net sales}}$	Operating profit before interest and taxes per dollar of sales
c. EBIT ratio	$\dfrac{\text{Net sales} - \text{CGS} - \text{S \& A expenses} + \text{Nonoperating income}}{\text{Net sales}}$	Earnings before interest and taxes per dollar of sales
d. Operating ratio	$\dfrac{\text{Operating expenses (CGS + S \& A expenses)}}{\text{Net sales}}$	Operating expenses per dollar of sales
e. Net profit margin	$\dfrac{\text{Net income}}{\text{Net sales}}$	Net income per dollar of sales
III Turnover ratios		
a. Total asset turnover	$\dfrac{\text{Net sales}}{\text{Total assets}}$	Ability of invested capital to produce gross revenue
b. Receivables turnover	$\dfrac{\text{Net credit sales}}{\text{Average receivables}}$	Quality and liquidity of receivables

TABLE 5-1 (contd.)

Core of Financial Ratios

Ratio	Method of Computation	Interpretation
c. Average collection period	$\dfrac{\text{Average receivables} \times 365 \text{ (or 360)}}{\text{Net credit sales}}$	Period required to collect average receivables
d. Inventory turnover	$\dfrac{\text{Cost of goods sold}}{\text{Average inventory}}$	Liquidity of inventory and tendency to overstock
e. Average day's inventory	$\dfrac{\text{Average inventory} \times 365 \text{ (or 360)}}{\text{Cost of goods sold}}$	Holding period of average inventory
f. Working capital turnover	$\dfrac{\text{Net sales}}{\text{Current assets} - \text{Current liabilities}}$	Indication of the cash cycle of the firm
IV Return-on-investment ratios		
a. Net-earning-power ratio	$\dfrac{\text{Net income}}{\text{Total assets}}$	Net earning power of invested capital
b. Earning power of total investment	$\dfrac{\text{EBIT}}{\text{Total assets}}$ also (EBIT ratio) × (Total asset turnover)	Ability of invested capital to produce income for all investors (bondholders and stockholders) — eliminates "leverage" effect from net profit-to-total-assets ratio
c. Net profit to common equity	$\dfrac{\text{Net income}}{\text{Total common equity}}$	Net earning power of common capital
V Leverage and capital-structure ratios		
a. Total-debt-to-equity ratio	$\dfrac{\text{Current liabilities} + \text{Long-term debt}}{\text{Total common equity}}$	Total amount of debt leverage per dollar of common equity
b. Total debt to total capital	$\dfrac{\text{Current liabilities} + \text{L.T.D.}}{\text{C.L.} + \text{L.T.D.} + \text{Pfd. Stk.} + \text{Total common equity}}$	Debt financing per dollar of total finance
also Total debt to total assets	$\dfrac{\text{Current liabilities} + \text{L.T.D.}}{\text{Total assets}}$	Asset security of debt sources of finance

c. Long-term-debt-to-equity ratio

$$\frac{\text{L.T.D.}}{\text{Total common equity}}$$

Long-term debt leverage per dollar of common equity

d. Tangible-assets debt coverage

$$\frac{\text{Total assets} - \text{Intangibles} - \text{Current liabilities}}{\text{L.T.D.}}$$

Asset security of long-term debt sources of finance

e. Total-debt-plus-preferred-to-equity ratio

$$\frac{\text{Current liab.} + \text{L.T.D.} + \text{Pfd. Stk.}}{\text{Total common equity}}$$

Debt and preferred leverage per dollar of common equity

f. Times-interest-earned ratio

$$\frac{\text{EBIT}}{\text{Long-term debt interest}}$$

Income security of long-term debt

g. Cash-flow-times-interest-earned ratio

$$\frac{\text{EBIT} + \text{Depreciation}}{\text{Long-term debt interest}}$$

Short-run ability to meet interest payments

h. Coverage of interest and sinking-fund payments

$$\frac{\text{EBIT} + \text{Depreciation}}{\text{Interest} + \text{Sinking fund}}$$

Coverage of interest and sinking-fund payments when depreciation exceeds sinking-fund payments

$$\frac{\text{EBIT} + \text{Depreciation}}{\text{Interest} + \text{Sinking fund} - (\text{Tax rate})(\text{Depreciation})}$$
$$\overline{} 1 - \text{Tax rate}$$

Coverage of interest and sinking-fund payments when depreciation is less than sinking-fund payments

i. Times-interest-earned plus preferred dividends

$$\frac{\text{EBIT}}{\text{Long-term debt interest} + \dfrac{\text{Preferred dividends}}{1 - \text{Tax rate}}}$$

Income security of the preferred stock

VI Asset-relation ratios

a. Plant and equipment to total assets

$$\frac{\text{Net plant} + \text{Net equipment}}{\text{Total assets}}$$

Proportion of operating-earning assets to total assets

b. Inventory to total assets

$$\frac{\text{Average inventory}}{\text{Total assets}}$$

Size of inventory and tendency to over-stock

c. Receivables to total assets

$$\frac{\text{Average receivables}}{\text{Total assets}}$$

Size of receivables and credit policy

d. Annual depreciation to plant and equipment

$$\frac{\text{Annual depreciation}}{\text{Gross plant and equipment}}$$

Regularity and uniformity of depreciation allowances

e. Approximate average asset life

$$\frac{\text{Net plant and equipment}}{\text{Normalized depreciation}}$$

Average life of plant and equipment

89

TABLE 5-1 (contd.)

Core of Financial Ratios

Ratio	Method of Computation	Interpretation
VII Common-stock-security ratios		
a. Book value per share of common stock	$\dfrac{\text{Total common equity}}{\text{No. shares outstanding}}$	Asset security of the common stock
b. Net tangible assets per share	$\dfrac{\text{Total common equity} - \text{Intangible assets}}{\text{No. shares outstanding}}$	Tangible asset security of the common stock
c. Leverage and capital-structure ratios	(see Part V)	Leverage risk of the common stock
d. EPS ratio	$\dfrac{\text{Net income available for common}}{\text{No. shares outstanding}}$	Earnings per share of common stock
e. DPS ratio	$\dfrac{\text{Dividends paid on common}}{\text{No. shares outstanding}}$	Dividends per share of common stock
f. Cash-flow-per-share ratio	$\dfrac{\text{Net income} + \text{Depreciation}}{\text{No. shares outstanding}}$	Cash earnings per share retainable for investment in assets
g. Pay-out ratio	$\dfrac{\text{Dividends paid on common}}{\text{Net income available for common}}$	Dividend security of the common stock and the dividend policy of the corporate management
VIII Yield and price ratios		
a. Net yield to maturity	To be read from bond tables or computed from equation 3.1	Expected annual rate of income return on funds invested in bonds
b. Current yield of preferred	$\dfrac{\text{Annual cash dividends}}{\text{Market price of pfd.}}$	Expected annual rate of income return of funds invested in preferred
c. Current yield of common	$\dfrac{\text{Annual cash dividends}}{\text{Market price of common}}$	Expected annual rate of dividend income return of funds invested in common
d. Price-earnings ratio	$\dfrac{\text{Market price of common}}{\text{Dollars earned per share of common}}$	Price of common relative to earnings

consuming. Stockholders are also concerned with corporate liquidity because dividend payments, like interest payments, may be jeopardized if the firm is short of cashable assets. Furthermore, the long-run earning power of the firm may be impaired if it becomes necessary to liquidate fixed assets to meet current liabilities.

The maintenance of profit margins is necessary if the firm is to be able to service its debt obligations, pay dividends, and increase earnings. The ratios in group II are designed to test the ability of the firm to control costs and keep profit margins intact. The long-run profitability of the firm is clearly far more important to bondholders and stockholders than the asset security of the firm's debt and equity. Because asset liquidation is only a final resort relied upon by the unprofitable firm, profit-margin indicators assume a most important role for all the firm's investors.

Turnover ratios (group III) indicate the ability of the firm to generate revenues from its asset investment. Even if profit margins are high, the firm may be unprofitable if a large investment in assets is required to generate a meager sales volume. In addition to indexing the revenue-generating capacity of the firm, turnover ratios may also serve to portray the liquidity of the firm along with the ratios in group I. In particular, the working capital ratios IIIb through IIIf may give clues to the cash cycle of the firm, that is, its ability to convert receivables and inventories into cash.

Profit ratios and turnover ratios lie behind a most-important group of comparisons – those describing return on investment. Indeed, the earning-power-of-total-investment ratio is simply the EBIT ratio times the total-asset-turnover ratio. Because a firm's return on investment is a function of both its ability to produce cheaply (margins) and sell in quantity (turnover), the rates of return on investment ratios are good summaries of the overall earning position of the firm.

The use of debt by the enterprise to improve earnings for shareholders is demonstrated by the ratios in group V (leverage and capital structure). These ratios serve further to test the asset security of debt sources and the risk accruing to bondholders and stockholders from financial leverage. The income security of bondholders and preferred-stock holders is also indicated by these ratios.

The asset-relation ratios (group VI) may be used to supplement some of the previously outlined groups. The composition of assets into earning and liquid parts is suggested by VIa. The ratios VIb and VIc are useful supplements to the liquidity and turnover ratios of groups I and III. Ratio VId is an indicator of the regularity and uniformity of depreciation allowances and may imply the necessity of adjusting the firm's depreciation accounts (see the "Adjustments to Financial Statements" section starting on page 93). Ratio VIe provides information about the average life of plant and equipment. It can also be used to determine whether reported earnings have been overstated (understated) when book depreciation has been inadequate (excessive).

The security of common stock may be determined from the ratios in group VII. The asset security, income security, dividend security, and leverage risk to shareholders are indexed by the ratios in this group.

The final group of ratios (VIII) describes the yields of the securities of the firm. As such, these ratios are the most important single group. The percentage rates of return to bondholders, preferred-stock holders, and common-stock holders are computed with these ratios. Hence, they play a very important role in the selection of the optimal portfolio of securities.

Another presentation of income-statement and balance-sheet ratios is on a common size basis. This form breaks down each category of income, expense, asset, liability, and so on into percentages. Thus, all revenue and cost items are expressed as percentages of net sales. All asset items are expressed as percentages of total assets, and all liability and net worth items are expressed as percentages of total liabilities and net worth. This form of computation allows the analyst to make immediate comparisons of all items in the income statements and balance sheets of a firm over time and among firms at a point in time.

Consider the income statement and balance sheet for the Ungar Corp. given below. Common-sized statements for each report are indicated in the parentheses next to each figure.

Net sales	$200,000	(100%)
Cost of goods sold	50,000	(25%)
Gross income	$150,000	(75%)
Selling expense	20,000	(10%)
Administrative expense	30,000	(15%)
Earnings before interest and taxes	$100,000	(50%)
Interest	40,000	(20%)
Earnings before taxes	$ 60,000	(30%)
Taxes	30,000	(15%)
Net income	$ 30,000	(15%)
Current assets		
Cash	$ 50,000	(10%)
Receivables	40,000	(8%)
Inventory	60,000	(12%)
Total current assets	$150,000	(30%)
Fixed asset	$350,000	(70%)
Total assets	$500,000	(100%)
Current liabilities	$100,000	(20%)
Bonds	200,000	(40%)
Net worth	200,000	(40%)
Total liabilities & net worth	$500,000	(100%)

ADJUSTMENTS TO FINANCIAL STATEMENTS

By necessity, ratio analysis depends on the use of externally reported accounting data. To the extent that accounting data do not accurately depict the real economic condition of the firm, ratios do not give a good picture of the position of the firm. Accounting practices do not always produce numbers that the financial analyst regards as adequate or useful. Hence, adjustments have to be made frequently to accounting reports so that the analyst can get the information he wants. When accounting practices vary among firms or industries, the analyst must also make adjustments in order to get comparable results.

We may divide the various adjustments to financial statements into several categories. Perhaps the most important type of adjustment is that resulting from the presence of *nonrecurring* items on income statements. The payment of back taxes or receipt of tax refunds, the results of litigation or renegotiation, profits or losses on the sale of fixed assets, adjustments to the market value of securities, the write-down or recovery of foreign assets, and the proceeds of life insurance policies collected are all income statement entries that cannot be expected to recur. The appropriate adjustment for these items is to transfer them from the income statement to a schedule of capital charges and credits and to adjust the deduction for income taxes accordingly.

A second type of adjustment may be required when allocations have been made from income to reserve accounts. Examples of this practice are commonly found in the establishment of valuation reserves, liability reserves, and net-worth reserves. As a rule, the analyst should add back to income all reserve appropriations that are not allowed as deductions for income tax purposes.

A reconciliation of reported taxable income with the income tax deduction indicated in the income statement is required when any substantial deviations exist. If corporate income taxes are approximately 50 percent, then net income before taxes should be about twice the deduction for taxes (and net income after taxes should just about equal tax payments). There are a number of explanations for deviations, and the analyst should explore all possibilities. Common examples include: (1) loss carry-backs and carry-forwards; (2) tax-exempt income; (3) dividends from domestic corporations; (4) profits and losses from the sale of capital assets; (5) minerals depletion allowances; and (6) investment company exemptions. In the United States, municipal bonds are generally exempt from federal income taxes. Thus, corporations that carry these items (such as banks and insurance companies) may have a lower average tax rate than companies that hold no such bonds. Only 15 percent of the dividend income received by domestic corporations paid by other domestic corporations is taxable in the United States. Firms that carry substantial holdings in common stocks (such as fire and casualty insurance companies) may thus have their taxes reduced by this exclusion. Profits on the sale of capital assets are taxed at preferred rates in the United States and are not taxed at all in some countries. If a company has sold assets at a profit, its tax bill may be lower than it would have been had the profit originated from operations. In the United States, oil and mining companies are given depletion "allowances" that are deductible from taxes. These allowances are based on a percentage of revenues.

Other tax discrepancies may result from management decisions. When depreciation is charged at a higher rate for tax purposes than on financial statements, the tax deduction item will be lower than expected unless a reserve is established to reflect the possibility of additional taxation. When allocations are made to reserves that are not allowed for tax purposes, the tax deduction may be larger than anticipated. Capital charges and credits that should be reflected in the equity accounts may affect the taxes paid by the corporation. Taxes may be higher or lower depending on whether a charge or a credit is involved. Interest payments made during the construction of plant (particularly for public utilities) are not a legitimate charge to income, although they are allowed as a deduction for tax purposes. This item should be capitalized as a construction cost (by adjustment if necessary), and shown as a discrepancy in the tax reconciliation (see p. 97).

The analyst's attitude toward tax discrepancies should be the following: Determine the reason for the difference. If the discrepancy is due to tax-exempt income or depletion allowances, the results should be accepted as reported. If the difference is due to capital gains, these transactions should be separated from the income statement as nonrecurring items and taxes should be adjusted accordingly. If the firm has a small tax or no tax due to loss carry-forwards, earnings should be computed on the basis of full tax assumption for that year. When discrepancies result from allocations to reserves that are not tax deductible, earnings should be restated after adding back these allocations.

Attempts to offset specific assets and liabilities should be scrutinized, because a distortion of the ratios may result. One common example of this practice is the netting of the current asset "government securities held in anticipation of taxes" against the current liability "accrued taxes," which tends to increase the current ratio.

Intangible assets (patents, goodwill, and so on) should be treated with great care, as their value on the books often has no relation to their market value or future income-generating capacity.

If a company leases a substantial amount of its assets (which may often be detected by the presence of sizable leasing expenses on the income statement) it may appear to have little debt and yet be heavily obligated by leasing contracts. To make the financial statements of different companies comparable, many analysts capitalize leases and treat them as debt. For example, if a company had annual leasing expenses of $100,000 and the analyst wished to capitalize them at 10 percent, he would add $1 million to the fixed asset and long-term debt accounts of the company's balance sheet.

Adjustments to financial statements should be made with caution. Although one goal of adjusting statements is the assurance of uniform data for making comparisons, the analyst should not adopt a doctrinaire approach. When it is felt that an adjustment is required in order to reflect more accurately the true economic position of the firm, the adjustment should be made. If the analyst is considering an adjustment because he feels the data for one firm over time or for a group of firms at a point in time are not comparable, he should ask himself whether the adjustment is being contemplated for sake of convenience or because it is really needed. In no case should an adjustment be made if the result is small. As a rule, if the impact of an item is less than 5 percent of the pertinent result (net income, total assets, and so on), it can safely be ignored.[2]

An income statement and a balance sheet for Raw Data, Inc., are provided below:

Raw Data Inc.
Consolidated Statement of Income
(thousands)

Net sales	$250,000
Cost of goods sold[1]	200,000
Gross income	$ 50,000
Selling and administrative expense	20,000
Net operating income	$ 30,000
Other income[2]	30,000
Earnings before interest and taxes	$ 60,000
Interest	5,000
Earnings before taxes	$ 55,000
Taxes	21,250
Net Income	$ 33,750

[1]Includes $10 million reserve for replacement of plant.

[2]Includes a $5 million tax refund, $10 million in profit from the sale of securities, $5 million in municipal bond interest, and $10 million in dividends from subsidiaries.

[2] Another form of adjustment is almost always made by the firm in the preparation of its financial statements. These are adjustments made necessary by common stock splits and stock dividends. If data are not adjusted for these changes, gross distortions may result. In the case of small stock dividends (that is, less than 5 percent), analysts frequently ignore the adjustment. It should be pointed out, however, that the cumulative effect of a large number of stock dividends of less than 5 percent can be significant.

Raw Data Inc.
Consolidated Balance Sheet
(thousands)

Current assets	$200,000
Net plant	400,000
Other assets[1]	300,000
Total assets	$900,000
Current liabilities	$200,000
Long-term debt	100,000
Net worth	
Common stock	$200,000
Retained earnings	250,000
Reserve for replacement of plant	150,000
Total net worth	$600,000
Total Liabilities and Worth	$900,000

[1]Includes $100 million in municipal bonds (at market) and a $200 million investment in subsidiaries.

Appropriate adjustments to the income statement and balance sheet would be:

1. Elimination of nonrecurring items from the income statement.
   a. Tax refund
   b. Profit on sale of securities (taxes should be reduced by .30 ×
      $10,000,000 = $3,000,000 when this item is taken out).[3]
2. The reserve for the replacement of plant should be deducted from cost of goods sold (that is, added back to income).

The adjusted income statement would appear as follows:

Raw Data Inc.
Adjusted Consolidated Statement of Income
(thousands)

Net sales	$250,000
Cost of goods sold	190,000
Gross income	$ 60,000
Selling and administrative expense	20,000
Net operating income	$ 40,000
Other income	15,000
Earnings before interest and taxes	$ 55,000
Interest	5,000
Earnings before taxes	$ 50,000
Taxes	$ 18,250
Net income	$ 31,750

[3]The U.S. corporation tax rate on capital gains is (as of this writing) the lesser of: (1) the corporation's tax rate on ordinary income; or (2) 30 percent.

The only change in the balance sheet would be the addition of the reserve for replacement of plant to retained earnings. The tax reconciliation may be made immediately:

Expected taxes (.5 × $55,000,000)	$27,500,000	
Reported taxes	21,250,000	
Discrepancy	$ 6,250,000	
Taxes saved on untaxed income:		
Municipal bond interest	2,500,000	(.5 × 5,000,000)
Tax refund	2,500,000	(.5 × 5,000,000)
Taxes saved from:		
Capital gains items	2,000,000	(.2 × 10,000,000)
Dividend exclusion	4,250,000	(.5 × 8,500,000)
Taxes computed on:		
Nondeductible replacement		
reserve	5,000,000	(.5 × 10,000,000)
	$ 6,250,000	

FINANCIAL STATEMENTS AND ACCOUNTING DATA

There are times when simply adjusting a firm's financial statements is insufficient to make them useful to the analyst. Even though the auditors may have certified a document as having been prepared "according to generally accepted accounting principles," this reassurance may mean very little. Unfortunately, accounting is an art and not a science, and there is no single "correct" way of recording business transactions. The accounting community frequently attempts to achieve *verifiable* results, which implies that reasonable men examining the same data would come to the same conclusions. These data are supposed to be supported by formal business documents that evidence "arm's-length" transactions and that leave little room for interpretation. Of course, if perfect verifiability were achieved (which never happens), it would be at the expense of the *utility* of statements. Many transactions do require interpretation for meaningful presentation, and judgment may play an important role. On the other hand, when opinions, estimates, and judgment become significant in interpreting financial events, the *objectivity* and *consistency* of reporting may suffer.

Consider an asset which was purchased two years ago for $100,000 with an estimated life of ten years and no salvage. Under the accounting principle of verifiability, it could objectively and consistently be determined that the asset cost $100,000, that under straight-line depreciation it would be valued at $80,000 today, and that the annual depreciation expense for the asset is $10,000. Unfortunately, only the first of these numbers may have any real economic meaning. The asset may be worth $90,000 today (due to price level changes) and the replacement depreciation might be closer to $11,250 ($90,000 ÷ 8 years). Nevertheless, the current value of the asset and its replacement depreciation are very subjective numbers. Reasonable men may have differing opinions on these figures.

Herein lies the dilemma. Verifiable, objective, consistent statements may not be terribly useful. On the other hand, statements in which opinion and judgment play a substantial role may lose comparability over time for a given firm and across firms at an instance in time. Moreover, statements that are subjective in nature are much more easily abused that those that are conservatively prepared. An unscrupulous management may prevail upon its accountants to prepare (and its auditors to certify) reports that are blatantly misleading if too much interpretative leeway is allowed.

The accounting community has recognized this problem, and since 1938 there has been an attempt to set standards for accounting procedures that would adhere to both the principles of verifiability and utility. In 1959, the American Institute of Certified Public Accountants established its Accounting Principles Board (APB) to issue "opinions" dealing with specific problem areas in accounting. These opinions have become a part of generally accepted accounting principles and departures from them must be disclosed in footnotes to financial statements or in the auditor's certification when the effect of any departure is material.

Although the APB opinions have strengthened the reporting process, the Board recently came under increasing attack for taking too long to reach decisions about important matters. Moreover, after colossal improprieties in the 1970-1973 period (when auditors certified statements that were misleading at best), it became increasingly apparent that the accounting community alone should not be charged with establishing financial accounting standards. Thus, in 1973 a new Financial Accounting Standards Board (FASB) was created to resolve some of the more significant outstanding disputes in financial accounting. The new Board is composed of CPAs, financial analysts, and former corporate officers, all of whom have severed existing ties with their respective accounting firms, investment institutions, or corporations to work impartially and on a full-time basis at the Board. Finally, there is current movement toward *requiring* that generally accepted principles (including FASB opinions) be employed, rather than merely requiring the notation of any deviation.

In many ways, the accounting and investments communities were at a crossroads in the early 1970s. As mentioned in Chapter 2, fundamental changes in the structure of the investments business are currently being effected. Similarly, the accounting profession is undergoing substantial alteration. There has been a general feeling that investors have lost confidence in the financial data they are provided and that this may account for the withdrawal of millions of small investors from the market in the early 1970s. There is no doubt that in recent years many firms have engaged in questionable practices to obfuscate their true financial position and that these practices have been at least condoned, if not endorsed, by the accountants who work for (and audit) these companies. One example after another of impropriety came to light between 1970 and 1973, from the Penn-Central case (where auditors certified statements indicating a strong position for the road in 1969 only to have the firm collapse not long after the publication of the 1969 annual report) to the scandalous Equity Funding fiasco (where auditors attested to the existence of assets that never existed and where earnings over a period of ten years were almost completely manufactured by the top management). These incidents shocked the public and the Securities and Exchange Commission, which has ultimate authority over the processes of financial accounting, and it seems likely at the time of this writing that the delegation of responsibility that the S.E.C. has made both to the investment and the accounting community for self-regulation may be in jeopardy unless substantial reform is quickly effected.

Until many of the more substantive issues are resolved, analysts are cautioned to observe the following points when examining financial statements:

1. Read the auditor's opinion carefully. An opinion containing "qualifications" should be immediately suspect. Auditor's statements with seemingly innocuous reservations may signal a future massive write-off or some other impending disaster. In addition, a change in auditors now must be accompanied by a statement of reasons for the change. If this statement even hints of disagreement over presentation of accounts and, especially, if the change is from a large auditing firm to a small one, the analyst should be put on his guard.

2. Examine the financial footnotes for changes in accounting policies during the year. A switch from accelerated to straight-line depreciation or a change from the LIFO to FIFO inventory evaluation method will tend to improve reported earnings. Be suspicious of overly complicated footnotes which appear to cloud rather than clarify issues. They are probably intended to do just that.

3. Scrutinize the "capitalized" portion of a firm's costs (that is, those costs written off over a period of time rather than expensed in the year incurred). Research and development, advertising, promotion, training, and engineering costs are particularly important items to check. By deferring costs a firm may be overstating current earnings. Small oil companies follow the practice of "full costing" whereby drilling costs are capitalized rather than written off as incurred. These figures may require adjustment.

In the latter 1960s and early 1970s, the capitalization of expenses, to improve current earnings, was often employed in conjunction with the "big bath". During the upward phase of the market cycle, a firm might capitalize every expense that it could in order to show earnings increases and thus boost the price of its stock. Sooner or later, the firm would be unable to sustain the earnings growth through this method; moreover, the asset side of the balance sheet would be so swollen with goodwill, deferred expenses, and the like as to defy credibility. This condition would often occur when the market was in a decline and the firm's stock was depressed. At this point, many firms would take the "big bath" by writing off everything that had accumulated on the balance sheet as an extraordinary charge. With the stock down anyway, the charge would have little price effect. The firm, however, would have "cleared the decks" to play the same game all over again in the next market upswing. The accounting community has gone on record against the "big bath"; how effective this position will be in preventing such abuses remains to be seen.

4. Pay particular attention to nonrecurring items and tax credits. Although the former are supposed to be separated out, many investors do not fully appreciate the importance of comparing strictly recurring, operating items exclusive of other sources of income.

5. For diversified companies, try to get management to show the sales and earnings for each broad business activity. These data must be filed now on the *10-K reports* required annually by the S.E.C. from corporations, but they rarely appear in reports to stockholders.

6. For firms that lease substantial portions of their assets, attempt to secure sufficient information from management so that these assets can be capitalized and put on the balance sheet. The capitalized lease should be added to both the fixed assets of the firm and to its long-term debt.

7. Be sure to attempt a tax reconciliation. If the firm maintains a single composite balance sheet item entitled "deferred taxes," try to discover what differences exist between expenses reported to the IRS and those indicated in the annual report. These differences should be justifiable in the opinion of the analyst, or the figures reported to shareholders should be adjusted to reflect the IRS numbers.

MERGERS AND FINANCIAL ANALYSIS[4]

A major set of problems develops for the analyst when a merger occurs. It is clear that the combination of two firms during an accounting period may distort the financial reports of the surviving company, particularly with regard to such general figures as sales, net income, and so on. Of course, placing the figures on a per share basis may reduce some of the distortion, but even per share numbers can differ widely after a merger, even though the firm's position may not have

[4]Parts of this section are adapted from Findlay and Williams, *An Integrated Analysis for Managerial Finance* (Englewood Cliffs, N.J.: Prentice-Hall, Inc., 1970); pp. 230–36. A more detailed discussion of the growth aspects of mergers is presented in Chapter 11.

altered considerably. The biggest problem for the analyst is making the figures comparable before and after the merger. This task is becoming more and more difficult as conglomerates assume a more important role in business.

Technically speaking, a combination of two or more companies in which one is the survivor is called a merger; if a totally new company absorbs the old companies, a consolidation has been effected. A combination of firms involved in different stages of the production of the same product is a vertical merger, and the combination of firms in totally unrelated lines of business is called a conglomerate merger. A combination of companies in the same business is called a horizontal merger.

A merger may be effected either by the purchase of a firm's assets or its stock. A purchase of assets generally requires only the approval of the board of directors of the purchasing company. In both cases, some form of approval by the stockholders of the selling company is required. A purchase of stock also generally involves the acquisition of the liabilities and assets of the firm. If the purchase is made in the form of cash or debt securities, any gain is taxable immediately either to the firm or to the shareholders (if distributed under a plan as a dividend in total or partial liquidation). The acquiring company, however, is often able to write up the assets for additional depreciation if a cash purchase is made. A purchase for stock will usually defer taxation to the holder until the stock is disposed of, but the purchasing company will only acquire the assets at their book value. In any case, the purchase may result from negotiations with the company or a direct tender offer to the stockholders for their shares. Dissenting stockholders may go to court to have a fair market value of their shares determined and demand payment in cash.

There are two methods of accounting for merger transactions. Under the *purchase method*, the assets and liabilities of the acquired firm are reported after the merger on the books of the acquiring firm at their "fair market value" (usually determined by appraisal). Individual assets are carried at their separate "fair values," and liabilities are similarly appraised and carried. Any difference between the actual price paid for the acquisition and its net (assets less liabilities) fair value is reported as "goodwill from acquisitions." At the date of combination, the retained earnings balance of the surviving company is carried forward, and the balance of the acquired firm is eliminated. After the combination, future financial statements depict only the historical data of the acquiring company.

Under the *pooling of interests method*, the assets and liabilities of the combining firms are reported after the merger at their previously established book values. No goodwill account results from this form of combination, and the retained earnings balances of the combining companies are added to obtain the new balance at the date of acquisition. After the merger, financial statements must be prepared as though the firms had been combined throughout the precombination period. Depictions of historical data (such as earnings per share) must be restated on the same basis.

When the purchase price of the acquired company exceeds its book value, the pooling-of-interests method of accounting for the transaction is frequently employed because of the treatment of assets. If these assets are mainly depreciable (fixed assets rather than current), the result produces higher earnings for the surviving company than would exist if the acquired assets were depreciated at their most recent exchange value. For example, suppose ABC bought the assets of XYZ for $25 million. These assets had a book value of only $20 million and were being depreciated on a straight-line basis with ten years remaining life. If ABC depreciated these acquired assets on their purchase value, an expense of $25,000,000 \div 10 = \$2,500,000$ would exist. On the other hand, by continuing to depreciate on the old book value basis, only $20,000,000 \div 10 = \$2,000,000$ of depreciation expense would be reported. The difference is a $500,000 pretax larger earnings amount than would prevail if the purchase method of accounting for merger had been used.

There is an obvious advantage to firms wishing to demonstrate "earnings growth" when the pooling of interest method is employed. Many abuses have resulted, however.[5] Some firms have gone so far as to pool assets, switch depreciation policy (from accelerated to straight-line), and put in asset accounts items that were formerly considered to be expenses of the current period, all in an attempt to understate costs and overstate earnings. Such practices have received very unfavorable publicity (and deservedly so), the upshot being that the term *dirty pooling* has been applied to the method.

In response to the clear-cut distortions that became prevalent, the accounting community has set forth rather rigorous standards to be applied before a merger can be considered a pooling of interests. The Accounting Principles Board of the A.I.C.P.A. issued Opinion 16 on "Business Combinations" and Opinion 17 on "Intangible Assets" to deal with pooling and associated problems. Opinion 16 details twelve criteria, all of which must be met in order that a combination be deemed a pooling of interest. These criteria restrict pools to autonomous concerns that have been independent (that is, neither constituent can hold more than 10 percent of the outstanding voting stock of the other). The combination must be effected in a single transaction or be completed under a single plan within one year, and it must involve the issuance of *voting common stock only* in exchange for the voting stock of the combined firm.[6] Other requirements restrict purely financial transactions two years before the merger, limit the reacquisition of voting shares after a plan to

---

[5]Other abuses, committed particularly by acquisition-minded conglomerates wishing to show an upward "trend" in earnings per share (and hence their market prices), are explored in Chapter 11.

[6]Previously, certain poolings were accomplished with the use of voting common stock, other securities, and even cash. These transactions were treated as part purchase, part poolings. Opinion 16 declares that only one method is acceptable. If nonvoting securities or cash are used as consideration for more than 10 percent of the voting shares of the company to be pooled, the merger must be treated as a purchase.

combine has been initiated, protect each shareholder's percentage ownership position, prohibit the existence of contingently issuable shares at the date of consummation of the agreement, preclude agreements to reacquire shares issued in a pooling, and restrict dispositions of assets of the combining companies for two years after the merger. The intention of these requirements is to reduce the improprieties associated with poolings of interest, but there is some question about whether the desired results will be attained.[7] One practitioner has observed:

> Even more significant, virtually any purchase can now be turned into a "mandatory" pooling. For example, assume that A Corporation wants to combine with B Corporation but only on a pooling basis. B's shareholders, however, consider A's shares a poor investment and demand cash. Solution: A issues its voting common stock to B's shareholders in a merger. The shares are registered and immediately sold in a secondary offering. Results: (1) A gets its pooling. (2) B shareholders receive cash. (3) Because the combination is not a reorganization for tax purposes (failing the taxation continuity of interest test), if the tax bases of assets received by A exceed the book bases carried over in the pooling, a permanent difference results . . . .
>
> Thus, it appears that the APB's aim to limit pooling usage can easily be by-passed. Unfortunately, a detailed "legislative" approach which eliminates judgment places a premium on deft maneuvering.[8]

It is no wonder that the analyst still casts a leery eye at many pooling-of-interest mergers. In general, the pooling method shows a higher reported net income and a lower asset base (thus, a much higher return on investment) than the purchase method. Pooling may also make possible the reporting of "instant earnings" in that earnings during the fiscal year in which a merger takes place become a part of the earnings of the acquiring company. (Of course, all previous years' earnings are also consolidated as well). Nevertheless, abuses can also occur with the purchase method. If the book value of the net fixed assets of the acquired firm is below the purchase price, the excess may be put on the books of the surviving company as "goodwill." If this amount is not amortized, as it should be, future costs will also be understated and earnings overstated. A.P.B. Opinion 17 does require that goodwill be amortized, but a period of up to forty years is allowed.

When the analyst encounters a merger, he is advised to examine the reasonableness of the transaction, regardless of whether the pooling or purchase method was employed. The acquired assets may be worth a higher purchase price (than their book value) because of the synergism of the combination (the $2 + 2 = 5$ effect). Equally possible, however, is that inflation and higher

---

[7]See S. P. Gunther, "Poolings, Purchases, Goodwill: A Review of APB Opinions 16 and 17," *The New York Certified Public Accountant,* January 1971, pp. 25–36.

[8]*Ibid.,* p. 35.

replacement costs account for at least part of the difference. In any event, the analyst should accept the transaction (market) price of the assets. If the firm used a pooling approach, the assets should be adjusted upward to their market values. If the purchase method were used, any unjustified "goodwill" should be classified as "fixed assets." In both instances, the assets should be depreciated on the merger exchange value, and no permanent goodwill account should be allowed without an appropriate annual amortization.

SPECIAL INDUSTRY RATIOS

Railroads

Several industries require special ratios in addition to those listed in Table 5-1.[9] The unique character of the railroads, for example, necessitates the computation of several financial and physical ratios that give a better picture of the operating characteristics of that industry than would be discerned from the standard core. The *maintenance ratio* indicates the effort the railroad is making in keeping its roadway and equipment in good repair. It is calculated by comparing the amount spent on maintenance to total operating revenues. This ratio is important because railroads tend to have heavy fixed charges (bond interest), and during lean times they are prone to let maintenance, which is postponable, lag behind. When the roads are "starving" their facilities, it is clear that expensive repairs may have to be done in the future, a fact that the analyst should know.

A second important railroad ratio is the *transportation* ratio. It is given by dividing transportation expenses by operating revenue and is a measure of the operating efficiency of the railroad. The physical measurement, *net ton-miles per train-hour,* is the best indicator of revenue efficiency and costs available to the analyst. Ton-miles are a good indicator of revenue efficiency. Such factors as car capacity utilized (tons per car), train size (cars per train), and miles per car-hour (train speed) are included in the ratio. Train-hours, similarly, are a convenient measure of cost. The advantage many of the western United States roads have over their eastern counterparts is due to their superior net ton-miles per train-hour ratio (resulting mainly from long-haul freight trains that carry a large number of cars).

[9]A more complete discussion of special ratios for specific industries is contained in Graham, Dodd, and Cottle, *Security Analysis,* 4th ed. (New York: McGraw-Hill Book Company, 1962); Badger, Torgerson, and Guthmann, *Investment Principles and Practices* (Englewood Cliffs, N.J.: Prentice-Hall, Inc., 1969); and Bellemore and Ritchie, *Investments: Principles, Practices and Analysis* (Cincinnati: South-Western Publishing Company, Inc., 1969).

Public Utilities

Analysis of public utility securities also requires several different ratios and some reinterpretations of the existing core. Many analysts believe, for example, that the operating ratio for public utilities should *exclude* depreciation allowances. This is a large item for most utilities, and differing estimations of plant life can significantly affect the amount charged to depreciation. Hence, comparisons of the operating efficiency of various utilities (control of wages, fuel costs, purchased power, operating taxes, maintenance, and so on) would be clouded if depreciation were included. With the separation of depreciation from the operating ratio, a new ratio, *depreciation as a percentage of operating revenue,* should be computed. This will indicate the consistency and relative size of depreciation in relation to operating revenues.

Physical ratios are also important for the public utilities. It is possible to compute the average *rate, usage,* and *bill* for residential and industrial users of electricity. These data are very useful in determining the factors underlying revenue patterns and can be crucial in assessing growth rates for public utilities. On the cost side, *system peak* and *load factors* are important, because the demand for electricity tends to be hourly and seasonal. If a utility has a capacity that is too small, consumer demand cannot always be accommodated (leading to brown- or blackouts under severe conditions). This causes irritation of, and occasional trouble with, regulating authorities. On the other hand, too large a capacity is expensive and can eat into profits. One way the utility can reduce the effects of this phenomenon is through encouraging off-peak demand. Its ability to do this is given by the *load-factor* ratio:

$$\frac{\text{total annual output}}{\text{hours in a year}} \div \text{peak load}$$

Thus, if a utility produces 1 million kwh (kilowatt hours) in a year and has a peak load of 200 kw, its load factor would be:

$$\frac{1,000,000}{8,760} \div 200 = 57 \text{ percent}$$

Airlines

For the airlines, a *load factor* is also important. Two types of load ratios are usually computed. The *passenger load factor* indicates the percentage of seats occupied during the year. It is compared with the *break-even passenger load factor,* which is the percentage of occupied seats required for the coverage of total costs. (A variation of this ratio may be computed to determine the occupancy percentage required to cover variable costs). Load factors are useful to determine how much excess capacity the airline has. Because the airlines are a high-fixed-cost industry, profit rates tend to rise rapidly as the passenger load factor exceeds the break-even factor.

Airline analysts calculate two efficiency ratios that are useful in appraising costs. The *average length of trip* is calculated by dividing the total annual miles flown by the number of flights scheduled during the year. Longer trips are generally less costly per mile than short ones. Hence, higher values for this ratio imply more profitable operations. Another efficiency ratio is the average number of hours each plane is in the air. The ability of the firm to utilize its equipment intensively is usually considered favorable because depreciation and maintenance costs do not vary proportionately with the number of miles flown or the time each plane spends in the air.

Commercial Banks

Financial institutions are unique and require special analysis. Commercial banks are highly levered, and the analyst must be careful to assess the *capital-to-deposits* ratio for them. In order to be profitable, a bank cannot maintain too large an amount of capital to deposits. Nevertheless, if the ratio is too low, a small decline in the value of the bank's assets (through loan defaults or losses on the bond portfolio) can eliminate the stockholders' investment and even threaten the position of depositors. For this reason, regulatory authorities will put pressure on a bank with a low ratio. Many analysts feel that ratios in the 7 to 9 percent range are optimal depending on the overall condition of the bank. Institutions with high *risk-assets-to-capital* ratios (risk assets include loans, discounts, municipal bonds, corporate bonds, and miscellaneous assets) should be in the upper end of the range, and banks with low risk-assets-to-capital ratios could be in the lower end. A final ratio for banks that should be examined closely is the *net-loan-losses-to-net-operating-income* ratio. Losses on loans are usually not deducted from net operating income but are reported separately. It might be expected that highly profitable banks (making riskier loans) should have a larger net-loan-loss ratio than less-profitable banks, although this is not always the case. Net loan losses above 5 percent of net operating income should be considered excessive in any event.

Life Insurance Companies

The reported profitability of life insurance companies depends to a large extent on the *legal reserves* that must be set aside out of premiums to meet future claims. This reserve will depend upon the mortality tables assumed by the company and the rate of interest it can earn on investments. If a conservative reserve policy is established by the company, it may report lower earnings than an equally profitable firm with a less-conservative policy. The analyst should examine the *mortality ratio* (ratio of actual mortality experienced to anticipated mortality) and the *interest ratio* (ratio of actual return on investment to expected return) to see if the reserves set aside have been excessive or insufficient.

Fire and Casualty Companies

Three special ratios are required for analyzing fire and casualty insurance companies. The *loss ratio* compares the loss and loss-adjustment expenses to net premiums earned. It gives some indication of the risk-selection ability of the firm. The *expense ratio* compares the commissions and acquisition expenses to net premiums written. It gives information about the cost-control abilities of the company. The *underwriting-gain-or-loss ratio* compares the loss and acquisition expenses to premiums earned. Underwriting gains or losses do not include investment income, which tends to be the major source of profits for stock fire and casualty companies.

Mutual Funds

For mutual funds, the *load* expresses the sales commission on the shares in terms of the gross amount paid. Thus, an 8½ percent load would imply that an investor would pay $100 for shares with an asset value of $91.50; note that an 8½ percent load corresponds to a ($8.50/$91.50) 9.3 percent *markup.* The *management fee,* usually expressed as a percentage of total assets per annum, is also of interest. *Brokerage fees to total income* (or, *securities sold to total assets*) will give some indications of the expenses generated by the managers in search of performance. The above factors are usually analyzed together, as the no-load funds are often run by brokerage firms and managed to generate sufficient management and brokerage fees in order to eliminate much of the advantage to investors of having no load. The *gross-redemption ratio* is given by (value shares redeemed/total value of shares); the *net-redemption ratio* is [(value of shares redeemed – value of new shares sold)/total value of shares]. Both these ratios give some indication of investor confidence in the fund; the latter also gives weight to management's ability to compensate for redemptions by the sale of new shares. The *cash ratio* for a fund is the cash and money-market instruments to total assets. A large ratio can imply (1) management bearishness on the market; (2) a preparation for anticipated net redemptions; or (3) a recent inflow of funds from the sale of new shares or portfolio liquidation that has not been employed. The most significant performance ratio is probably the annual return, which is given by:

$$\frac{\text{Asset value per share (end of year)} + \text{Dividends paid} - \text{Asset value per share (beginning of year)}}{\text{Asset value (beginning of year)}}$$

This return can then be compared over time to that of other funds or some market index.

PROBLEMS

1. Below are income statements and balance sheets for the Wynn Corp. for the years 1973 and 1974.

Wynn Corp.
Consolidated Statement of Income
(thousands)

	1973	1974
Net sales	$114,868	$170,356
Cost of goods sold	108,086	154,094
Operating depreciation	168	187
Gross income	$ 6,614	$ 16,075
Selling and administrative expenses	760	2,540
Net operating income	$ 5,854	$ 13,535
Other income	35	474
Earnings before interest and taxes	$ 5,889	$ 14,009
Income taxes	2,660	6,720
Net income available for common	$ 3,229	$ 7,289
Common dividends	732	1,465
Balance carried to surplus	$ 2,497	$ 5,824
add surplus beginning period	7,115	9,612
Surplus end of period	$ 9,612	$ 15,436

Wynn Corp.
Consolidated Balance Sheets
(thousands)

	1973	1974
Current assets		
Cash	$ 3,625	$ 4,633
Receivables	13,896	20,468
Inventories	34,430	59,341
Total current assets	$ 51,951	$ 84,442
Net plant and equipment	$ 2,228	$ 3,084
Investment in subsidiaries	$ 1,253	$ 1,315
Total assets	$ 55,432	$ 88,841
Current liabilities		
Payables	$ 9,840	$ 20,707
Notes	15,000	27,000
Accruals	1,572	2,938
Reserves	2,498	5,851
Total current liabilities	$ 28,910	$ 56,496
Fixed liabilities	$ – 0 –	$ – 0 –
Net worth		
Common stock (1,000,000 shares)	$ 14,657	$ 14,657
Paid in surplus	2,252	2,252
Earned surplus	9,612	15,436
Total net worth	$ 26,521	$ 32,345
Total liabilities and worth	$ 55,432	$ 88,841

a. Prepare common size statements for the Wynn Corp.

b. Compute all the ratios indicated in Table 5-1 for the Wynn Corp. for 1973 and 1974. The following information will be required:

(1) Daily operating expenditures — about $500,000 (Note: this may be determined by dividing annual operating expenditures by the number of days in the year. If operating expenses are expected to be higher in the next year than in the last one for which financial data are published, a budget for that year must be obtained. Also, the simple division of the number of days in the year into annual operating expenditures assumes that cash flows out evenly during the year. For seasonal businesses, this may not be a realistic assumption.)

(2) Market price of the stock as of the end of 1974 — $146 per share.

c. From the financial statements you have, try to decide what type of firm Wynn is. The asset mix of the enterprise should be of use in making this determination.

d. Analyze the position of Wynn. Would you consider it a profitable operation? Does the firm appear to be a risky venture?

2. Compute the following ratios for Raw Data (example problem on pages 95–97) on an unadjusted and an adjusted basis:

a. Current ratio

b. Gross profit margin

c. Operating income ratio

d. EBIT ratio

e. Net profit margin

f. Total asset turnover

g. Earning-power-of-total-investment ratio

h. Net-profits-to-common-equity ratio

i. Total-debt-to-equity ratio

Which ratios differ when the statements are adjusted? Why? Does the position of the firm appear better or worse after the adjustments are made?

3. Hampstead Ltd. posted the following financial statements for 1974 (thousands):

Net sales	$100,000	Current assets	$ 50,000
Cost of goods sold[1]	50,000	Plant (net)	200,000
Gross income	$ 50,000	Copyrights[3]	10,000
Other expenses[2]	40,000	Total assets	$260,000
Net income before tax	$ 10,000		
Tax	0	Liabilities	$100,000
Net income	$ 10,000	Net worth	160,000
		Total liabilities and worth	$260,000

[1]Includes depreciation charges of $10 million based on straight-line depreciation. For tax purposes, $20 million was deducted based on accelerated depreciation. The auditors feel the straight-line figure is an adequate figure for real economic depreciation.
[2]Includes an $8 million loss from litigation allowed as a tax deduction.
[3]Copyrights are valued at their acquisition price. A conservative appraisal of their economic value is about $100 million.

a. Prepare an adjusted income statement and balance sheet for Hampstead.

b. Reconcile the firm's tax payment. Assume the normal tax rate for Hampstead is 50 percent.

c. Compute these ratios for Hampstead on an unadjusted and an adjusted basis:

    (1) Gross profit margin

    (2) EBIT ratio

    (3) Net profit margin

    (4) Total asset turnover

    (5) Earning-power-of-total-investment ratio

    (6) Net-profits-to-common-equity ratio

    (7) Total debt-to-equity ratio

4. A public utility has an annual output of 55 million kwh. Its peak load is 10,000 kw. Determine its load factor.

5. The Power and Wealth Fund has a net asset value of $20 per share, a management fee of 1 percent of assets per year, and the following marginal load schedule:

First $5000	8½%
Next 20,000	5
Next 40,000	3
Thereafter	½

If Mr. Timid pays a total of $100,000 for shares, how many will he get?

6. The Central Railroad has the following income statement (thousands):

Operating revenues:	
Freight	$ 95,097
Passenger	8,398
Other	4,905
Total operating revenue	$108,400
Operating expenses:	
Transportation	$ 45,500
Maintenance of way & structure	14,217
Maintenance of equipment	19,157
Traffic, other & special amortization	10,906
Total operating expenses	$ 89,780
Net railway operating income	$ 18,620
Less intermediate items:	
Payroll & other taxes	7,564
Net equipment & joint facility rents	5,207
Payments for guaranteed expenses	1,325
Rent for leased roads	1,121
Dividends and interest	(558)
Rent and miscellaneous (net)	(1784)
Net intermediate items	$ 12,875

Earnings before interest and taxes	$ 5,745
Interest on debt	5,173
Earnings before taxes	$ 572
Taxes	272
Net income	$ 300

Determine the following ratios for Central:

    a. Transportation ratio
    b. Total-maintenance ratio
    c. Operating ratio
    d. EBIT margin
    e. Net margin

COMPREHENSIVE CASE

As an investment analyst, you are reviewing the following income statement and balance sheet for the Boheme Corporation, a manufacturer of hippie attire:

Boheme Corporation
Statement of Income for the Year 1974

Sales		$200,000
Less:		
Cost of goods sold	$100,000	
Selling, general & admin. expenses	65,000	
Depreciation[1]	10,000	175,000
Earnings before Interest and Taxes		$ 25,000
Less:		
Interest		5,000
Earnings before taxes		$ 20,000
Less:		
Taxes		4,000
Net income		$ 16,000
Preferred dividends		1,000
Net income to common shareholders		$ 15,000
Common dividends		5,000
Earnings retained		$ 10,000

[1]For tax purposes, the firm uses accelerated depreciation. Charges amounting to $22,000 were deducted for 1974.

Boheme Corporation
Balance Sheet as of December 31, 1974

Current Assets:	
Cash	$ 5,000
Receivables	5,000
Inventories	10,000
Total current	$ 20,000
Fixed assets:	
Gross plant	$100,000
Less:	
Accumulated depreciation	30,000
	$ 70,000
Other assets	10,000
Total assets	$100,000
Current liabilities	
Accounts Payable	$ 10,000
Wages Payable	6,400
Total Current	$ 16,400
Bonds (10's '81)	50,000
Preferred stock (10%, $10 par)	10,000
Common stock ($1 par)	10,000
Retained earnings	13,600
	$100,000

1. You are considering the purchase of the Boheme 10's of 1981, which were issued when the firm was organized three years ago. The bonds are selling at 90¾ (that is, 90.75 percent of each $1000 par value). Interest is paid annually on December 31, and any purchase you make would be on January 2, 1975. The bonds mature on December 31, 1981. You have determined the following data from the 1972 and 1973 annual reports of the company:

	1972	*1973*
Sales	$50,000	$100,000
Gross margin	40.0%	45.0%
EBIT margin	14.0%	10.0%
Net margin	3.2%	4.0%
Asset turnover	.625X	1.1X
Return on investment		
(EBIT/Total assets)	8.75%	11.0%
Total debt to total capital	.75	.74
Interest coverage	1.4X	2.0X

a. Make any necessary adjustments to the 1974 statements.

b. Reconcile the firm's tax payment. Assume a normal tax rate of 50 percent.

c. Compute the above seven ratios for 1974.

d. What favorable factors might influence your purchase of these bonds? What unfavorable ones?

e. What other information might you wish to have in making your evaluation?

f. What is the yield to maturity of the Boheme 10's '81?

g. If you thought the firm was less risky today than it was when the bonds were issued, would you be willing to accept a return lower than 10 percent?

h. How do you account for the current price of the bonds?

2. You are considering the purchase of Boheme common stock. In order to value the security, you have attempted to project future sales and earnings for 1975. You are convinced that sales will increase according to the past pattern (that is, up by 100%) and the EBIT margin will be about the same as it was in 1974. You assume debt levels and the tax rate will remain constant.

a. Determine sales, earnings before interest and taxes, and net income to common shareholders for 1975.

b. Earnings per share of common were $.16 in 1972 and $.40 in 1973. Determine EPS for 1974 and projected EPS for 1975.

c. The firm paid no dividend in 1972 or 1973 but did pay out one-third of 1974 earnings. Cash dividends per share are expected to double in 1975.

(1) How much in dividends were paid in 1974?

(2) What projected pay-out rate is expected for 1975?

d. The P/E multiple for Boheme (in Table 5-1) averaged 20X in 1972 and 1973. What was the average price of the stock for each year?

e. As of January 2, 1975, Boheme was selling at $15 per share. What is the current P/E multiple based on 1974 earnings?

f. What may account for this change in the multiple?

g. Based on the current price of Boheme and your expectations about the future of the company, would you buy it?

REFERENCES

Badger, Torgerson, and Guthmann, *Investment Principles and Practices.* Englewood Cliffs, N.J.: Prentice-Hall, Inc., 1969.

Bellemore, Douglas H., and John C. Ritchie, Jr., *Investments: Principles, Practices and Analysis,* 3rd ed. Cincinnati: South-Western Publishing Company, Incorporated, 1969.

Brilloff, Abraham, *Unaccountable Accounting,* New York: Harper and Row, 1972.

Findlay, M. C., and Edward E. Williams, *An Integrated Analysis for Managerial Finance,* Chaps. 8 and 18. Englewood Cliffs, N.J.: Prentice-Hall, Inc., 1970.

Graham, Benjamin, David L. Dodd, and Sidney Cottle, *Security Analysis,* 4th ed. New York: McGraw-Hill Book Company, 1962.

Gunther, S. P., "Poolings, Purchases, Goodwill: A Review of APB Opinions 16 and 17," *The New York Certified Public Accountant,* January 1971, pp. 25–36.

How to Read a Financial Report. New York: Merrill Lynch, Pierce, Fenner, and Smith, N.D.

Myer, John Nicholas, *Financial Statement Analysis,* 4th ed. Englewood Cliffs, N.J.: Prentice-Hall, Inc., 1969.

Welsch, G. A., Zlatkovich, C. T., and J. A. White, *Intermediate Accounting*, 3rd ed. Homewood: Richard D. Irwin, Inc., 1972.

6

Forecasting
Techniques

NAIVE FORECASTS

We found in the previous chapter that the most important variables indicating the worth and security of bonds and stocks were those relating to the future income-generating abilities of the firm. Because bond interest, sinking-fund payments, and common stock dividends are paid out of *future* rather than past revenues, it is imperative that the analyst forecast the position of the firm he is investigating as far into the future as possible.

Forecasting techniques vary from the most simple naive projections to the development of complicated regression models of the firm's total activities. Budgets and financial statements play a role in almost every kind of forecasting technique, although the sophistication of the use of these data may vary considerably.

Analysts have been making naive forecasts for years. Before the advent of the computer, practically all forecasts were simplistic by necessity. Some of the more common naive techniques consist of making linear extrapolations of past performance. For example, if a firm's earnings have been growing at 20 percent compounded annually, the analyst may simply add this amount to current earnings in order to get next year's earnings. The main weakness of such an approach is obvious in that no consideration is given to the underlying determinants of earnings. Furthermore, the analyst is assuming blindly that past performance will always be repeated. (This assumption is explicit even in many of the more-sophisticated techniques.)

The use of ratios with naive projections has long been the mainstay of financial analysis. A frequently used procedure is to project sales one or two years into the future and then apply historical ratios to generate *pro forma* income statements and balance sheets. When it appears to the analyst that various ratio patterns might change in the near future, he incorporates these adjustments into his analysis.

We may consider an example. Suppose the Recensement Data Gathering Corporation has shown rapid growth in recent years. Sales have advanced by 30 percent annually, and profits have been growing by 40 percent. Ratios for Recensement for the past three years are given below:

Ratio	1972	1973	1974
Current	2.40	2.80	2.60
Gross margin	.22	.23	.24
EBIT ratio	.15	.16	.17
Net margin	.06	.07	.09
Asset turnover	3.00	3.25	3.60
Long-term debt to capital	.09	.08	.06

Sales for 1974 were $500,000. The analyst believes the past growth rate will continue for next year. He also feels that the current ratio will remain at about the 1974 level, that the long-run gross margin should be about 24 percent of sales, and that the EBIT and net margins will continue at 1974 levels. Long-run improvement in turnovers is anticipated, however, and the analyst feels 3.80 is an accurate total asset turnover projection. The firm has $10,000 in long-term debt that should not change next year. The fixed asset investment should increase to about $150,000. Earnings for 1975 could be projected using a simple extrapolation of the earnings growth rate:

$$1974 \text{ earnings} = (.09)(\$500,000) = \$45,000$$

$$(.4)(\$45,000) = \$18,000$$

$$1975 \text{ earnings} = \$45,000 + \$18,000 = \$63,000$$

A less-naive approach might be to prepare a *pro forma* income statement and balance sheet given the sales growth and ratio assumptions made above:

Recensement Data
Pro forma **Statement of Income**

Sales [(500,000) + (.3) (500,000)]	$650,000
Cost of goods sold [(.76) (650,000)]	494,000
Gross margin	156,000
Other expenses	45,000
EBIT [(.17) (650,000)]	110,500
Interest and taxes	52,200
Net income [(.09) (650,000)]	$ 58,500

Pro forma Balance Sheet

Current assets	$ 21,000
Fixed assets	150,000
Total assets [(650,000) ÷ (3.8)]	$171,000
Current liabilities [(21,000) ÷ (2.6)]	$ 8,000
Long-term debt	10,000
Net worth	153,000
	$171,000

Notice that the earnings growth rate indicated by the second approach is less than that of the first:

$$(58,500 - 45,000) \div 45,000 = 30 \text{ percent}$$

This growth rate was implicit in the assumptions made in the second approach. If sales are growing by a given percentage and the net margin is assumed to be constant, then the earnings growth rate must equal the sales growth rate. In this instance, as in all examples in which ratio values are assumed, the analyst should be sure that he is not making internally inconsistent assumptions.

REGRESSION AND CORRELATION ANALYSIS

Naive forecasting techniques are reasonably satisfactory if the analyst is projecting only one or two years into the future. When longer forecasts are needed, however, more sophisticated approaches are required. For a number of firms, there are no underlying long-run trends in performance. If it appears to the analyst that a firm's activities are more or less stable (that is, sales, costs, and earnings do not vary by much), then there really is no forecasting problem. There are not many firms in this category, however. Much more likely is the case of the *cyclical* firm that evidences no long-run trends but that does have a consistent performance in the short run. Forecasting the position of a cyclical enterprise *may* be accomplished by the use of *regression and correlation analysis*, provided continuation of an upswing (or a downswing) in activities prevails.[1] It must be remembered, however, that changes from an upswing to a downswing position (or vice versa) cannot be predicted with least-squares techniques. Statistical procedures are available for attempting this problem, but they are beyond the scope of this book.

The use of multiple regression and correlation analysis and corporate modeling allows the analyst to specify more accurately values for a far larger

[1] A review of regression and correlation analysis is provided in Appendix B.

number of variables than the naive methods. Like the naive techniques previously discussed, however, regression analysis assumes some underlying trend in the data being examined. If no trend is there (short run or long run), the regression results will be of little value for forecasting purposes. Indeed, when neither a negative nor a positive trend appears to be evident within a set of data, the analyst must either assume that past performance will be repeated or rely on the crudest of naive techniques — hunch.

A typical analysis employing regression procedures will begin with a forecast of aggregate economic activity. Some securities analysts prepare their own predictions of such variables as GNP, prices, the level of interest rates, and so on. Others depend upon the large econometric models, such as those developed at the University of Pennsylvania's Wharton School and the Brookings Institution, to generate aggregate predictions. Once the aggregate projection is made, the analyst then concentrates on developing a model of the industry in which he is interested. Finally, a model is prepared for specific firms (or a firm) within that industry. Typically, the results of the aggregate forecast are fed into the industry model, and the output from the industry model is used as input for the firm projection. At each stage of developing his forecast, the analyst must be careful to select those independent variables that make *a priori* sense as determinants. Although it is possible to generate "good" statistical results (that is, high R^2 values that are also statistically significant) by correlating any two or more variables, it would be difficult for an analyst to defend a forecast that, say, based a prediction of sales on the phases of the moon. Even if high sales and a full moon correlated with a very good, statistically significant fit, one would be hard pressed to find an economic explanation for the phenomena.

EXAMPLES

1. Peason-Jackson is a large, nationwide publisher of college textbooks. Textbook sales seem to depend on a number of factors, but two variables stand out as being particularly significant: family median income (Y) and the total college population (P). An analyst has determined the following equation to project total annual textbook sales:

$$S_i = 140.3 + 12.7(Y) + 59.4(P)$$

Where S_i is measured in millions, Y in thousands, and P in millions. For next year, if $Y = \$8,200$ and $P = 6,500,000$, a projection of S_i would be:

$$S_i = 140.3 + 12.7(8.2) + 59.4(6.5)$$
$$S_i = 630.54 \text{ or } \$630,540,000.$$

2. Sales for Peason-Jackson are clearly a function of industry sales. It has also been determined that a high correlation exists between the firm's sales and one other variable, the number of salesmen employed by the firm (N). The following equation has been fitted:

$$S_p = -50.6 + .18\ (S_i) + .03\ (N)$$

where S_p is measured in millions. A prediction for Peason-Jackson sales for next year if $N = 1280$ would be:

$$S_p = -50.6 + .18\ (630.54) + .03\ (1280)$$
$$S_p = 101.30 \text{ or } \$101,300,000.$$

INDEPENDENT VARIABLES AND SENSITIVITY ANALYSIS

Two major problems confront the analyst when he uses multiple regression analysis to forecast: (1) What are the key independent variables? and (2) How sensitive are the final forecasted results to changes in the values of the independent variables? The first of these questions is difficult to answer. Frequently, the analyst will try a number of combinations of variables, examining the coefficients of partial determination, R^2, and the statistical significance of his results in order to find the combination that yields the best prediction. The second problem can be handled through the use of *sensitivity analysis*. Simply explained, sensitivity analysis seeks to demonstrate how large a change in the value of a single independent variable is required to alter *significantly* the forecasted outcome. Because the values assigned to the exogenous variables in a system of forecasting equations are rarely known with certainty, it may be necessary for the analyst to try likely values first and then examine his results as less-likely values are used. It is clear, of course, that forecasted results for a dependent variable are no more accurate than the input assumed for the independent variables.

Sensitivity analysis may be employed in a number of contexts. The independent variables in any regression equation may be subjected to sensitivity tests. Many analysts have attempted to forecast stock prices directly without going through the extensive fundamental analysis that we recommend in this book. When such an approach (direct forecasting) is employed, sensitivity analysis may become a necessary supplement. Consider the case of the Second Philadelphia Corp., an investment banking house that attempts to forecast stock prices with regression analysis. The following equation is used:

$$P_t = f(\bar{P}_{t-1}, D_{t-1}, S_t, L, r, i)$$

Where: P_t is the stock price in period t.

$\bar{P}_{t-1}$ was the average stock price in the previous period.

D_{t-1} was the dividend in the previous period.

S_t is expected sales per share in period t.

L is the degree of financial leverage (debt to equity) for the firm expected in period t.

r is the rate of return on investment (EBIT to total assets) expected in period t.

i is the prime rate of interest expected in period t.

For National Motors, the regression equation below has been determined:

$$P_t = -6.50 + (.76)\bar{P}_{t-1} + (.15)D_{t-1} + (1.34)S_t$$
$$- (8.24)L + (12.54)r - (26.12)i$$

Values for each independent variable have been estimated for period t as:

$$S_t = \$10$$
$$L = .40$$
$$r = .25$$
$$i = .06$$

The average share price for National during the previous period was $22. The firm paid a dividend of $1 per share in the previous period. A projection of the stock price would provide:

$$P_t = -6.50 + (.76)(22.00) + (.15)(1.00) + (1.34)(10.00)$$
$$-(8.24)(.40) + (12.54)(.25) - (26.12)(.06)$$
$$= -6.50 + 16.72 + 0.15 + 13.40 - 3.30 + 3.14 - 1.57$$
$$= \$22.04$$

Because future sales for National are not known with certainty, sensitivity analysis may be employed to examine the differences in share prices produced by various sales estimates. If economic conditions are good, sales may be $11.00 per share. If they do not change from the past period, the $10.00 figure will prevail. If conditions deteriorate, sales per share could fall to $9.00. Sensitivity analysis could be applied to these three possible events:

1. If S_t = $11.00, P_t becomes $23.38
2. If S_t = $9.00, P_t becomes $20.70
3. Thus, a 10 percent deviation in sales per share can produce a 6 percent variation in forecasted price (that is, 1.34/22.04).

The analysis could be applied to other variables as well. Suppose i might be .05, .06, or .07. The best event (i = .05) would add $.26 to the share price, and the worst one (i = .07) would reduce the price by $.26. This does not appear to be a very sensitive variable.

The forecasting procedure used by Second Philadelphia, even when supplemented by sensitivity analysis, leaves much to be desired. We are not given R^2, the coefficients of partial determination, or F test values to measure statistical significance. Furthermore, one could suspect the presence of *serial correlation*, given the fact that one of the independent variables is a lagged version of the dependent variable. In any case, forecasting equations of this general sort should be used with great care. A more difficult, but also more adequate, method is to project stock "values" (rather than prices) using a series of equations indicating fundamental relationships such as company revenues to industry revenues, costs to revenues, and so on. The comprehensive case at the end of this chapter employs a simplified version of this method.

DISCRIMINANT ANALYSIS

Multiple regression analysis and corporate modeling are used by the securities analyst primarily as tools to discern good investment prospects from bad ones. There are other techniques that are gradually coming into use by the financial community (although they have been employed by statisticians elsewhere for some time) to measure prospective asset performance. One of the more interesting of these techniques is *discriminant analysis*. This approach may be used to find those financial characteristics that best discriminate profitable investments from unprofitable ones. The method assumes that observations come from two distinct universes, the profitable and the unprofitable. Suppose we have examined the price appreciation of common stocks and have identified two characteristics as being important: growth in sales and growth in earnings. We have examined each of these characteristics for a number of stocks and have compared them with the growth in share price. From these data, we have plotted each security on a scatter diagram (see Figure 6-1). The circles indicate investments that turned out to be unprofitable (showing a price decline), and the

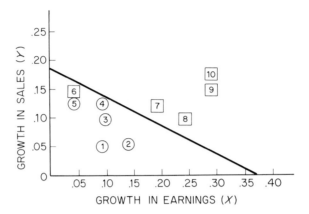

Figure 6.1   Discriminant Scatter Diagram

boxes indicate investments that turned out to be profitable (showing price appreciation). Now, we want to determine which of those investments we would have made given a specified criteria for sales and earnings growth. In order to do this, we must find the parameters for the following discriminant function:

$$f = a(X) + b(Y) \qquad\qquad (6.1)$$

where X is the growth rate of earnings and Y is the growth rate of sales. The parameters should be such that the average value of f for profitable investments (f_p) is significantly larger than for unprofitable ones (f_u). In Figure 6-2, these values are indicated for the universes of profitable and unprofitable investments. Note that some profitable investments could be misclassified as being unprofitable (and, hence, unsuccessfully discriminated) and some unprofitable investments could be misclassified as being profitable.

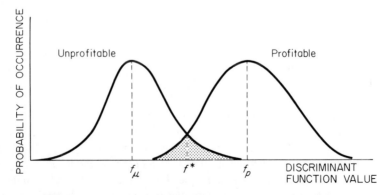

Figure 6.2   Discriminant Function for Profitable and Unprofitable Investments

The coefficients a and b in equation 6.1 may be computed by the following:

$$a = \frac{S_{yy}d_x - S_{xy}d_y}{S_{xx}S_{yy} - S^2{}_{xy}} \tag{6.2}$$

$$b = \frac{S_{xx}d_y - S_{xy}d_x}{S_{xx}S_{yy} - S^2{}_{xy}} \tag{6.3}$$

where S_{xx} and S_{yy} are the respective variances of X and Y; and S_{xy} is the covariance of X and Y. The difference between the average of X's for profitable investments and unprofitable ones is d_x. The difference between the average of Y's for profitable and unprofitable investments is d_y. The solution of equations 6.2 and 6.3 gives us $- a/b$, the slope of the discriminant boundary line.

Once we know a and b, we may compute f values for our securities. Our objective is to find f^* (Figure 6-2), which will serve as a cutoff point for investments. Although some profitable investments might have values less than f^* and some unprofitable ones might have a value greater than f^* (the shaded area in Figure 6-2), the use of this value will minimize the probability of predicting that an unprofitable investment will be profitable (or a profitable investment will be unprofitable). Once f^* is determined, we may immediately compute the Y-intercept of the discriminant line as f^*/b.

The ten securities in Figure 6-1 have the following X and Y values and profit characteristic:

Security	X	Y	Profitable or Unprofitable
1	.10	.05	Unprofitable
2	.15	.06	Unprofitable
3	.12	.10	Unprofitable
4	.10	.12	Unprofitable
5	.05	.12	Unprofitable
6	.05	.14	Profitable
7	.20	.12	Profitable
8	.25	.10	Profitable
9	.30	.15	Profitable
10	.30	.18	Profitable

If $a = 2.0$ and $b = 4.0$, f_i values for each security may be computed:

$$f = a(X) + b(Y)$$
$$f_1 = 2(.10) + 4(.05) = .40$$
$$f_2 = 2(.15) + 4(.06) = .54$$
$$f_3 = 2(.12) + 4(.10) = .64$$

$$f_4 = 2(.10) + 4(.12) = .68$$

$$f_5 = 2(.05) + 4(.12) = .58$$

$$f_6 = 2(.05) + 4(.14) = .66$$

$$f_7 = 2(.20) + 4(.12) = .88$$

$$f_8 = 2(.25) + 4(.10) = .90$$

$$f_9 = 2(.30) + 4(.15) = 1.20$$

$$f_{10} = 2(.30) + 4(.18) = 1.32$$

Next, we may rank the securities by f_i values and profit characteristic (P or U):

$$f_1 = .40 \quad U$$

$$f_2 = .54 \quad U$$

$$f_5 = .58 \quad U$$

$$f_3 = .64 \quad U$$

$$f_6 = .66 \quad P$$

$$f_4 = .68 \quad U$$

$$f_7 = .88 \quad P$$

$$f_8 = .90 \quad P$$

$$f_9 = 1.20 \quad P$$

$$f_{10} = 1.32 \quad P$$

Notice that the solution would provide an area of overlap for values between .64 and .88. As a convention, we might adopt the midpoint between these values (.76) as the cutoff point. If this were done, no unprofitable investments would have been selected, but profitable investment 6 would have been bypassed.

Empirical Studies Using Discriminant Analysis

Several noteworthy studies have been made using multiple discriminant analysis to discern good performance in realized investment returns. One, by Marc Nerlove, found that seven variables best discriminated good performance from bad. They were: (1) growth of sales; (2) retention of earnings; (3) growth in earnings; (4) long-run dividends; (5) leverage; (6) the firm's product mix; and

(7) the relationship of fixed plant to total assets.[2] Another study, by Fred B. Renwick, sought to determine the causes of good portfolio performance.[3] He found four variables that best discriminated among three portfolios, one yielding high returns, another yielding low returns, and a control portfolio yielding mixed returns. Renwick's choice of discriminant variables were profitability of the firm (net operating income to total assets), the sales growth rate, the retention rate, and the degree of leverage.[4]

Although discriminant analysis has proved to be very helpful as a tool for exploratory research, some authorities feel that it is most appropriately applied to explain past relationships rather than to predict future ones. The statistical foundation for the procedure is not terribly strong, and it should be employed only by those who understand the method very well. Nevertheless, in capable hands the technique can provide added insight into the problem of classification.

PROBLEMS

1. An analyst is trying to forecast the future performance of Liggett Ltd. From talking with officials of the firm, he has determined the following:

(1) The firm plans to increase its net investment in fixed assets by $1 million over the next two years, with $400,000 being added in the first year (1975).
(2) The firm plans to introduce several new products that should produce substantial added revenue.
(3) Advertising expenses associated with the introduction of the new product lines should increase selling expenses by 20 percent.
(4) Management has introduced better cost controls over operations. Already, these added controls have cut operating expenses tremendously.

The analyst has computed the following ratios for the past five years for Liggett:

	1970	1971	1972	1973	1974
Sales increase from previous year	.10	.12	.09	.10	.11
Gross margin	.30	.28	.29	.33	.35
EBIT margin	.15	.14	.15	.17	.19
Net margin	.05	.05	.05	.06	.07
Total debt to capital	.60	.58	.56	.54	.51
Current ratio	4.20	4.30	4.30	6.80	7.60

[2]Marc Nerlove, "Factors Affecting Differences Among Rates of Return on Investments in Individual Common Stocks," *Review of Economics and Statistics*, August 1968, pp. 122–36.

[3]Fred B. Renwick, "Asset Management and Investor Portfolio Behavior: Theory and Practice," *Journal of Finance*, May 1969, pp. 181–206.

[4]Another application of discriminant analysis (to determine potential corporate bankruptcies) is considered in Chapter 8.

a. Reconstruct the 1974 income statement for Liggett. The firm has no nonoperating revenues or expenses. It has outstanding $5 million in long-term debt on which it pays 5 percent interest. The firm pays 50 percent of earnings before taxes in income taxes. Sales for 1974 were $5 million.

b. Reconstruct the balance sheet for Liggett as of December 31, 1974. (Note: The total asset turnover for 1974 was .50 times.)

c. Prepare *pro forma* income statements and balance sheets for 1975 and 1976. The analyst has made the following assumptions:

(1) Sales will increase by about 10 percent annually from current lines. New lines will increase sales by about $500,000 in 1975 and then follow the 10 percent pattern.

(2) Cost control efforts should produce continued savings. The gross margin should advance to about .37.

(3) Administrative expenses are relatively stable at $300,000 per year. Selling expenses tend to be about 10 percent of sales but will increase to 12 percent with the addition of the new product lines.

(4) The new plant and equipment will be financed this way: in 1975, $200,000 worth of current assets will be converted into fixed assets, and $200,000 of earnings will be retained. In 1976, $200,000 will be converted from current to fixed assets, $200,000 will be retained, and current liabilities will be increased by $200,000.

d. Compute the following *pro forma* ratios for Liggett for 1975 and 1976:

(1) EBIT margin

(2) Net margin

(3) Total asset turnover

(4) Total debt to capital

(5) Book value per share (100,000 shares outstanding)

(6) Earnings per share

(7) Dividends per share

(8) Pay-out ratio

(9) Current ratio

e. Evaluate Liggett's prospects for the next two years. Examine these specific points:

(1) What accounts for Liggett's improved earning power?

(2) What rate of growth in earnings is anticipated from 1974 to 1975? From 1975 to 1976?

(3) What accounts for the larger increase in earnings than in sales?

f. Liggett debt is in the form of 5 percent bonds due in 1984. The bonds were sold in 1964 at par. By 1970, the firm had no other outstanding long-term debt.

(1) What two ratios might the analyst examine to determine the asset and income security of the debt?

(2) Compute these ratios for 1974 and *pro forma* 1975 and 1976.

(3) What will happen to the security of the bonds if the projections made above are correct?

g. Liggett stock sells for $70 per share as of December 31, 1974.

(1) What is the P/E multiple for 1974?

(2) What are the dividend yields *pro forma* for 1975 and 1976? (Assume the 1974 P/E will continue for 1975 and 1976.)

(3) If one purchased Liggett today at $70 and sold it at the end of 1976, what would his return be? (Assume dividends are paid out annually and that the current price reflects the recent payment of the 1974 dividend).

2. What independent variables might you consider regressing in order to predict sales in the following industries:

a. Automobiles

b. Steel

c. Railroads

d. Public utilities

3. Enumerate possible independent variables for regressing with sales for firms in the following types of business:

a. Popular records

b. Baby food

c. Luxury automobiles

d. Color television

e. Housing construction

4. You are given the following model for predicting the sales of the Strauss Corporation:

$$S = -47 + .16(X_1) + .12(X_2) + 1.45(X_3)$$
$$(.92) \qquad (.14) \qquad (.63)$$
$$R^2 = .75$$

Where: S = Strauss sales (in thousands)

X_1 = industry sales (in thousands)

X_2 = an index of prices charged by Strauss' competitors

X_3 = advertising expenditures made by Strauss (in thousands)

Suppose industry sales for next year are estimated to be $1,200,000, your index of prices is expected to be 114, and Strauss' annual report states that the firm plans to spend about $100,000 on advertising next year. Predict sales from the equation. Interpret the coefficients of partial determination and the R^2 value.

5. Test the sensitivity of Strauss' sales (above) to each independent variable. Continuous distributions for the variables have been determined where:

$$\bar{X}_1 = \$1,200,000 \qquad \sigma_{x_1} = \$200,000$$
$$\bar{X}_2 = 114 \qquad \sigma_{x_2} = 10$$
$$\bar{X}_3 = \$100,000 \qquad \sigma_{x_3} = 0$$

a. Test each variable to $\pm\sigma$. Assume the variables are normally distributed.

b. Suppose the analyst wished to test the sensitivity of low values of industry sales on Strauss' sales. The lowest values, which could occur only 5 percent or less of the time, will be considered "acceptable risks."

(1) At what value for industry sales will the analyst be 95 percent confident that sales will be no lower than this value?

(2) How sensitive would Strauss' sales be to these low values?

6. Reconsider the discriminant function developed in the example constructed on page 124.

a. Using the cutoff criteria developed in the example, choose among the following investments:

Investment	f Value
1	.52
2	.60
3	.82
4	.96
5	1.54

b. Suppose investments 1 and 3 turn out to be unprofitable and investments 2, 4, and 5 turn out to be profitable? How good has your decision rule been?

c. What implicit assumption is made when the criteria developed for a sample set of alternatives (such as that suggested in the example problem) is used for another set (such as that indicated in number 6a)?

COMPREHENSIVE CASE

A complete corporate model for Windsor Mobile Homes, Inc. has been prepared by an analyst. His equations are indicated to be:

$$SA = 14.8 + .01(GNP) + .34(FA) - 1.84(INT) \quad (1)$$
$$CGS = 3.4 + .45(SA) \quad (2)$$
$$SE = .6 + .12(SA) \quad (3)$$
$$OE = 1.3 + .09(SA) \quad (4)$$
$$CA = 2.4 + .38(FA) \quad (5)$$
$$CL = 1.3 + .45(CA) \quad (6)$$

Where: GNP = gross national product (in billions of dollars)

         FA = the firm's fixed asset investment (in millions of dollars)

        INT = the prime rate of interest (in percents)

         SA = the firm's sales (in millions of dollars)

         SE = selling expenses for the firm (in millions of dollars)

         OE = other expenses for the firm (in millions of dollars)

         CA = the firm's level of current assets (in millions of dollars)

         CL = the firm's level of current liabilities (in millions of dollars)

1. The analyst has projected GNP for the next year to be $1,450 billion. He believes the firm will increase its fixed asset investment to about $21.5 million. The prime rate of interest is expected to be about 4 percent. Given these values for the variables exogenous to the system, solve the six equations given above.

2. Prepare a projected income statement for next year. The firm has outstanding $20 million in long-term debt at 6 percent. This level is not expected to change next year. The firm is taxed at 50 percent.

3. Prepare a projected balance sheet for next year.

4. Repeat the above for the year after next. Assume the following:
   a. GNP = $1,550 billion
   b. FA = $22.5 million
   c. INT = 5 percent

5. To which of the independent variables are Windsor sales most sensitive? From what you know about Windsor's industry, can you specify any reason for this result?

REFERENCES

Clelland, Richard C., et al., *Basic Statistics with Business Applications.* New York: John Wiley & Sons, Inc., 1966.

Kane, Edward J., *Economic Statistics and Econometrics.* New York: Harper & Row, Publishers, Incorporated, 1968.

Nerlove, Marc, "Factors Affecting Differences Among Rates of Return on Investment in Individual Common Stocks," *Review of Economics and Statistics*, August 1968, pp. 122–36.

Renwick, Fred B., "Asset Management and Investor Portfolio Behavior: Theory and Practice," *Journal of Finance*, May 1969, pp. 181–206.

Yamane, Taro, *Statistics: An Introductory Analysis*, 2d ed. New York: Harper & Row, Publishers, Incorporated, 1967.

7

Analysis
of Fixed Income
Securities I

FORECASTS AND BOND ANALYSIS

Fixed-income securities are generally purchased because of the reduced risk associated with returns generated by these instruments. A *bond* obligates the issuing firm (or government) to pay interest at a specific rate, at a particular interval, and in a prescribed manner. Also, payments of principal are to be made periodically according to the terms specified in the *indenture* (the contractual agreement between the issuer and holder of the bond). The mere fact that a security takes the form of a fixed-income instrument does not insure the safety of the security. Indeed, the common stocks of some enterprises are less risky than the bonds of others. Nevertheless, the bond form does generally set a maximum payment ceiling (the coupon rate), and lesser amounts will be paid only if the issuer encounters financial difficulty.

Determining the probability that a firm (or other issuer) will be unable to meet coupon or principal payments is the primary responsibility of the bond analyst. Clearly, this task requires a complete analysis of the present and future financial position of the firm, and the bond analyst will employ the techniques outlined in the previous two chapters to determine this position.

A recommended procedure is to forecast the earnings of the firm as far into the future as possible. In the ideal case, the analyst will be able to project throughout the life of the bond. Given this forecast, the analyst may then prepare annual probability distributions of interest (and principal) payments.

From this set of distributions, the risk and return from purchasing the instrument may be determined.

We may consider an example of the appropriate methodology. An analyst has constructed a corporate model for the Consolidated Electric Appliance Corp. He wishes to use this model in order to determine the risk and return associated with Consolidated's 5 percent subordinated debenture due on December 31, 1979. The bond pays interest semiannually, although the analyst is assuming annual payments to simplify his calculations.

Consolidated grossed $120 million in 1974. A revenue-forecasting equation has been generated with a reasonably good fit by means of multiple regression analysis:

$$R = 72.72 + .004(Y) + 4.26(P)$$

where:

R = annual revenue (in millions)

Y = per capita income of individuals in Consolidated's
sales area

P = population of Consolidated's sales area
(in millions)

Analysis of past income statements has revealed that Consolidated incurs annual operating fixed costs of $80 million (including $40 million in depreciation) and has a variable cost ratio of about .2. Interest payments on the firm's bond indebtedness has totaled $5 million annually. The firm pays an average income tax of 40 percent.

1. Forecast total revenues for Consolidated for 1975–1979 assuming the following values:

	Y	P
1975	$3,000	8.75 million
1976	3,125	9.00
1977	3,300	9.40
1978	3,500	9.60
1979	3,800	10.00

The forecasted revenues would be:

1975 $72.72 + (.004)(3,000) + (4.26)(8.75) = \$122.00$ million

1976 $72.72 + (.004)(3,125) + (4.26)(9.00) = \$123.56$

1977   72.72 + (.004)(3,300) + (4.26)(9.40) = \$125.96

1978   72.72 + (.004)(3,500) + (4.26)(9.60) = \$127.62

1979   72.72 + (.004)(3,800) + (4.26)(10.00) = \$130.52

2. Prepare simplified *pro forma* income statements for 1975–1979.

(in millions)

	1975	1976	1977	1978	1979
Revenues	\$122.00	\$123.56	\$125.96	\$127.62	\$130.52
Fixed operating costs	80.00	80.00	80.00	80.00	80.00
Variable operating costs	24.40	24.71	25.19	25.52	26.10
EBIT	17.60	18.85	20.77	22.10	24.42
Interest	5.00	5.00	5.00	5.00	5.00
EBT	12.60	13.85	15.77	17.10	19.42
Taxes	5.04	5.54	6.31	6.84	7.77
Net income	\$ 7.56	\$ 8.31	\$ 9.46	\$ 10.26	\$ 11.65

3. Compute the times-interest-earned ratio expected for 1975–1979.

$$1975 \quad \frac{17.60}{5.00} = 3.52X \qquad\qquad 1978 \quad \frac{22.10}{5.00} = 4.42X$$

$$1976 \quad \frac{18.85}{5.00} = 3.77X \qquad\qquad 1979 \quad \frac{24.42}{5.00} = 4.88X$$

$$1977 \quad \frac{20.77}{5.00} = 4.15X$$

4. How far would revenues have to decline before interest payments would be endangered in 1975?

Revenues	\$ (X)	\$106.25
Fixed operating costs	80.00	80.00
Variable operating costs	(.2)(X)	21.25
EBIT	\$ 5.00	\$ 5.00

$$X - 80.00 - (.2)(X) = 5.00$$

$$X = \$106.25 \text{ million}$$

Revenues would have to decline by 11.5 percent from 1974 revenues and be 12.9 percent under the 1975 projection before interest payments would be jeopardized.

5. What probability would one assign to the event: 1975 revenues ≤ $106.25 million? This is the toughest question the analyst must answer, and it is obviously a very subjective matter. A decline in revenues of the magnitude indicated would be possible for firms in many industries. If Consolidated were a railroad, for example, the probability of such an event might be reasonably high. For a public utility, however, the chances of a decrease in revenues of over 3 or 4 percent is not great. Manufacturing concerns have varying patterns of revenue volatility, and the best guide may be to examine the experience of past years.

6. Does the regression result help the analyst in determining the probability of interest-payment jeopardization? One of the major characteristics of regression techniques is that they only indicate trends (positive or negative). Thus, a regression estimator will not, by itself, aid the analyst in determining the probability that his projection will be worse than expected. However, the analyst may examine other statistics that will aid him in this determination. Initially, he may inspect the R^2 value to check on the closeness of fit among the variables. A low R^2 might reduce his confidence in the estimated value and may cause him to reexamine the historical data (the regression inputs) to determine whether large declines had been experienced in the past. Next, he might consider the standard error of the estimate. If the analyst believes the underlying distribution is essentially normal, then the standard error of the estimate may be used to determine the probability $P\ (R \leqslant \$106.25$ million). Suppose the revenue distribution for Consolidated is normally distributed with a standard error of $2 million. Then, $P(R \leqslant \$106.25$ million) $\cong 0$. For $R \leqslant \$106.25$ million, a value almost 8 standard errors [that is, $(122-106)/2$] from the expected value would have to occur. The probability of this event is extremely small.

7. What other variables, in addition to revenue variability, would the analyst have to examine in order to determine the probability that interest payments would be jeopardized? From the example above, the reader can recognize the importance of *operating leverage* on interest payments. A relatively small decline in revenues (11.5 percent) would completely wipe out EBIT for Consolidated. This is true because of the high level of fixed operating costs incurred by the company. For a firm with a lower degree of operating leverage, a larger decline in revenues could be tolerated before interest payments would be endangered. Thus, in addition to the stability of revenues, the analyst should examine the cost structure of the firm in order to determine the probability of interest-payment default. A high level of fixed costs or an increasing percentage of costs to total revenues (declining profit margins) can be as detrimental to interest-payment coverage as revenue declines. These points are illustrated more rigorously in the appendix to this chapter.

8. Suppose revenues did indeed fall to $106.25 million. Would the firm default on its bond interest payments? Not necessarily. Interest payments are made out of cash flows — not just earnings before interest and taxes. A firm may continue to pay interest on its indebtedness even though it is losing money.

Several sources of funds other than earnings can be employed. (a) Cash generated from depreciation flows, for example, may be used to pay interest rather than replace plant and equipment. When a firm uses depreciation flows for this purpose, of course, its long-run earnings potential is reduced. (b) A firm may have built up a stock of cash that may be used to make interest payments. If the cash flows of the firm are independent over time, then the cash account may be used for interest payments during bad years and replenished during good years. If, as is more likely, the flows are dependent over time, then one bad year would follow another and the cash account would be soon depleted. (c) The firm may borrow to meet interest obligations. Nevertheless, loans are granted for such purposes rarely, and then only when it appears that the firm is temporarily suffering an earnings decline. (d) Railroads have a habit of meeting debt charges by deferring maintenance of equipment and right of way. Hence, they allow deterioration of facilities that eventually must be repaired or replaced. This is the reason that the rail analyst examines the maintenance ratio when analyzing the position of a railroad. Although all these methods of continuing interest payments under depressed conditions may delay default, there is a tendency for them to be stopgap measures that only postpone the inevitable.

COVERAGE RATIOS AND INCOME SECURITY

In addition to using the forecasting tools employed in the previous section, the analyst will also use several ratios to aid him in the determination of possible default. He will frequently compute the times-interest-earned ratio for past years and compare the firm's ratio with that of other firms in the same business. He will also examine the trend of the ratio for the firm over time. Of course, these ratios should not be substitutes in analysis for forecasting. Rather, they should serve as additional data to give added perspective to the results obtained from projections.

When a firm has several bond issues outstanding, it is possible to compute several variations of the times-interest-earned ratio. The simplest of these ratios is computed by adding all interest payments and dividing this sum into earnings before interest and taxes (EBIT). The resulting ratio is called the *overall-interest-coverage ratio*. A second group of ratios, called *cumulative-deduction-coverage ratios*, attempts to differentiate among bonds on the basis of their claim on earnings (and assets in the case of liquidation) in order to show a higher coverage for more-secure obligations. The interest coverage of claims is computed in order of priority. First, the interest requirement for the most senior security is divided into EBIT to obtain its coverage ratio. Next, the claims of junior securities are added to the denominator of the coverage ratio successively in order to determine the coverage of each issue. Although the exact arrangement of priorities can be ascertained only from the indentures of the relevant securities, the general order of priority is: first mortgage bonds and equivalents (for example, equipment trust certificates, collateral trust agreements, and so on), second mortgage bonds, debentures, subordinated debentures, junior subordinated debentures, preferred stock, and, finally, common stock. A third method of computing coverage ratios is the *prior deductions method*. Instead of adding the interest requirement of senior issues to the denominator as in the cumulative deduction method, this approach subtracts them from the numerator (EBIT). The coverage is then computed as [(EBIT - prior charges)/interest on security under analysis]. The computation may produce the absurd result that a junior obligation appears to be safer than a senior issue. Although this method gives no useful information, many investment banking houses once employed it to give a deceptively good picture for a bond they were about to underwrite. It should be avoided by the analyst. These three methods of computing coverage ratios are illustrated below.

The long-term debt section of the balance sheet of the Atlantic and Pacific R.R. is as follows (in order of earnings claim):

First mortgage 5's of 1985	$ 24,200,000
Second mortgage 8 1/8's of 1979	20,000,000
Collateral trust notes 4's of 1975	50,000,000
Subordinated debentures 9's of 1990	6,000,000
	$100,200,000

Earnings before interest and taxes for Atlantic and Pacific is $10,750,000. The overall interest coverage would be:

(.05)(24.2 million) =	$1,210,000
(.08125)(20 million) =	1,625,000
(.04)(50 million) =	2,000,000
(.09)(6 million) =	540,000
	$5,375,000

$$10,750,000/5,375,000 = 2.0X$$

The cumulative coverage for each issue would be:

First mortgage bonds

$$(10,750,000)/(1,210,000) = 8.9X$$

Second mortgage bonds

$$(10,750,000)/(1,210,000 + 1,625,000) = 3.8X$$

Collateral trust notes

$$(10,750,000)/(1,210,000 + 1,625,000 + 2,000,000) = 2.2X$$

Subordinated debentures

$$(10,750,000)/(1,210,000 + 1,625,000 + 2,000,000 + 540,000) = 2.0X$$

Notice that the coverage for the most junior issue is the same as the overall coverage.

The prior deduction coverage for each issue would be:

First mortgage bonds
$$(10,750,000)/(1,210,000) = 8.9X$$
Second mortgage bonds
$$(10,750,000 - 1,210,000)/(1,625,000) = 5.9X$$
Collateral trust notes
$$(10,750,000 - 1,210,000 - 1,625,000)/(2,000,000) = 3.9X$$
Subordinated debentures
$$(10,750,000 - 1,210,000 - 1,625,000 - 2,000,000)/(540,000) = 10.9X$$

Note the absurd result here indicating greater security for the subordinated debentures than for the first mortgage bonds.

PROTECTION IN CASE OF FINANCIAL DIFFICULTY

The major determinants of the firm's ability to make its interest payments are the volume of interest payments the firm owes in each period and the earnings available for those payments. Other tests used to determine the safety of the coupon and principal payments for a bond were discussed in Chapter 5. The degree of *financial leverage* possessed by the firm may be indicated by various debt-to-equity and debt-to-total-capital ratios. The asset security of obligations may be tested by computing several asset-coverage ratios (such as the tangible asset debt coverage). Although the capital-structure and asset-coverage ratios do provide additional information about the position of the firm's debt obligations, they are most useful as indicators of what the holders might receive in case of liquidation or reorganization. Because the primary reason for bond purchases is the *avoidance* of any problems associated with payment default or delay, the analyst should not be satisfied simply because a firm has little indebtedness or a bond is well secured by assets in case of difficulty. Of course, once the analyst is confident that coupon and principal payments are adequately protected by future earnings, added security provided by low indebtedness and large asset holdings can be considered a safety hedge in case a very poor state of events develops.

When financial difficulties do occur for a company, there are several courses of action available. If creditors believe that the firm will never be able to earn enough to repay its obligations, they may sue to place the firm in bankruptcy. If it is decided that the firm should be *liquidated*, a referee is appointed to sell the firm's assets at the best price he can obtain. The funds received are used first to pay for the cost of liquidation (legal fees and so on). Next, any back taxes, wages payable, and certain other claims are paid. Secured creditors are entitled to the proceeds obtained from the sale of the assets against which they have claims. In case their claims are not fully satisfied, they become general creditors for the balance owed them. Remaining funds are distributed to the general creditors. If funds are insufficient to meet all obligations, they are pro-rated by size of claim. When the general creditors are satisfied, distribution is made to subordinated creditors and then preferred stockholders. The balance, if any, goes to the common stockholders.

Because the process of bankruptcy is expensive administratively, many creditors will make great concessions to avoid the procedure. A frequently employed method is simply to give the debtor an *extension*, that is, more time to pay the obligation. This method is particularly attractive if interest payments are still being made (fully or partially) and only principal payments are being missed. A second method, used generally where interest payments have been stopped, is the *composition*, by which less than the total amount due is accepted as full payment of the obligation. Many creditors are willing to accept such an arrangement, because the funds become available for investment elsewhere fairly quickly and also the settlement may be greater than that which could be obtained from legal proceedings.

It may be decided that a firm should be *reorganized* rather than liquidated under bankruptcy. This is almost always the case for companies engaged in providing a vital public service (such as public utilities and railroads). Under reorganization, a *receiver* is appointed by the courts to operate the business until a satisfactory plan can be worked out. This process may take months or even years. Some railroads, for example, have been in receivership for twenty years before a reorganization could be accomplished. The reorganization plan is determined by a referee who decides upon a new capital structure for the firm. The objective of the new structure is to make it possible for the firm to become viable again. This usually means that the firm will not be overly burdened with fixed charges. Because interest on income bonds must be paid only if earned, this security has become a standard part of many reorganizations, particularly for railroads. (The poor reputation generally accorded income bonds in the past is no doubt accounted for by its use in reorganizations).

Reorganization may take place under two rules. The *absolute priority* rule settles claims with strict regard to their legal priority, and all senior claims must be satisfied in full before junior claims can be settled. Under *relative priority*, all claimants participate in the reorganization (including common stockholders), although heavier losses are apportioned to junior claims than senior. One method of distributing new securities under relative priority is to allocate on the basis of the market values of the old securities. We may consider a couple of examples.

The Singleton Publishing Co. is in financial difficulty. The company has been unable to meet interest payments on its subordinated debentures for two years, and preferred stock dividends have been passed for five years. Junior bondholders have granted two extensions of interest payments, but they are unwilling to grant a third. Lawyers for the company have polled the bondholders about the possibility of a composition, but full payment was demanded. Hence, the firm has petitioned to be declared bankrupt.

A balance sheet for Singleton is given below:

Cash	$ 50,000	Current liabilities	$ 200,000
Receivables	100,000	Mortgage bonds	300,000
Inventories	350,000	Subordinated debentures	300,000
Fixed assets	500,000	Preferred stock	100,000
	$1,000,000	Common equity	100,000
			$1,000,000

Receivables could be factored for 80 percent of their book value. Inventories can be sold at 70 percent of book value, and fixed assets could be liquidated at 40 percent of book value. It is expected that liquidation costs would be about $100,000. Among the firm's current liabilities are $50,000 in wages payable, and $10,000 in accrued taxes. Mortgage bondholders have a prior claim against all fixed assets. Upon liquidation, creditors would receive the following proceeds:

Cash	$ 50,000
Receivables	80,000
Inventories	245,000
Fixed assets	200,000
	$575,000

(a) First mortgage bondholders would have claim to $200,000 from the sale of fixed assets and would become general creditors for the balance of $100,000. (b) Liquidation costs, wages payable, and accrued taxes would have a claim against $160,000. (c) The balance ($575,000 − 200,000 − 160,000 = $215,000) would go to the general creditors. Other current liabilities are $140,000. The balance owed to first mortgage bondholders is $100,000. Subordinated debenture holders have a claim of $300,000. Thus, the payment to current liabilities would be 14/54 × $215,000 ≅ $55,000, first mortgage bondholders would initially get an additional 10/54 × $215,000 ≅ $40,000, and subordinated holders would claim 30/54 × $215,000 ≅ $120,000. However, because the debentures are subordinated to the mortgage bonds, the bondholders are entitled to have satisfied any remaining claims against the portion due the debentures. Thus, $60,000 would be transferred from the debenture claim to the mortgage bondholders. In sum, the mortgage bondholders would be paid in full, the other liability holders would be paid about 39 percent of their claim, and the debenture holders would receive about 20 percent of their claim.

The New York and Pennsylvania Railroad is being reorganized. Data from the trustee's files indicate:

	Current Book Value (in millions)	Trustee's Desired Structure (in millions)	Current Market Value (in millions)
First mortgage bonds	$ 100	$ 0	$ 80
Second mortgage bonds	150	0	90
Debentures	150	100	90
Subordinated notes	300	0	150
Income bonds	0	100	0
Preferred stock	0	100	0
Common stock	300	200	90
	$1,000	$500	$500

Reorganization under absolute priority would result in the following: The $100 million first mortgage bonds would get $100 million of debenture bonds. First mortgage bondholders would thus get $1,000 in debentures for each $1,000 first mortgage bond held. Second mortgage bonds would get $100 million of income bonds plus $50 million of preferred stock. Second mortgage bondholders would thus get $667 in income bonds and $333 in preferred stock for each $1,000 bond held. Current debenture holders would get $50 million in preferred stock and $100 million in common stock, or $333 worth of preferred and $667 worth of common for each $1,000 debenture held. Subordinate note holders would receive $100 million in common, or $333 worth of common for each $1,000 in notes held. Common stock holders would get nothing.

Reorganization under relative priority would be somewhat more complicated. Because the total market value of securities is $500 million and securities to be distributed are valued at $500 million, each class of holder would get the following if the basis for reorganization were market values: (a) First mortgage bondholders would get $80 million in debentures, or $800 worth of debenture for each $1,000 first mortgage bond held. (b) Second mortgage bondholders would get $20 million in debentures plus $70 million in income bonds, or $133 worth of debenture and $467 worth of income bonds for each $1,000 second mortgage bond held. (c) Debenture bondholders would get $30 million in income bonds and $60 million in preferred stock, or $200 in income bonds and $400 in preferred stock for each $1,000 debenture held. (d) Subordinated note holders would receive $40 million in preferred stock plus $110 million in common stock, or $133 in preferred stock and $367 in common stock for each $1,000 note held. (e) Common stockholders would get $90 million in common stock, or three shares for every ten now held.

PROBLEMS

1. An analyst is attempting to value the 5 percent first mortgage bonds of the Central Railroad. The bonds are due in ten years and pay an annual coupon. The analyst has forecasted C.R.R. revenues as follows (in millions):

1975	$106	1980	$126
1976	108	1981	131
1977	114	1982	117
1978	105	1983	109
1979	118	1984	112

The analyst believes that revenues are normally distributed with a standard error of the estimate of $10 million.

An examination of past income statements has indicated that C.R.R. has annual fixed operating expenses of $50 million (including $10 million depreciation) and a variable cost ratio of .4. The company has several bond issues outstanding including $100 million of first mortgage bonds, $50 million of second mortgage bonds, and $50 million of subordinated debentures that have coupons of 5 percent, 6 percent, and 8 percent respectively. The firm pays 50 percent of earnings before taxes in corporate income taxes.

    a. Prepare *pro forma* income statements for C.R.R. for 1975–1984.

    b. Compute the expected times-interest-earned ratio (based on total interest) for 1975–1984.

    c. How low could revenues be in the poorest year for the firm to be able to just meet interest payments out of earnings before interest and taxes?

    d. What is the probability that the firm will earn less than its total interest payments in the poorest year?

    e. Do you think the firm will default in this year? Why or why not?

    f. What is the overall probability of default? (Use the average forecasted revenue figure.)

    g. Suppose forecasted revenues were as follows (in millions):

1975	$126	1980	$108
1976	131	1981	106
1977	118	1982	105
1978	117	1983	109
1979	114	1984	112

Would this rearrangement of forecasted revenues influence your subjective judgment about the riskiness of the issue?

    h. The probability computed in problem 1f assumes that revenues are independent from one year to the next. If revenues were in fact dependent, with poor years auguring poorer ones, would this influence your opinion about the probability of default?

2. Reconsider the Central Railroad (above).

a. Compute the overall interest coverage, the cumulative deduction coverage, and the prior deduction coverage for 1975 (*pro forma*) for the road's indebtedness.

b. Compute the overall interest coverage and the cumulative deduction coverage for 1978 and 1981 (*pro forma*).

c. Suppose revenues for C.R.R. are $100 million. Compute the overall interest coverage and the cumulative deduction coverage. Is a default possible? What advantages would senior debt holders have?

3. A balance sheet for Ronald-Race Motors, Ltd. is provided below (in millions):

Cash	$ 25	Current liabilities	$ 50
Receivables	75	Senior debentures	50
Inventories	100	Subordinated debentures	200
Fixed assets	300	Common equity	200
	$500		$500

The firm is in financial difficulty and has just omitted payment of interest on the subordinated debentures. If the firm were forced into liquidation by these bondholders, receivables and inventories could be collected and sold at 2/3 and 1/2 of their respective book values. Fixed assets could be sold at 1/3 of their book worth. Among the current liabilities are $20 million in accrued wages and $15 million in accrued taxes. Legal fees and liquidation costs would amount to $30 million.

The company has offered a composition of 80 percent in a new issue of income bonds that would have a coupon of 6 percent and a maturity of 50 years. The present subordinated debentures have a coupon of 8 percent. Should the subordinated debenture holders press for liquidation or accept the composition?

4. The Ronald-Race subordinated debenture holders have decided to sue for bankruptcy, but the courts have ruled that the firm is engaged in too vital an activity for liquidation. The firm will be reorganized under absolute priority according to the following structure:

	Trustee's Desired Structure (in millions)	Current Market Value (in millions)
Senior debentures	$	$ 40
Subordinated debentures		100
Preferred stock (6,000,000 shs.)	60	—
Common stock (12,000,000 shs.)	120	100
	$180	$240

Current liabilities will be continued in the new structure at book value.

a. Determine what the other creditors would receive.

b. Determine what the long-term creditors would receive if the reorganization were done under relative priority.

c. Suppose the preferred stock issue paid 8 percent and sold in the market after reorganization at $10 per share. Suppose the new common stock began trading at $12. Would the old subordinated debenture holders have fared better by accepting the composition? What other alternative would they have had before reorganization?

APPENDIX

The Risk Structure of Interest Rates

In the appendix to Chapter 4, we established that the structure of rates on long-term securities will be related to the expected future short-term rates. Furthermore, it seems reasonable to expect that the greater potential price volatility of long-term securities resulting from a change in the actual or expected level of interest rates should cause them to command a higher nominal rate of interest in the form of a risk premium. This risk (called *interest-rate risk*) is the result of bond price changes caused by interest rate changes and is considered a part of the liquidity preference version of term structure theory (see Chapter 4). It should be borne in mind that this is the one risk that exists even for government securities (except the very short term).[1] Indeed, it might be argued that there is no such thing as a riskless long-term investment.[2]

Once we depart from the world of federal government securities, *default risk* becomes quite prominent in our discussion of the structure of market returns. Although many readers might be tempted to view this risk as solely involving the probability of the security in question becoming worthless, such is not a general case. Even if an issuer enters bankruptcy, the securities generally command some positive market price on the basis of expected liquidation payments or a possible reorganization. Thus, it is the possibility of partial payments and even full payments made behind schedule that constitute the difficult problems in the analysis of default risk. Consider the Ale Corp., which issued a five-year note at 6 percent with interest payments to be made annually. It is estimated that there is a .8 probability that the note will be paid on schedule, a .1 probability that the interest for years three and four will be skipped and paid at the end of year five, and a .1 probability that, aside from skipping interest in years three and four, the firm will enter bankruptcy in year

---

[1] It might be argued that inflation risk, or, more precisely, the change in expected rate of inflation risk, exists for all investments, including (especially) money.

[2] Even the investment in short-term securities involves risking the actual income to be earned in future periods. Thus, it might be even more correct to say that it is impossible to avoid all risks.

five and the holder will receive a total liquidation payment of $1000 at the end of year seven. The expected return on this note would be:

a. 6 percent if the note is paid on schedule.

b. Year	CF	PV@5%	PV	PV@6%	PV
0	−1000	1.000	−1000	1.000	−1000
1+2	+60	1.859	+111.60	1.833	+110
5	+1180	.784	+925.12	.747	+881.46
			+36.72		−8.54

≈ 5.8 percent if interest in years three and four is deferred until year five.

c. Year	CF	PV@2%	PV	PV@1%	PV
0	−1000	1.000	−1000	1.000	−1000
1+2	+60	1.942	+117	1.97	+118
7	+1000	.871	+871	.933	+933
			−12		+51

≈ 1.8 percent if interest in years three and four is missed, and the firm enters bankruptcy in year five.

$$r = (.8)(.06) + (.1)(.058) + (.1)(.018) = 5.56\%$$

Because the possibility of default, no matter how remote, exists for all nongovernment securities, it is necessary that they offer a nominal yield in excess of the riskless rate merely to possess an expected return equal to the riskless rate. As illustrated in the example above, the bond possessed a nominal yield of 6 percent and an expected yield of 5.56 percent. This factor alone would cause the yield curve for a homogeneous set of risky securities to lie above the yield curve for government securities. As a practical matter, however, risky securities generally offer an *expected* return in excess of the riskless rate. As a result, their nominal yield exceeds the riskless rate by a risk premium as well as the expected value of any default loss. In addition, this risk premium becomes larger as the security becomes riskier. Three hypothetical probability distributions of expected returns are given in Figure 7A-1 (it is assumed the bonds are held until maturity). The certain return for government bonds is illustrated as case A. Case B is a moderately risky, and C a quite risky, bond. It will be observed that the distributions for both B and C are greatly skewed. Receipt of the nominal yield is generally the best possible outcome (sometimes a call above par will increase the return), with various degrees of default trailing down to the left.[3] The figure has been drawn with the expected return on the

[3]It should be noted that the distribution of returns becomes more symmetrical as the holding period considered becomes shorter. In this discussion, we have assumed that the bond is held until maturity. If we chose instead a one-year holding period, where return would be final price plus income compared to initial price, the probability distribution of returns would likely be close to normal.

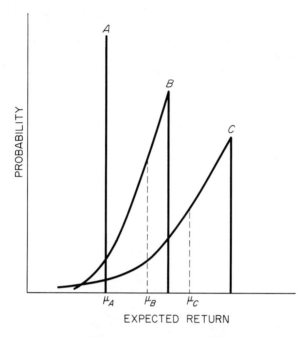

Figure 7A.1 Probability Distributions of Return for Three Hypothetical Bonds of Varying Risk Held to Maturity.

risky bonds in excess of the riskless rate. The theoretical justification for this observed market behavior is based upon investor aversion to risk in general and, especially, to the direction of skewness.

In terms of the analytical framework espoused by this book, default risk is a function of (1) the level and variation of gross revenues earned by the issuer; (2) the size of fixed charges against that income; and (3) the size of additional resources, such as working capital or bank credit, to meet the obligation. Let us begin by illustrating the difference in effect between variable and fixed charges against income. It should be noted that the effect of fixed charges is the same whether they are the result of operating (salaries and so on) or financial (interest) leverage.

Let:

S_i = i^{th} possible level of sales

$\mu_s, \mu_{avc}, \mu_{afc}$ = expected value of sales, expected value of sales minus variable costs, expected value of sales minus variable and fixed costs

$\sigma_s, \sigma_{avc}, \sigma_{afc}$ = standard deviation of sales, standard deviation of sales minus variable costs, standard deviation of sales minus variable and fixed costs.

VC = variable cost (a fixed percentage of sales)

FC = fixed costs, with reinvestment assumed equal to depreciation so that accrual and cash flow data are equal

$$Z = (1 - \frac{VC}{S})$$

p_i = probability of ith level of sales occurring

Then:

$$\mu_s = \sum_{i=1}^{n} S_i \, p_i \qquad\qquad (7A.1)$$

$$\sigma_s = \sqrt{\sum_{i=1}^{n} (S_i - \mu_s)^2 \, p_i} \qquad\qquad (7A.2)$$

$$\mu_{avc} = \sum_{i=1}^{n} (ZS_i) \, p_i = Z(\sum_{i=1}^{n} S_i p_i) = Z\mu_s \qquad\qquad (7A.3)$$

$$\sigma_{avc} = \sqrt{\sum_{i=1}^{n} (ZS_i - Z\mu_s)^2 \, p_i} = \sqrt{Z^2 \sum_{i=1}^{n} (S_i - \mu_s)^2 \, p_i}$$

$$= Z\sigma_s \qquad\qquad (7A.4)$$

Therefore:

$$\frac{\sigma_{avc}}{\mu_{avc}} = \frac{Z\sigma_s}{Z\mu_s} = \frac{\sigma_s}{\mu_s} \qquad\qquad (7A.5)$$

The point of equations 7A.1 through 7A.5 is to demonstrate that the presence of variable costs does not change the risk of the cash flow. In other words, the probability that sales minus variable costs will be less than zero is the same as the probability that sales will be less than zero.[4] The variable costs reduce the mean value of the flow, of course, but they also tighten the dispersion of outcomes proportionally. Compare this with the result when fixed charges are also present:

$$\mu_{afc} = \sum_{i=1}^{n} (ZS_i - FC) \, p_i = Z(\sum_{i=1}^{n} S_i p_i) - FC = Z\mu_s - FC \qquad\qquad (7A.6)$$

[4] Assuming, of course, that $VC/S < 1$.

$$\sigma_{afc} = \sqrt{\sum_{i=1}^{n} [(ZS_i - FC) - (Z\mu_s - FC)]^2 \, p_i}$$

$$= \sqrt{\sum_{i=1}^{n} [ZS_i - FC - Z\mu_s + FC]^2 \, p_i}$$

$$= \sqrt{Z^2 \sum_{i=1}^{n} (S_i - \mu_s)^2 \, p_i} = Z\sigma_s \qquad (7A.7)$$

Therefore:

$$\frac{\sigma_{afc}}{\mu_{afc}} = \frac{Z\sigma_s}{Z\mu_s - FC} > \frac{\sigma_s}{\mu_s} \qquad (7A.8)$$

Thus, the presence of fixed charges will increase the risk of the firm's flows and the probability that the flow will be exhausted before a given security holder's claim is satisfied. If we redefine FC in 7A.8 as those fixed charges relating to a given holder's claim and all charges of greater priority, we can see how the variation increases as we move to more junior securities. We can also see that, because operating fixed charges generally have the highest priority, if these are large, *ceteris paribus,* even the most senior bondholder may be in a precarious position.[5] For this reason, firms with large operating fixed charges may usually issue only a modest amount of debt without paying substantial risk premiums. Finally, however, it should be noted that some firms can have large operating and financial fixed charges (that is, FC large in relation to μ_s) at reasonable rates if the variation in revenue (σ_s) is small (for example, public utilities).

Recall that resources other than annual cash flow may be used to meet fixed-charge requirements. In any given year, the firm's cash balance, marketable securities held, and, in some cases, its unused lines of bank credit could be added directly to the cash flow in the denominator of equation 7A.8 in order to reduce the probability of funds available being inadequate to settle claims. The same statement could be made over the life of a bond issue if we could assume that the distributions of annual cash flows were independent over time (for example, the cash drawn down by an abnormally low sales figure in one year could be replenished by an equally high figure in subsequent years). When the flows are dependent, as they are likely to be in reality, one bad year follows another, and, the firm will soon run out of cash. The existence of liquidity balances, therefore, will afford protection to security holders against short-run fluctuations in the issuer's flows, but not against a long-run trend. Let us consider an example.

The Peel Corp. has $\mu_s = \$10$ million and $\sigma_s = \$3$ million, with sales normally distributed. The variable cost ratio (VC/S) is .6 and operating fixed costs are $1 million. Peel has senior bonds outstanding with interest require-

---

[5]Because the default upon even the most junior issue can throw the firm into bankruptcy, senior holders must join the junior and common-stock holders in being concerned that all fixed charges are met.

ments of $500,000 and junior bonds requiring $300,000. The probability that each will be fully paid is:

$$(1) \quad Z = .4; \quad \frac{Z\sigma_s}{Z\mu_s - OFC - FC_s} = \frac{1.2\overline{m}}{4\overline{m} - 1\overline{m} - .5\overline{m}}$$

$$= \frac{1.2\overline{m}}{2.5\overline{m}} \; ; \; P(X \geqslant 0) = P(X \geqslant \mu - 2.08\sigma) = .9812$$

$$(2) \quad \frac{1.2\overline{m}}{2.2\overline{m}} \; ; \; P(X \geqslant 0) = P(X \geqslant \mu - 1.84\sigma) = .9671$$

If Peel held $1 million in cash that could be used to meet obligations, the probabilities would become:

$$(1) \quad \frac{1.2\overline{m}}{3.5\overline{m}} \; ; \; P(X \geqslant 0) = P(X \geqslant \mu - 2.92\sigma) = .9982$$

$$(2) \quad \frac{1.2\overline{m}}{3.2\overline{m}} \; ; \; P(X \geqslant 0) = P(X \geqslant \mu - 2.67\sigma) = .9962$$

A generally reliable indicator of default risk is the bond rating assigned by Moody or Standard and Poor. (See Chapter 8). Empirical work has shown that default loss has corresponded fairly well with these ratings. This does not imply that we can automatically class bonds with the same rating as being of equivalent risk; there are still bargains to be found by the diligent analyst. Nor does this mean that we can observe a neat Aaa yield curve lying on top of the government yield curve (with an Aa yield curve on top of it, and so on), all curves moving up and down and changing slope together. For one thing, it has been observed that the yield spread between high-grade and low-grade bonds narrows near the peak of the cycle (either because the good business has finally reached the marginal firm and made the interest payment more secure or else because euphoric investors are buying everything in sight) and widens at the trough (for the opposite reasons). It has also been argued that the yield curve for very risky securities may slope down, as the greatest risk of default occurs when the issue is near to maturity and can be neither repaid nor refunded.[6]

There are other factors that prevent the market structure of returns from being a nice set of equal-risk yield curves lying on top of each other. The fact that municipal bond interest is tax exempt causes the nominal yield curve for at least high-grade municipals to lie under the government curve. The 85 percent intercorporate dividend exclusion has also caused the apparent return on preferred stock to lie below the (less-risky) yield on bonds of the same issuer. (See Chapter 8). The presence of a call feature may make the actual maturity of an issue indeterminate, thus confusing its location on any yield curve. In addition, market segmentation and other institutional factors affect the risk structure of yields as well as the term structure. The fact that many financial institutions are effectively precluded from investing in lower quality securities

[6]See Ramon Johnson, "Term Structures of Corporate Bond Yields as a Function of Risk of Default," *Journal of Finance*, May 1967, pp. 313–45.

undoubtedly causes yield differentials (both nominal and expected) to be greater than they would otherwise be.[7]

A concluding note should be made regarding equities. Because stock possesses a theoretically infinite life, the return on stocks of a given risk would appear as a point (at maturity = ∞) rather than an entire yield curve. Preferred stocks are rather well behaved in this regard, in that their yields should be comparable, after the adjustment for tax factors discussed above, to the yields on long-term bonds of similar risk, and the yields should move together. The case of common stock is more difficult, because the amount and timing of income is not contractual and can only be estimated. It is generally assumed that the return on common should be high, as it is the most risky security a firm can issue. Yet, this return cannot be precisely measured *ex ante* if the income stream is not known.

Finally, portfolio and capital market theory (to be discussed in Chapters 16 and 17) suggest that security pricing and risk premiums should not be based upon an individual security's risk considered in isolation, but rather upon its contribution to portfolio risk. We must therefore defer further discussion on this point until then.

Appendix Problems

1. The Baxter Corporation has issued a ten-year note at 7 percent with interest payments to be made annually. The following estimates have been made regarding payment.

Event	Probability
(1) All payments as due	.75
(2) Interest in years six and following paid one year late — deficiency made up at end of life of issue	.10
(3) Interest in years six and following paid one year late and only one-half amount due — deficiency made up at end of life of issue	.05
(4) #3 with difference not made up	.04
(5) Company in difficulty during year three — coupon negotiated down to 3 percent	.03
(6) Company enters bankruptcy midway through year five — total bondholder recovery is 50 percent of par value	.02
(7) Company enters bankruptcy now — no recovery	.01
	1.00

[7]We return to this point in Chapters 19 and 20. A more complete discussion of risk structure and the various factors contributing to it may be found in James C. Van Horne, *The Function and Analysis of Capital Market Rates* (Englewood Cliffs, N.J.: Prentice-Hall, Inc., 1970), Chaps. 5–7.

    a. What is the expected value of the return on this note?

    b. Graph the probability distribution of possible rates of return.

    c. Comment upon the dispersion and skewness of this distribution.

    2. The Jet Corporation has $\mu_s = \$100$ million and $\sigma_s = \$30$ million. Operating fixed costs are $50 million. The variable cost ratio is .2. Senior debt has an annual interest requirement of $5 million and junior debt requires $8 million.

    a. What is the expected value of net income before interest and taxes?

    b. What is the probability that each issue will be fully paid?

    c. How would your answer to b change if the firm held an extra $5 million in cash?

    3. Rework problem 2 assuming that operating fixed costs are $20 million and the variable cost ratio is .5.

    4. Assume the following data:

Issue	Yield
Treasury bills	5 percent
Government bonds (25 yr.)	6½ percent
Aaa corporate bonds (25 yr.)	7 percent
Aaa municipals (25 yr.)	5 percent

Analyze the components of the 5 percent yield on municipals in terms of risk and tax premia to the marginal investor. Include a determination of his tax rate.

REFERENCES

Barges, Alexander, "Growth Rates and Debt Capacity," *Financial Analysts Journal,* January–February 1968, pp. 100–104.

Beaver, William H., "Financial Ratios as Predictors of Failure," *Empirical Research in Accounting: Selected Studies*, 1966, (a supplement to the *Journal of Accounting Research*), pp. 71–127.

Donaldson, Gordon, *Corporate Debt Capacity*. Homewood, Ill.: Richard D. Irwin, 1971, first published, 1961.

Findlay, M.C., and E. E. Williams, *An Integrated Analysis for Managerial Finance,* Chap. 11. Englewood Cliffs, N.J.: Prentice-Hall, Inc., 1970.

Fisher, Lawrence, "Determinants of Risk Premiums on Corporate Bonds," *Journal of Political Economy*, June 1959, pp. 217–37.

Hickman, W. Braddock, *Corporate Bond Quality and Investor Experience*. Princeton, N.J.: Princeton University Press for the NBER, 1958.

Horrigan, James O., "The Determination of Long-Term Credit Standing with Financial Ratios," *Empirical Research in Accounting, op. cit.,* pp. 44–70.

Johnson, Ramon, "Term Structures of Corporate Bond Yields as a Function of Risk of Default," *Journal of Finance*, May 1967, pp. 313–45.

Myer, John W., *Financial Statement Analysis*, 4th ed. Englewood Cliffs, N.J.: Prentice-Hall, Inc., 1971.

Van Horne, James C., *The Function and Analysis of Capital Market Rates*. Englewood Cliffs, N.J.: Prentice-Hall, Inc., 1970.

8

Analysis of Fixed Income Securities II

METHODS OF PRINCIPAL REPAYMENT

The security of coupon payments is clearly an important matter for the financial analyst. Nevertheless, the security of principal payments may be equally important. Legally, a bond may be considered in default if either interest or principal payments are in arrears. The repayment of principal may be accomplished in several ways. Most common for corporate bonds is repayment by way of a *sinking fund.* This arrangement obligates the issuer to begin repaying a certain percentage of the issue after some year in the life of the issue. Thus, a bond indenture may specify that no sinking fund payments be made for the first five years of the life of an issue, that 10 percent of the issue be paid over the next eight years, and that the remaining 20 percent be paid in the final (that is, fourteenth) year of the life of the issue. Sinking-fund payments may be made by depositing the appropriate percentage of the par value with the trustee of the issue. In many cases, sinking-fund requirements may also be met by going out into the market and purchasing the equivalent par amount at market prices. Thus, if a bond is selling at a discount, the issuer may satisfy the sinking fund requirement by paying less than the amount that would be placed on deposit with the trustee. For example, a 10 percent sinking-fund requirement on a $10 million issue could be satisfied with $0.9 million if the bonds were purchased in the market at 90. Sinking-fund requirements of this form may exert upward pressure on bonds selling at a discount, as the presence of the issuer in the market decreases the supply of the obligation.

Funds placed on deposit with the trustee may be used to retire the appropriate part of the issue at par by lot drawing, or they may be invested in equivalent securities with comparable yields. In the latter case, funds accumulate until the issue matures. Then, the other securities are sold, and the issue is paid off. In the former case, the existence of the sinking fund reduces the average life of the bond issue, which in turn reduces the risk exposure of the investor. The redemption process under a lot-drawing sinking-fund arrangement is essentially random. The investor does not know when his bonds will be redeemed, and thus he cannot know the precise life of the debt. Because the going rate of interest tends to be related to the maturity of the issue (see Chapter 4), the life of the bond is important to the investor. Analysts frequently compute the *yield to average life* of the bond, rather than the yield to maturity, when a lot-drawing sinking fund is used to pay off an issue. The yield to average life is computed by determining the *expected life* of a bond. The expected life is then substituted for the maturity of the obligation in making the yield calculation. Suppose a bond sells in the market at 90. It has a 6 percent coupon with sinking-fund payments equal to 10 percent of the issue coming due over each of the next five years. Fifty percent of the issue has already been repaid. The average life remaining for the bonds outstanding is given by:

Year	Probability	
1	.2	.2
2	.2	.4
3	.2	.6
4	.2	.8
5	.2	1.0
	Average life 3.0 years	

Thus, if the yield to maturity of the issue were computed, the results would be (using the shortcut formula):

$$\text{yield to maturity} \simeq \frac{60 + \dfrac{1000 - 900}{5}}{\dfrac{1000 + 900}{2}} \simeq \frac{80}{950} = 8.42\%$$

or (using present-value tables):

yield to maturity @ 8%	3.993(60)	= 239.58
	.681(1000)	= 681.00
		920.58
@ 9%	3.890(60)	= 233.40
	.650(1000)	= 650.00
		883.40

interpolating, yield $\cong$ 8.54%

The yield to average life would provide the following yields, however:

$$\text{yield to average life} \simeq \cfrac{60 + \cfrac{1000 - 900}{3}}{\cfrac{1000 + 900}{2}} \simeq \frac{93}{950} = 9.79\%$$

yield to average life @ 9%	2.531(60)	= 151.86
	.772(1000)	= 772.00
		923.86
@ 10%	2.487(60)	= 149.22
	.751(1000)	= 751.00
		900.22

yield $\simeq$ 10.0%

The higher yield develops because the principal payment ($1,000) is five years away in the case of the yield to maturity calculation but only three years in the future (expected) in the yield to average life computation.

If the firm is required to satisfy the sinking-fund requirement by a lot drawing at par, then the yield to average life is the appropriate indicator of expected investor return. Furthermore, if the indenture requires that a premium over par be paid to investors whose bonds are chosen, this figure should be used in place of par value in the above computations. On the other hand, an indenture that allows the firm to satisfy its obligation either by lot drawings or by the purchase of bonds in the open market requires a more complicated analysis. In the case of bonds selling at a premium, it is to the corporation's advantage to employ a lot drawing at par. This implies that yield to average life is the appropriate investor concept of expected return (assuming the current pattern of interest rates remains constant in the future). For bonds at a discount, the firm would presumably enter the market to satisfy its obligation. If bond markets were reasonably efficient, the purchases by the issuer would not affect the pattern of rates, and yield to maturity would reflect the investor's expected return; this result would also apply in the special case in which the investor chose to hold his bonds to maturity. In "thin" markets, it is possible that the purchases by the issuer would force the price upward and result in a return greater than the yield to maturity to those investors who sold their bonds at the right time; it is unlikely that the expectation of this profit is great, however, and yield to maturity remains the best measure even in this case. It should be pointed out, additionally, that the coupon on a bond that does not allow the issuer the right to purchase in the market to satisfy sinking-fund requirements may be lower than for an equivalent bond that grants that privilege.[1]

A second method of repaying principal is by means of *serial obligation.* In this case, a part of the issue is scheduled to mature each year until the entire

[1] See F. Jen and J. Wert, "The Effect of Sinking Fund Provisions on Corporate Bond Yields," *Financial Analysts Journal,* March –April 1967, pp. 125 –31.

issue is repaid. The investor knows in advance when his bond will mature, and coupon rates are adjusted according to maturities. Serial obligations are seldom used by corporate issuers, although government and municipal bonds are often of the serial type. Because the investor knows the maturity of a serial issue at the time of purchase, the yield to maturity on his bond is the appropriate return measure. The result may then be compared to yields on other bonds of the same specific maturity.

A final method of repayment is the *lump-sum payment*. In this case, the entire issue is repaid at the maturity date. This method is used frequently by public utilities that simply "roll over" debt (that is, replace a maturing issue with a new one). The federal government also tends to repay its debt on this basis. This form of repayment is satisfactory if the issuer is a top credit and has no difficulty in selling new bonds as old obligations come due. Lesser credits may have difficulty, however, in replacing debt, and the result may be detrimental to the holder of the maturing issue. It should be noted that bonds with an escrow sinking fund are technically lump-sum payment obligations from the standpoint of the investor. Nevertheless, this feature does provide additional lender protection. The yield to maturity is the appropriate return criterion for lump-sum payment bonds.

PREDICTION OF FUTURE DEFALCATION

The security of interest and principal payments may be measured by use of the interest-and-sinking-fund-coverage ratio (discussed in Chapter 5). The historical pattern of this ratio along with *pro forma* calculations of it based on projections of earnings before interest and taxes constitutes a good overall test of the ability of the firm to meet interest and sinking-fund payments.

Reconsider the EBIT projections for Consolidated Electric Appliance (page 133). Suppose the firm had $100 million outstanding in the 5 percent subordinated debenture, with sinking-fund payments of 5 percent due in 1975-1976, 10 percent in 1977-1978, and the balance (70 percent) due in 1979. The coverage of interest and sinking-fund payments, given the EBIT forecast, would be:

$$\frac{\text{EBIT} + \text{Depreciation}}{\text{Interest} + \text{Sinking fund}} \qquad \frac{1975}{\frac{17.60 + 40.00}{5.00 + 5.00}} = 5.76\text{X}$$

(Interest falls by 5 percent $\dfrac{1976}{\dfrac{18.85 + 40.00}{4.75 + 5.00}} = 6.04\text{X}$
to 4.75 million)

	1977
(Interest falls by 5 percent to 4.50 million)	$\dfrac{20.77 + 40.00}{4.50 + 10.00} = 4.19X$

	1978
(Interest falls by 10 percent to 4.00 million)	$\dfrac{22.10 + 40.00}{4.00 + 10.00} = 4.44X$

	1979
$\dfrac{\text{EBIT + Depreciation}}{\text{Int.} + \dfrac{\text{Sinking fund} - (\text{tax rate})(\text{Dep.})}{1 - (\text{tax rate})}}$	$\dfrac{24.42 + 40.00}{3.50 + \dfrac{70.00 - (.4)(40.00)}{1 - (.4)}} = .69X$

These ratios are respectable, although one might wonder whether interest or principal payments on the bonds would be in jeopardy in 1979. This prospect is unlikely. The firm will probably roll over its debt as it comes due. Given the stability of the firm's EBIT, it should have no difficulty refunding the issue in 1979.

Other ratios may be employed in a multiple discriminant analysis (see discussion in Chapter 6) to predict possible defalcation. Edward Altman examined twenty-two ratios as indicators of corporate bankruptcy.[2] He selected the five that best predicted eventual collapse and developed the following discriminant function:

$$Z = 0.012X_1 + 0.014X_2 + 0.033X_3 + 0.006X_4 + 0.999X_5 \qquad (8.1)$$

Where: X_1 = working capital/total assets

X_2 = retained earnings/total assets

X_3 = EBIT/total assets

X_4 = market value equity/book value of total debt

X_5 = sales/total assets

X_1 through X_4 are expressed as whole numbers (10 percent = 10), and X_5 is expressed as a decimal (10 percent = .10). Altman found that firms with a Z value above 2.99 were "nonbankrupt" and those below 1.81 were "bankrupt." A value of Z = 2.675 as a cutoff provided the least misclassifications.

[2]See E. I. Altman, "Financial Ratios, Discriminant Analysis and the Prediction of Corporate Bankruptcy," *Journal of Finance,* September 1968, pp. 589 – 609.

The Altman function might be applied to Consolidated Electric Appliance. Suppose the firm is expected to have the following ratios in 1975:

Working capital/Total assets	=	.15
Retained earnings/Total assets	=	.20
EBIT/Total assets	=	.07
Market value equity/Book debt	=	1.50
Sales/Total assets	=	.50

The Altman Z value for the firm would be:

$$Z = (.012)(15) + (.014)(20) + (.033)(7) + (.006)(150) + (.999)(.5) = 2.09$$

Although this value is below the cutoff of $Z = 2.675$, it is unlikely that Consolidated is on the verge of imminent collapse. In the first place, the universe to which Consolidated belongs (assets well over $25 million) is not exactly the same as that upon which Altman based his study. Other ratios may be important in discriminating potential bankruptcies for larger concerns. Altman studied firms with a total asset size of $1 million to $25 million, and it might be misleading to use his equation for every case. The analyst should prepare his own discriminant function where circumstances warrant. Moreover, it would be unwise for an analyst to depend entirely on a discriminant function to determine a potential bankruptcy. All evidence should be considered, particularly the forecasts that have been made of the firm's future-earnings capacity. If a poor earnings forecast and generally weak ratios combine with a discriminant value below the cutoff, the analyst might expect trouble in the future.

HOLDING PERIOD RISKS

In addition to the factors previously considered in determining the yield and security of a bond, one other variable must be assessed: the desired holding period of the bond. It will be recalled from Chapter 4 that the aggregate level of interest rates may vary as economic conditions change, and that bond prices move inversely with the market rate of interest. Thus, there is a market risk in holding a bond as well as the business and financial risk associated with the issuer. A precipitous decline in bond prices, caused by higher rates of interest, can reduce the flexibility of the bondholder and *force* him to hold an obligation until maturity (the so-called *lock-in effect*) in order to avoid realizing capital losses. Of course, an opportunity loss occurs whether or not it is realized. Moreover, if planning or necessity requires the sale of a bond prior to maturity, then the prevailing rate of interest at the time of sale can produce either a capital loss or gain for the holder. The extra risk resulting from interest rate changes that produce lock-ins or capital losses must be considered when a bond is purchased.

To some extent, the desired holding period for a bond may be affected by factors outside the control of the investor. It was mentioned earlier that sinking-fund requirements satisfied by lot drawing may reduce the holding period for the bondholder. Furthermore, most bonds are *callable.* When a bond is called, the expected holding period may be reduced for the investor. Nevertheless, many bond indentures contain *deferred call protection* for a specified period of time (usually five to ten years). Moreover, bonds are called for refunding only when the issuing firm may refinance at a rate lower than the current coupon. Hence, the best call protection for the investor during high interest-rate periods is provided by purchasing bonds issued in the past at lower coupons. These bonds will sell at large discounts from par and thus would necessarily appreciate substantially before the market price of the issue approached the call price and made a call feasible for the issuer. Two similar bonds, one selling at a large discount and the other offering a large coupon, may sell at different yields to maturity because of this implicit difference in call protection.

Bonds are typically callable at prices somewhat above par, at least until near the maturity date, but a substantial drop in interest rates (causing bond prices to advance) may encourage the issuer to call an issue even at a premium. The result is to shorten the actual maturity of the bond. Also, the call possibility may prevent the bond from rising to a substantial premium in case interest rates do fall significantly after the issue date.

The bond indenture may contain several call price schedules that may affect the investor. One schedule will indicate call prices for refunding purposes. Another may specify call prices in future years for sinking fund purposes. A third schedule may indicate the prices at which all or part of the issue may be called if funds are raised by the debtor from sources other than a new issue sold at a lower cost (an asset conversion, for example). The premium on these schedules will usually decline to par as the set maturity date approaches.

Consider a bond that has twenty-two years remaining before maturity but is callable at 104 in two years. The bond is selling at a premium, and it is expected that the issue will be called at the first opportunity. The market price of the bond is 111, although equivalent risk bonds with similar coupons and maturities having longer call protection sell at higher prices. A noncallable bond of a similar credit with a twenty-year maturity was recently sold to yield 6 percent, while the coupon on the bond under analysis is 9 percent. The yield to maturity on the callable bond would be:

$$\text{yield to maturity} = \frac{90 + \dfrac{1,000 - 1,110}{22}}{\dfrac{1,000 + 1,110}{2}} = \frac{85}{1,055} = 8.06\%$$

The yield to first call would be:

$$\text{yield to first call} = \frac{90 + \dfrac{1,040 - 1,110}{2}}{\dfrac{1,040 + 1,110}{2}} = \frac{55}{1,075} = 5.12\%$$

Which yield should the analyst use? The answer would depend on his long-run forecast of interest rates. If he believed that rates would continue as they are at the time of analysis, or if he believed they would fall further, the bond would almost certainly be called, and the correct yield would be the yield to first call. On the other hand, if the analyst expected rates to rise, particularly if he suspected an increase to a level beyond the current coupon on the bond, an argument could be made for using the yield to maturity. Needless to say, if the analyst expected interest rates to fall, he might be advised to concentrate his attention on bonds with greater call protection (for example, deep discount bonds) that would not necessarily be called. The appropriate yield computation in this instance would, of course, be the yield to maturity. Furthermore, if the analyst expected rates to increase, the decision to purchase long-term bonds in the first place might be challenged.

The effect of the call privilege on corporate bond yields varies depending on money-market conditions. Yield differentials on bonds with different call characteristics (premiums offered and deferment periods) tend to increase during periods of high interest rates and to decline when interest rates are low. Jen and Wert found that during 1960–1964 the yield differential on newly issued utility bonds was near zero when coupon rates were low but was positive when rates were high.[3] Pye found the effect of a five-year deferment was to depress rates. In fact, his results showed that the yield to maturity on a freely callable thirty-year bond during periods of tight money was almost 100 basis points higher than on a bond with a deferred call.[4] The overall effect of the call privilege has been to reduce realized yields on corporate bonds which were issued when interest rates have been high. In a study comparing 434 utility bonds issued between 1956 and 1964, Jen and Wert found that many issues were called as interest rates fell and

[3]F. Jen and J. Wert, "The Value of the Deferred Call Privilege," *National Banking Review,* March 1966, pp. 369–78. An extension of the study is made by Jen and Wert, "The Deferred Call Provision and Corporate Bond Yields," *Journal of Financial and Quantitative Analysis,* June 1968, pp. 157–69.

[4] G. Pye, "The Value of Call Deferment on a Bond: Some Empirical Results," *Journal of Finance,* December 1967, pp. 623–36.

that the effective yield realized by investors in bonds issued during high-interest periods was only a little greater than the yield realized on bonds issued in moderate interest-rate periods.[5]

BOND TABLES AND BOND-RATING AGENCIES

The primary objective of the security analyst in evaluating a bond is the determination of the expected rate of return from the instrument and the risk associated with that return. Various yield calculations, including yields to maturity, average life, and first call, have been mentioned. Rarely will the analyst use either the shortcut formula we have discussed above or present-value tables in computing the yields on a bond. Instead, he will have a complete set of bond tables. (See Figure 8-1). Bond tables are based on present-value tables such as those appearing in Appendix C, but they require absolutely no additional calculation. The analyst looks up the yield on, say, a 7¾ percent coupon issue due in eighteen years and six months selling at 95¾ and finds a yield immediately of 8.20 percent.

The analyst may also depend on rating agencies to help him assess the riskiness of a bond issue. Both Moody and Standard & Poor rate the bonds of seasoned companies, and much can be learned from comparing the respective ratings of various issues given by these two independent agencies. Moody rates the highest grade, nonspeculative bond as Aaa. Such bonds have little risk of default and are of the highest quality. The equivalent S&P rating is AAA. Just under the highest rating is the Moody Aa and the S&P AA. Double-A bonds are also of high quality, but they are somewhat less secure than the triple-A's. Medium quality bonds are rated A and Baa by Moody and A and BBB by Standard & Poor, the single A bond being a slightly better credit. Bonds rated Ba (Moody) and BB (S&P) and below are considered to be speculative bonds that have some definite default possibility. Although many analysts depend on the rating agencies for an independent, unbiased analysis of the credit-worthiness of a bond, the original analyst will do his own research into the risk condition of a bond issuer.[6] Furthermore, the analyst will always bear in mind that the price of even the highest-rated bonds will fall if the general level of interest rates

[5]F. Jen and J. Wert, "The Effect of Call Risk on Corporate Bond Yields," *Journal of Finance,* December 1967, pp. 637–51. Also, see R. Johnson, "The Value of the Call Privilege," *Financial Analysts Journal,* March–April 1967, pp. 134–38; and G. Pye, "The Value of the Call Option on a Bond," *Journal of Political Economy,* April 1966, pp. 200–205.

[6]Many analysts find that bonds with the same ratings tend to sell at nearly identical yields even though there may be risk differences within a rating class. Thus, the analyst who does his own investigating may find opportunities that would go undiscovered if he relied solely on the rating agencies to assess risk.

7¾% YEARS and MONTHS

Yield	18-6	19-0	19-6	20-0	20-6	21-0	21-6	22-0
4.00	148.69	149.58	150.44	151.29	152.12	152.94	153.74	154.52
4.20	145.35	146.15	146.94	147.72	148.47	149.21	149.94	150.65
4.40	142.10	142.84	143.55	144.25	144.94	145.61	146.27	146.91
4.60	138.96	139.62	140.27	140.90	141.52	142.13	142.72	143.30
4.80	135.90	136.50	137.09	137.66	138.22	138.76	139.29	139.81
5.00	132.94	133.48	134.00	134.52	135.02	135.50	135.98	136.44
5.20	130.07	130.55	131.02	131.47	131.92	132.35	132.78	133.19
5.40	127.28	127.71	128.12	128.53	128.92	129.30	129.68	130.04
5.60	124.57	124.95	125.32	125.67	126.02	126.36	126.68	127.00
5.80	121.95	122.28	122.59	122.91	123.21	123.50	123.79	124.06
6.00	119.40	119.68	119.96	120.23	120.49	120.74	120.98	121.22
6.10	118.15	118.41	118.67	118.92	119.16	119.39	119.62	119.84
6.20	116.92	117.16	117.40	117.63	117.85	118.06	118.27	118.48
6.30	115.71	115.93	116.15	116.36	116.56	116.76	116.95	117.14
6.40	114.52	114.72	114.92	115.11	115.30	115.48	115.65	115.82
6.50	113.34	113.53	113.71	113.88	114.05	114.21	114.37	114.52
6.60	112.18	112.35	112.51	112.67	112.82	112.97	113.11	113.25
6.70	111.04	111.19	111.34	111.48	111.61	111.74	111.87	111.99
6.80	109.92	110.05	110.18	110.30	110.42	110.54	110.65	110.76
6.90	108.81	108.92	109.04	109.15	109.25	109.35	109.45	109.55
7.00	107.71	107.82	107.91	108.01	108.10	108.19	108.27	108.36
7.10	106.64	106.72	106.81	106.89	106.96	107.04	107.11	107.18
7.20	105.57	105.65	105.72	105.78	105.85	105.91	105.97	106.03
7.30	104.53	104.59	104.64	104.70	104.75	104.80	104.84	104.89
7.40	103.50	103.54	103.58	103.62	103.66	103.70	103.74	103.77
7.50	102.48	102.51	102.54	102.57	102.60	102.62	102.65	102.67
7.60	101.48	101.50	101.51	101.53	101.55	101.56	101.58	101.59
7.70	100.49	100.49	100.50	100.51	100.51	100.52	100.52	100.53
7.80	99.51	99.51	99.50	99.50	99.49	99.49	99.48	99.48
7.90	98.55	98.54	98.52	98.50	98.49	98.47	98.46	98.45
8.00	97.61	97.58	97.55	97.53	97.50	97.48	97.45	97.43
8.10	96.67	96.63	96.60	96.56	96.53	96.49	96.46	96.43
8.20	95.75	95.70	95.66	95.61	95.57	95.53	95.49	95.45
8.30	94.85	94.79	94.73	94.68	94.62	94.57	94.53	94.48
8.40	93.95	93.88	93.82	93.75	93.69	93.64	93.58	93.53
8.50	93.07	92.99	92.92	92.85	92.78	92.71	92.65	92.59
8.60	92.20	92.11	92.03	91.95	91.88	91.80	91.73	91.67
8.70	91.34	91.25	91.16	91.07	90.99	90.91	90.83	90.76
8.80	90.49	90.39	90.29	90.20	90.11	90.02	89.94	89.86
8.90	89.66	89.55	89.44	89.34	89.25	89.15	89.07	88.98
9.00	88.84	88.72	88.61	88.50	88.40	88.30	88.20	88.11
9.10	88.02	87.90	87.78	87.67	87.56	87.45	87.35	87.26
9.20	87.22	87.09	86.97	86.85	86.73	86.62	86.52	86.42
9.30	86.43	86.30	86.16	86.04	85.92	85.80	85.69	85.59
9.40	85.66	85.51	85.37	85.24	85.12	85.00	84.88	84.77
9.50	84.89	84.74	84.59	84.46	84.33	84.20	84.08	83.97
9.60	84.13	83.97	83.83	83.68	83.55	83.42	83.30	83.18
9.70	83.38	83.22	83.07	82.92	82.78	82.65	82.52	82.40
9.80	82.64	82.48	82.32	82.17	82.02	81.89	81.76	81.63
9.90	81.92	81.75	81.58	81.43	81.28	81.14	81.00	80.87
10.00	81.20	81.02	80.86	80.70	80.54	80.40	80.26	80.13
10.20	79.79	79.61	79.43	79.26	79.11	78.95	78.81	78.67
10.40	78.42	78.23	78.05	77.87	77.71	77.55	77.40	77.26
10.60	77.09	76.89	76.70	76.52	76.35	76.19	76.03	75.88
10.80	75.79	75.59	75.39	75.20	75.03	74.86	74.70	74.55
11.00	74.53	74.32	74.12	73.93	73.74	73.57	73.41	73.26
11.20	73.30	73.08	72.88	72.68	72.50	72.32	72.15	72.00
11.40	72.10	71.88	71.67	71.47	71.28	71.10	70.93	70.78
11.60	70.93	70.71	70.49	70.29	70.10	69.92	69.75	69.59
11.80	69.79	69.56	69.35	69.14	68.95	68.77	68.60	68.43
12.00	68.68	68.45	68.23	68.03	67.83	67.65	67.47	67.31

Source: Financial Publishing Co., 82 Brooklyne Avenue, Boston, Mass. 02215

Figure 8-1   A Bond Table

increases.[7] Investors who bought 2½ percent triple-A bonds in the early 1950s thinking that no decline in price could occur have been very chagrined to see these issues quoted at thirty- and forty-point discounts from par as a result of rising interest rates in the 1960s.

The fact that even highly rated bonds may carry some risk can be seen by considering an example. Suppose an analyst is investigating the Royal Corp. 5's of 1994. The bonds have an S&P rating of AA and a Moody rating of Aa. A complete analysis of the future prospects for the firm reveals that these debentures have an expected times-interest-earned multiple of 8.8X over the life of the issue. The firm has two mortgage bonds senior to this issue that have 16.4X and 9.2X coverage. The 5's of 1994 have sinking-fund requirements of 10 percent per year beginning in 1984, and the interest-plus-sinking-fund coverage of this issue plus the two others average 5X. It is expected that the firm will be able to make sinking-fund payments out of cash flow and finance planned expansion from new-debt issues and retained earnings. The 5's of 1994 are callable in 1984, although the analyst does not expect them to be called. Assuming the current year is 1974, and the bonds sell at 80, the yield to maturity of the issue would be:

$$\text{yield to maturity} = \frac{50 + \dfrac{200}{20}}{\dfrac{800 + 1000}{2}} = \frac{60}{900} = 6.67\%$$

Now, suppose the analyst feels that interest rates may increase somewhat over the next ten years, which is the holding period he envisages for maintaining the bond in portfolios supervised by his firm. He has attached the following probability distribution to rates on issues equivalent in risk to the Royal 5's 1994 after a decade:

Probability	Yield to Maturity
.6	7.80
.3	6.30
.1	5.00

Thus, he believes that ten years from now there are six chances in ten that yields will be higher than those currently prevailing (6.67 percent) on equivalent risk bonds. On the other hand, he feels that rates could be as much as 167 basis points (1.67 percent) lower. Given his yield forecast, the analyst could

---

[7]Indeed, the prices of low-risk bonds are *more* responsive to interest rate changes than those of high-risk obligations. The pure interest rate component of yield is higher for low-risk bonds than for high-risk ones (where the risk component is greater). Thus, an upward shift in the overall structure of rates will produce a larger proportional change in the yields of high-grade bonds than for lower-grade issues. For a discussion of this point within the context of the risk and term structure of yields, see the appendix to Chapter 7.

determine the price at which the Royal 5's of 1994 would sell in 1984. If rates rose to 7.80 percent, the bond price would be:

$$7.80 = \frac{50 + \dfrac{1000 - X}{10}}{\dfrac{1000 + X}{2}} \qquad X \simeq 80$$

or about $800. Notice that the number of years to maturity of the issue ten years from now is ten years (that is, twenty years – ten years).[8] Thus, there would be a probability of .6 that the bond price *would not change,* because it currently sells for $800. If yields fell to 6.30 percent, the future bond price would be:

$$6.30 = \frac{50 + \dfrac{1000 - X}{10}}{\dfrac{1000 + X}{2}} \qquad X \simeq 90$$

or about $900. If yields declined to 5.00 percent, the price of the bond ten years hence would be:

$$5.00 = \frac{50 + \dfrac{1000 - X}{10}}{\dfrac{1000 + X}{2}} \qquad X \simeq 100$$

Obviously, if yields fell to the coupon rate of the issue, it would advance to par.

Given his estimates of the future price of the Royal 5's of 94, the analyst could determine the yield his clients would get if they bought the bond today (1974) and sold it in ten years. If future yields rose to 7.80 percent and the price of the bond remained at 80, his clients' return would be:

$$\text{Yield} = \frac{50 + \dfrac{800 - 800}{10}}{\dfrac{800 + 800}{2}} = \frac{50}{800} = 6.25\%$$

[8]The analyst has used the yield-to-maturity calculation for 1984–1994 rather than the yield to average life because sinking-fund requirements can be met through market purchases. Because his forecast of interest rates precludes a call (unless rates drop well below 5 percent between 1984–1994), the yield to first call has also been ignored.

If future yields fell to 6.30 percent, and the price of the bond advanced to 90, the clients' return would be:

$$\text{Yield} = \frac{50 + \dfrac{900 - 800}{10}}{\dfrac{900 + 800}{2}} = \frac{60}{850} = 7.06\%$$

Finally, if yields declined to 5.00 percent (bond price at par), the clients' return would be:

$$\text{Yield} = \frac{50 + \dfrac{1000 - 800}{10}}{\dfrac{1000 + 800}{2}} = \frac{70}{900} = 7.78\%$$

Hence, the probability distribution of returns to the analyst's clients if they bought this issue is:

Probability	Yield (to 1984)
.6	6.25 percent
.3	7.06 percent
.1	7.78 percent

Although the Royal Corp. is a good credit (double A), the analyst feels there is some slight chance that a default could occur. He has predicted the following default probabilities for the Royal 5's 1994:

Default (Years Hence)	Probability
1 - 9	.00
10	.02

If a default occurs in year 10, the analyst expects that liquidation would give debenture holders 40 percent of the par value of the investment plus the coupon. The expected return in the case of default would be:

$$\text{Yield} = \frac{50 + \dfrac{400 - 800}{10}}{\dfrac{400 + 800}{2}} = \frac{10}{600} = 1.67\%$$

Because the shortcut equation does not always provide accurate results in the case of a deep discount situation (such as a price of 40), the analyst has verified the results using present-value tables:

$$
\begin{array}{lll}
\text{@ 1\%} & (9.471)(50) = & 473.55 \\
              & (.905)(400) = & \underline{362.00} \\
              &   & 835.55
\end{array}
$$

$$
\begin{array}{lll}
\text{@ 2\%} & (8.983)(50) = & 449.15 \\
              & (.820)(400) = & \underline{328.00} \\
              &   & 777.15
\end{array}
$$

Interpolating, i = 1.60%

Including the possibility of default, a refined probability distribution of returns could be computed. The expected return and standard deviation are also provided:

Return (X_i)	Probability (p_i)		Expected Return
6.25%	(.6)(.98) =	.588	3.6750%
7.06	(.3)(.98) =	.294	2.0756
7.78	(.1)(.98) =	.098	.7624
1.60	(1.0)(.02) =	.020	.0320
		1.000	$\overline{X}$ = 6.5450%

$X_i - \overline{X}$	$(X_i - \overline{X})^2 p_i$
6.25 − 6.55 = − .30%	(.09)(.588) = .0529 × 10^{-4}
7.06 − 6.55 = .51	(.26)(.294) = .0764
7.78 − 6.55 = 1.23	(1.51)(.098) = .1480
1.60 − 6.55 = −4.95	(24.50)(.020) = .4900
	σ^2 = .7673 × 10^{-4}

$$E(R) = 6.55\%$$
$$\sigma = \sqrt{.00007673} = .88\%$$

The analyst may conclude that although the Royal 5's of 1994 have a yield to maturity of 6.67 percent, the expected yield if the issue were held for ten years would be only 6.55 percent. Furthermore, even though the issue is rated AA, there is a probability of .588 that only 6.25 percent would be earned (due to an increase in interest rates) and a probability of .020 that a meager 1.60 percent would be obtained (if the issue defaulted).

ANALYSIS OF MUNICIPAL BONDS

U.S. government obligations do not require the kind of analysis that has been discussed above. Indeed, it is generally assumed that short-term governments are virtually riskless, and the so-called pure rate of interest is approximated by the yield on short-term government obligations. Long-term U.S. governments (notes and bonds) do carry some price fluctuation (market) risk because the prices of all bonds vary as interest rates change. Hence, even the safest bonds regarding coupon and principal security can sell at large discounts.

Analyzing municipal bonds requires a slightly different procedure from that employed in corporate-bond evaluation. Unlike federal issues, municipals cannot be assumed to be default-risk free.[9] Although state-government issues, and bonds guaranteed by state governments, are for all practical purposes free of default risk, various city, county, and district bonds may have considerable coupon and principal risk associated with them.

General obligation municipal bonds are secured by the "full faith and credit" of the issuer. There are several ratios that the analyst may examine to test the security of these obligations:

1. Municipal debt as a percentage of assessed valuation of taxable real estate. This ratio indicates the singular importance of property taxes as a source of municipal finance.[10] Ratios from 8 to 10 percent are considered acceptable by most analysts, although higher ratios may be approved when other taxation sources, such as sales taxes, are available.

2. Per capita debt. This ratio indicates the total debt of the municipal authority per resident. To the extent that the number of taxpayers (rather than the value of property) is significant to a municipal's tax base, this ratio is important. Depending on the population of the issuing authority, per capita debt of from one-hundred to four-hundred dollars is acceptable, with larger amounts permitted for larger municipal issuers.

3. Debt service as a percentage of the municipal budget. When more than one-quarter of a municipal budget goes for debt service (interest plus debt retirement), the ability of the authority to meet its obligations is considered in jeopardy.

A second form of municipal is the *revenue bond.* The security of these

[9]In addition to market-price (interest-rate) and default risks, many municipals are subject to liquidity risks. A number of these issues are quite thinly traded and may require considerable markdowns for quick sale.

[10]Recent court rulings in the United States have brought into doubt the long-run importance of property taxes in financing municipal governments. If other forms of taxation take the place of property taxes, new ratios to assess the security of municipal bonds will have to be devised. Furthermore, if federal revenue sharing becomes a significant source of funds to municipalities, it may be that the municipal bond will no longer be important as a financial instrument.

issues depends upon the "profitability" of the project that the bond has financed. Revenue bonds may be analyzed in a similar manner to corporation issues, and earnings coverage becomes the most important element. Thus, the net revenue generated by a turnpike authority would be the best single factor to consider in appraising the riskiness of the issue. Public projects that are privately financed are not expected to earn large profits. Hence, coverage ratios should not be expected to be as high as those for corporate bonds. Ratios of 1½ to 2 times charges are considered quite acceptable.

Municipal issues are generally tax exempt. That is, no federal income tax is due on the income earned from these bonds. Furthermore, state income taxes payable in the state of issue are generally waived. Thus, a purchaser of a New York City general obligation bond who lived there would pay neither federal, state, nor city income taxes on interest from the issue. Suppose the New York City General Obligation 6's of 1981 are selling at par. A resident of the state is considering the purchase of the bonds. He is in the 50 percent marginal federal tax bracket (adjusted for the deduction of state income taxes) and the 10 percent State of New York bracket. The equivalent pretax yield he would have to earn to equal his tax-free New York City bond would be:

$$\text{Pretax yield} = \frac{\text{Yield on municipal}}{1 - \text{marginal tax bracket}}$$

$$= \frac{.06}{1 - .6}$$

$$= 15 \text{ percent}$$

ANALYSIS OF PREFERRED STOCK

Preferred stock is considered to be a fixed income security because preferred dividends are usually paid at a specific rate.[11] Although preferred stocks are called stock and are treated legally as equity (preferred dividends must be paid out of after-tax dollars and preferred holders have a prior claim against earnings and assets only over common-stock holders), the nature of the instrument makes it necessary to consider preferred stocks as essentially the most junior form of bond. Hence, the analysis of preferred stocks proceeds very much like that discussed for corporate bonds. The basic tools of forecasting and ratio computations of profitability, income security, and asset security are the same.

[11]Participating preferreds may give preferred holders a return above the fixed payment after a specified amount has also been paid to common stockholders. These issues should be evaluated essentially as preferred stocks when the probability of extra payment is small and as common stocks when the probability is great.

The only different ratio that is employed is the times-interest-earned-plus-preferred-dividends ratio (which was discussed in Chapter 5).

We may reconsider the EBIT projections for Consolidated Electric Appliance Corp. (page 156). Suppose that, in addition to the subordinated debenture issue, the firm had $20 million in $5 preferred stock (par $100). The total annual preferred dividend is ($20,000,000)(.05) = $1,000,000. The times-interest-earned-plus-preferred-dividends coverage for the 1975 projection would be:

$$\frac{\text{EBIT}}{\text{Interest} + \dfrac{\text{Preferred dividend}}{1 - \text{tax rate}}} = \frac{17.60}{5.00 + \dfrac{1.00}{1 - .4}} = \frac{17.60}{6.67} = 2.64X$$

For years 1976–1979, we find:

$$1976, \frac{18.85}{6.42} = 2.94X \qquad 1978, \frac{22.10}{5.67} = 3.90X$$

$$1977, \frac{20.77}{6.17} = 3.37X \qquad 1979, \frac{24.42}{5.17} = 4.72X$$

Consolidated $5 preferreds sell in the market for $75 per share. Assuming that the issue is not callable, the return would be:

$$\frac{5}{75} = 6.67\%$$

If the issue were callable in twenty-five years at par, and if it were believed that Consolidated would call the issue, the return would become:

$$\frac{5 + \dfrac{100 - 75}{25}}{\dfrac{100 + 75}{2}} = \frac{6}{87.5} = 6.86\%$$

Preferreds frequently yield less than the junior bonds of the same company. This is due to the fact that in the United States preferred dividends are 85 percent exempt from taxation for corporate holders (to reduce the impact of the double taxation of dividends) and can be included in the $100 dividend tax exclusion for individuals. In Canada, a rather large dividend *credit* is allowed to individuals for all dividends, common and preferred, paid by qualifying Canadian corporations. Bond interest paid by these concerns is fully taxed, however.

PROBLEMS

1. A firm has just floated a fifteen-year, 7 percent coupon bond at par. Sinking-fund payments of 10 percent must be made after the tenth year, with the balance being paid in the last year.

    a. If the firm could satisfy sinking-fund payments through purchase in the open market, what would the appropriate yield be?

    b. If the firm were forced to redeem at par by lot drawing, what yield would the issue have?

    c. Suppose the bond sold at a premium after issue and the firm could satisfy sinking-fund requirements either by market purchases or lot drawings. What yield would the analyst be most inclined to use?

2.

    a. The indenture of the twenty-year Blue Corp. bonds provides for a sinking fund to retire 5 percent of the issue per year beginning in year eleven. What is the expected life of a Blue bond (also called the average life of the issue)?

    b. If the Blue bonds are issued at $950 with an $80 coupon, compute the yield to maturity and the yield to average life.

3. The Central Railroad (see problems 1 and 2 in Chapter 7) has a sinking-fund requirement on its 5's of 1979 (first mortgage bonds) beginning in 1975 of 20 percent. Equivalent payments must be made in 1976–1979. Determine the coverage of interest and sinking-fund payments over this period, given the EBIT projections.

4. Suppose C.R.R. plans to refund its 6's of 1990 (second mortgage) and 8's of 2000 (subordinated debentures) and has no sinking-fund requirements on these bonds. How would this information influence your judgment about the safety of the 5's of 1979? In any case, would you feel the first mortgage bond to be lacking in principal payment security?

5. In addition to its three bond issues, the Central Railroad has a $40 million, 7 percent preferred issue (par $100). Ignoring any sinking-fund payments on the railroad's debt obligations, compute the interest and preferred-dividends coverage for the projections made for 1975–1984.

6. C.R.R. preferred sells at $60. The issue is callable at par in ten years. What is the current yield on the issue? What is the yield-to-call-date?

7. Evaluate the safety of the C.R.R. preferreds. What is the likelihood that the preferred dividend will be passed during 1975–1984?

8. Suppose C.R.R. passes the preferred dividend in 1975. Would it matter if the issue were a cumulative preferred (rather than a noncumulative)?

9. What legal rights might the preferred stockholders have if the C.R.R. dividend were passed in 1975 and again in 1976?

10. An analyst has determined the following discriminant function for large U.S. public corporations (assets over $100 million):

$$Z = 0.04X_1 + 0.09X_2 + 1.50X_3$$

Where: X_1 = EBIT to total assets (times 100)

          X_2 = EBIT to interest payments (as calculated)

          X_3 = sales to total assets (as calculated)

Determine Z for Consolidated Electric Appliance (see text discussion). Re-examine page 133 to find the times-interest-earned ratio for Consolidated as projected for 1975. If values greater than $Z = .99$ indicate a firm comes from the universe of "nonbankrupts," classify Consolidated.

11.

 a. Commercial Credit Ltd. 9's of 1989 were sold five years ago in 1969. The bond had a ten-year call protection and is callable in 1979 at 105. The current price (1974) is 110. Compute the yield to maturity and first call for the issue.

 b. Which is the appropriate yield for the analyst to use if he expects interest rates on equivalent risk issues to be 8 percent in 1979?

12. A 7 percent, twenty-five-year bond was issued two years ago with five years call protection. It may be called in year six at 107 and is currently selling for 109. Compute the yield to maturity and yield to first call.

13.

 a. The bonds of the Net Corp. were issued seven years ago with a maturity of twenty-five years. The indenture provided for retirement of 6 percent of the issue per year beginning at the end of year eleven. What is the average life of the issue now?

 b. Net bonds have a 5 percent coupon and sell for $900. Compute the yield to maturity and yield to average life.

 c. Instead of the above, assume that the Net bonds were issued with a 9 percent coupon, ten years' call protection, callable at the end of year eleven at 106, and currently sell for 110. Compute the yields to maturity and to first call.

14. The C.B.D.&F. Railroad has a set of collateral trust bonds due in eight years. We are considering recommending this Ba, BB rated issue for a three-year holding period for our speculative accounts. The bonds carry a 6 percent coupon and can be bought at 84. We feel that the bonds should advance in price over the next three years, as interest rates fall, although there is some chance of decline. Our estimated price probability distribution is given as follows:

Probability	Price
.1	81
.3	87
.6	93

The bonds carry some default possibility, because the cumulative-deduction-times-interest-earned multiple on forecasted income is only 2.4X for next year and 2.7X for the following two. The bonds are serial obligations, hence no sinking-fund payments are made. We estimate default yields to year three as follows:

Year	Default Yield	Probability
1	−28.4%	.03
2	−22.8	.05
3	−17.0	.08

a. If the bonds were purchased, what would be their yield to maturity?

b. Suppose the bonds were held for three years. Determine a probability distribution of expected returns, assuming the prices estimated above.

c. Assuming the probability-of-default schedule given above, determine the distribution of returns from purchasing the bond.

d. What is the expected return and standard deviation of returns from the bonds?

e. Do these bonds appear to be good speculative prospects? Why or why not?

15. Evaluate the bond mentioned on page 168 in light of the following:*

	Debt as a Percentage of Taxable Real Estate	Per Capita Debt	Debt Service Requirements as a Percentage of Budget
New York City	14	500	10
Philadelphia	11	450	8
Los Angeles	9	350	6

*The data given are fictitious and do not represent approximations of the actual ratios of these cities.

Philadelphia bonds yield 6.45 percent to maturity and Los Angeles bonds yield 5.45 percent. Would you expect the New York City 6's of 1981 to sell at par in light of these alternative yields? Determine an appropriate yield employing the following formula:

$$\text{Yield} = i + (.100)(D) + (.003)(P) + (.250)(B)$$

Where: i = pure rate of interest

D = debt as a percentage of taxable real estate

P = per capita debt

B = debt as a percentage of budget

Suppose i = .02 percent (tax-adjusted equivalent yield for taxable short-term governments).

COMPREHENSIVE CASE

Reconsider the position of Consolidated Electric Appliance. (See Chapter 7.) Assume the following projections of per capita income and population for Consolidated's sales area:

	Y	P
1975	$3,000	8.75 million
1976	3,100	8.50
1977	3,200	8.30
1978	3,300	8.10
1979	3,400	8.00

1. Forecast total revenues for 1975–1979 and prepare *pro forma* income statements.

2. Compute the times-interest-earned ratio for each period.

3. How far would revenue have to fall to endanger interest payments? Is this very likely, given the revised projections?

4. Sinking-fund payments for Consolidated are given on page 156. Determine the coverage of interest and sinking-fund payments for the revised projections.

5. Consolidated 5's of 1979 are selling at 90. Given the sinking-fund assumptions made above, determine:
   a. The yield to maturity of the issue
   b. The yield to average life.
Assume the bond is bought in 1974.

6. The issue is callable today at 105, in 1975 at 104, in 1976 at 103, and in 1977 at 102. The probability that interest rates would fall enough to justify a call in 1975 and 1976 is considered remote, but a call might be possible in 1977 if interest rates fell below 4.5 percent on equivalent issues. Determine the yield to possible call for the issue.

7. Consolidated 5's are rated AA by S&P and Aaa by Moody. Default risks are considered minimal, but an increase in interest rates could produce a capital loss (or frozen position) before the issue matures. Interest rates for next year on equivalent risk issues are forecasted according to the following distribution:

Probability	Yield
.2	7.4 percent
.5	6.8
.3	6.2

What is the probability that a capital loss would be incurred (on paper) by next year?

8. Suppose the issue were sold next year. Given the above probabilities, what would the expected return be? The standard deviation of returns?

REFERENCES

Altman, E. I., "Financial Ratios, Discriminant Analysis and the Prediction of Corporate Bankruptcy," *Journal of Finance,* September 1968, pp. 589–609.

Atkinson, T. R., *Trends in Corporate Bond Quality.* New York: Columbia University Press, 1967.

Findlay, M. C., and E. E. Williams, "Toward More Adequate Debt Service Ratios," Paper delivered before the Financial Management Association, San Antonio, October 12, 1972.

Jen, F., and J. Wert, "The Deferred Call Provision and Corporate Bond Yields," *Journal of Financial and Quantitative Analysis,* June 1968, pp. 157–69.

_____ , "The Effect of Call Risk on Corporate Bond Yields," *Journal of Finance,* December 1967, pp. 637–51.

_____ , "The Effect of Sinking Fund Provisions on Corporate Bond Yields," *Financial Analysts Journal,* March–April 1967, pp. 125–31.

_____ , "The Value of the Deferred Call Privilege," *National Banking Review,* March 1966, pp. 369–78.

Johnson, R., "The Value of the Call Privilege", *Financial Analysts Journal,* March–April 1967, pp. 134–38.

Pye, G., "The Value of the Call Option on a Bond," *Journal of Political Economy,* April 1966, pp. 200–205.

_____ , "The Value of the Call Deferment on a Bond: Some Empirical Results," *Journal of Finance,* December 1967, pp. 623–36.

9

Common Stocks:
Basic Analysis

THE PROCEDURE OF ANALYSIS

The most difficult task of the security analyst is the appraisal of common stock. The variables involved are more numerous and complicated than in bond analysis, and the forecasting abilities of the analyst become far more crucial. Equities do not promise shareholders a fixed income, and the pattern of flows generated by common stocks is typically volatile.

Because equities are risky securities, the expected returns from purchasing them tend to be higher than those earned from bonds.[1] Equity dividend yields have not equaled bond yields in recent years, but the combined returns from dividends and price appreciation have been somewhat greater on the average. Furthermore, all equities are not more risky than bonds. Indeed, the common shares of most blue-chip investment grade companies are *less* risky than the debt obligations of many other concerns. No one would argue, for example, that the shares of AT&T were more risky than the mortgage bonds of most railroads. Of course, AT&T common would be a bit more risky than AT&T bonds.

[1]A study of the returns earned on common stocks over the period 1926–1960 indicated that an investor who bought an equal dollar amount of each stock listed on the NYSE in January 1926 would have earned a compounded annual rate of return of 8.7 percent. The variability in returns for investors buying and selling within this span was great, however. An investor who bought in June 1932 and sold in December 1940 would have earned a compounded annual return of 20.8 percent, but one who bought in September 1929 and sold in June 1932 would have lost 49.1 percent. See L. Fisher and J. H. Lorie, "Rates of Return on Investment in Common Stocks," *Journal of Business*, January 1964, pp. 1–12, 15–17.

The basic procedure for evaluating equity securities begins very much like the one recommended for bond analysis. First, aggregate economic projections are made utilizing the techniques explained in Chapter 6. Next, a comprehensive evaluation of the industry in question is prepared. Finally, the future earnings position of the firm is forecasted as far as possible into the future. Probability estimates are attached where appropriate to such significant variables as sales, pertinent cost figures, and most importantly, net income. Because a major element of the cash return generated by a common stock is the dividend it pays, a careful projection of the future dividend policy of the firm must be made.

Ratio analysis can be a very useful supplement to the forecasting procedures outlined above (see Chapter 5). Various profit, turnover, and return-on-investment ratios may be computed for the firm in past years and for other comparable enterprises in the industry. These ratios may be used as performance criteria in evaluating the future prospects for the firm. A recommended policy is to compute *pro forma* ratios based on the projected data generated from the equations used to forecast sales, costs, and net income. These *pro forma* ratios may then be compared with past ratios and industry averages to measure relative performance. Ratios may also be used to verify the reliability of projections made with regression techniques. Thus, if the *pro forma* net profit margin resulting from a regression forecast was quite a bit higher than the firm had ever previously experienced, the analyst might wish to revise his projecting equations. The two sets of tools, forecasting equations and ratio analysis, should not be considered as mutually exclusive alternatives. Rather, they should be complementary methods of investigation.

DETERMINING CAPITAL OUTLAYS AND
FUTURE FINANCING

In order to illustrate a comprehensive procedure of analysis, we shall again consider Consolidated Electric Appliance (see Chapters 7 and 8). We assume that the analyst has done all the background work that was required for bond analysis. These same data are used in the common-stock appraisal, and there is no need to repeat the explanation here. In the analysis of a common stock, however, two other projections must be made before an accurate forecast of future earnings may be determined. Capital investment is the lifeblood of the firm, and any growth predictions must by necessity include explicit forecasts of a company's asset acquisition policy. Furthermore, because capital investment requires financing, the analyst must project the sources of finance available to the firm in the future. Either capital investment or future financing policy may not be important enough to consider in bond analysis (we ignored both in Chapters 7 and 8 for the sake of convenience); however, they constitute a crucial part of the equity analysis.

Reconsider the revenue forecast and subsequent *pro forma* income statements made on pages 132-33 for C.E.A. Assume that the following data have been gathered from past C.E.A. financial statements (in the manner described in Chapter 5):

C.E.A. Selected Ratios, 1970–1974

	1970	1971	1972	1973	1974
Current ratio	3.2X	3.4X	3.9X	2.8X	3.3X
EBIT ratio	.133	.145	.159	.124	.133
Net profit margin	.059	.063	.071	.053	.058
Fixed asset turnover	.59X	.65X	.69X	.57X	.61X
Net-earning-power ratio	.035	.041	.049	.030	.035
Total debt to equity	.96	.94	.92	.95	.93
Dividend-payout ratio	.77	.78	.79	.85	.81

From the *pro forma* statements we can determine *pro forma* EBIT ratios and net profit margins for 1975-1979:

	1975	1976	1977	1978	1979
EBIT/Sales	.144	.153	.165	.176	.187
Net income/Sales	.062	.067	.075	.082	.089

We observe that there is a clear upward trend in both ratios for the *pro forma* data. The historical ratios, however, show an upward movement from 1970-1972 and then a sharp drop in 1973. All indications point to a substantial capital outlay in that year. Hence, the current ratio improves (as cash is built up), the profit margins advance (as sales increase faster than costs, which are mainly fixed), and the fixed asset turnover increases (as plant is depreciated while sales rise). In 1973, when the capital outlay seems to have been made, cash is expended (hence the decline in the current ratio), fixed costs increase (thus the decline in profit margins), and plant is added at a faster rate than sales increase (therefore the drop in asset turnover).

The analyst should realize that the extremely good initial results produced by his projection equations are to some extent due to the high degree of operating and financial leverage characteristic of the firm. When he forecasts an increase in sales and holds fixed costs and interest payments constant, he guarantees rather handsome improvements in profits. It would appear that an occasional capital addition would be required to sustain the improved sales pattern that the analyst foresees. Thus, the analyst's assumption of the constant level of fixed costs should be revised. Ideally, he could make a forecast of capital outlays (and subsequent higher fixed costs) from the long-run capital budget of the firm. If this information is unavailable to him, he will have to make estimates of the revenue-generating capacity of the plant and assume additions as forecasted output increases beyond the indicated capacity level.

In light of this further research, our analyst has decided that a large capital outlay will have to be made towards the end of his forecast period. The increased capacity resulting from the 1973 additions will be used by about 1978, he believes, and further improvements in revenues will depend on larger capacity. How might the analyst go about predicting the required capital outlay for 1978? The analyst has discovered from the history of the asset-turnover ratio that an extra dollar of sales requires about $1.61 in added fixed assets. He came to this conclusion by averaging the fixed asset turnover ratio from 1970–1974 and dividing the result into $1.00 of sales. Thus, the average turnover has been .62. This means that for each $1.61 in fixed assets purchased, annual sales have been able to advance by about $1.00 (that is, $1.00/$1.61 = .62). Of course, the analyst realizes that this is only a very crude method of determining necessary capital outlays and that it rests upon an assumption that the long-run relationship between fixed assets and sales is constant.

We know from our projections that sales are expected to increase from $120 million in 1974 to $127.62 million in 1978. If capacity is added in 1978 to accommodate a similar expansion from 1979–1983, C.E.A. will have to make an outlay of $(1.61)(\$7.62 \text{ million}) = \$12.27$ million in that year. The added plant will raise fixed costs because depreciation charges will be higher. Suppose our analyst has determined that about one-half of fixed operating costs are depreciation charges. Further, he has found that fixed assets are depreciated on a straight-line basis over an average of five years (some plant lasts for twenty years, but most equipment is useful for only two or three years). The added depreciation charge for 1978 through 1983 would be:

$$(.2)(\$12.27 \text{ million}) = \$2.45 \text{ million}$$

An important question now must be raised concerning the method(s) the firm might employ to finance its required added plant. In order to sustain output at existing levels, it must be assumed that the company has at least reinvested depreciation flows (hence keeping the level of fixed assets constant from 1975–1977). The 1978 outlays could be financed from three sources, specifically: retention of earnings, the sale of new shares, and the sale of more bonds. How might the analyst decide what course C.E.A. will follow? A check of the equity accounts from past balance sheets will reveal whether or not the firm has a history of stock issues. If it does not, chances are that it will not sell shares in the future. Computation of past dividend-payout ratios will indicate something about the retention policy of the firm. A rather constant ratio might give some indication about future policy. Finally, a calculation of past debt-to-equity ratios may provide some information about the debt policy of the firm. Again, if a stable ratio is approximated, the analyst might get some indication about future debt levels. For C.E.A., the average dividend payout over 1970–1974 has been:

$$(.77 + .78 + .79 + .85 + .81)/5 = .80$$

Thus, the average retention rate has been .20. If this level of retention (payout) continues for 1975–1977, we can compute the amount that would be available for reinvestment as:

$$(.20)(7.56 + 8.31 + 9.46) = \$5.07 \text{ million}$$

Because the last major addition to capital was made in 1973, retained earnings for 1974 would also be available. Data from pages 132-33 allow us to reconstruct the 1974 income statement:

Revenue	$120.00 (million)
Fixed operating costs	80.00
Variable operating costs	24.00
EBIT	16.00
Interest	5.00
EBT	11.00
Taxes	4.40
Net income	$ 6.60

If the payout ratio was .81 in 1974, then retained earnings must be:

$$(.19)(6.60) = \$1.25 \text{ million}$$

Thus, the total amount of retention from 1974–1977 would be $5.07 million + $1.25 million = $6.32 million. It is likely that the analyst will find that the firm's current ratio will be increasing during 1974–1977, because retained earnings would take the asset form of added cash and/or marketable securities. In 1978, liquidity would be reduced as cash and marketable securities were converted into plant and equipment.

Now, if the firm maintains its past capital structure (about .94 debt to equity), it should be able to sell debt in 1978 to raise (.94)($6.32 million) = $5.94 million. Adding this to the amount of retained earnings, we find:

$$\$6.32 \text{ million} + \$5.94 \text{ million} = \$12.26 \text{ million}$$

This amount almost exactly equals the $12.27 million needed for expansion.

Thus, it is possible to recast the *pro forma* income statements for C.E.A. over 1975–1979 making more accurate assumptions about the firm's future asset purchases, its future financing, and its future fixed cost structure.[2] The projections are made below assuming: (1) the 1978 bond issue is sold at the beginning of the year at a 6 percent coupon cost; (2) the dividend payout remains at about .80; and (3) C.E.A. has 1 million common shares outstanding.

Consolidated Electric Appliance Corp.
Pro forma **Statement of Income**
(in millions)

	1975	1976	1977	1978	1979
Revenues	$122.00	123.56	125.96	127.62	130.52
Fixed operating costs	80.00	80.00	80.00	82.45	82.45
Variable operating costs	24.40	24.71	25.19	25.52	26.10
EBIT	17.60	18.85	20.77	19.65	21.97
Interest	5.00	5.00	5.00	5.36	5.36
EBT	12.60	13.85	15.77	14.29	16.61
Taxes	5.04	5.54	6.31	5.72	6.64
Net income	7.56	8.31	9.46	8.57	9.97
Dividends	6.05	6.65	7.57	6.86	7.98
Retained earnings	$ 1.51	1.66	1.89	1.71	1.99
EPS	$ 7.56	8.31	9.46	8.57	9.97
DPS	$ 6.05	6.65	7.57	6.86	7.98

COMPREHENSIVE CASE

Below, you will find 1973 and 1974 income statement and balance sheets for Winstone Inc., a manufacturer of ladies apparel.

Winstone Inc.
Statements of Profit and Loss

	1973	1974
Net sales	$11,486,842	$17,035,617
Less operating expenses:		
Cost of goods sold	10,808,614	15,494,047
Selling expenses	16,871	38,520
Administrative expenses	49,736	57,067
Interest on short-term debt	26,333	92,444
Total operating expenses	10,901,554	15,682,078

[2]There may be long-run increases in other fixed cost items besides depreciation. These are ignored in this example, but the analyst should attempt to forecast them where possible.

Winstone Inc.
Statements of Profit and Loss (cont.)

	1973	1974
Net operating income	585,288	1,353,539
Other income (net) [1]	3,651	47,456
Net income before income taxes	588,939	1,400,995
Less income taxes	266,000	672,000
Net available for common	322,939	728,995
Less common dividends	73,287	146,575
Balance carried to surplus	249,652	582,420
Add surplus beginning of period	711,549	961,201
Surplus end of period	$ 961,201	$ 1,543,621

[1] Includes $56,938 in federal taxes refunded in 1973, and $56,996 in taxes refunded in 1974.

Winstone Inc.
Balance Sheets

	1973	1974
Current assets:		
Cash	$ 362,572	$ 464,360
Accounts receivable	1,389,676	2,046,867
Inventories	3,443,137	5,934,183
Total current assets	$5,195,385	$8,445,410
Fixed assets:		
Net property	$ 143,803	$ 223,233
Tools and dies, net	28,415	3,345
Investment in subsidiaries	50,591	81,910
Total fixed assets	$ 222,809	$ 308,488
Deferred expenses:		
Prepayments	$ 46,722	$ 30,619
Other assets:		
Leasehold improvements	$ 41,044	$ 44,708
Misc. deposits, etc.	37,322	46,873
Long-term receivables	–	8,022
Total other assets	$ 78,366	$ 99,603
Total Assets	$5,543,282	$8,884,120
Current liabilities:		
Accounts payable	$ 984,061	$2,070,703
Notes payable	1,500,000	2,700,000
Accrued expenses	157,173	293,548
Tax reserve	223,833	545,193
Other current liabilities	26,000	40,000
Total current liabilities	$2,891,066	$5,649,484
Fixed liabilities:	–	–

Winstone Inc.
Balance Sheets (cont.)

	1973	1974
Net worth:		
Common stock (1 million shs.)	$1,465,749	$1,465,749
Paid in surplus	225,266	225,266
Earned surplus	961,201	1,543,621
Total net worth	$2,652,216	$3,234,636
Total liabilities and worth	$5,543,282	$8,884,120

Key ratios for Winstone for 1970-1972 and for the industry in 1974 are given as follows:

Ratio	1970	1971	1972	Industry Average
Current	1.4X	1.7X	1.9X	2.6X
Gross margin	.02	.03	.04	.07
Net margin	(loss)	.01	.02	.03
Total asset turnover	2.1X	2.0X	2.0X	2.0X
Net-earning-power ratio	—	.02	.04	.06
Total debt to equity	.86	.94	1.00	.75
Book value per share	$2.18	$2.27	$2.40	—
Dividend payout	nil	nil	.30	.48
P/E multiple	—	42X	20X	14X
EPS	($.02)	$ .09	$ .19	—

1. Adjust the income statements and balance sheets for 1973 and 1974. Prepare adjusted statements. Reconcile the firm's tax payment in light of the fact that expected taxes should be 50 percent of net income before taxes.

2. Compute the above ratios for 1973 and 1974. Use adjusted data where it is appropriate to do so (that is, net margin, net earning power, dividend payment, and P/E multiple). Compute EPS on an unadjusted and an adjusted basis. The average market price for Winstone shares was $5 in 1973 and $9 3/8 in 1974.

3. What favorable and unfavorable trends do you observe for Winstone?

4. An analyst has determined the following projection equation for the ladies apparel industry:

$$S_I = 240 + (.07) \, GNP + (1.23) \, WOM$$

Where S_I = industry sales (in millions)

GNP = gross national product (in billions)

WOM = number of women between ages of 14 and 65 (in millions)

The analyst has obtained GNP and population forecasts from the Departments of Commerce and Labor. (Note: the numbers are assumed and do not represent actual forecasts by either the U.S. Dept. of Commerce or the Dept. of Labor).

Year	GNP (billions)	Women 14–65 (million)
1975	$1,553	90.5
1976	1,620	91.3
1977	1,710	92.1
1978	1,806	91.0
1979	1,926	90.5

Given the above, project industry sales from 1975 –1979.

5. The following projection equation for Winstone has also been computed:

$$S_W = -1.54 + (.05)S_I + (.02)SEL$$

Where: S_W = Winstone sales (in millions)

S_I = industry sales (in millions)

SEL = Winstone selling expenditures (in thousands)

The analyst has found out from Winstone's management that they plan a continued aggressive campaign to increase their share of the market. The selling expense budget is expected to double each year from 1975 to 1979. From this information, forecast Winstone's sales for 1975–1979.

6. Since Winstone entered the apparel business twelve years ago, its market share has averaged 3.7 percent. In recent years (1970–1974), there has been a distinct upward trend, however, and the analyst believes the firm could achieve 10 percent of the market eventually. From the forecasts of industry and firm sales, compute Winstone's projected market share from 1975 to 1979. Are these figures consistent with the analyst's expectations about Winstone's eventual potential?

7. The analyst notes that Winstone operated near the break-even point from its inception in 1962 until 1971. The firm lost money during its first five years of operations and also incurred deficits in 1969 and 1970. He is convinced that the enterprise has passed the critical stage, however, and that future years will be profitable. He recognizes that the large improvements in margins experienced from 1970 to 1974 cannot continue and were characteristic of a firm moving away from its break-even point. He feels that the firm should be able to achieve the industry average gross margin in the future, however. If this is true, what would the dollar gross margin be for 1975–1979?

8. In order to make possible the rather large increases in sales that are projected, it is clear that the firm's asset base will have to expand. The firm must carry larger volumes of receivables and inventories in order to compete, and these items will increase along with necessary additions to fixed plant. The analyst expects the asset turnover to be steady at about

2.0X. If this is the case, how much in added assets will be required from 1975 to 1979?

9. The analyst believes that the short-term debt position of the firm is dangerously high. Management argues, however, that the high percentage of current to fixed assets allows the firm to have substantial amounts of short-term liabilities. Management points to the low cost of this source of finance (only $92 thousand was paid in interest in 1974, even though liabilities equaled $5.6 million). It appears that management will not consider a long-term debt issue and will finance future growth out of retained earnings and increases in current liabilities. The analyst has prepared *pro forma* statements for 1975 with this in mind:

Winstone Inc. *Pro forma* **Statement Profit and Loss, 1975** (in thousands)			Winstone Inc. *Pro forma* **Balance Sheet, 1975** (in thousands)	
Sales	$23,000		Total assets	$11,500
CGS	21,390			
Gross margin	1,610			
Selling expense	77		Current liabilities	$ 7,726
Adm. expense	50		Fixed liabilities	—
Interest	112		Common stock	1,466
Net operating income	1,371		Paid in surplus	225
Other income (net)	(23)		Earned surplus	2,083
Net income before tax	1,348			$11,500
Taxes (50%)	674			
Net available for common	674			
Dividends	135			
Balance carried to surplus	539			
Add surplus, beg.	1,544			
Surplus, end of period	$ 2,083			

Note: 1. Gross margin equals .07 sales.
2. Selling expense is assumed equal to the budgeted amount (as projected above).
3. Administrative expenses are assumed to be $50,000 for 1975 and are expected to increase by about $20,000 annually.
4. Interest is assumed to equal 2.0 percent of the total current liabilities of the previous year.
5. Other income is assumed to be −$23,000 in 1975, and zero thereafter.
6. Taxes equal 50 percent of NIBT.
7. The dividend payout ratio is assumed to be .20.
8. Total assets equal .5 sales.
9. Common stock and paid in surplus are assumed constant.

From the above data, construct *pro forma* income statements and balance sheets for 1976–1979.

10. Recapitulate earnings per share and dividends per share as follows:
   a. Reported, 1970–1974
   b. Adjusted, 1973–1974
   c. Projected, 1975–1979.

REFERENCES

Bellemore, Douglas H., and John C. Ritchie, Jr., *Investments: Principles, Practices and Analysis,* 3d ed., Cincinnati: South-Western Publishing Company, Incorporated, 1969.

Cohen, Jerome B., and Edward D. Zinbarg, *Investment Analysis and Portfolio Management,* Homewood, Ill.: Richard D. Irwin, Inc., 1967.

Fisher, L., and J. H. Lorie, "Rates of Return on Investment in Common Stocks," *Journal of Business,* January 1964, pp. 1–12, 15–17.

Graham, B., D. Dodd, and S. Cottle, *Security Analysis,* 4th ed., New York: McGraw-Hill Book Company, 1962, part IV.

Solomon, Ezra, "Economic Growth and Common-Stock Value", *Journal of Business,* July 1955, pp. 213–221.

10

Common Stocks:
Valuation Models

DOLLAR RETURNS FROM COMMON SHARES

Dollar returns from common stocks are derived from two sources: (1) the dividends paid by the firm, and (2) the price appreciation of the security. The ability of a firm to pay dividends, of course, depends upon its earning power. A firm that generates only a negligible return on its asset investment will obviously be in no position to pay dividends. Nevertheless, even firms that obtain very good returns on investment sometimes elect not to pay large dividends. Such firms may be able to benefit stockholders more by retaining earnings and reinvesting in profitable assets. This procedure will produce higher earnings in the future and improve the long-run dividend paying potential of the firm.[1] Furthermore, such a policy may allow stockholders in high income-tax brackets a substantial tax saving. Cash dividends are normally taxed at ordinary income rates, whereas capital gains are given preferential treatment. When a firm retains earnings for reinvestment in profitable projects, it improves its long-run earnings stream. This improvement should be reflected in the price of the firm's shares. Thus, by retaining earnings, the firm may in effect raise the price of its stock. Investors would then have a capital gain rather than the ordinary income that they would get if a dividend were paid.

---

[1]The economics of dividend policy from the standpoint of the corporation is discussed at greater length in Findlay and Williams, *An Integrated Analysis for Managerial Finance* (Englewood Cliffs, N.J.: Prentice-Hall, Inc., 1970), Chap. 14.

Common shares may be categorized by the above characteristics. The shares of firms that do not generate large returns on their investment in assets but that pay out in cash dividends most of what they do earn are called *income shares.* These stocks sell almost entirely on a pure dividend yield basis, because appreciation from retained earnings is limited. Income stocks may be above-average-risk securities issued by declining firms that have exhausted their most profitable reinvestment opportunities. Many railroad, fire and casualty insurance, and undiversified tobacco equities would be included in this group. On the other hand, income stocks may also be lower-than-average-risk securities issued by firms that have their return on investment regulated by government. These equities, which are usually stable and relatively safe even during periods of recession,[2] may retain earnings and show capital appreciation. Nevertheless, their growth rates are constrained by the regulated rate of return that they are allowed to earn on plant and equipment. The best examples of the low-risk income stock are the shares of most American public utilities.

Equities that pay a rather constant dividend over time may be evaluated much like a preferred stock. One buys such a security for income, and its worth to the investor is the dividend stream that is produced. Hence, the return from purchasing such a stock is easily determined by the general yield equation for an asset:

$$P_0 = \frac{D_0}{(1+i)^0} + \frac{D_1}{(1+i)^1} + \ldots + \frac{D_\infty}{(1+i)^\infty}$$

$$P_0 = \sum_{t=0}^{\infty} \frac{D_t}{(1+i)^t} \qquad (10.1)$$

Where: P_0 is the price of the stock

D_t is the dividend expected in year t

i is the rate of return earned on the stock

In this equation, it is assumed that dividends are paid annually and that a dividend will soon be paid (hence the D_0 value). The first assumption is usually

[2] Shares that are stable and relatively recession-proof are also called *defensive shares.* All defensive shares are not income stocks, however. Food and drug companies are considered to be defensive securities, and their dividend yields are generally low. Their shares also have growth potential. Gold-mining and distillery stocks are also typically classified as defensive stocks, and many of these securities (particularly the gold-mining shares) pay no dividends at all.

violated in the real world because firms have a tendency to pay quarterly dividends. In this case, the equation could be revised to:[3]

$$P_0 = \Sigma\Sigma \; \frac{D_t/4}{\left(1 + \dfrac{i}{4}\right)^{4t+k}}$$

(10.2)

Nevertheless, the difference between equations 10.1 and 10.2 is small, and for all practical purposes the former may be used even if dividends are paid more often than once per year. Of course, the total dividend paid during the year (and not just the quarterly payment) should be used with equation 10.1. The second assumption, that a dividend soon will be paid, may or may not be valid depending on the date of computation. If a dividend has just been paid, and another one will not come for a year, equation 10.1 may be amended to become:

$$P_0 = \sum_{t=1}^{\infty} \frac{D_t}{(1+i)^t}$$

(10.3)

Returning to equation 10.1, if it is assumed that D_t is constant, the equation may be rewritten as:

$$P_0 = D \sum_{t=0}^{\infty} (1+i)^{-t}$$

(10.4)

We know that:

$$\underset{t \to \infty}{\text{Lim}} \; \Sigma(1+i)^{-t} = \frac{1}{i}$$

(10.5)

Thus,

$$P_0 = \frac{D}{i}$$

(10.6)

Or,[4]

$$i = \frac{D}{P_0}$$

(10.7)

[3] See the discussion on compounding periods in Appendix A.

[4] A similar proof obtains under conditions of continuous compounding. Here, $P_0 = \int_0^{\infty} D(t)e^{-it}dt$. Now, if $D(t)$ and i are assumed constant, then:

$$P_0 = D\left[-\frac{1}{i}e^{-it}\right]_{t=\infty} - D\left[-\frac{1}{i}e^{-it}\right]_{t=0} = \frac{D}{i}.$$

Equation 10.7 is the simplest form of yield expression. It only applies where the dividend payment is reasonably constant and will be paid for a very long time into the future. These are not totally unrealistic assumptions for some income stocks, particularly certain public utility equities. Thus, if the Elmira Gas Co. has paid a dividend of one dollar consistently over the past thirty years and expects to continue to do so in the future, its yield could be easily determined given the market price (P_0) of the stock. If Elmira common sold for ten dollars, its yield would be:

$$\$1/\$10 = 10\%$$

Similarly, assuming investors wished a 10 percent return from Elmira, the price of the stock could be determined, given the dividend payment:

$$\$1/.10 = \$10$$

Stocks that sell entirely on a dividend yield basis are becoming less important to investors. These stocks show no long-run growth in price, although gains (and losses) can be enjoyed (suffered) depending on movements in the overall rate of interest and changes in the risk position of the issuing company. Hence, an investor might buy Elmira Gas at ten dollars this year and see the price advance next year if the yield that investors expected from the stock declined. Suppose that overall rates of interest in the market fell such that investors required only a 9 percent rate of return on Elmira next year. Its price would become:

$$\$1/.09 = \$11.11$$

Thus, the investor who bought the stock this year at $10 would have his dollar dividend *plus* a capital gain of $1.11. It should be remembered, of course, that the gain had nothing to do with the growth of Elmira.[5] It resulted entirely from a change in overall interest rates. A similar gain could have been earned on Elmira bonds. This point is explored more fully in the next section.

HOLDING-PERIOD RETURNS

As in the case for bonds and preferred shares, the holding period for equities may be important. Because no one holds a security infinitely (as implied in

---

[5]Capital gains resulting from growth in corporate earnings are quite different in character from interest-rate- (or risk-change-) produced gains. The former are discussed in the next chapter.

equation 10.1), it is possible for capital gains (or losses) to occur if one sells the security. Changes in price may result from changes in the returns demanded by investors. Differences in demanded returns will occur: (1) if market interest rates change; (2) if the risk complexion of the firm alters; or (3) if expectations about dividends beyond the holding period vary. Thus, if an investor paid P_0 for a stock today with the expectation of selling for P_n in n years, his return would be given by:

$$P_0 = \sum_{t=0}^{n} \frac{D_t}{(1+i)^t} + \frac{P_n}{(1+i)^n} \tag{10.8}$$

The best estimate at $t = 0$ of P_n is:

$$P_n = \sum_{t=n+1}^{\infty} \frac{D_t}{(1+i)^{t-n}} \tag{10.9}$$

Equation 10.8 is, of course, a restatement of equation 10.1, because a substitution of 10.9 into 10.8 will produce 10.1. To see this point more clearly, consider the following example:

Grand Union Power pays a dividend of two dollars per share. The same dividend amount has been paid annually in the past for a number of years, and it is expected that this dividend will be paid in the future. The company is about ready to declare its annual dividend. Mrs. Ima Widow is considering a purchase of G.U.P. common. She plans to hold the stock for five years. Her investment counselor has told her that interest rates should be lower then and that G.U.P. should be in an even stronger financial position than it is now. The stock now sells for 23 3/8 per share. Her advisor believes that it will yield about 8 percent in five years. If this is the case, the price five years from now would be:

$$P_5 = \frac{\$2}{.08} = \$25$$

If Grand Union does sell at the expected price in five years, Mrs. Widow's expected return would be:

$$P_0 = \sum_{t=0}^{5} D_t(1+i)^{-t} + 25(1+i)^{-5}$$

At $i = 12$ percent, $D_0 = 2(1.000) = 2.00$

$D_1 \ldots D_5 = 2(3.605) = 7.21$

$P_5 = 25(.567) = \underline{14.18}$

$\$23.39$

Her return would be about 12 percent, as she paid $23.375 for the stock.

Notice that in the example, G.U.P. was on the verge of paying its annual cash dividend. If it had just paid the dividend, we would expect the market price to be two dollars lower, or 21 3/8. If she bought just after the payment, her yield would still be about 12 percent:

$$P_0 = \sum_{t=1}^{5} D_t(1+i)^{-t} + 25(1+i)^{-5}$$

At $i = 12$ percent, $D_1 \ldots D_5 = 2(3.605) = \quad 7.21$

$$P_5 = 25(.567) \quad = \quad \underline{14.18}$$
$$\$21.39$$

THE DIVIDEND STREAM –
EARNINGS MULTIPLIER MODEL

Equities that evidence marked volatility in their sales, earnings, and dividend patterns are called *cyclical shares.* Aggregate economic activity has a distinct impact on the performance of these securities, and their evaluation depends on an accurate forecast of the business cycle. Typical cyclical shares include most steel, airline, automobile, railroad, and capital-goods-producer stocks.

An equation such as 10.8 may be used to determine the expected return on cyclical stocks. It must be remembered, however, that the dividend payments of these shares cannot be assumed to be constant. Thus, a projection of the expected dividend to be paid in each year of the holding period must be made. Furthermore, the anticipated price at the end of the holding period must be forecasted. Such a forecast is more difficult for a cyclical share than an income stock because factors other than the general level of interest rates and corporate risk are also important. In order to deal with terminal price expectations, we shall attempt to predict the price-earnings multiplier that will apply in the last year of the holding period.

A P/E multiple is simply the ratio of market price to earnings. It has been used by analysts in the past to determine the "value" of a security, and it can be a useful surrogate for expected return. Indeed, in the case of a firm that has a constant earnings stream and pays all earnings out in dividends, the P/E multiple is the inverse of the expected return. This can be seen by reconsidering equation 10.7:

$$i = \frac{D}{P_0}$$

if $D = E$, then

$$i = \frac{E}{P_0}$$ (10.10)

or

$$\frac{P_0}{E} = \frac{1}{i}$$ (10.11)

When all earnings are not paid out in dividends and when earnings grow, the P/E multiple and the expected rate of return may differ.[6] Nevertheless, there is a rough general relationship between the two.

The determinants of the P/E multiple may be given as follows:

$$M = f(i, \sigma, g)$$ (10.12)

Where: M is the firm's P/E multiple

i is the general market rate of interest

σ is a measure of the riskiness of the firm

g is the growth rate in the firm's earnings stream

Multiples can be expected to be negatively related to i and σ and positively related to g. Many analysts feel that corporate risk is the primary determinant of multiples except for concerns with exceptionally high earnings growth rates (above 10 percent compounded annually for at least ten years). For most firms, a general measure of this risk is indicated by their S&P rating.[7] These ratings may be used to select an appropriate multiple range for a given security (see Table 10-1).[8] Whether a stock sells in the upper or lower end of the range will depend on the general level of interest rates and the growth potential of the firm. Historical multiples may also be used to establish a range of multiples for a firm. Thus, if a firm has sold between 12 and 14 times earnings for the past ten years, it is likely that it will sell in that general range in the future (barring very large movements in the rate of interest and assuming the riskiness and growth potential of the firm do not change radically).

---

[6] When the firm re-invests retained funds at i, the P/E multiple will also equal the inverse of the expected rate of return. See Chap. 11.

[7] A more comprehensive risk measure will be developed in Chapter 11.

[8] The multiples indicated in table 10.1 do not apply to rapidly growing concerns in the short run. Multiples of 30 and higher are frequently observed for these securities.

TABLE 10-1

Common Stock P/E Multiples[9]

S&P Rating	Description	Multiple Range for Industrials and Rails	Multiple Range for Utilities, Banks, and Life Insurance Stocks
A+	Excellent	14–15	18–20
A	Good	12–13	15–17
A–	Above average	10–11	12–14
B+	Average	8–9	9–11
B	Below average	6–7	6–8
B–	Low	4–5	4–5
C	Lowest	2–3	2–3

We may employ the expected terminal data multiple in a revised form of equation 10.8:

$$P_0 = \sum_{t=0}^{n} \frac{D_t}{(1+i)^t} + \frac{(M)\,(E_n)}{(1+i)^n} \qquad (10.13)$$

In this equation, M is the P/E multiple expected in year n (the terminal date of the holding period), and E_n is the forecasted earnings per share for year n. The value $(M)(E_n)$ should approximate the expected share price at period n. Thus, an investor can take his EPS forecast for year n, apply an appropriate multiple, and obtain a reasonable estimate of the price that he will receive when he sells his shares.

Two caveats should be indicated about the use of P/E multiples at a point in time. First, daily disturbances in stock market prices may produce wide ranges of multiples during any one year. Thus, if a stock sold between 20 and 30 during a year and earned two dollars per share, its multiple would range from 10 to 15 depending on the market price used. A good practice is to select a "normalized" price for computing the multiple. Where no clear growth pattern in price is indicated, the analyst may simply average the year's high and low prices to get a normalized value. In the above instance, the normalized price would be 25 and the resulting multiple would be 12–13. When a growth pattern is present, an argument may be made for using the year-end price or even the year's high price to compute the multiple.

The second caveat concerns the earnings figure used to estimate the stock price at the terminal holding date. For cyclical stocks, it may be that the earnings figure forecasted for the terminal year is substantially above (or below)

[9]The guidelines in this table were developed over many years by Dr. J. C. Dolley, Emeritus Professor of Finance, The University of Texas at Austin. Although admittedly only a first approximation, these heuristics are felt by the authors to reflect normative multiple patterns.

average. Although there is a tendency for the prices of cyclical stocks to do well in above-average years and poorly in below-average ones, rarely do they match the extremes of the earnings pattern. Thus, multiples for cyclical stocks tend to fall in very good years (as earnings rise faster than stock prices) and rise in bad ones (as earnings fall faster than prices). This phenomenon should be borne in mind when forecasting the terminal price for these securities.

AN ILLUSTRATION OF ESTIMATING COMMON STOCK RETURNS

We may employ Table 10-1 to discern another major category of common shares – the *blue-chip stocks*. Equities of the largest concerns that have long and unbroken records of earnings and dividend payments fall into this category. Blue-chip stocks are rated A+ and A by S&P and are considered to be the lowest overall risk form of common share. The evaluation of most blue chips may be approached in the same manner as that described for the analysis of cyclical shares. The problems associated with terminal-date pricing are not so significant in the case of these stocks, however. Even those blue chips that are also cyclical stocks (for example, U.S. Steel, Bethlehem Steel, and so on) do not have wide movements in reported earnings per share. Many high-grade blue chips are income stocks (the public utilities in particular), and some are even *growth stocks* (discussed and analyzed in the next chapter). The blue-chip companies are household words, such as American Telephone, Standard Oil of New Jersey,[10] Du Pont, General Motors, General Electric, and Eastman Kodak.

We may illustrate much of the discussion above with an example. Reconsider the earnings and dividend projections made for Consolidated Electric Appliance (page 180). Notice that C.E.A. has a reasonably high dividend payout. This would tend to place the firm in the income-stock category. If it is also a large, high-quality company with a long record of earnings and dividend payment, it may also be considered a blue-chip stock. Notice further that the projected compounded annual growth rate for C.E.A. is not terribly large. Comparing the EPS projection in 1979 with that of 1975, we find a compounded annual growth rate of:

$$9.97 \ (X) = 7.56$$

$$X = 7.56/9.97 = .758$$

Examining the present value tables, a factor of .763 is found for four years (the time interval from the end of 1975 to the end of 1979) at a rate of 7 percent.

[10]Standard's new name, Exxon, is probably not a household word yet, but it probably will become one. The firm is a solid blue chip in any case.

Thus, the growth rate is just over 7 percent, which is not sufficient to classify the stock as a "growth" equity.

C.E.A. common now (that is, the end of 1974) sells for $138 per share. The P/E multiple for C.E.A. and the current dividend yield may be computed from examining the 1974 income statement (see page 178). The firm earned $6.60 per share and paid a dividend of $5.35 ($6.60 – $1.25). The P/E multiple is thus:

$$\frac{138.00}{6.60} = 21X$$

The current dividend yield is:

$$\frac{5.35}{138.00} = 3.9\%$$

C.E.A. is rated A+ by S&P. In the past, the stock has sold at a P/E multiple of 18 – 22X. It is expected that interest rates will be slightly lower in 1979 than they are currently, that the risk position of the firm will be more or less unchanged, and that growth prospects for the company beyond 1979 will be about the same as they were during 1975–1979. Given these expectations, we may determine a reasonable P/E multiple for 1979 earnings. An A+ rated industrial should have a multiple in the 14–15 range (Table 10-1), although with some growth prospects a multiple above this range could be justified. The suggested range (14–15) is somewhat lower than the historical multiple at which C.E.A. has been selling. The current multiple is 21. If risk and growth are unchanged over the 1975–1979 period but interest rates fall slightly, a very modest increase in the suggested multiple range might be allowed. A 1979 multiple of 20 would not be an unreasonable projection, considering the firm's historical multiple, its growth prospects, and the projected decline in interest rates.

Given the 1979 multiple selected above, we may estimate the stock price for 1979:

$$(20)\ (9.97) = \$199.40$$

Suppose a purchase of C.E.A. were made today at 138. We may compute the compounded annual rate of return expected by an investor who projected the dividend stream outlined on page 179 and the terminal price indicated above. Assuming the dividend is paid annually and that the 1974 dividend has already been paid, we find:

at 12 percent,

$$
\begin{array}{rcl}
(6.05)\ (.893) &=& 5.40 \\
(6.65)\ (.797) &=& 5.30 \\
(7.57)\ (.712) &=& 5.39 \\
(6.86)\ (.636) &=& 4.36 \\
(7.98)\ (.567) &=& 4.52 \\
(199.40)\ (.567) &=& \underline{113.06} \\
&& 138.03
\end{array}
$$

The expected return would be 12 percent.

PROBLEMS

Amalgamated Telephone pays an annual dividend of five dollars. The firm has a stable earnings record and does not anticipate changing the dividend in the future.

1. If an investor wished to earn 8 percent on Amalgamated, how much would he pay per share?

2. Suppose the market price of Amalgamated were fifty dollars per share. How much would it yield?

3. If market rates of interest increased such that investors felt Amalgamated should yield 12.5 percent, at what price would it sell?

4. Suppose an investor bought Amalgamated at 50. He held the stock for ten years and earned a return of 10 percent. If the stock just paid a dividend, at what price did the investor sell the stock at the end of ten years?

5. Amalgamated was purchased at 50. The lowest possible return an investor would accept on the investment is 6 percent. If the dividend were maintained, how far could the price of the stock decline in ten years so that just 6 percent would be realized? What would have to be the expected return on Amalgamated from year ten onward for this price to prevail?

COMPREHENSIVE CASE

Review the analysis you made for Winstone, Inc. (Comprehensive Case, Chapter 9).

1. Categorize Winstone as an income, defensive, cyclical, blue-chip, and/or a growth stock.

2. What is Winstone's current dividend yield (1974)?

3. Winstone has an S&P rating of B+. Between now and 1979, it is expected that the firm will become a much larger firm and will be somewhat less risky. The high level of current liabilities will leave the firm

more risky than others in the same industry, however. It is expected that interest rates will not change appreciably by 1979. Determine a reasonable P/E multiple for 1979 earnings.

4. Price the stock for 1979, given the multiple you selected above.

5. Winstone may be purchased today at 9 3/8. From the projections made above, what rate of return would an investor expect from Winstone during 1975–1979? (Assume the dividend is paid annually and that the 1974 dividend has already been paid).

REFERENCES

Brittain, J., *Corporate Dividend Policy*. Washington, D.C.: Brookings Institute, 1966.

Findlay, M. C., and E. E. Williams, *An Integrated Analysis for Managerial Finance,* Chap. 14. Englewood Cliffs, N.J.: Prentice-Hall, Inc., 1970.

Gordon, M., "Dividends, Earnings, and Stock Prices," *Review of Economics and Statistics,* May 1959, pp. 99–105.

————, *The Investment, Financing and Valuation of the Corporation*. Homewood, Ill.: Richard D. Irwin, 1962.

————, "The Savings, Investment, and Valuation of a Corporation," *Review of Economics and Statistics,* February 1962, pp. 37–51.

Vickers, D., "Profitability and Reinvestment Rates: A Note on the Gordon Paradox," *Journal of Business,* July 1966, pp. 366–70.

Walter, J., "Dividend Policy and Common Stock Prices," *Journal of Finance,* March 1956, pp. 29–41.

————, "Dividend Policy: Its Influence on the Value of the Enterprise," *Journal of Finance,* May 1963, pp. 280–91.

————, *Dividend Policy and Enterprise Valuation*. Belmont, Calif.: Wadsworth Publishing Co. Inc., 1967.

11

Common Stocks: Growth and Risk Analysis

DIVIDENDS AND EARNINGS GROWTH

An equity that evidences much-better-than-average increases in sales and earnings for a consistent period of time is called a *growth stock*. These shares outperform the economy and most other equities in their respective industries. Growth companies typically pay negligible dividends because they can do better for their shareholders by retaining earnings and reinvesting in plant and equipment. They are aggressive in their search for new, profitable opportunities, and they typically spend a great deal on research and development. Many growth stocks are also blue chips, with such stock market stars as IBM, Xerox, and Polaroid as prime examples.

When a stock shows a sustained earnings growth pattern over a long period of time, the dividend-paying potential of the security increases. For this reason, shareholders are willing to pay large P/E multiples for growth stocks. Indeed, some of the leaders among the growth equities have sold at 50 and even 100 times current earnings. Although most investors who pay these prices for growth securities believe that they are purchasing equities for capital gains, they are in fact buying a growing expected *future* dividend stream. Price appreciation occurs, of course, and this is due to the improved dividend paying abilities of the firm. Even though the firm may pay no dividend for years, as it retains earnings and grows, the fact that it *could* pay a larger dividend (and eventually will when its growth rate declines) produces the share price appreciation.

Equation 10.8 is a very appropriate valuation model for growth shares: Reiterating,

$$P_0 = \sum_{t=0}^{n} \frac{D_t}{(1+i)^t} + \frac{P_n}{(1+i)^n} \qquad \text{(10.8 Restated)}$$

In general, the first term on the right-hand side of the equation will be small, because dividend payments in the near future will, in all likelihood, be negligible or even nonexistent. The return to investors is produced by the price appreciation from P_0 to P_n; and, as we indicated above, P_n is determined by the dividend stream remaining beyond period n. Reiterating equation 10.9:

$$P_n = \sum_{t=n+1}^{\infty} \frac{D_t}{(1+i)^{t-n}} \qquad \text{(10.9 Restated)}$$

The relationship between share price movements and the timing of future dividend payments can be seen with an example. Suppose the Alpha, Beta, and Gamma Corporations are expected to maintain the following pattern of dividend payments:

Year	Alpha	Beta	Gamma
1	$1.00	$0.00	$0.00
2	1.00	0.25	0.00
3	1.00	0.50	0.00
4 and beyond	1.00	1.00	1.00

Shareholders desire a 10 percent return and will pay prices for each firm's shares that will produce a 10 percent yield. Notice initially that each company will pay $1 per year forever beginning in year 4. Thus, the price of each share should be ($1.00/.1) = $10 at the beginning of year 4 and thereafter, with the 10 percent return represented by the $1 dividend in relation to the $10 price. For Alpha, the same analysis applies presently. The current price should be $10 and should remain there for the next three years.[1] For Gamma, the price pattern would be:

$$P_0 = 0 + \frac{P_3}{(1.10)^3} = \$10(.751) = \$7.51$$

$$P_1 = \$10(.826) \qquad = \quad 8.26$$

$$P_2 = \$10(.909) \qquad = \quad 9.09$$

$$P_3 \qquad\qquad\qquad\quad = 10.00$$

[1]Within each year, the price of the stock would tend to rise as the dividend payment date approached. Theoretically, the price would be $10 right after a dividend payment and would rise to $11 just before the next payment. Once the dividend were declared (and shareholders as of a given record date were scheduled to receive their $1 per share), the stock would sell "ex-dividend" and would fall back to $10.

Thus, Gamma holders receive their 10 percent return totally in the form of price increases for the first three years. It should be stressed that the price increase does not occur by magic, but rather because the present value of the future dividend stream rises as the stream moves nearer to the present by the passage of time. The Beta price pattern would be:

$$P_0 = 0 + \$.25(.826) + .50(.751) + 10(.751) = 8.09$$

$$P_1 = \$.25(.909) + .50(.826) + 10(.826) = 8.90$$

$$P_2 = \$.50(.909) + 10(.909) = 9.54$$

$$P_3 = 10.00$$

Thus, in year 1 the total return is from price change $(.81/8.09 = 10\%)$. In years 2 and 3, it comes from both price change and dividends $[(.64 + .25)/8.90 = 10\%]$; $[(.46 + .50)/9.54 = 10\%]$.

DETERMINANTS OF EARNINGS GROWTH

It will be recalled from Chapter 10 that substituting the price change equation 10.9 into equation 10.8 produces the basic dividend valuation model stated in equation 10.1. Reiterating,

$$P_0 = \frac{D_0}{(1+i)^0} + \frac{D_1}{(1+i)^1} + \ldots + \frac{D_\infty}{(1+i)^\infty} \qquad \text{(10.1 Restated)}$$

Rather than attempting to designate expected dividends over period $t = 0$ to $t = \infty$, it is operationally more feasible to estimate the approximate growth rate of dividends over time. Given an expected dividend growth rate g, we may revise equation 10.1 to the following:

$$P_0 = \frac{D(1+g)^0}{(1+i)^0} + \frac{D(1+g)^1}{(1+i)^1} + \ldots + \frac{D(1+g)^\infty}{(1+i)^\infty}$$

$$P_0 = \sum_{t=0}^{\infty} \frac{D(1+g)^t}{(1+i)^t} \qquad (11.1)$$

In this instance, $D_0 = D(1 + g)^0$, $D_1 = D(1 + g)^1$, and so on. Under conditions of continuous compounding, equation 11.1 becomes:

$$P_0 = \int_0^\infty D e^{gt} e^{-it} dt \qquad (11.2)$$

which may be integrated, assuming g and i are constant and $g < i$, to produce:[2]

$$P_0 = \frac{D}{i-g}$$ (11.3)

Equation 11.3 is a useful summary of the variables determining the price of a growth stock. It can be rewritten in an even more informative way:

$$i = \frac{D}{P_0} + g$$ (11.4)

This, in effect, tells us that the two components of the return on a growth stock are the dividend yield (D/P_0) and the growth in expected dividends. When the firm's retention rate (b) is expected to be constant, the dividend growth must equal the growth in earnings. Under these assumptions, the shares will sell at a constant P/E multiple (assuming interest rates also remain constant), and the earnings growth must equal the growth in share price.[3] Thus, if D/E and P/E are constant, then equation 11.4 indicates the total return to stockholders from dividends (D/P_0) and from capital gains (g).

The factors that determine the rate g are very important and should be understood by the analyst. Foremost in importance is the rate of return that the firm generates on its investment in assets. A broad indication of this rate may be obtained from examining the earning-power-of-total-investment ratio over time (EBIT/total assets). This ratio is the best single measure of the pretax return that the firm generates on its assets and should be scrutinized carefully for every growth stock. A second factor is the degree of financial leverage assumed by the

[2]

$$P_0 = \int_0^\infty D e^{gt} e^{-it} dt = \int_0^\infty D e^{-t(i-g)} dt$$

$$= D \left[-\frac{1}{i-g} e^{-t(i-g)} \right]_{t=\infty} - D \left[-\frac{1}{i-g} e^{-t(i-g)} \right]_{t=0}$$

$$= D \left[-\frac{1}{i-g} e^{-\infty} \right] - D \left[-\frac{1}{i-g} e^{-0} \right]$$

$$= \frac{D}{i-g}$$

For the above to be valid, g must be less than i. If $g \geqslant i$, price would increase without limit in the perpetual model. See David Durand, "Growth Stocks and the Petersburg Paradox," *Journal of Finance*, September 1957, pp. 348-63. The Petersburg Paradox is also discussed in Chapter 15.

[3] The return (i) in all future periods is constant by definition. If the dividend growth rate (g) is also assumed to be constant, it must follow from equation 11.4 that D/P is constant. D equals $(1-b)E$ by definition. It may therefore be deduced that $(1-b)E$ will grow at rate g and, if $(1-b)$ is assumed to be constant, E will grow at rate g and E/P will be constant. Furthermore, if E grows at rate g, then P must also grow at this rate. We may conclude that D/P, E/P, P/E, and D/E will be constant and D, E, and P will all grow at rate g.

firm and the spread between payments to bondholders and the earning power of total investment. The size of this spread will determine the residual return remaining for stockholders. A third factor that is also of crucial importance is the retention ratio, b (1 - the dividend-payout ratio). Every dollar retained and reinvested should be reflected in the growth rate.

Growth and Earnings Retention

We may be somewhat more specific about the determinants of g. Suppose a corporation is entirely financed by equity capital. Moreover, suppose that increases in equity come about solely from the retention of earnings. In this case, growth in earnings (dividends) before tax would be given by:

$$g = br \qquad (11.5)$$

Where: b is the rate of earning retention

r is the return on assets (EBIT to total assets)

On an after-tax basis, 11.5 would become:

$$g = b(1-t)r \qquad (11.6)$$

This would follow because the growth in assets would be determined by b and the return on assets would be r. The after-tax return on assets would be $(1-t)r$. Multiplying $(1-t)r$ times the rate of growth of the asset base would produce the rate of growth of earnings. We may consider an example. Suppose International Copy Machines is a growth company. It now has the following income statement and balance sheet (simplified):

Income Statement Period $t=0$		Balance Sheet As of $t=0$	
Sales	$1,000,000	Assets	$1,000,000
Expenses	750,000		
EBIT	250,000	Bonds	– 0 –
Taxes	125,000	Equity	1,000,000
N.I.	$ 125,000		$1,000,000

In the steady state (all things remaining the same), the firm would have a return on its asset base (EBIT to total assets) of .25. The firm finances entirely by retaining earnings. If it elected to retain no earnings (pay out all earnings in dividends), the asset base could not grow, sales would not increase, and net income would remain the same over time (that is, the firm would *not* be a growth company). This can be verified through the use of equation 11.6.

$$g = (0) \, (1-.5) \, (.25) = 0$$

On the other hand, if the firm decided to retain, say, 40 percent of its earnings, the asset base would increase by $(.4) \, (125,000) = \$50,000$. The new asset base would be $1,050,000$. Given the extra assets, and assuming the return on investment continued at .25, the new income statement generated in period $t = 1$ would be:

Income Statement
Period t=1

EBIT	$262,500*
Taxes	131,250
N.I.	$131,250

*(.25) ($1,050,000)

This would represent a growth in net income of $[(131,250 - 125,000)/125,000] = 5.0$ percent. Equation 11.6 would give us the same result:

$$g = (.4) \, (1-.5) \, (.25) = .05$$

Suppose the firm retained all its earnings. The growth rate would be:

$$g = (1.0) \, (1-.5) \, (.25) = .125$$

Growth and Leverage

Of course, to use equation 11.6 to determine corporate-earnings growth rates, it must be assumed: (1) that the firm finances entirely with retained earnings; and (2) that the tax rate and the rate of return on investment remain constant. Neither of these assumptions may hold in the real world, although this fact should not be terribly important. Assumption (1) can be relaxed easily enough, and a revised equation can be formulated for a firm that employs debt as well as equity finance. The revised equation is:[4]

$$g = [(1-t)(b)] [L(r-c) + r] \tag{11.7}$$

Where: L is the leverage ratio (debt to equity)
employed by the firm

c is the average coupon rate of interest paid on
corporate debt

The only difference between equations 11.7 and 11.6 is that any extra return on investment above the interest payments made to bondholders is shown to influence the stockholders' earnings growth rate. Thus, if International finances half with bonds and half with equity ($L = 1$), it would earn $(1 - t)r$ on the asset investment made possible by equity sources (for example, $.5 \times .25 = 12.5$ percent). If it retained b percent of its earnings, the growth produced by equity sources would be $b(1 - t)r$. If $b = .4$ (60 percent dividend payout), $g = .4 \times 12.5 = 5.0$ percent. Bond sales would produce another $(r - c)$ return on the assets financed with debt sources. If $c = 6$ percent, $r - c$ would be $.25 - .06 = .19$. Thus, the earnings growth resulting from debt finance would be $b(1 - t)L(r - c)$, or $(.4)(.5)(1)(.19) = 3.8$ percent. The total growth rate would be 5.0 percent (from equity sources) plus 3.8 percent (debt sources), or 8.8 percent. This example is presented numerically in Table 11.1.

Equation 11.7 can be used by the analyst to determine whether the firm is getting favorable or unfavorable leverage. If $r > c$, leverage would be favorable,

---

[4]This equation is developed in the appendix to this chapter. If it may be assumed that the tax rate, interest cost, and debt-equity ratio will be constant over time, then we may define $R = (1 - t) [L(r - c) + r]$ as the after-tax return on equity and, furthermore, equation 11.7 may be restated as $g = bR$. If we may further assume, as is often done in the case of regulated utilities, that earnings retained will earn at the required return on equity (i), then $R = i$. Solving equation 11.4, we obtain:

$$i = \frac{D}{P_0} + g$$

$$i = \frac{D}{P_0} + bR$$

$$i = \frac{(1 - b)E_0}{P_0} + bi$$

$$i - bi = (1 - b)\frac{E_0}{P_0}$$

$$(1 - b)i = (1 - b)\frac{E_0}{P_0}$$

$$i = E_0/P_0$$

Thus, in this special case, the inverse of the P/E ratio will provide the expected return on the stock.

TABLE 11.1

Growth and the Levered Firm

International Copy Machines
Balance Sheet
Beginning Period t=0

Assets	$1,000,000
Bonds (6%)	$ 500,000
Equity	500,000
	$1,000,000

International Copy Machines
Income Statement
For Period t=0

EBIT	$250,000
Interest	30,000
EBT	$220,000
Taxes	110,000
N.I.	$110,000
Dividends	66,000
Retained Earnings	$ 44,000

International Copy Machines
Sources and Uses of Funds
For Period t=0

Retained Earnings	$44,000
Bond Sale	44,000
	$88,000
Asset Purchases	$88,000

International Copy Machines
Balance Sheet
Beginning Period t=1

Assets	$1,088,000
Bonds (6%)	$ 544,000
Equity	544,000
	$1,088,000

International Copy Machines
Income Statement
For Period t=1

EBIT	$272,000*
Interest	32,640
EBT	$239,360
Taxes	119,680
N.I.	$119,680

*(.25 × 1,088,000)

Growth in Net Income

$$\frac{119,680 - 110,000}{110,000} = 8.8\%$$

and debt financing would improve the shareholders' net rate of return (net income to stockholders' equity) and earnings growth rate. If $r < c$, leverage would be unfavorable, and debt financing would reduce the return to shareholders and the earnings growth rate.[5] In the case of International (above), suppose $r = .05$ and $c = .08$. If the firm retained all its earnings, but had no bond finance, the after-tax growth rate would be:

$$g = (1)(.5)(.05) = .025$$

If the firm financed half with bonds and half with equity, however, the growth rate would be:

$$g = [(.5)(1)] \ [(1)(-.03) + (.05)]$$
$$= (.5)(.02)$$
$$= .01$$

Thus, the rate of growth would be reduced from 2.5 percent to 1.0 percent.

Although equation 11.7 is an improvement over equation 11.6 in that debt finance is included as a variable, it still harbors the assumptions of a constant rate of taxation and a constant rate of return on investment. To the extent that tax rates fall, it should be obvious that earnings growth rates should improve. Similarly, if better cost controls (margins) or improved sales-asset relationships (turnovers) can be effected, higher growth rates could be obtained. The analyst should be very careful to use existing EBIT/total asset ratios as a surrogate for return on investment *only* if that relationship is expected to hold in the future.[6] Otherwise, *pro forma* expected ratios should be used.

MERGERS AND GROWTH[7]

In many cases, it is possible for a company to grow and acquire assets over time by the acquisition of other firms.[8] The attractiveness of such an acquisition is a

---

[5] The optimal leverage position would not necessarily be where $c = r$. In fact, it will usually be the case that the firm will have an optimal capital structure where $c < r$. See Edward E. Williams, "Cost of Capital Functions and the Firm's Optimal Level of Gearing," *Journal of Business Finance*, Summer 1972, pp. 78–83.

[6] Equations 11.6 and 11.7 also assume that the only source of equity finance is the retention of earnings. Empirically, this is not a bad assumption because stock sales now account for only a negligible part of the total financing arranged by major U.S. corporations in any one year.

[7] Partially adapted from Findlay and Williams, *An Integrated Analysis for Managerial Finance* (Englewood Cliffs, N.J.: Prentice-Hall, Inc., 1970), pp. 230–36.

[8] See William W. Alberts, and Joel E. Segall, eds., *The Corporate Merger* (Chicago: University of Chicago Press, 1966).

function of the profitability of the assets (both tangible and intangible) to be acquired and the form and amount of payment to be made.

Mergers may occur for any number of reasons. Perhaps the oldest and strongest motivation is the simple desire to increase power over the market. The increased market power resulting from a merger may raise profits through "operating economies," such as bulk purchases, reciprocal purchases, advertising discounts, better channels of distribution (everything from more freight cars when needed to more shelf space), and better access to and bargaining position for external funds.[9] Merger also allows a firm to acquire large numbers of talented management and research personnel and at the same time to gain increased market power to sell whatever they produce. Galbraith goes so far as to suggest that modern corporations are willing to undertake risky research ventures because their control of the market will enable them to sell whatever results from the project.[10]

In other cases, merger may occur because the acquired company is a bargain; poor management, inadequate capital, stock market disfavor, a poor year, or other factors may reduce the price of the stock to the point that the firm is worth a great deal more than the cost of acquiring it. The acquired firm may have vast sums in the form of liquid assets, such that the acquiring firm could raise more money by merging with it than by selling securities on the market. It is further possible that the acquired firm would have tax-loss carry-forwards that could be used to reduce future tax liabilities of the merged company.

There are two remaining arguments for merger that must be examined rather closely. The first is diversification. If a firm is able to acquire other firms whose earnings do not correlate very closely with its own (coefficient of correlation less than +1, and the closer to -1 the better), the probability distribution for earnings of the new firm should show less dispersion (be less risky) than for the old firm. If one dollar of earnings for the merged firm is less risky, it should be discounted at a lower rate in imperfect markets. This would result in an increase in the price of the stock and shareholder well-being. The merger would thus serve a valid economic function. It should be pointed out, however, that such diversification could also be achieved by shareholders in their own portfolios.[11]

Much is written about the growth resulting from mergers. To the extent that the merged firms are able to interact and combine their talents to do things that neither could do before (the synergism or "2 + 2 = 5" effect), a valid

[9]The eventual goal of many large firms would seem to be complete autonomy from the requirements of the capital markets.

[10]J. K. Galbraith, *The New Industrial State* (Boston: Houghton Mifflin Company, 1967).

[11]See Chapter 16. In perfect markets, as shown in Chapter 17, the price effects of such a merger would be nil.

justification for the merger, and perhaps an increase in stock price, may exist. On the other hand, the merger of firms in totally different lines of business with no subsequent interaction may create value through diversification but not through real growth, although growth may appear to occur. Consider the following:

Ming-Trico-Vaugn is a conglomerate. It has 5 million shares outstanding and earns $6 per share. Because of MTV's growth characteristics, it sells at 40 times current earnings ($240 per share). The Stagnant Steel Co. has 4 million shares outstanding and earns $2 per share. Because of its poor growth prospects and inherent risk, the market will only pay 10 times current earnings ($20) for Stagnant stock. MTV has proposed a merger with Stagnant. No changes will take place in Stagnant's operations and the current management will remain intact. The merger will merely make Stagnant one of a growing list of companies controlled by MTV. A merger offer has been tendered giving Stagnant holders one new MTV share for each ten Stagnant shares outstanding. Because this amounts to an offer of $240 for $200, virtually every Stagnant shareholder has accepted the proposal.

Just after the merger, the chairman of MTV has his accountants prepare a new consolidated statement of income. In order to purchase Stagnant, 400,000 additional MTV shares have been issued. Thus, the new capitalization of the company is 5,400,000 shares. Upon consolidating the net income of the two firms, the accountants report a revised total income of:

$$(6.00) \ (5,000,000) + (2.00) \ (4,000,000) = \$38,000,000$$

Dividing this figure by the new capitalization of 5,400,000 shares produces an earnings per share of:

$$(\$38,000,000/5,400,000) = \$7.04$$

Thus, without changing operations at all, MTV has been able to show a fantastic increase in earnings of $[(7.04 - 6.00/(6.00)] = 17.3$ percent!

Of course, an efficient and rational market would realize that the above transactions were merely financial, and unless the merger reduced the riskiness of MTV there should be no increase in the price of MTV shares. In fact, because MTV paid a premium of 20 percent above the value of Stagnant shares, it might be argued that the price of MTV shares should *fall*. Unfortunately, there is considerable empirical evidence that this has not been what has happened (at least in the short run).

Suppose that MTV and Stagnant had perfectly positive (+1) earnings correlations. Suppose further that rational markets prevailed and MTV stock did not increase after the "new" earnings per share had been announced. What would have happened to the earnings multiplier (P/E) of MTV stock?

$$\$240/\$7.04 \simeq 34 \text{ times}$$

Thus, the multiple would have fallen from 40X to 34X. Of course, this would be quite rational, because the merged company would be riskier than the premerger MTV (Stagnant was riskier than MTV) and the future earnings growth rate from operations would be reduced (Stagnant had very poor earnings growth prospects).

In a less "efficient" market, the old multiple of 40X might hold (or even a higher one given the new "growth" in earnings). If this were the case, MTV common would advance to:

$$(40) \; (\$7.04) = \$281.60$$

Assume that this did indeed happen, and MTV set about to find yet another merger partner. Suppose it found a company, call it Stagnant II, and consummated a merger on the same terms as with Stagnant I. What would be the effect on MTV earnings?

a. Price of Stagnant II stock: $20

b. Price markup given to effect merger: 20 percent

c. Price offer to Stagnant II: $24

d. Price of MTV stock: $281.60

e. Number of MTV shares given for each Stagnant II share: $24.00/281.60 = .085$

f. Number of new MTV shares issued: $(.085) \; (4,000,000) = 340,000$

g. New total earnings: $38 million + $8 million = $46 million

h. New earnings per share: $46,000,000/5,740,000 = \$8.01$

i. Earnings growth: $[(8.01 - 7.04)/(7.04)] = 13.8$ percent

We see in this example how it is possible to combine companies without growth in order to acquire a "growth" company. As indicated in the discussion above, a company must find ever-larger merger partners if the apparent growth rate is not to decline. In addition, the market must be willing to assign a constant P/E ratio to earnings of ever-declining quality. On the other hand, if companies can be bought with convertible securities, warrants, or other kinds of "funny money," the apparent growth rate can be made even more spectacular.

The analyst should be aware of the difference between growth achieved from improved operations and growth induced from merger. Although the theoretical distinction between buying individual assets to increase output (and hopefully profits) and purchasing other firms to accomplish the same ends are not great, the practical differences may be enormous. Purely financial transactions (such as those illustrated in the example above) should be viewed with suspicion by the analyst unless there are clear-cut, real economic benefits accruing to the merging enterprise. Operating economies, improved market position, better managerial talent, and so on are all justifiable grounds for a merger. Unfortunately, these elements have not always been ingredients in the business combinations of recent years.

AFTER-TAX RATES OF RETURN AND GROWTH

The after-tax return on an investment in common stock will depend on the tax position of the investor and the taxation climate in which he finds himself. For growth stocks, capital-gains taxation becomes relatively more important than taxes levied on dividends. Employing the symbols of equation 10.8, the after-tax dividend received in each period t is $(1 - m_t)D_t$ where m_t is the marginal income tax bracket of the investor in period t. The capital gain secured by the investor is simply $P_n - P_0$. His tax on the gain is $k_n(P_n - P_0)$ where k_n is the capital-gains tax rate the investor is subject to at period n. His after-tax capital flow is thus: $P_n - [(k_n)(P_n - P_0)]$. His after-tax return would be given by i in the following equation.

$$P_0 = \sum_{t=0}^{n} \frac{(1-m_t)D_t}{(1+i)^t} + \frac{P_n - [k_n (P_n - P_0)]}{(1+i)^n} \qquad (11.8)$$

An investor purchases a stock that pays a dividend of two dollars per year. He plans to hold the stock for five years. The stock now sells at $18X$ earnings of five dollars per share. It is expected that this multiple will apply in five years when EPS will be six dollars. The after-tax dividend return that the investor would get in periods $t = 1$ through $t = 5$ (the dividend in $t = 0$ has just been paid) depends upon his marginal tax bracket. If this is 40 percent, his after-tax return would be:

$$(1-.4)(\$2) = \$1.20$$

If the investor pays capital gains taxes at one-half his marginal rate, his after-tax capital flow would be:

$$\$108 - [(.2)(108-90)] = \$104.40$$

The investor's after-tax rate of return would be:

at 5 percent,	(4.329) (1.20)	= $ 5.19
	(.784) (104.40) =	81.85
		$87.04
at 4 percent,	(4.452) (1.20)	= $ 5.34
	(.822) (104.40) =	85.82
		$91.16

∴ about 4.3 percent

COMMON STOCK RISK ANALYSIS

In addition to the expected return estimate that the analyst has made, he needs to have some basic measure of the riskiness of the security he is analyzing.[12] Many analysts rely entirely on agency ratings to determine risk, and others use ratio analysis to discern the overall liquidity, profitability, leverage, and so on of the firm whose common stock is being considered. These methods are useful, but by themselves are inadequate. If the analyst has prepared probability distributions in estimating the expected return from the investment, he may use these distributions to determine the deviations around the expected values. A simple example will serve to explain. Suppose an analyst has specified a probability distribution for the sales of the Ace Co. He has also determined a conditional distribution of costs given each level of sales.[13] Finally, he has calculated an overall distribution of net income and dividend payments.

Sales (in millions)	Total Expenses	Net Income
100 (.3)	70 (.2)	30 (.06)
	80 (.6)	20 (.18)
	90 (.2)	10 (.06)
90 (.5)	65 (.1)	25 (.05)
	75 (.7)	15 (.35)
	85 (.2)	5 (.10)
80 (.2)	60 (.2)	20 (.04)
	70 (.5)	10 (.10)
	80 (.3)	0 (.06)

If the firm has 10 million shares outstanding, the data may be grouped into a distribution of EPS:

EPS	Probability
$3.00	.06
2.50	.05
2.00	.22
1.50	.35
1.00	.16
.50	.10
.00	.06
	1.00

[12] In the material to follow, we shall be attempting to measure the "absolute" or "total" risk associated with a common stock. Nevertheless, the important risk variable is the "nondiversifiable" or "systematic" element — that risk that cannot be diversified away in an efficient portfolio. When we begin constructing optimal portfolios in Chapter 16, the reader will observe that there are two parameters required for evaluation: (1) the expected return from holding a security; and (2) the covariances among returns of all securities in the portfolio. At this point, however, it should be noted that the variance is required before covariances may be estimated.

[13] A more complicated set of conditional probability distributions could be prepared to take into account various categories of expenses.

From this, the analyst may construct a dividend payment distribution. Suppose he believes that management will pay a maximum dividend of two dollars but will distribute less if earnings are low. Within the range of EPS from one dollar to two dollars, he believes a .75 payout will take place. Below earnings of one dollar, no dividend will be paid. The DPS distribution would be:

DPS	Probability
$2.00	.11
1.50	.22
1.12½	.35
.75	.16
.00	.16
	1.00

The expected value of EPS and DPS and their standard deviations may be computed. They equal:

	EPS	DPS
μ =	$1.50	$1.06
σ =	.72	.58

The analyst may repeat the above process for each year in the anticipated holding period of the security. Suppose he obtained the following:

Year	EPS	DPS
1	μ = $1.50	$1.06
	σ = .72	.58
2	μ = 1.80	1.20
	σ = .85	.64
3	μ = 2.00	1.40
	σ = .95	.76

Thus, he would have expected values and deviations for EPS and DPS over the three-year holding period. He could next determine a distribution of multiples to get the expected price in three years. Assume he forecasts the following:

P/E Multiple	Probability
10X	.6
12X	.4

This distribution could be combined with the earnings distribution for year three to obtain a distribution of prices. Ideally, each multiple should be combined with each EPS to get the distribution. If the EPS distribution were

EPS	Probability
$3.50	.2
2.00	.6
.50	.2

and if it were assumed that the level of multiple was independent from the forecasted EPS (an assumption that may not hold), the price distribution would be:

Multiple	X	EPS	=	Price
		$3.50 (.2)		$35.00 (.12)
10X (.6)		2.00 (.6)		20.00 (.36)
		.50 (.2)		5.00 (.12)
		3.50 (.2)		42.00 (.08)
10X (.4)		2.00 (.6)		24.00 (.24)
12		.50 (.2)		6.00 (.08)

Grouping the data:

Price	Probability
$42.00	.08
35.00	.12
24.00	.24
20.00	.36
6.00	.08
5.00	.12
	1.00

The expected price and its standard deviation would be: $\mu = \$21.60$, $\sigma = \$10.50$.

In the example presented above, all the separate return distributions were assumed to be independent. Most likely, they will not be. Generally, if a firm does poorly in the early years of an investment holding period, it will continue to do poorly. Thus, the dividend distributions of later years may well depend upon the outcomes in previous years. Furthermore, the EPS distribution in the terminal year will almost always be correlated with the dividend distribution of that year. Finally, the value of the P/E multiple in the terminal year will most likely be influenced by the earnings and dividend performance in earlier years. Thus, the analyst should attempt to construct conditional probabilities, where appropriate, for all the distributions involved.

Suppose an analyst has projected the following distributions for a stock that is to be held for two years:

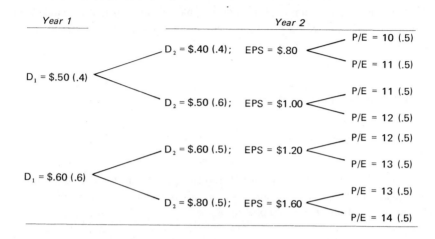

Year 1	Year 2	

Eight outcomes (with associated probabilities) would be possible:

	D_1	D_2	P_n	Prob.
a.	$.50	$.40	$ 8.00	.08
b.	.50	.40	8.80	.08
c.	.50	.50	11.00	.12
d.	.50	.50	12.00	.12
e.	.60	.60	14.40	.15
f.	.60	.60	15.60	.15
g.	.60	.80	20.80	.15
h.	.60	.80	22.40	.15
				1.00

The yield from each combination (a–h) can be computed, given the current market price of the security, which is assumed to be $8, and placed in a probability distribution.

Combination	Yield	Probability
a	5.6%	.08
b	10.4	.08
c	23.1	.12
d	28.2	.12
e	40.7	.15
f	46.1	.15
g	68.1	.15
h	74.1	.15

The expected yield from this distribution is 41.8 percent with a standard deviation of 22.6 percent.

For situations where more outcomes are designated (and where the time span is longer) many combinations are possible. In these instances, hand calculation becomes exceedingly tedious, and again the analyst must rely on the computer to do the computational work.

RISK MEASURES FOR COMMON STOCK RETURNS

The Independent Case

Once the analyst has specified his DPS and terminal price distributions for each year, he may compute an overall return-risk measure for the equity under investigation. If it is assumed that all distributions are independent, the following equations may be employed:[14]

$$V_\mu = \sum_{t=0}^{n} \frac{\bar{D}_t}{(1+i)^t} + \frac{\bar{P}_n}{(1+i)^n} \tag{11.9}$$

and,

$$\sigma = \sqrt{\sum_{t=0}^{n} \frac{(\bar{D}_t^\sigma)^2}{(1+i)^{2t}} + \frac{(\bar{P}_n^\sigma)^2}{(1+i)^{2n}}} \tag{11.10}$$

Where: V_μ is the present value of the dividend stream and terminal selling price.

$\bar{D}_t$ is the expected dividend in period t.

$\bar{P}_n$ is the expected terminal price at period n.

i is the rate of return from the investment.

σ is the overall standard deviation around the present value.

D_t^σ is the standard deviation of dividends in period t.

P_n^σ is the standard deviation around the expected market price at period n.

[14]See Frederick S. Hillier, "The Derivation of Probabilistic Information for the Evaluation of Risky Investments," *Management Science*, April 1963, pp. 443–57.

Referring back to the first example constructed in the previous section (the Ace Co.), we may solve for V_μ and σ. Suppose an investor wished to determine the probability of earning at least 10 percent on the purchase of the stock. The present value of his projected return stream would be:

$$V_\mu = \frac{(1.06)}{(1.10)^1} + \frac{(1.20)}{(1.10)^2} + \frac{(1.40)}{(1.10)^3} + \frac{(21.60)}{(1.10)^3} = \$19.13$$

If the current market price of the stock were 19 1/8, the investor would expect to obtain the 10 percent return. If the current market price were lower, he would expect a larger return. If it were higher, he would expect a lower return.

The risk from purchasing the stock would be:

$$\sigma = \sqrt{\frac{(.58)^2}{(1+.10)^2} + \frac{(.64)^2}{(1+.10)^4} + \frac{(.76)^2}{(1+.10)^6} + \frac{(10.50)^2}{(1+.10)^6}}$$

$$= \$7.94$$

If the stock were selling at $11.19 (that is, $19.13 - $7.94) and the underlying distributions were normal, the investor would consult table C.5 (see Appendix C) to determine the probability that he would earn less than 10 percent:

$$P(X|X \leqslant V_\mu - 1\sigma) \approx .16$$

The Perfectly Correlated Case

At the opposite extreme from having completely independent flows is the case of perfectly correlated returns. In this instance, any deviation from the mean value of a flow in any particular period would be matched by deviations in all other periods in exactly the same manner. The present value of the dividend stream and terminal selling price would be the same as in the independence case (equation 11.9), but the overall standard deviation around the present value would be given by:

$$\sigma = \sum_{t=0}^{n} \frac{D_t^\sigma}{(1+i)^t} + \frac{P_n^\sigma}{(1+i)^n} \qquad (11.11)$$

If the flows in the above example were perfectly correlated, the risk from purchasing the stock would be:

$$\sigma = \frac{.58}{(1+.10)^1} + \frac{.64}{(1+.10)^2} + \frac{.76}{(1+.10)^3} + \frac{10.50}{(1+.10)^3}$$

$$= \$9.52$$

Not surprisingly, the overall risk is greater when returns are perfectly correlated than when returns are independent.

The Mixed Case

In the real world, it will be unusual for returns to be either perfectly correlated or independent. A more likely situation would be a mixture of the two with parts of the return stream being independent and other parts being perfectly correlated. In this more realistic case, the present value of the stream would still be given by equation 11.9, but the overall standard deviation would be much more complex:[15]

$$\sigma = \sqrt{\left(\sum_{t=0}^{n} \frac{(D_t^\sigma)^2}{(1+i)^{2t}} + \frac{(P_n^\sigma)^2}{(1+i)^{2n}}\right) + \sum_{k=1}^{m} \left(\left[\sum_{t=0}^{n} \frac{(D_t^\sigma)^{(k)}}{(1+i)^t}\right] + \frac{(P_n^\sigma)^{(k)}}{(1+i)^n}\right)^2} \qquad (11.12)$$

where D_t^σ and P_n^σ are the dividend-price standard deviations for the independent portion of the flow returns; and $(D_t^\sigma)^k$ and $(P_n^\sigma)^k$ are the dividend-price standard deviations for stream k of a perfectly correlated portion of the flow returns.

Reconsidering our example, suppose it can be determined that the dividend stream is perfectly correlated. That is, poor corporate performance in period $t = 1$ that results in a lower dividend payment than the expected value would also mean poor performance in period $t = 2$ and $t = 3$. Because the stock price at period $t = 3$ depends on future dividends (beyond $t = 3$), and these dividends would also be influenced by the poor performance of earlier years, at least part of the variation in stock price for $t = 3$ would be perfectly correlated with the dividend-stream variations. Nevertheless, there may be other factors influencing stock prices (such as the overall level of interest rates or simply random events) so that part of the variation in stock price is also independent. Assume that we can determine that about 80 percent of the stock price variation in period $t = 3$ is traceable to the riskiness of the dividend stream, and 20 percent results from other (independent) factors. Given this information, we could reformulate equation 11.12 to get the overall deviation for the investment:

$$\sigma = \sqrt{\frac{(P_3^\sigma)^2}{(1+.10)^6} + \left(\sum_{t=1}^{3} \frac{(D_t^\sigma)^{(1)}}{(1+.10)^t} + \frac{(P_3^\sigma)^{(1)}}{(1+.10)^3}\right)^2}$$

$$= \sqrt{(2.10)^2(.564) + [(.58)(.909) + (.64)(.826) + (.76)(.751) + (8.40)(.751)]^2}$$

$$= \$8.09$$

---

[15] *Ibid.*

Notice that the overall riskiness of the mixed case lies between the extremes of independence and perfect correlation.

Determining a Distribution of Rates of Return

The above formulations can also be used to generate a distribution of rates of return. The following steps should be employed:

1. Compute V_μ and σ for an initial value of i.

2. Determine the number of standard deviations that would equalize the present price of the stock and V_μ (that is, solve $V_\mu + Z\sigma = P_0$ for Z).

3. Find $P(X \mid X \leq V_\mu + Z\sigma)$ from table C.5. This will be the probability that V_μ will be less than the present price of the stock at the given i and is, in turn, the probability that the rate of return will be less than i.

4. Plot the probability determined above on a cumulative probability distribution.

5. Iterate steps 1–4 above varying i in order to generate a complete cumulative probability distribution.

6. Convert the cumulative distribution to a discrete probability distribution of rates of return.

7. For a two-parameter description, the fiftieth percentile of the cumulative probability distribution will provide an estimate of the mean (expected) rate of return. Dividing the interquartile range by 1.35 will provide an estimate of σ.

Thus, the analyst would have a percentage rate of return expected from the purchase of a stock and the standard deviation around that percentage. There are other approaches to the problem of generating μ and σ statistics of rates of return. The next section examines one such method in detail.

SIMULATION AND RISK EVALUATION

When the analyst has specified distributions with many more possible outcomes than we have dealt with above, manual calculations are not feasible and the computer must be employed. It is, of course, possible to attempt a deterministic solution on a computer that would merely compute a probability distribution of returns employing all observations from all distributions. Greater flexibility at less cost can usually be obtained by employing a Monte Carlo simulation.[16] This method often provides an approximate solution when a deterministic solution is too expensive by employing techniques of random sampling from the distributions of variables.

Monte Carlo simulation can perhaps best be explained by the case in which all variables are assumed to be independent of each other. The steps are as follows:

1. Determine a probability distribution for each variable (see Figure 11-1).

2. Transform any continuous distributions into discrete distributions, with each discrete interval representing 1 percent (or .1 percent or some other convenient interval) of the distribution.

3. Determine the midpoint of each interval in each discrete distribution.

4. Assign a number from 1 to n (where n represents the number of intervals into which each distribution was divided) to each interval. For example, if a distribution were divided into 100 intervals, the first percentile would be assigned the number 1, the second would be assigned 2, and the hundredth, 00.

5. The distribution of returns should also be divided into intervals (say, whole percentages) and counters defined (for example, .5 percent $\leqslant i_1 < 1.5$ percent; 1.5 percent $\leqslant i_2 < 2.5$ percent, and so on) which are initialized at zero (that is $i_1 = i_2 = \ldots i_n = 0$).

6. Generate from the computer, or select from a table, a two-digit (if fewer than 101 intervals are employed) random number for the first independent distribution (which would be D_1 in Figure 11-1).

7. Determine the interval on the distribution that was assigned a number corresponding to the random number generated and select the midpoint.

8. Repeat steps 6 and 7 for the remaining distributions such that there is one observation for each variable.

9. Compute the rate of return for this set of observations. For the example given, this would require inputing the simulated variables to the formula:

$$P_0 = \sum_{t=1}^{6} \frac{D_t}{(1+i)^t} + \frac{P_6}{(1+i)^6}$$

and solving for i.

10. The i computed in step 9 would then be assigned to the appropriate interval in the return distribution and the counter for that interval would be incremented by one. For example, if the first computation yielded an $i = 5.7$

---

[16]Cf. David B. Hertz, "Risk Analysis in Capital Investment," *Harvard Business Review*, January–February 1964, pp. 95–106; and Hertz, "Investment Policies that Pay Off," *Harvard Business Review*, January–February 1968, pp. 96–108.

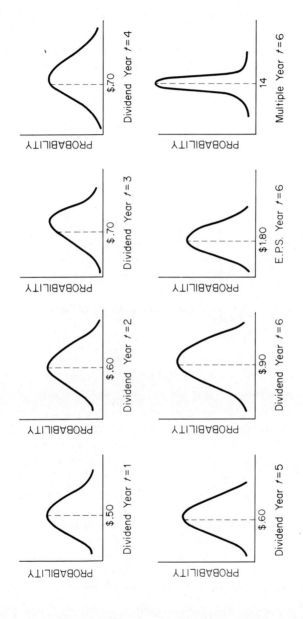

Figure 11-1 Pre-Simulated Independent Probability Distributions of Dividend Payments, Terminal Year E.P.S., and Terminal Year Multiples

percent, then i_6 would be incremented and, at the end of the first iteration, $i_{1-5} = i_{7-n} = 0$ and $i_6 = 1$.

11. Repeat steps 6-10 a large number of (N) times in order to generate a frequency distribution of i's.

12. Each counter can then be normalized to provide a probability distribution [for example, $i_1/N = P(i|.5$ percent $\leqslant i < 1.5$ percent)], as in Figure 11-2.[17]

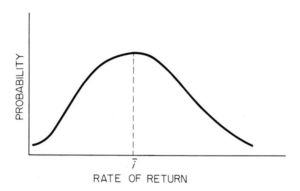

Figure 11-2   Simulated Probability Distribution of Rates of Return

13. From this distribution, μ_i, σ_i, or any other desired statistic may be computed. The larger N is, the better will be the resulting estimate (as in any random sampling situation).

Dependent relationships among variables may also be simulated. If two variables are perfectly correlated (positively or negatively) with each other, the distributions may simply be combined and simulated as one variable; the same result is obtained if the same random number is used for both distributions on each iteration. Partial dependence is somewhat more troublesome, but one possible solution is illustrated in Figure 11-3. Here the interval from which the value for the first variable is selected on a given iteration determines the distribution used to select the value for the second variable. For example, if a random number between 1 and 30 is selected for variable U in Figure 11-3 on a given iteration (that is, a value from the lowest 30 percent of possible outcomes), then the random number selected for variable V will be applied to distribution V_1.

[17]Although figure 11-2 is actually a discrete distribution of one hundred interval values, it is drawn as being approximately continuous.

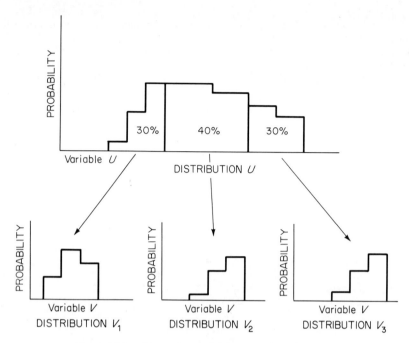

Figure 11-3   Simulation with Semi-Dependent Variables

PROBLEMS

1. Supergrow, Ltd., is expected to pay no dividends for ten years. From year eleven and thereafter, the firm is expected to pay three dollars per share annually.

a. If investors require a 12 percent return for holding Supergrow, what price pattern would the stock evidence?

b. What pattern would prevail if the firm paid a dividend of one dollar for years one to five, two dollars for six to ten, and three dollars thereafter?

c. What pattern would prevail if the firm paid three dollars throughout?

2. The Uni Corp. currently has the ability to pay a dividend of two dollars per year forever. By retaining all earnings for ten years, however, a dividend of ten dollars per year forever could be paid beginning in year eleven. If Uni shareholders require a 15 percent return, what would be the current price of the stock under each of the policies?

3. A firm pays a dividend of one dollar per share. The market price of the firm's shares is 20, and the market expects dividends to grow by 10 percent annually. What return would investors obtain from purchasing this security, assuming a constant future dividend payout ratio and P/E multiple?

4. Equatoroid Camera, Ltd., is a growth company. The firm is primarily financed by retained earnings, pays 50 percent of earnings in taxes, and earns 25 percent on its asset investment. If the firm retains 80 percent of its earnings, what is its rate of growth?

5. Suppose Equatoroid finances with debt as well as equity. The firm tries to maintain a debt-equity ratio of .4. What would its growth rate be if it paid bondholders a rate of 6 percent?

6. A simplified income statement and balance sheet for Dynamic Sinculator is given below:

Income Statement			Balance Sheet	
Revenues	$100,000,000		Assets	$50,000,000
Expenses	59,000,000			
EBIT	41,000,000		Bonds	$20,000,000
Interest	1,000,000		Net worth	30,000,000
EBT	40,000,000			$50,000,000
Taxes	20,000,000			
N.I.	20,000,000			
Dividends	4,000,000			
R.E.	$ 16,000,000			

Other data:

Market price per common share	80
Number of shares outstanding	5 million

a. Compute the following relationships:
   (1) EBIT/Total assets
   (2) Debt/Equity
   (3) Retention rate
   (4) Average tax rate
   (5) EPS
   (6) DPS
   (7) P/E multiple
   (8) Dividend yield
   (9) Coupon rate on bonds

b. Assuming that all the relationships are constant in the future, determine the dividend growth rate for Dynamic Sinculator.

c. What would the earnings growth rate be? The rate of growth in the share price?

d. What would the annual growth in assets be?

e. What would the growth in sales be, given a constant total-asset turnover?

f. What return would investors expect from a purchase of Dynamic, given the above assumptions?

g. Would this sort of return be a feasible expectation? What difficulties might arise?

7. In a perfect market, what should be the price of MTV shares (example, pages 209-10) after the purchase of Stagnant I? of Stagnant II?

8. International Transportation and Telecommunication has 10 million shares outstanding and earns $2 per share. As a "growth" conglomerate, the firm's stock sells at 50 times current earnings. The Sinking Offshore Shipping Co. has 5 million shares outstanding and sells at $10 per share based on current EPS of $1. International plans to merger with S.O.S. by offering shares in the ratio of current market prices.

a. What is the ratio of exchange of International shares for S.O.S. shares?

b. How many International shares would be outstanding after the merger?

c. What will be the new International EPS?

d. What apparent "growth" has taken place?

e. Given the fact that International is heavily engaged in transportation, what diversification effects might the merger make possible?

f. Suppose the merged company were riskier than the premerger International. What price and P/E multiple might an efficient market pay for the merged company's stock?

g. Suppose the market retained the old P/E multiple that existed for premerger International. What would the new market price of the merged company be?

h. Trace the "growth effect" if International could find yet another Sinking Offshore Shipping Co.

9. An investor is in the 50 percent marginal income tax bracket. He pays capital gains taxes at a rate of 25 percent. He is considering the purchase of a stock that now sells at $100 per share. The stock has an EPS of $4, which should grow by 10 percent compounded annually. The stock pays a dividend of $1, which should be increased to $1.20 after two years and to $1.50 for the fifth year of holding. The investor believes the current P/E multiple will prevail in five years when he plans to sell the stock. If the investor wants to earn at least 6 percent on his investment *after taxes,* should he purchase the shares?

10. An analyst has prepared the following sets of probability distributions for a stock (sales and costs in millions):

	Years 1–2	Year 3
Sales	25 (.4)	30 (.3)
	30 (.6)	40 (.7)
Costs	.6 of Sales (.5)	.6 of Sales (.5)
	.7 of Sales (.5)	.7 of Sales (.5)

a. Prepare net income and EPS distributions for the three years. The firm has 10 million shares outstanding.

b. The analyst expects the firm to pay out one third of earnings in dividends. Determine the expected dividend and its standard deviation for years 1–3.

c. The following P/E multiple distribution is anticipated by the analyst for year 3.

P/E Multiple	Probability
16X	.4
18X	.6

Determine the distribution of market prices for year 3.

d. Compute the expected market price and standard deviation for year 3.

e. Suppose an investor wished to earn 20 percent on this stock. What maximum price would he pay today, given the expected values of the dividend and terminal price distributions?

f. Assume the stock currently sells at the price to yield 20 percent. Determine the standard deviation of the present-value price distribution if the returns are assumed to be independent. Determine overall σ assuming the returns are perfectly correlated.

g. Assume the stock sells at $16. What is the probability that a return below 20 percent will be earned?

11. An investor expects the following flows from an investment:

Year	Dividend	Terminal Selling Price
1	$\mu = \$10, \sigma = \$1$	
2	$\mu = 10, \sigma = 1$	
3	$\mu = 10, \sigma = 1$	
4	$\mu = 10, \sigma = 1$	
5	$\mu = 10, \sigma = 1$	$\mu = \$100, \sigma = \$10$

a. For $i = 8$ percent, what is the present value of the flows, assuming the distributions are independent?

b. What is standard deviation of the distribution?

c. If the current price of the security is $94, what is the probability that the investor will earn less than 8 percent?

12. An analyst has simulated the future performance of a security. He has obtained a distribution with $\mu_i = 12$ percent and $\sigma = 4$ percent.

a. If the distribution is approximately normal, what is the probability that the investment will lose money?

b. What is the probability that the return will be 12 percent or greater?

c. What is the probability that the return will exceed 20 percent?

d. Suppose the distribution of returns for the security were positively skewed. Might this influence the analyst's judgment about the riskiness of the security? What if it were negatively skewed? Can you suggest a better measure of risk in these instances?

COMPREHENSIVE CASE

An analyst has prepared the following flow diagram for dividends, terminal EPS, and terminal multiple for the Random Corp. common shares:

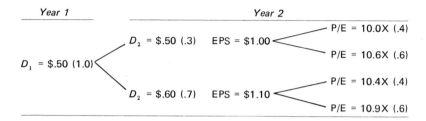

1. What possible outcomes (and associated probabilities) are present?

2. What is the yield for each outcome if the current price of the stock is $10?

3. Specify the probability distribution of yields. What is the mean of the distribution? The variance? The standard deviation?

4. Describe the symmetry of the distribution.

5. What is the semivariance of the distribution? Can any argument be made for using the semivariance as a measure of risk rather than the standard deviation (or variance)?

APPENDIX

Growth-Rate Equations for the Levered Firm[18]

This appendix develops equation 11.7, which appears in the text on page 205. If a firm had debt as well as equity in its structure according to some optimal (or at least constant) combination, asset growth would result from earnings retention (and possibly stock sales, which we shall ignore) and bond flotations. Thus, asset growth would be dependent upon b (the retention rate) and the relationship between debt (B) and equity (S). We shall assume that earning assets (A) equal debt plus equity, that is,

$$A = B + S \qquad (11A.1)$$

If the firm earns r on its asset base, then earnings before interest and taxes (EBIT) would be:

$$EBIT = rA \qquad (11A.2)$$

[18]The arguments in this appendix were developed by Edward E. Williams and J. J. Seneca, "Dividend Policy, Growth, and Retention Rates: U.S. Public Utilities 1958–1967," *Public Utilities Fortnightly*, March 15, 1973, pp. 23–27.

From EBIT, interest (c) is paid to bondholders, leaving for common shareholders before taxes:

$$E_b = \text{EBIT} - cB \qquad (11A.3)$$

After-tax earnings are given by:

$$E = (1 - t)(\text{EBIT} - cB) \qquad (11A.4)$$

If dividends (D) are paid to shareholders, $E-D$ is left to the firm for reinvestment in assets.
    Now, we know that asset growth is:

$$\Delta A = \Delta B + \Delta S \qquad (11A.5)$$

Furthermore, retaining earnings will increase S such that:

$$\Delta S = E - D \qquad (11A.6)$$

If there is an optimal relationship (L) between the firm's debt and equity,

$$\Delta B = L \Delta S \qquad (11A.7)$$

We wish to know by how much earnings (E) will grow if earnings are retained and bonds are sold to maintain an optimal B/S combination. Let the growth rate in earnings be:

$$g = \Delta E/E \qquad (11A.8)$$

We have established the relationship between E and EBIT, thus:

$$\Delta E = (1-t)(\Delta \text{EBIT} - c\Delta B) \qquad (11A.9)$$

Furthermore, we know from 11A.2 that EBIT is simply the return on assets times the asset base. Extra EBIT resulting from expanding the asset base would thus be:

$$\Delta \text{EBIT} = r\Delta A \qquad (11A.10)$$

Now, if we substitute (11A.10) into (11A.9), we find:

$$\Delta E = [(1-t)] \, [(r\Delta A)-(c\Delta B)] \qquad (11A.11)$$

We know ΔA from 11A.5. Thus, by substituting that equation into 11A.11, we find:

$$\Delta E = [(1-t)] \ [r(\Delta B+\Delta S) - c\Delta B] \qquad (11A.12)$$

This equation may be expanded,

$$\Delta E = [(1-t)] \ [r\Delta B + r\Delta S - c\Delta B] \qquad (11A.13)$$

Rewriting,

$$\Delta E = [(1-t)] \ [r\Delta B - c\Delta B + r\Delta S] \qquad (11A.14)$$

Factoring within the second term of the right-hand member of the expression, we find:

$$\Delta E = [(1-t)] \ [(r-c)(\Delta B) + (r\Delta S)] \qquad (11A.15)$$

We know ΔB from equation 11A.7 and ΔS from 11A.6. Substituting these equations into 11A.15, we find:

$$\Delta E = [(1-t)] \ [(r-c)L(E-D)+r(E-D)] \qquad (11A.16)$$

Factoring within the second term of the right-hand member of the expression once again, we find:

$$\Delta E = [(1-t)] \ [(E-D)] \ [(r-c)L+r] \qquad (11A.17)$$

Thus, the growth rate (equation 11A.8) would be:

$$g = \Delta E/E = \frac{[(1-t)] \ [(E-D)] \ [L(r-c)+r]}{E} \qquad (11A.18)$$

which may also be written as:

$$g = \left[(1-t)\right] \left[(1-\frac{D}{E})\right] \left[L(r-c)+r\right] \qquad (11A.19)$$

Because b equals $(1 - D/E)$, we can simplify to produce:

$$g = [(1-t)(b)] \ [L(r-c)+r] \qquad (11A.20)$$

which is also equation 11.7 in the text.

REFERENCES

Alberts, William W., and Joel E. Segall, eds., *The Corporate Merger.* Chicago: University of Chicago Press, 1966.

Baumol, W., and B. Malkiel, "The Firm's Optimal Debt-Equity Combination and the Cost of Capital," *Quarterly Journal of Economics,* November 1967, pp. 547-78.

Baxter, N., "Leverage, Risk of Ruin, and the Cost of Capital," *Journal of Finance,* September 1967, pp. 395-404.

Beranek, W., *The Effects of Leverage on the Market Value of Common Stocks.* Madison: Bureau of Business Research and Service, Univ. of Wisconsin, 1964.

Brigham, E., and M. Gordon, "Leverage, Dividend Policy, and the Cost of Capital," *Journal of Finance,* March 1968, pp. 85-103.

Dellenbarger, Lynn E., *Common Stocks Valuation in Industrial Mergers.* Gainesville: University of Florida Press, 1966.

Durand, David, "Growth Stocks and the Petersburg Paradox," *Journal of Finance,* September 1957, pp. 348-63.

Findlay, M. C., and E. E. Williams, *An Integrated Analysis for Managerial Finance,* Chap. 18. Englewood Cliffs, N.J.: Prentice-Hall, Inc., 1970.

―――, "Capital Allocation and the Nature of Ownership Equities," *Financial Management,* Summer 1972, pp. 68-76.

―――, "Toward a More ⟨Adequate Debt Service Measure," Paper delivered before the Financial Management Association, San Antonio, October 1972.

Galbraith, J. K., *The New Industrial State.* Boston: Houghton Mifflin Company, 1967.

Goudzwaard, M. B., "Conglomerate Mergers, Convertibles, and Cash Dividends," *Quarterly Review of Economics and Business,* Spring 1969, pp. 53-62.

Hertz, David, "Risk Analysis in Capital Investment," *Harvard Business Review,* January-February 1964, pp. 95-106.

―――, "Investment Policies that Pay Off," *Harvard Business Review,* January-February 1968, pp. 96-108.

Hillier, Frederick S., "The Derivation of Probabilistic Information for the Evaluation of Risky Investments," *Management Science,* April 1963, pp. 443-57.

Jaaskelainen, V., "Growth of Earnings and Dividend Distribution Policy," *Swedish Journal of Economics,* September 1967, pp. 184-95.

Lintner, J., "The Cost of Capital and Optimal Financing of Corporate Growth," *Journal of Finance,* May 1963, pp. 292-310.

―――, "Optimal Dividends and Corporate Growth under Uncertainty," *Quarterly Journal of Economics,* February 1964, pp. 49-95.

Little, I. M. D., "Higgledy Piggledy Growth," *Bulletin of the Oxford Institute of Statistics,* November 1962, pp. 387-412.

Miller, M., and F. Modigliani, "Dividend Policy, Growth, and the Valuation of Shares," *Journal of Business,* October 1961, pp. 411-33.

Modigliani, F., and M. Miller, "The Cost of Capital, Corporation Finance and the Theory of Investment," *American Economic Review,* June 1958, pp. 261-97.

Williams, Edward E., "Cost of Capital Functions and the Firm's Optimal Level of Gearing," *Journal of Business Finance,* Summer 1972, pp. 78-83.

————, and J. J. Seneca, "Dividend Policy, Growth, and Retention Rates: U.S. Public Utilities 1958-1967," *Public Utilities Fortnightly,* March 15, 1973, pp. 23-27.

Wright, F., I. Young, and A. Barton, "The Effect of Financial Structure on the Market Value of Companies," *Australian Economic Papers,* June 1966, pp. 21-34.

12

Common Stocks: Further Considerations

ASSET VALUES AND COMMON STOCK APPRAISAL

Throughout the previous discussion of common-stock returns, the focus was on the dividend-paying ability of the equity and its possible price appreciation. Under very special circumstances, however, the analyst may wish to consider assets as well as earnings in computing the yield equation. There are instances in which a substantial volume of assets may not produce a large future earnings stream. If it is possible that these assets will be transformed into another form of higher yielding asset, or if it is conceivable that the assets will be distributed to stockholders, then the value of such assets should be assessed.[1]

Firms that maintain large cash balances or that hold substantial amounts of liquid securities will often show a poor earnings record. If it appears possible that the liquidity of these firms will be reduced through the purchase of earning assets, the analyst should take this into account in projecting the future earnings stream for the firm. Also, if it is possible that the firm will pay a liquidating (or partially liquidating) cash dividend to shareholders, the amount of this distribution should be included in the analyst's yield equation. If a firm maintains its liquidity at the expense of earning assets and it appears that none of this surplus liquidity will be distributed to shareholders, the analyst should

[1]See B. Graham *et al., Security Analysis*, 4th ed. (New York: McGraw-Hill Book Company, 1962), Chap. 41.

not consider the extra liquidity in evaluation (except to the extent that substantial liquidity may reduce the riskiness of the firm).[2]

Financial companies (banks, savings and loan associations, insurance companies, and so on) frequently hold large volumes of liquid assets (cash, marketable securities). On occasion, a financial company will have a poor earnings record for this reason. Such firms offer an opportunity for an imaginative management to increase the firm's return on investment by reducing liquidity (switching from cash into mortgages or even consumer loans). When the analyst believes there is a strong chance for such a policy change, he should attempt to quantify the possible results. This is a very difficult task, and it sometimes requires assumptions about management behavior that are always difficult to make. Nevertheless, the analyst who can shrewdly make such judgments is rewarded highly.

Certain nonfinancial concerns will have book values that exceed the market price of the firm's shares. Such firms rarely offer good investment returns to investors because their asset holdings are generally worth much less than the stated book values. Many American railroads, for example, sell at large discounts from book value. They do so because the earning power of their asset holdings is low. Furthermore, the possibility of converting into more profitable assets (or liquidating) is very small because of regulatory constraints. Manufacturing concerns that have substantial assets that produce little cash flow frequently cannot liquidate these assets, except at distress prices. Hence, for all practical purposes, their asset "values" have no real significance. An exception is the firm that generates a large cash flow but that shows negligible net income (perhaps due to substantial depreciation charges). Such a firm can use its cash flow to reinvest in more profitable ventures, or it can pay out partial liquidating dividends to shareholders. If it is likely that either of these events will transpire, the analyst should include the possibility in his appraisal. Firms that do not have a large cash flow but do have large working capital positions (particularly cash) may also have the option of converting into higher yielding assets or paying a liquidating dividend. It usually requires a change in management for this to occur, however.

EXAMPLE

1. An analyst has projected the EPS stream for the Leafy Tobacco Co. for the next five years:

[2]High levels of liquidity frequently prompt tender offers to purchase controlling interest in the firm. The effect of these offers is usually to increase the price of the company's shares. If the probability of a tender offer looms significant, the analyst should attempt to quantify its expected value.

1975	$.30
1976	.28
1977	.26
1978	.28
1979	.30

The firm pays a $.24 dividend per year and has done so for ten years. The stock now sells for $3 per share, and the current P/E multiple is expected to be maintained in the future. The yield from purchasing Leafy shares for a five-year holding period would be: At 8 percent,

$$(3.99)(\$.24) + (.681)(\$3) = \$3.00$$

2. Leafy (above) has a book value of $5 per share and a net cash value (cash minus *all* liabilities) of $1.50 per share. The analyst feels that Leafy could pay out a partial liquidating dividend, but management shows no disposition toward this idea. Furthermore, there appears to be no chance that a new management team will take over in the near future. More likely, current management has shown some interest in diversifying into the manufacture of candy where it is felt that a return of at least 10 percent could be earned (net). Suppose the diversificiation took place in two years and the current net cash value per share were invested. Reprojected EPS would be:

$$(.10)(\$1.50) = \$.15$$

1975	$.30
1976	.28
1977	.41
1978	.43
1979	.45

3. The analyst believes Leafy would increase its dividend to $.30 per share in 1978 if the diversification plan were accepted. Furthermore, he believes the market would value Leafy at 12X earnings in 1979 if the firm diversified. Projected dividends and the 1979 market price given these assumptions would be:

	DPS	Market Price
1975	$.24	
1976	.24	
1977	.24	
1978	.30	
1979	.30	(12)($.45) = $5.40

4. The return earned on Leafy stock if the diversification plan were adopted and the analyst's assumptions proved to be correct would be: At 20 percent,

$$
\begin{aligned}
(.833)\,(\$.24) &= \$\ .20 \\
(.694)\,(\ .24) &= \quad.17 \\
(.579)\,(\ .24) &= \quad.14 \\
(.482)\,(\ .30) &= \quad.14 \\
(.402)\,(\ .30) &= \quad.12 \\
(.402)\,(5.40) &= \underline{\ 2.17} \\
&\quad\ \$2.94
\end{aligned}
$$

The return would be just under 20 percent.

5. The analyst believes the probability that the firm will diversify is .2. The expected return and the standard deviation of the two possible outcomes would be:

$$
\begin{array}{ll}
(.8)\,(\ 8.0) = \ 6.4 & \quad 8.0 - 10.4 = (-2.4)^2 = \ 5.76(.8) = \ 4.61 \\
(.2)\,(20.0) = \ \underline{4.0} & \quad 20.0 - 10.4 = (9.6)^2 \ = 92.16(.2) = \underline{18.43} \\
\qquad\qquad\quad 10.4 & \qquad\qquad\qquad\qquad\qquad\qquad\qquad\quad 23.04
\end{array}
$$

$$
\mu = 10.4\% \qquad \sigma = \sqrt{23.04} = 4.8\%
$$

STOCK PRICES AND THE ISSUANCE OF NEW SHARES

The dynamic aspects of common-stock analysis pose some of the more perilous problems for the analyst. This is particularly true because many analysts think in static terms and find it hard to cope with the secondary and tertiary effects of a change in a variable. Perhaps the greatest confusion is evidenced over the subject of new-share issues. When a firm goes to the market to sell additional shares, the obvious short-run consequence is a reduction of current earnings per share. *Dilution* is the term applied to this phenomenon, and many analysts feel that the effect of issuing new shares (and the subsequent dilution) will depress share prices.[3] Thus, if XYZ has 1 million shares outstanding selling at $20 per share and it sells another 100,000 shares, one might suppose that the price per share would fall (see Figure 12-1). Suppose XYZ earned $1.00 per share ($1 million).

[3]See Harry G. Guthmann and Archie J. Bakag, "The Market Impact of the Sale of Large Blocks of Stock," *The Journal of Finance*, December 1965, pp. 617–32. Also, see Eugene Lerner and Rolf Auster, "Does the Market Discount Potential Dilution?" *Financial Analysts Journal*, July–August 1969, pp. 118–21; and Sidney Leveson, "Have We Solved the Dilution Problem?," *Financial Analysts Journal*, September–October 1968, pp. 69–70.

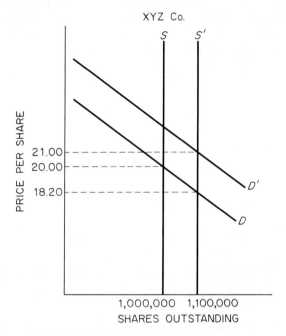

Figure 12-1   Price Effect of New Share Issue

If another 100,000 shares were issued, the adjusted earnings per share would be:

$$1,000,000/1,100,000 = \$.91$$

If a multiple of 20X were applied to the adjusted earnings, a price of (20) (.91) = $18.20 would prevail. Thus, the shift in the XYZ share supply curve from *S* to *S'* would tend to depress the stock's price.

Of course, only part of the story has been told. It is usually the case that the secondary effects of selling new shares are very positive, and the real position of the firm may *improve* rather than deteriorate as a result of the issue. The sale of new shares may allow the firm to raise needed capital to expand facilities, improve sales, and increase long-run profits. If long-run earnings per share *increase* by an amount larger than the short-run dilution produced by the creation of new shares, the price of the firm's stock should *rise* rather than fall. Suppose XYZ earnings increased to a long-run EPS of $1.05 as a result of the new share issue. It might be expected here that demanders would begin *bidding up* share prices given these improved expectations. In fact, if the multiplier of 20X held, we might expect the stock price to *rise* to: (20) ($1.05) = $21. This would be effected by a shift in the demand curve from *D* to *D'* (see Figure 12-1). Although it cannot be argued that every new issue of shares will produce increases in long-run earnings sufficient to offset the dilution effect, one should not merely assume that a new issue will depress prices. Rather, one should attempt to assess the long-run impact on earnings resulting from raising new capital.

EXAMPLE

Cameo, Ltd. has 10 million shares outstanding. An analyst has forecasted revenues, EPS, and DPS for the next four years under the assumption that the firm's asset investment will grow only by the amount of earnings retained. His projections are given below:

Year	Revenue (000)	Total Expenses (000)	EPS	DPS
1975	$100,000	$ 80,000	$2.00	$1.00
1976	120,000	90,000	3.00	1.50
1977	150,000	105,000	4.50	2.00
1978	200,000	130,000	7.00	3.00

The firm has an asset investment of $50 million in 1975. Retained earnings for 1975 are projected at $10 million. Thus, the asset investment for 1976 is forecasted at $60 million. Retained earnings for 1976 are expected to be $15 million. The asset investment for 1977 is thus projected to be $75 million. Retained earnings are projected at $25 million for 1977. The asset investment for 1978 is forecasted to be $100 million. Notice that the analyst is assuming a constant asset turnover for each year:

Year	Revenue (000)	Total Assets (000)	Turnover
1975	$100,000	$ 50,000	2X
1976	120,000	60,000	2X
1977	150,000	75,000	2X
1978	200,000	100,000	2X

He is also using the following net income equation:

$$\text{Net Income} = \text{Sales} - (30,000,000 + .5\ \text{Sales})$$

Now, suppose Cameo sells at $105 per share. The analyst believes the current P/E multiple is high but justifiable in light of the earnings pattern predicted for 1975–1978. He does not feel the expected growth rate beyond 1978 will match the 50 percent compounded annual rate of earnings-per-share growth forecasted for 1975-1978, however. Thus, he expects the multiple to fall to about 20 times earnings in 1978. Given the analyst's expectations, the stock would yield: At 9 percent,

$$(.917)(1.00) + (.842)(1.50) + (.772)(2.00) + (.708)(3.00) + (.708)(140.00) = \$104.96$$

Cameo has announced an offering of 500,000 new shares to current stockholders at $100 per share.[4] The dilution of projected EPS resulting from the offering would be:

		EPS
1975	20,000,000/10,500,000 =	$1.90
1976	30,000,000/10,500,000 =	2.86
1977	45,000,000/10,500,000 =	4.28
1978	70,000,000/10,500,000 =	6.67

Cameo plans to expand immediately with the $50 million it has raised. The analyst feels that the firm will have excess capacity for awhile. He projects an asset turnover of 1.8X in 1975 and 1976, 1.9X in 1977, and 2.0X in 1978. His new net-income equation is:

$$\text{Net Income} = \text{Sales} - (60{,}000{,}000 + .5\ \text{Sales})$$

Reprojected total assets, revenues, total expenses, EPS and DPS for Cameo over 1975-1978 assuming dividends are about one-half earnings would be:

Year	Total Assets (000)	Revenues (000)	Expenses (000)	EPS	DPS
1975	$100,000	$180,000	$150,000	$ 2.86	$1.43
1976	115,000	207,000	163,500	4.14	2.12
1977	136,750	259,825	189,913	6.66	3.33
1978	171,706	343,412	231,706	10.64	5.32

Suppose the market felt that the risk offered by investing in Cameo had not changed and that 9 percent was still an adequate return from the security. What price should the stock *advance to* at the time of the new offering, given the above forecast?

$$(.917)(1.43) + (.843)(2.12) + (.772)(3.33) + (.708)(5.32) + (.708)(212.80) = \$160.10$$

Thus, rather than declining, Cameo stock should in fact *rise* as a result of the new share offering.

[4]This procedure of selling shares is done through a rights offering. A discussion of the valuation of common stock rights is contained in Chapter 14.

STOCK DIVIDENDS AND STOCK SPLITS

Another area that presents problems for many analysts is the evaluation of *common stock dividends* and *stock splits*. The payment of a stock dividend is merely a method by which the firm "capitalizes" retained earnings into the permanent capital accounts (common stock, and common stock excess over par). For some firms, such as commercial banks, the transfer of retained earnings into permanent capital may be required by law. For most firms, however, the payment of a stock dividend is simply a way of distributing more shares to the existing stockholders. No real economic change occurs from the distribution. The net worth of the firm does not alter, and shareholders maintain the same percentage ownership in the firm after the declaration of a stock dividend that they had before it. The only real difference is that shareholders have a greater number of shares, which, of course, should be worth proportionately less per share.

Although there is no economic reason for most firms to pay stock dividends, many do pay them. Some managements believe they can fool shareholders by paying out stock rather than cash. Others contend that investors in high tax brackets prefer stock dividends to cash dividends because the extra stock accruing from a stock dividend may be sold if funds are needed. A cash dividend would be taxed at regular rates, whereas only the profit resulting from the sale of additional shares would be taxed (and then at more favorable capital-gains rates). Nevertheless, it would not be necessary that a stock dividend be paid for the investor to obtain funds. He could simply sell some of his original holding of shares. Even if the stock had appreciated in value since his purchase, he would be equally well off by selling a percentage of his original holding as by receiving an equivalent percentage as a stock dividend which he would liquidate.

Splitting a firm's stock is similar to a stock dividend in that the real economic position of the investor does not change. He has more pieces of paper, but his percentage ownership in the firm is the same. The stock split does have an accounting effect in that the par value of the stock is reduced by the inverse of the split (a 2:1 split reduces the par value by one half), but this change is not terribly important. Par value has absolutely no meaning in terms of stock price value (except when a firm issues shares below their par value), and many companies no longer assign par values to their stock.

Three arguments are made to justify splits economically. The first is that splits are an omen of growth. The second is that cash dividends may increase after a split. The third is that investors prefer shares selling in some optimal price range (usually $20 to $80). The first argument is without merit because the *rate* of sales and earnings growth will be the same regardless of the number of shares the firm has outstanding. Only the sale of *new* shares, which brings in added capital for investment, can affect sales and earnings growth.[5] The second argument is behaviorally correct in that many firms do increase their dividend payout after a split. Nevertheless, an increase in payout can be accomplished without a split. Furthermore, if the firm is growing rapidly, a better policy would be to *reduce* the payout and reinvest in profitable projects. This might positively affect the well-being of shareholders more than the payment of a cash dividend! The third argument is the only real justification for a split. If investors really do prefer stocks selling in some given range, when a stock price advances out of that range it should be split. It is hard to imagine, however, that many investors would rather have one hundred shares at $50 per share than ten shares at $500. The investment is $5,000 regardless. Many popular growth issues such as I.B.M., Xerox, and Polaroid sell at prices well over $100 per share, and the brokerage commission is actually *less* for the same dollar investment in higher-priced shares than lower-priced ones. Of course, at very high prices (one share at $5,000, for example), share divisibility becomes impossible, and some investors are priced out of the market. There is little argument that shares selling at these prices should be split, unless management wishes to keep the shares out of the hands of small investors. The latter policy will undoubtedly produce a lower total market value for the firm.

Although the accounting and economic effects of the stock split are of questionable significance, many analysts and investors alike greet the news of a pending split enthusiastically. Of course, this fact in itself may justify the decision of a firm to split its shares by producing a self-fulfilling prophecy. Nevertheless, the only real effect of a split is the creation of more shares, which should sell at lower prices. It seems obvious that an investor who owns one hundred shares of a stock selling at $10 per share, earning $1, and paying $.50 in cash dividends would be no better off owning two hundred shares of the same stock selling at $5 per share, earning $.50, and paying $.25 in dividends.

---

[5]The "omen of future growth" argument is adopted by Fama, Fisher, Jensen, and Roll in a recent article. They suggest that when a split is announced, it is interpreted by the market as a sign of confidence on the part of the company's directors in the firm's future earnings growth. Moreover, if the firm increases the dividend payout at the time of the split, this may be interpreted as a sign that management believes that the new dividend rate will be sustainable in the future. According to this view, then, price increases in the months immediately preceding a split are due to an alteration in expectations concerning the future earning potential of the firm rather than to any intrinsic value of the split in and of itself. Unfortunately, the FFJR findings indicate that the market makes unbiased forecasts about the growth implications of a split and that these forecasts are fully reflected in the price of the shares at the time of the split. As a result, only those individuals who knew about an effective dividend increase following the split *before* its announcement (the directors, for example) could profit from the split. Thus, even if splits were an "omen of future growth", it would be impossible for outsiders to benefit from such information. See E. Fama, L. Fisher, M. Jensen, and R. Roll, "The Adjustment of Stock Prices to New Information," *International Economic Review,* February, 1969 pp. 1–21.

EXAMPLES

1. A firm has the following capital structure:

Common stock ($10 par, 1 million shares)	$ 10,000,000
Common stock, excess over par	20,000,000
Retained earnings	70,000,000
	$100,000,000

The firm declares a 10 percent stock dividend. For stock dividends less than 20 to 25 percent, market price rather than book value is used to determine the recapitalization. The firm's market price is $150 per share. The transfer of the dividend from retained earnings into permanent capital is thus:

$$(.10)(150,000,000) = \$15,000,000$$

The new structure would be:

Common stock ($10 par, 1.1 million shares)	$ 11,000,000
Common stock, excess over par	34,000,000
Retained earnings	55,000,000
	$100,000,000

2. Suppose the firm above declared a 3:1 split. The capital structure would become:

Common stock ($3.33 1/3 par, 3 million shares)	$ 10,000,000
Common stock, excess over par	20,000,000
Retained earnings	70,000,000
	$100,000,000

FINANCIAL ANALYSIS AND ACCOUNTING DATA

In this final section, we issue a caveat to the analyst about the data that he has at his disposal for analysis. The historical numbers that he uses to prepare ratios and forecasting equations are generally based on figures that have been taken from the published financial statements of the firm being analyzed. Although these statements may have been prepared "according to generally accepted accounting principles," there may be significant variation in the real economic meaning of financial reports. Obvious inconsistencies in the methodology of preparation (for example, when a firm switches from LIFO to FIFO inventory valuation, or from accelerated depreciation to straight-line) require adjustments to the documents prepared by the accounting community (see Chapter 5). More subtle problems may exist, however, which cannot easily be handled by making simple adjustments.

One of the more plaguing difficulties with financial statements is that they are prepared on the assumption of stable prices. To the extent that prices change over time, the reported asset values on the firm's balance sheet (and perhaps the liability values as well) will be inaccurate. Further, because accounting costs are usually based on historical prices, a misstatement about the value of an asset may well result in an inaccurate depiction of net income. Moreover, net income in one period may not be equivalent to an identical net income in another if the aggregate level of prices has changed. If a firm earns $1.00 per share in 1974 and $1.05 in 1975, it really has shown no improvement if the overall price level has also risen by 5 percent.

Another problem is that the market values of a firm's assets may have no relationship to their book values. Price-level changes, variances from depreciation estimates, and the insistence of accountants upon valuing assets at the lower of cost or market (an example of the doctrine of "conservatism") make the balance sheet an unreliable statement about the value of the enterprise. Of course, the accountants themselves beg off, claiming that financial analysts expect too much from published statements. One respected former practitioner has observed:

> . . . accountants in their most solemn pronouncements have made it quite clear that the financial statements they prepare do not even purport to provide information about solvency and profitability. For instance, anyone might be pardoned for thinking that a conventional balance sheet is prepared to show the financial strength of a company by listing its obligations against its resources and to establish its net value. But this is not at all how a balance sheet is defined in accounting texts.[6]

Thus, when the analyst finds that return on total investment has increased from 20 percent to 21 percent, it is not clear that an improvement has taken place. Earnings figures from one year to the next (and across firms for any given year) are not strictly comparable, and total investment can become completely incomparable over time.

What is the unfortunate analyst to do under such circumstances? The answer, of course, is to make the best of the situation. Adjustments to published statements should be made whenever there is good justification to do so. Otherwise, the analyst should bear in mind always the limitations of the data that he

---

[6]Howard Ross, *The Elusive Art of Accounting* (New York: The Ronald Press, 1966), p. 9.

has used in making his appraisal. A report based on less-than-perfect data is better than no report at all. Security analysis has always been a tentative undertaking. It is perhaps less so today than it was a few years ago. Nevertheless, all the powerful statistical tools that the analyst now has at his disposal have not reduced the process to a scientific procedure. Analysis is an artful endeavor. It has been in the past and will always be a matter of rational guess work.[7]

PROBLEMS

1. The Old Conservative National Bank has demonstrated the following earnings and dividend pattern for the past ten years:

	EPS	DPS
1965	$1.18	$ .90
1966	1.20	.90
1967	1.23	.90
1968	1.19	.90
1969	1.23	.90
1970	1.27	.90
1971	1.30	1.00
1972	1.24	1.00
1973	1.26	1.00
1974	1.30	1.00

The 1974 balance sheet for the bank is given below (in millions):

Cash	$ 20	Demand deposits	$ 50
Marketable securities	50	Savings deposits	60
Loans	50	Common stock (1 million shs)	20
Investments	30	Surplus	10
Banking house	10	Undivided profit	20
Total assets	$160	Total liab. & worth	$160

[7]There is growing empirical evidence that successive changes in reported corporate income are independent. This implies that accounting income behaves randomly over time. Early research to indicate complete randomness is reported by I. M. D. Little, "Higgledy Piggledy Growth," *Institute of Statistics, Oxford,* November 1962, pp. 387–412. More recent findings suggest that accounting income follows a submartingale. See Ray Ball and Ross Watts, "Some Time Series Properties of Accounting Income," *Journal of Finance,* June 1972, pp. 663–81. Under a submartingale, one observation becomes the basis for expectations about the next. Thus, a certain amount of serial correlation in successive income amounts is indicated. If corporate income does in fact follow a submartingale, attempts by accountants to "smooth" the results (by means of such practices as ignoring "extraordinary items") will be meaningless. Indeed, such attempts would tend to *increase* the variance of future income changes by making the probability distribution of such income asymmetric. (Note: a more detailed discussion of the statistical properties of the submartingale and its application to security prices is contained in Chapter 19.)

The bank earned an average of 5 percent on its marketable securities in 1974, 10 percent on its loans, and 8 percent on its investments (mainly government bonds). It also earned $1 million in gains on its portfolio and grossed $3.5 million from customer services. The bank incurred operating costs of $9.9 million and paid an average rate of 4 percent on its savings accounts. Its average tax rate is 50 percent.

    a. Reconstruct the bank's 1974 income statement.

    b. Old Conservative must maintain a 20 percent reserve requirement against demand deposits and a 4 percent reserve against savings accounts. What are its excess reserves? (Note: Legal reserves consist of bank vault cash plus deposits held with the district Federal Reserve Bank.)

    c. Suppose the bank placed its excess reserves in new loans. What would be its added net return?

    d. In addition to placing its excess reserves in new loans, suppose the bank generated $1,000,000 in new demand deposits, set aside the appropriate reserves, and invested the balance in new loans. If the cost of generating the new accounts and making the new loans were $40,000, what added return would the bank earn?

    e. Suppose the bank reduced its marketable security investment by $20 million and placed $20 million more in loans. How much added net income would be earned?

    f. Old Conservative now sells for $20 per share. The stock price has increased at the same rate as long-run earnings (about 2 percent per year). What return have investors been getting?

    g. An analyst believes there is a chance that a new management team is about to take over at Old Conservative. If this happens, the policies outlined in c, d, and e above will be adopted. Forecast 1975 earnings assuming the new management takes over (assume all other variables except those affected by the policy changes will remain constant).

    h. What factors positively affecting the bank's P/E multiple would exist if the policy changes were made? What negative factors?

    i. Suppose the P/E remained constant. Project the price of the shares at the end of 1975 if the policy changes are made.

    j. What return would an investor earn from purchasing the shares if the price indicated above were obtained? Assume an increase in the dividend for 1975 to $1.50 per share.

    k. The analyst feels the probability that management will change is about .4. Determine the expected return and the standard deviation of the two possible outcomes.

2. Jiminex, Inc., earned $30 million in 1974. Projections for 1975 indicate a net income of $33 million. The firm has 5 million shares outstanding, pays out about three-quarters of net income in common dividends, and sells at $60 per share.

    a. Compute EPS and DPS for 1974 and projected EPS and DPS for 1975.

    b. Investors expect Jiminex to evidence earnings increases at about 10 percent annually for a long time. What is the current return from purchasing Jiminex shares?

    c. Suppose Jiminex sells 1 million new shares at the current market price. What earnings and dividend dilution would result?

d. An analyst believes that the capital raised by Jiminex will increase its earnings growth rate to 12.5 percent. If the market agrees with this analysis and is willing to continue to accept the same return as before (calculated in b above), what must happen to the price of Jiminex shares?

3. An investor bought one hundred shares of Amalgamated Rubbish two years ago. He paid $90 per share then, and the stock now sells at $100. The stock paid a $5 cash dividend last year and will soon do so again.

a. When the stock pays its cash dividend, what should happen to the stock price?

b. Suppose Amalgamated declares a 5 percent stock dividend in place of the cash dividend. What should happen to the price of the stock?

c. What tax would the investor pay on his cash dividend if he is in the 40 percent marginal tax bracket?

d. Suppose a stock rather than a cash dividend were declared. If the stock dividend were 5 percent and the investor elected to sell the extra shares, what would his after-tax return be? (He pays capital-gains taxes at a rate of 20 percent).

e. Compare this with his return if a cash dividend were paid.

f. Would your calculation above justify the payment of a stock dividend for tax reasons?

4. Suppose Amalgamated (above) were split 5 for 1. What should the new market price be? (Assume no dividends, cash or stock, are paid.)

COMPREHENSIVE CASE

1. Select a firm from one of the following industries for analysis:

Public utilities	Tobacco
Railroads	Textile
Airlines	Paper
Banking	Publishing
Life insurance	Drug
Automobiles	Steel
Chemicals	Office equipment
International petroleum	Motion picture
Food	Metals

2. Examine financial statements for the firm for the past five years. Make appropriate adjustments to the financial statements, and reconcile the firm's actual tax payment with expected taxes.

3. Compute all significant ratios for the firm over the five-year period.

4. Determine a least-squares forecasting equation for the sales of the industry. Use this equation, if appropriate, in preparing a sales-forecasting equation for the firm.

5. Project revenues for the industry and the firm for the next five years.

6. Forecast expenses for the firm for the next five years using either least-squares equations or ratio analysis. Estimate net income, earnings per share, and dividends per share.

7. Prepare *pro forma* income statements and balance sheets for the forecasting period. Determine probable additions to plant and equipment, and estimate possible sources of finance.

8. Compute the ratios calculated above (number 3) from the *pro forma* statements. Reconcile any discrepancies between historical patterns and the projected values.

9. Categorize your firm as an income, defensive, cyclical, blue-chip, or growth stock.

10. Determine the current dividend yield for the stock.

11. Examine the historical P/E multiples for the firm. Try to assess the level of interest rates, the riskiness of the firm, and the growth potential for the stock in five years. From these data, project a P/E multiple for earnings at the end of the five-year holding period.

12. Given the current price of the firm's stock and the dividend and terminal price projections made above, compute the return expected from a purchase of the security.

REFERENCES

Ball, R. and R. Watts, "Some Time Series Properties of Accounting Income," *Journal of Finance,* June, 1972, pp. 663-81.

Baumol, W., P. Heim, B. Malkiel, and R. Quandt, "Earnings Retention, New Capital and the Growth of the firm," *Review of Economics and Statistics,* November, 1970, pp. 345-55.

Fama, E., L. Fisher, M. Jensen, and R. Roll, "The Adjustment of Stock Prices to New Information," *International Economic Review,* February, 1969, pp. 1-21.

Graham, B., D. Dodd, and S. Cottle, *Security Analysis,* 4th ed. New York: McGraw-Hill Book Company, 1962.

Guthmann, H., and A. Bakag, "The Market Impact of the Sale of Large Blocks of Stock," *Journal of Finance,* December 1965, pp. 617-32.

Lerner, E., and R. Auster, "Does the Market Discount Potential Dilution?" *Financial Analysts Journal,* July-August 1969, pp. 118-21.

————, and W. Carleton, "The Integration of Capital Budgeting and Stock Valuation," *American Economic Review,* September 1964, pp. 683-702.

Leveson, S., "Have We Solved the Dilution Problem?," *Financial Analysts Journal,* September-October 1968, pp. 69-70.

Little, I. M. D., "Higgledy Piggledy Growth," *Institute of Statistics, Oxford,* November, 1962, pp. 387-412.

Ross, H., *The Elusive Art of Accounting*, New York: The Ronald Press, 1966.

Williams, E. E., "A Note on Accounting Practice, Investor Rationality, and Capital Resource Allocation," *Financial Analysts Journal*, July–August 1969, pp. 37–40.

Williamson, John, "Profit, Growth, and Sales Maximization," *Economica,* February, 1966, pp. 1–16.

13

Convertible Securities

THE NATURE OF CONVERTIBLE SECURITIES

There are a variety of instruments that may be converted into or exchanged for common stock. Warrants, common-stock subscription rights, purchase and sale options, and convertible securities are the most important examples. The valuation of any instrument that has the potential of becoming common stock must, of course, depend on an initial evaluation of the common shares of the company in question. The underlying value of semiequities also depends on other variables. In this chapter, we shall assume that a complete evaluation of the firm's common shares has been made according to the suggested methods outlined in the eight previous chapters. The other important variables will be considered as additional determinants of the value of the instrument being analyzed.

Debentures and preferred stocks may have a feature that allows the holder to convert these fixed-income securities into common stock. Convertible bonds and preferreds are very much alike in many respects. Nevertheless, it should be remembered that the interest on convertible bonds is deductible in the computation of the income taxes of the issuer like any other bond and that the coupon payments are a legal obligation that must be met along with sinking-fund requirements if any exist. Convertible preferreds, on the other hand, are similar to straight preferreds in that dividends are declared out of after-tax earnings. Furthermore, dividends on convertible preferreds may be passed during unprofitable years. Many convertible preferreds are cumulative, of course, and all arrearages on such issues must be paid before any common dividends may be issued. Because preferreds are considered to be equity securities, the use of a convertible preferred in a merger would usually constitute a tax-free exchange for the holder.

The convertible security is both a fixed-income instrument and potentially common equity. Thus, it must be analyzed as a bond (or preferred) *and* as common stock. All the evaluation techniques required for scrutinizing a fixed-income security (Chapters 7 and 8) plus those employed in common stock analysis (Chapters 9 through 12) must be called into play when a convertible is being considered. The convertible security contains several added characteristics that are not found in straight bonds or common stocks. A *conversion ratio* will be included in the indenture of the convertible bond (and in the share certificate of the preferred). This ratio indicates the number of common shares that may be obtained from surrendering the convertible instrument to the corporation. For example, a debenture with a conversion ratio of 20 would provide its holder with 20 common shares if he elected to convert the bond into common stock. If the bond were a $1,000 par issue, this would mean that for each $50 par amount, one common share would be obtained. The par value divided by the conversion ratio is termed the *conversion price.* Conversion ratios and prices are usually altered to reflect stock dividends and splits, although small stock dividends (3 percent or less) are sometimes ignored.

Because convertible security holders have the advantage over straight bond and preferred holders of sharing in the well-being of the firm if it is a profitable enterprise, one would expect that a price would be paid for the privilege. In general, convertible issues yield less than do equivalent straight issues. The coupon on a convertible bond will always be set at a lower rate than would be the case if the issue were straight debt. This is also true for the dividend rate on a convertible preferred.

When a convertible security is sold, the conversion price is usually set somewhat above the current market price of the common stock. The difference between these prices is called the *conversion premium.* Expressed as a percentage, the conversion premium equals: (conversion price – market price)/(market price). Conversion premiums vary from negligible amounts to more than 25 percent. Unseasoned firms may have to issue convertible securities in order to sell debt at all, and the conversion premium for bonds sold by such concerns would be small. Seasoned companies, on the other hand, will frequently sell convertibles at large premiums during very bullish periods.

The demand for convertibles is enhanced in bull markets by the presence of a number of institutional investors who are prohibited from holding common stocks but who can buy convertible debentures. The added demand from such purchasers tends to increase conversion premiums and to lower yields from what they otherwise might be. Another element of demand that has the same effect is induced by the greater borrowing power available through ownership of convertibles rather than pure equities. In the past, regulated margin requirements have been lower on convertibles than on common shares. Moreover, banks will frequently lend more on a convertible issue than on the underlying issue of common stock. The results may be favorable for the speculator who wishes to improve the leverage position of his portfolio, but they also imply higher premiums and lower yields for convertibles.

The dual nature of the convertible security means that it has two different fundamental values. The *conversion value* accrues from the right to convert the security into common stock. If a bond could be converted into 20 shares of common stock, and the price of the common were $60 per share, the conversion value of the bond would be $1,200. The bond would not sell for less than this price because arbitragers could always buy the bond and convert it into common. The *bond* (or *investment*) *value* derives from the income-generating power of the instrument. This value is the price at which the security would sell even if it had no conversion feature. The value of the instrument as straight debt (or straight preferred) constitutes another floor below which the price of the issue will not fall (regardless of the price of the common stock). A lower price would imply a higher yield than could be obtained on equivalent straight debt (or preferred) securities, and again arbitragers would bid up the price until yields were equalized.

THEORETICAL PRICE BEHAVIOR OF CONVERTIBLES

We have observed that a convertible security cannot fall below the greater of its conversion or investment values. It can sell above either of these, however, and it frequently will because of the option value of the instrument.[1] Premiums above floor values are limited for convertibles, however, because most convertibles are callable by the issuing corporation. A convertible may sell above the call price set by the issuer but only because the instrument can be converted into common stock. No one would pay a premium over the conversion value at such prices because a call by the issuer would force conversion. A bond selling well above its call price may very likely be called, and anyone who paid more than the conversion value of the bond would lose the difference.

The theoretical price behavior of a convertible security is illustrated in Figure 13-1. Suppose that a bond has a ten-year maturity remaining and is now callable at 105; it has a coupon of 5 percent and a conversion price of $50 per share; and equivalent straight-debt issues currently yield 6 percent. The

---

[1] For a more detailed discussion of premiums, see Chapter 14.

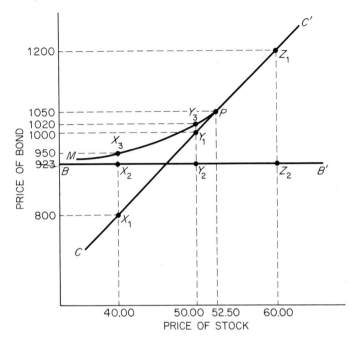

Figure 13-1   Theoretical Price Behavior of a Convertible Security

investment value of the issue is:

$$.06 = \frac{50 + \dfrac{1000 - X}{10}}{\dfrac{1000 + X}{2}}$$

$$X = \$923$$

The bond would not sell below this value unless the yields on equivalent straight-debt issues also fell or the risk of the issuer increased. The bond value floor is given by line BB' in Figure 13-1. Now, let us suppose that the price of the common is $40 per share. The conversion value of the bond would be $(20 \times 40) = \$800$. In Figure 13-1, this is given as point X_1 on line CPC'. Does this mean that the market price of the bond is $800? Definitely not. The investment value floor is $923 (point X_2 on line BB'). Furthermore, if the market wishes to pay a premium for the option value of the bond, it may sell at an even higher price, say $950 (that is, point X_3 on the actual price line MPC').

    What would happen at a common stock price of $50? The investment value would not change unless the increase in the price of the stock resulted from a reduction in the riskiness of the firm or a lowering of all market rates of interest. In either of these cases, the yield on equivalent straight-debt issues would fall, and the investment value of the bond would rise. Let us assume, however, that these variables are held constant and that the difference in the stock price occurs for other reasons (see the discussion on the determinants of stock prices in Chapter 10). At a price of $50, the conversion value of the bond would now be $(20 \times 50) = \$1000$ (point Y_1 in Figure 13-1). The investment value would still be $923 (point Y_2). Let us suppose a slight premium continues to exist and that the market price of the bond is $1020.

What would develop at a common stock price of $60? The investment value would remain at $923 (point Z_2). The conversion value would become $(20 \times 60) = \$1200$ (point Z_1), and this would be the market price of the issue. No one would pay more because the issue would have been in the callable range beyond a price of $1050. Hence, at point P the market price line MPC' would join the conversion value line CPC'. When the market price of the common stock advanced to $52.50, the conversion value of the bond would exactly equal the call price. Market bond prices could be justified above this price only to the extent that the market price of the common stock also advanced.

REASONS FOR CONVERTING

The conversion of a security into common stock may occur for two reasons: (1) the convertible may be called by the issuing corporation; and (2) the yield from holding common stock may exceed the yield from holding the convertible. In the first instance, a convertible selling substantially above its call price may be called by the issuer. If this is done, the holder has the option of converting to common or accepting cash payment at the call price. Because the convertible would sell above its call price only if the conversion value of the bond exceeded the call price, the rational investor would always convert into common. Even if he did not (or could not for legal or institutional reasons) wish to hold common stock, it would be wise to convert and sell the common rather than accept the call price cash payment.

The second reason for conversion may best be considered with an example.[2] Suppose an investor holds a convertible bond that has a conversion ratio of 10 and that the common stock of the issuing firm sells at 150. The conversion value of the bond would be $1500. Suppose further that the bond is now callable at 105 ($1050). The bond would sell in the market for $1500,

---

[2] Voluntary conversion can also occur because of an increase in the conversion price over time or the effects of taxes and transactions costs. An example of the latter results when an investor is short common stock and chooses to deliver by purchasing the convertible and converting rather than buying the common outright. One might do this if the commissions on the bond were less than the equivalent amount of common stock (and no premium existed on the convertible).

because a call would be a definite possibility. Now, let us assume that the bond is a 4 percent coupon (and thus pays $40 per year in interest) and that the common stock pays a dividend of $5 per share. If one converted into common, the dividend return would be (10 X 5) = $50. Hence, many holders might decide to convert into common in order to obtain the larger dollar yield. No capital-gain potential would be lost, because any percentage appreciation by the convertible would be matched by an exact percentage appreciation in the common. On the downside, however, the common stock could depreciate by a larger percentage than might be observed for the convertible. This is true because at some point a premium above the conversion value may tend to develop for the convertible (the area indicated by the *MP* segment of line *MPC'* in Figure 13-1). Furthermore, a lower limit on the price decline of the convertible may be set by the investment value of the security. Thus, if one expected a large percentage depreciation by the common, one might elect to hold the convertible. A wiser policy, of course, would be to sell the convertible if one were all that pessimistic. Indeed, one might also sell the stock short or buy a put (see Chapter 14).

A caveat should be issued concerning the lower limit on the price decline of a convertible. In the past, many investors have bought convertibles believing that the downside risk was minimized for the reasons mentioned above. They were very surprised to find their bonds selling at huge discounts as the price of the underlying common stock plummeted. Their error was in assuming a static situation in which the investment value of the bond did not change as the stock price fell. One reason for a decline in the price of a stock may be a deterioration in the earning capacity of the firm. This will increase the riskiness of the firm and will hence raise the rate that the firm would have to pay on straight-debt issues. This, in turn, will reduce the investment value of all the firm's bonds and thus will increase the downside potential of convertible issues. An increase in the general level of interest rates will produce the same effect. Additionally, price deterioration in the common stock may dampen investor enthusiasm about the future. This will manifest itself in the form of lower premiums above the conversion value. Hence, as stock prices fall, the premiums that convertible holders had been counting on to reduce any decline in convertible prices may tend to disappear.

VALUATION OF CONVERTIBLES

A valuation model for convertible bonds that is similar to the bond-pricing equation developed in Chapter 3 may be constructed. Reiterating the straight-bond valuation formula:

$$P_0 = \sum_{t=1}^{n} \frac{C_t}{(1+i)^t} + \frac{P_n}{(1+i)^n} \qquad \text{(3.3 Restated)}$$

Where:

P_0 is the current price of the bond

C_t is the annual dollar coupon paid on the bond

P_n is the par value of the bond

i is the yield to maturity of the bond

n is the number of years to maturity

In the case of the convertible, the time horizon for holding the bond will be shorter than the number of years to maturity if the bond is converted. Thus, if a convertible is called, or if an investor elects to convert in order to get a higher dividend yield on the common, the bond would not be held to maturity. A revised equation taking conversion into account would be:

$$P_0 = \sum_{t=1}^{N} \frac{C_t}{(1+k)^t} + \frac{TV}{(1+k)^N} \qquad \text{(13.1)}$$

Where:

TV is the terminal value of the convertible

k is the expected rate of return from holding the convertible

N is the expected holding period $(N \leqslant n)$

Two obvious problems develop when considering 13.1 as a valuation model. First, how does one estimate N, the expected holding period? And second, how is the terminal value (TV) of the bond determined? An approach to these problems is developed by Eugene Brigham.[3] Suppose we let CV_t be the conversion value of a bond at period t. We know from the discussion on pages 252–53 that this value must increase approximately linearly with increases in the stock price. Thus, if the current stock price is S_0, growth in the stock price over time would be given by:

$$S_t = S_0 (1+g)^t \qquad \text{(13.2)}$$

Where:

S_t is the stock price at period t

g is the annual growth

[3] Eugene F. Brigham, "An Analysis of Convertible Debentures: Theory and Some Empirical Evidence," *Journal of Finance*, March 1966, pp. 35–54.

and CV_t would be given by:

$$CV_t = S_0 \ (1+g)^t R \qquad (13.3)$$

In equation 13.3, R is the conversion ratio. Now, if the issuing firm has a policy of calling bonds when the ratio of the market price of the common (S_t) to the conversion price (S_c) reaches a given level, 13.3 could be rewritten as:

$$CV_t = \frac{S_0}{S_c} \ (1+g)^t M \qquad (13.4)$$

where M is the issue price of the bond. Notice that M/S_c equals R, the conversion ratio.

The terminal value (TV) of the bond would be that price prevailing when the bond is called. When the call takes place, the conversional value CV_t equals TV. Hence,

$$TV = \frac{S_0}{S_c} \ (1+g)^N M \qquad (13.5)$$

This equation can be solved to find N.[4]

We may consider an example. Suppose the Grant Co. has outstanding an 8 percent debenture that is currently callable at 102. The bond will be callable at 101 in two years and at par in four years. The bond is also convertible into twenty shares of Grant common, which now sells for $25 per share. It is expected that the share price will grow at an annual rate of about 6 percent, and it is believed that the company will call the issue when the price of the common is 20 percent greater than the conversion price.[5] Because the bond is convertible into twenty shares of stock, the conversion price is $1000/20 = $50. If the current market price of the stock is $25, it will take:

$$\$50 = \$25(1+.06)^t$$

$$t = 12$$

---

[4] By logarithms,

$$N = \frac{(\log S_c - \log S_0) + (\log TV - \log M)}{\log (1+g)}$$

A more efficient procedure for calculating N would be to use compound interest tables (Appendix C).

[5] Technically, this decision rule is normally expressed in terms of calling the bond when its call price is at least 15 to 20 percent below its market price (assumed equal to its conversion value at these levels). The issuer allows this margin to be certain that any price weakness caused by the call announcement (for reasons of potential dilution or increased floating supply of shares) or other market factors will not be so great as to cause shareholders to accept the call price in lieu of converting.

years before the common reaches the conversion price. Because it is believed that the company will call the issue only after the price of the common is 20 percent greater than the conversion price (i.e., $60), it will require:

$$\$60 = \$25(1+.06)^t$$

$$t = 15$$

years before the bond is called. The conversion value of the bond will equal $(20)(\$60) = \$1,200$ at that time, and this amount must be the price at which the bond will be selling in 15 years. Because the bond is callable at par, no premium would be paid above the conversion value. Thus, the terminal value of the bond would have to equal the conversion value.

An investor who bought the Grant bonds today would expect the following stream over the next fifteen years:

$$P_0 = \sum_{t=1}^{15} \frac{80}{(1+k)^t} + \frac{1200}{(1+k)^{15}}$$

If the bond had a current price of 76½, the investor would expect a return of:

at 12%,

$$(80)(6.811) = 544.88$$
$$(1200)(.183) = \underline{219.60}$$
$$764.48$$

just under 12 percent on his convertible.

PROBLEMS

1. Jones owns a ZEX convertible bond, 6s92. The bond is convertible into fifty shares of ZEX common and is now callable. The current price of ZEX common is $25 per share. The company has just announced the call of the 6s92 at 108. What should Jones do?

2. Smith owns an S.P.C. convertible, 3s78. The bond is convertible into twenty S.P.C. shares. The bond is callable at 110, although the current price of the bond is only 89. S.P.C. common pays a dividend of $2 per share and sells for $40 per share. Should Smith convert?

3. The Iowa Corporation has issued 4 percent convertible debentures (par value $1,000), which may be exchanged for twenty shares of common. The price of the common is $40 per share. What are the conversion ratio, conversion price, and conversion premium of the bond?

4. The Bravo Corporation has issued convertible debentures at a par of $500. They may be exchanged for twenty shares of stock currently selling for $22. What are the conversion ratio, price, and premium?

5. The Smetina Corp. has outstanding a ten-year, 6 percent coupon debenture that is convertible into 100 shares of common. The common stock of Smetina sells for $7 per share, and an equivalent straight-debt issue now yields 8.9 percent to maturity.

   a. What is the conversion value of the convertible? The bond (investment) value?

   b. The market price of Smetina common when the convertible was sold was $8. If the convertible was sold at par ($1,000), what conversion premium was paid by purchasers?

   c. The Smetina convertible sells now at 85. What premium are investors paying beyond the greater of the conversion or investment value of the bond? What accounts for this premium?

   d. The Smetina convertible is callable at 104 in two years. If the price of Smetina common rose to $11, at what price would the convertible sell? Would a premium be possible?

   e. Suppose Smetina common increased in price over the next year from $7 to $11. Suppose further that the convertible sold in the market at its conversion value. What percentage gain would each security evidence?

   f. Suppose Smetina common fell in price to $3 and that the investment value of the convertible did not change. What percentage loss would each security show?

   g. Assume that the decline in the price of Smetina common was due to a deterioration in the fundamental position of the firm (an increase in risk) and an increase in general level of interest rates. If the Smetina straight-debt issue now yields 12.5 percent to maturity, what are the new conversion and investment values of the bond?

   h. Given the conditions in g above, what percentage loss would the convertible evidence if it sold at no premium over the greater of its investment or conversion value?

6. An analyst has forecasted the following EPS for the Cote Co.:

1975	$1.00
1976	1.20
1977	1.50
1978	2.00
1979	2.50

Cote has typically sold at a P/E multiple of 20X and the analyst expects this multiple to hold in the future. The firm has a policy of paying out about half of its earnings in dividends. Cote has a 4 percent convertible debenture outstanding due in 1979. The bond may be converted into fifty shares of common and would currently yield 6.3 percent as straight debt. The bond is currently callable at 108. The price of Cote common now (1974) is $16 per share.

   a. What are the conversion and bond values of the 4s79?

   b. If the bond is called, what should the investor do?

c. Suppose the bond is not called. What annual return would convertible holders expect over the five years remaining to maturity? The current (1974) price of the bond is 96¼.

APPENDIX

The Baumol-Malkiel-Quandt Model

Professors Baumol, Malkiel, and Quandt have constructed a comprehensive valuation model based upon the investor's subjective probability distribution of future market prices of the common stock.[1] According to them, the value C of a convertible must be either:

$$C \geqslant P(t)S + \int_0^{\bar{B}/P(t_0)S} f(i, t_0) \; [\bar{B} - i(t)P(t_0)S] \; di(t) \qquad (13A.1)$$

Where:

C is the value of the convertible at $t=0$

$P(t)$ is the expected market price of the stock at time t

S is the number of shares of common stock into which the convertible can be exchanged

$\bar{B}$ is the bond value of the convertible

$i(t)$ is a price relative of the market price of the stock at the time the convertible is evaluated ($t=0$)

or,

$$C \geqslant \bar{B} + \int_{\bar{B}/P(t_0)S}^{\infty} f(i, t_0) \; [i(t)P(t_0)S - \bar{B}] \; di(t) \qquad (13A.2)$$

The first term of the right-hand member of expression 13A.1 is the conversion value of the bond.[2] The second term is the expected value difference between the bond value of the convertible and lower expected future conversion values. This second term may be viewed as an "insurance" value of the convertible at time $t = 0$ (that is, the integral of all future occurrences where the bond value of the convertible exceeds its conversion value times the probability of occurrence, $f(i, t_0)di(t)$). The lower limit of the integral is zero, because the

---

[1]William J. Baumol, Burton G. Malkiel, and Richard E. Quandt, "The Valuation of Convertible Securities," *Quarterly Journal of Economics,* February 1966, pp. 48–59.
[2]This amount is assumed to remain constant over time.

price of the stock cannot fall below this amount. The upper limit is $\bar{B}/P(t_0)S$, because the bond value equals the conversion value at this amount.

The first term of the right-hand member of expression 13A.2 is the straight bond value of the convertible. The second term is the expected value difference between the conversion value and lower expected straight bond values. In this case, the value of the convertible must be at least equal to its straight bond value plus the value of the conversion feature. The conversion feature will add to the straight bond value only when $\bar{B}/P(t_0)S > \bar{B}$. Because the stock price could (theoretically) rise to ∞, the lower limit of the integral is $\bar{B}/P(t_0)S$ and the upper limit is ∞.

A modification of equation 13.1 is presented by Baumol-Malkiel-Quandt:

$$C \geqslant \frac{R}{(1+\frac{\rho}{2})} + \frac{R}{(1+\frac{\rho}{2})^2} + \ldots + \frac{R}{(1+\frac{\rho}{2})^{2n}} + \frac{C_b}{(1+\frac{\rho}{2})^{2n}} \qquad (13A.3)$$

Where:

R is the semiannual bond coupon[3]

n is the number of years in the investor's horizon

C_b is the actuarial value of the bond at the end of the horizon (determined by equation 13A.2 at the end of the horizon period)

ρ is the appropriate rate of discount

When $C = \bar{B}$, ρ is the bond yield on the convertible. If $C = P(t)S$, ρ is the stockholders' equity capitalization rate.[4] If $C > \bar{B} > P(t)S$ or $C > P(t)S > \bar{B}$, ρ is between these two rates.

REFERENCES

Baumol, William J., Burton G. Malkiel, and Richard E. Quandt, "The Valuation of Convertible Securities," *Quarterly Journal of Economics,* February 1966, pp. 48–59.

Bladen, A., *Techniques for Investing in Convertible Bonds.* New York: Salomon Bros. and Hutzler, 1966.

Brigham, Eugene F., "An Analysis of Convertible Debentures: Theory and Some Empirical Evidence," *Journal of Finance,* March 1966, pp. 35–54.

[3] Equation 13.1 simplifies the usual semiannual payment condition by assuming annual payments.

[4] See Chapter 10.

Cretien, Paul D., Jr., "Convertible Bond Premiums as Predictors of Common Stock Price Changes," *Financial Analysts Journal,* November-December 1969, pp. 90-95.

Gruen, Tobias, "Investment and Trading Opportunities in Convertible Securities," *Commercial and Financial Chronicle,* January 7, 1971.

————, "Taking Another Look at Investment and Trading Opportunities in Convertible Securities," *Commercial and Financial Chronicle,* July 8, 1971.

Pilcher, C. James, *Raising Capital with Convertible Securities.* Ann Arbor, Michigan: Bureau of Business Research, University of Michigan, 1955.

Pinches, George E., "Financing with Convertible Preferred Stocks, 1960-1967," *Journal of Finance,* March 1970, pp. 53-64.

Poensgen, Otto H., "The Valuation of Convertible Bonds," Parts I and II, *Industrial Management Review,* Fall 1965 and Spring 1966, pp. 77-92 and pp. 83-98.

Vinson, Charles, "Pricing Practices in the Primary Convertible Bond Market," *Quarterly Review of Economics and Business,* Summer 1970, pp. 47-60.

Weil, R.L., J. Segall, and D. Green, "Premiums on Convertible Bonds," *Journal of Finance,* June 1968, pp. 445-64.

14

Speculative Securities

COMMON-STOCK WARRANTS

In 1942, the common-stock warrants of R.K.O. were selling for $.0625 each. Four years later, they were selling for $13 — a two-hundred-eight-fold increase. In 1948, Hoffman Radio warrants were priced at a nickel apiece. Two years later, they sold as high as $25 each — a five-hundred-fold increase. Universal Picture warrants sold at $39 in 1945, but by 1947 they had fallen to $1.50. Between August 1956 and December 1959, General Tire common advanced from $50 to $280 (adjusted) — a 460 percent increase. The General Tire $60 warrants went from $7.25 to $215, however, in the same span — a 2,865 increase. More spectacularly, the $70 warrants went from $4.50 to $205 — a 4,455 percent increase.[1]

From these examples, it can be seen that fabulous profits (and losses) have been obtained through speculating in common-stock warrants. Although it is unlikely that any one person actually bought or sold these warrants at the times indicated in the above illustrations, it is nonetheless obvious that price movements of large magnitudes have occurred for many common-stock warrants in the past, and the risk-seeking investor should consider these instruments as an attractive speculative vehicle.

[1]The most dramatic performance in the history of common stock warrants was the 123,077 percent increase in the price of Tri-Continental warrants witnessed from 1942 to 1962. See Fred Pease, "The Warrant: Its Powers and Its Hazards," *Financial Analysts Journal*, January–February 1963, pp. 25–32.

Characteristics of Warrants

A *common-stock warrant* is simply a legal instrument issued by a corporation that grants the holder the right to purchase the common stock of the corporation at a stated price within a stated period of time. Thus, there are three basic elements to the common-stock warrant. The first of these, the *privilege of exchange,* is the most essential element. This privilege entitles the holder to exchange the warrant for common stock, usually on the basis of one warrant for one share of stock. The second, the stated *price of exchange* or *option price,* is the price for common above which the warrant becomes mathematically valuable. This option price may be fixed over the life of the warrant or may change, usually rising as the age of the warrant increases. The final element, the stated *period of time,* is the duration of the life of the warrant. This period may vary from a few days to perpetuity. An example will illustrate these three elements. Allegheny Corp. has an issue of 3¾ perpetuals that have been outstanding for quite some time. Each warrant of this issue is exchangeable for one share of common stock at $3.75 for the remainder of the life of the company. Thus, when the price of Allegheny common advances beyond 3¾, the warrant assumes a mathematical value. This mathematical value is precisely the difference between the price of the stock and $3.75.

Common-stock warrants may come into being in various ways. The most typical of these include the following:

1. Through the sale of common stock and the warrants together as a unit.
2. Through exchange as a result of a reorganization.
3. Through sale to underwriters at a nominal price – part of their actual compensation.
4. Through separate public sale (rare).
5. Through attachment as a bonus to senior securities.

The way a warrant comes into being may give some indication as to the future performance of the common stock of the company in question and, consequently, to the future value of the warrant. Warrants that result from reorganizations, where stockholders and other junior-security holders are given warrants in the reorganized company for their old securities, may be suspect. The fact that the company had to be reorganized might give some indication as to the future uncertainty for the common and hence the warrant. Although amazing comebacks in such cases have been witnessed (the St. Louis Southwestern R.R. is a prime example), during the period after reorganization warrants tend to be depressed.

When warrants are used as partial compensation for investment bankers or as a "sweetener" for other issues, no indication is given about the future performance of the warrant. Many well-established firms employ the second of these practices, and on occasion both are employed by established firms. The use of the warrant as a sweetener for the sale of another issue, particularly debenture or other forms of bond issue, is an alternative to issuing a convertible security (discussed in Chapter 13). Several advantages exist for the purchaser of the senior security with warrants attached over the senior issue convertible into common stock. First, the holder has the option of selling the warrant and retaining the original issue. The convertible holder obviously cannot do this. Second, the life of the warrant cannot be reduced or terminated at the option of the company, whereas many convertible issues are callable after a period of time. Finally, as Graham, Dodd, and Cottle point out, ". . . because of the speculative attractiveness attaching to warrants alone they usually command a greater premium in the market over their realizable value than would a comparable convertible issue."[2]

Valuing Warrants

Determining the worth of a warrant would be a simple matter if warrants sold at their mathematical value. Because there is value associated with the option element of a warrant, however, warrants generally sell above their mathematical worth.[3] The determinants of the price of a warrant may be specified as:

$$P_w = f(P_o, T_n, P_c, D_i, F_c) \qquad (14.1)$$

Where: P_w = market price of the warrant

P_o = option or exercise price of the common

T_n = duration of the issue, that is, time remaining before expiration

P_c = current price of the common

D_i = potential dilution, that is, ratio of the number of warrants outstanding to the number of common shares outstanding

F_c = the future common stock price

---

[2]Graham, Dodd, and Cottle, *Security Analysis,* 4th ed. (New York: McGraw-Hill Book Company, 1962), p. 614. Although this may be a slight exaggeration, it appears possible that risk-assuming speculators in an imperfect market may bid up the price of warrants to establish larger premiums beyond pure mathematical value than would be the case for a comparable convertible security. See the discussion of market premiums that follows.

[3]There is a tendency for the actual price of a warrant to approach its mathematical value as the price of the common stock rises significantly beyond the exercise price.

From the discussion above, we may observe that P_o and P_c have a definite quantifiable relationship to the value of the warrant. These two variables determine the mathematical value of the warrant, which may be expressed as follows:

$$V = (P_c - P_o)N \tag{14.2}$$

Where: V is the mathematical value of the warrant

N is the number of shares that may be purchased with one warrant

P_c and P_o are as in equation 14.1

To consider a simple example, if the stock of the XYZ Co. were currently selling in the market place at $25 per share, and each warrant allowed the purchase of one share of common stock at $15 per share, the mathematical value of the XYZ Co. warrants would be $10 per warrant.

Warrant Premiums and Maturities

The variables T_n, D_i, and F_c determine the premium that one would be willing to pay above the pure mathematical value of the warrant. T_n suggests something quite important regarding the nature of a stock warrant: a warrant is really nothing more than a long-term option enabling its owner to obtain the common stock at a fixed price in the future. Obviously, this option has a value that exists even when the common stock is selling substantially below the option price. This is true because the stock *might* rise above the option price at some point during the life of the warrant. Such a possibility has a value that is incorporated into the premium paid for the warrant. The value related to the variable T_n might appear to be intuitively obvious: the longer the time remaining in the life of the warrant, the more valuable the option privilege becomes. Unfortunately, the empirical relationship is not so easily discerned.

Attempts to quantify the effects of longevity on the value of the warrant have produced some evidence to suggest that this variable becomes important only as the warrant approaches expiration. Several studies, for example, have found that maturity differences are not important beyond a specific number of years.[4] Other writers argue that although isolated empirical investigations have

---

[4] A report prepared by the Investment Bankers Association of America placed the cutoff at two years. See *Federal Income Taxation of Compensatory Options (Including Warrants) Granted to Underwriters and Other Independent Contractors* (Washington, D.C.: Investment Bankers Association, 1963), p. 54. Others have posited cutoffs of from four to ten years. See S. T. Kassouf, *Evaluation of Convertible Securities* (New York: Analytical Publishers Co., 1966); G. Giguere, "Warrants: a Mathematical Method of Evaluation," *The Analysts Journal,* November–December 1958, pp. 17–25; J. P. Shelton, "The Relation of the Price of a Warrant to the Price of Its Associated Stock," *Financial Analysts Journal,* July–August 1967, pp. 88–99.

observed a truncation effect, there are no theoretical grounds for such a phenomenon. This view is adopted by Miller, who maintains that warrants often expire with the price of the common below the option price, although given more time the common *could* rise to produce a mathematical value for the warrant.[5] In a study of warrant price behavior over the period 1960–69, he finds that maturity differences influence premiums throughout the life of the warrant. Given two price relatives, common price to option price and warrant price to option price, empirical data are fitted to functions of the form $Y = aX^b$, and a graphical representation similar to Figure 14-1 is depicted. In this diagram, the

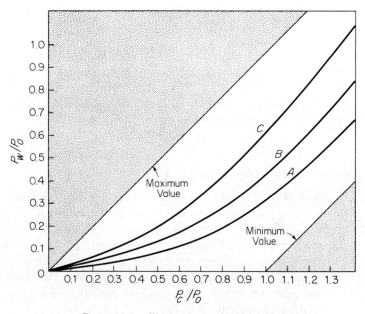

Figure 14-1   Warrant Longevity Value Model

warrant price relative (P_w/P_o) is the dependent (Y) variable, and the common-stock price relative (P_c/P_o) is the independent (X) variable. The maximum relative is given where $(P_w/P_o) = (P_c/P_o)$. Values where $(P_w/P_o) > (P_c/P_o)$ are not possible, because this would imply $P_w > P_c$ (that is, the warrant price exceeded the common stock price). The minimum relative is given where $[(P_c/P_o) - 1] = [(P_w/P_o)]$. Values where $[(P_c/P_o) - 1] > [(P_w/P_o)]$ imply $(P_c - P_o) > P_w$. This condition is not possible because if the mathematical value of the warrant exceeded its market price, arbitragers would buy the warrant, exercise it, and sell the common until $(P_c - P_o) = P_w$. Possible relatives are given by

[5] Jerry D. Miller, "Effects of Longevity on Values of Stock Purchase Warrants," *Financial Analysts Journal*, November–December 1971, pp. 78–85.

functions A, B, and C. These functions represent warrants of specific maturity categories with increasing slopes corresponding to longer maturities. Thus, if function A were the fit of warrants with maturities of one year or less and B were the fit of warrants with maturities of one to two years, the latter group would command a larger premium than the former. Symbolically,

$$\frac{P_{w(B)}/P_{o(B)}}{P_{c(B)}/P_{o(B)}} > \frac{P_{w(A)}/P_{o(A)}}{P_{c(A)}/P_{o(A)}}$$

thus:

$$P_{w(B)}/P_{c(B)} > P_{w(A)}/P_{c(A)}$$

Miller found this sort of relationship empirically where the functional relationship ranged from $Y = .2753\ (X)^{1.8545}$ for warrants of six-month to one-year maturities to $Y = .5509\ (X)^{1.2155}$ for perpetual warrants. The R^2 exceeds 0.94 for four of his six functions, indicating a reasonably good empirical fit.

Warrant Premiums, Dilution, and Dividends

The second of the key variables in the determination of the value of the premium applied to a given warrant issue is D_i, the potential dilution of earnings and dividends resulting from the exercise of warrants after the option price is reached. Because common stock warrants do not receive dividends, holders of warrants may elect to exercise their option to buy common stock in order to enjoy the income from dividends that the common pays. This, of course, assumes that the common stock is paid a dividend, and many of the companies that issue common-stock warrants do not pay dividends. It also assumes that the premium has become insignificant relative to the dividends that are paid. Thus, if XYZ common is selling at $25 per share, its outstanding warrants are selling at $10.25, and the exercise price is $15, some holders would exercise the purchase option if the dividend were large enough. The fact that additional shares are issued at less than the market price per share may produce a long-run dilution in earnings per share. This would occur if the present value of earnings generated from plant and equipment purchased with the funds obtained from the sale of new shares to warrant holders were less than the price paid by warrant holders for their shares. A dilution in long-run earnings would affect the market price of the common stock and hence the value of the warrant. In this instance, the presence of a substantial volume of warrants might serve to depress the market price per warrant.

It can be argued in this case that exercise would not take place because the rational holder of the warrants would simply sell at the market price of $10.25 and buy the common at $25, for a cost of $14.75 per share, a price lower than the $15 option price. This would indeed be true if it were not for the "turn of the market" — brokerage commissions, taxes, and so on. In this example, if the "turn" were larger than the $.25 differential, the option to purchase at $15 would be exercised. Thus, if the differential, which is actually the premium, is less than the turn, exercise may occur. If it is larger than the turn, exercise will not occur.

All this assumes, of course, that the extra dividends received from holding common are more valuable to the holder than the prospective return from holding the warrant. In the above case, if the common rose in price by 20 percent (from 25 to 30), the warrant would have to rise to at least 15 (the mathematical value of the warrant), which is almost a 50 percent increase. Thus, the speculator who expected higher prices for XYZ common would probably prefer to hold the warrant regardless of the XYZ dividend. This illustrates the major attraction of warrants to the risk-seeking investor. Price movements for warrants are generally magnified in percentage terms from a given change in the price of common. The phenomenon operates both positively and negatively. If XYZ fell by 20 percent, from 25 to 20, the warrant could fall by as much as 50 percent because the mathematical value of the warrant would now be only 5. Even if a larger premium developed at the lower warrant price, which frequently happens, the percentage decline in the price of the warrant would be magnified.

There is empirical evidence to demonstrate that firms with high dividend payouts tend to have slower rates of earnings growth.[6] This retardation of earnings growth may tend to reduce the attractiveness of warrants that may be exercised for high-yield common stocks. The negative impact of high cash payouts on warrant values has been recognized in studies that have found dividend yields to have a negative regression coefficient, with higher yields indicating lower warrant values.[7]

Warrants and Common-Stock Prices

The final key variable in the determination of the value of the premium to be applied to a given issue of common-stock warrants is F_c, the future price of the common stock. In many ways, this variable is the most important one for the determination of the value of the warrant, and undoubtedly it is the most difficult to handle. The ideal way of approaching this variable is to follow the procedures indicated previously for analyzing a common share. The important factors here are the expected future earnings of the company, the expected future dividends, and the expected future multiplier to apply to the earnings of the company per common share when the stock is to be sold. The analysis proceeds in the manner described in Chapters 5 through 12 of this book.

[6] See Edward E. Williams and J. J. Seneca, "Dividend Policy, Growth, and Retention Rates: U.S. Public Utilities 1958–1967," *Public Utilities Fortnightly,* March 15, 1973, pp. 23–27.
[7] See J. P. Shelton, "The Relation of the Price of a Warrant to the Price of Its Associated Stock," *op. cit.*

Suppose an analyst has forecasted the following earnings-per-share pattern for the Keystone Corp. for the next five years:

1974	$1.00
1975	$1.20
1976	$1.50
1977	$2.00
1978	$2.50

The analyst expects an earnings multiple of 20 to hold in 1978, and he believes the firm will maintain a dividend payout of about 50 percent over the period. Keystone common sells at 26¼. If a purchase were made at the beginning of 1974 for holding until 1978, the following return would be expected:

	1974	*1975*	*1976*	*1977*	*1978*
DPS	$.50	$.60	$.75	$1.00	$ 1.25
Market price at terminal date				20 X 2.50 =	50.00
Dollar returns	$.50	$.60	$.75	$1.00	$51.25
@ 16%	.826	.743	.641	.552	.476
Annual present value	$.41	$.45	$.48	$.55	$24.40

Total present value = $26.29

Thus, if the stock were purchased at $26.25, a return of about 16 percent could be earned.

Keystone Corp. also has a set of warrants expiring in 1990. The warrants give the holder the right to buy one share of common for each warrant held at a price of $30 per share. The mathematical value of the warrant currently is:

$$V = (P_c - P_o)N$$

$$= (\$26.25 - \$30.00)(1)$$

$$= -\$3.75$$

although the warrant sells in the market for $5. Thus, investors are paying a premium of $8.75 over the mathematical value of the warrant. Investors evidently feel that the future prospects for Keystone are sufficiently bright to produce a stock price substantially above the exercise price during the life of the warrant. Is this optimism justifiable?

To answer this, we may determine the price of Keystone warrants in 1978, given the above assumptions. If there were no premium existing then, the warrant price would be:

$$P_w - V = 0$$

$$P_w = V = (P_c - P_o)N$$

$$P_w = (50 - 30)1 = \$20$$

and it could be higher if a premium continued. An investor who bought the warrant would have an expected return of at least:

$$(X)(\$20) = \$5$$

$$X = .25$$

At 32 percent, a dollar received five years hence is worth $.25 today. Thus, the expected return would be about 32 percent. This compares with an expected return of only 16 percent for the common.

Suppose, however, that the analyst is incorrect in his estimates and that the following EPS pattern and multiple prevail:

1974	$ .80
1975	$1.00
1976	$1.20
1977	$1.40
1978	$1.50 (multiple in 1978 = 17 times earnings)

Common-stock holders would earn only 1.7 percent rather than the expected 16 percent:

Dollar return		@2%			@1%	
.40	X	.980 =	.39	X	.990 = $	.40
.50	X	.961 =	.48	X	.980 =	.49
.60	X	.942 =	.57	X	.971 =	.58
.70	X	.924 =	.65	X	.961 =	.67
.75	X	.906 =	.68	X	.951 =	.71
25.50[a]	X	.906 =	23.10	X	.951 =	$24.25
			$25.87			$27.10

return = 1.7 percent

[a]17 X 1.50 = 25.50

Given the revised data, warrant holders would *lose* even if the premium remained constant:

(a) $V = (P_c - P_o)N$

$= (25.50 - 30.00)1$

$= -\$4.50$

(b)   Premium $= P_w - V$

$\$8.75 = P_w - (-\$4.50)$

$P_w = \$4.25$

(c)   at -3 percent, $(.863)(\$5.00) = \$4.31$

Thus, we observe that under favorable conditions, the warrant return would be double that of the common stock (32 percent versus 16 percent). Under unfavorable ones, however, the common stock investment earned 1.7 percent, and the warrant investment lost 3 percent. Warrants are thus seen to be riskier than common stocks because their returns are levered. That is, good returns on a common stock produce better ones for warrants. Poor returns produce poorer ones.[8]

COMMON-STOCK SUBSCRIPTION RIGHTS

Common-stock subscription rights are a unique form of warrant that comes into being when a company sells additional shares to its own stockholders through a rights offering. New shares must be sold in this manner when stockholders have retained the *preemptive right* in the firm's charter to maintain their proportionate ownership share of the company. When a firm plans a rights offering, each shareholder receives rights according to the number of shares held. These rights

---

[8]We find from the above example that the *expected* common-stock price is a crucial variable in determining the returns expected to be earned on a warrant purchase. Volatility in stock price movements can also be important. It might be argued that the warrants of a firm whose common had sold from $40 to $60 ($\mu = \$50$) would be more "valuable" than those of an identical firm whose common ranged only from $45 to $55 ($\mu = \$50$). Unfortunately, empirical evidence on the desirability of common stock volatility for warrant holders is mixed. Even the importance of volatility is not accepted. Van Horne found that volatility was a very important determinant of warrant values, but Shelton discovered it to be an insignificant factor. See J. C. Van Horne, "Warrant Valuation in Relation to Volatility and Opportunity Costs," *Industrial Management Review,* Spring 1969, pp. 19–32; and J. P. Shelton, *op. cit.*

allow the purchase of new shares at a stated subscription price. Thus, rights are simply warrants with a very short maturity. They have value because the stated subscription price is always set below the then-existing market price of the firm's shares. Hence, shareholders will generally exercise their rights by buying new shares, or they will sell them to someone else who may exercise them. Only foolish investors will allow their rights to expire without exercising or selling them, although such people do exist.[9]

The mechanics of a rights offering are quite simple. First, the board of directors of the company announces a rights offering to shareholders listed on the books as of the record date. These shareholders will receive rights to buy additional shares that may be exercised any time between the date of the rights distribution and the expiration date. In the period between the announcement and the last date one may purchase the stock to become a shareholder by the record date (the former is called the "ex" date and is five business days before the record date), the common stock is said to be selling "rights-on" or "cum-rights." This means that any purchase of the common stock between those dates carries with it the right to buy additional new shares. After the ex date, the common stock sells "rights-off" or "ex-rights." Then, the common stock and warrants trade as separate instruments (a market for the warrants on a "when issued" basis generally is established soon after the announcement date), and the purchase of a share in the open market no longer carries with it the right to buy new shares from the company.[10]

During the period when the stock is selling cum-rights, the theoretical or mathematical value of each right is:

$$R_o = \frac{P_c - P_s}{N + 1} \tag{14.3}$$

Where: R_o = the theoretical or mathematical value of a right when the stock is selling cum-rights

P_c = the market price of the stock rights-on

P_s = the subscription price per share

N = the number of rights required to purchase one new share of stock

[9] If the market price of shares falls below the subscription price during the offering and stays there until the expiration date, the rights will have no value and nothing would be lost by not exercising them. Indeed, in this instance, shares might be brought more cheaply in the market than through subscription.

[10] On the ex date, when the common stock begins to sell ex-rights, its price must fall by the value of the right. If it does not, then we may conclude that the price of the common stock would have risen during that trading day had it not been the ex date. Thus, suppose a stock is selling at $15 the day before the ex date and has rights attached worth $1. If the stock still sells at $15 the next day, while the rights trade separately at $1, then the stock would otherwise have gone from $15 to $16.

On the ex date, the price per share should fall to:

$$P_x = \frac{(P_c \times N) + P_s}{N + 1}$$

(14.4)

Where: P_x = price of the stock ex-rights

And the value of the right becomes:

$$R_x = \frac{P_x - P_s}{N}$$

(14.5)

Where: R_x = the theoretical or mathematical value
of a right when the stock is selling
ex-rights

The theoretical value of a right is very much like the mathematical value of a warrant. Frequently, investors are willing to pay a premium for the option value of the right. These premiums are usually smaller than those paid for a warrant because the exercise life of a right is usually short.

EXAMPLE

The Edmundston Co. has announced a rights offering that will allow shareholders to subscribe to one new share for each 20 now held (20 rights to buy one new share). The firm's stock now sells for $101, and the subscription price will be $80 per share.

a) The theoretical value of each right is:

$$R_o = \frac{P_c - P_s}{N + 1}$$

$$= \frac{101 - 80}{21}$$

$$= \$1$$

b) When the stock goes ex-rights, its price should fall to:

$$P_x = \frac{(P_c \times N) + P_s}{N + 1} = \frac{(101)(20) + 80}{21} = \$100$$

c) If the price of the stock is \$100 when it goes ex-rights, the theoretical value of each right would be:

$$R_x = \frac{P_x - P_s}{N}$$

$$= \frac{100 - 80}{20}$$

$$= \$1$$

COMMON-STOCK OPTIONS

There exists a form of option that is not sold by a corporation on its own shares but rather by other individuals on shares that they hold (or promise to acquire). A *call* option gives the purchaser the right to buy a certain common stock (or other security) at a stated price for a given period of time. A *put* option allows the holder to sell a stock at a stated price for a given period of time. A *straddle* is the purchase of a put and call on the same security for the same period of time at the same price. A *spread* is similar to a straddle except the put price is set below the call price. If the option is written at the current market price of the stock, which is usually the case, the spread put would be below the market price, and the call would be above it. Combinations of options are also possible. A *strip* is a straddle plus a put. A *strap* is a straddle plus a call.

A call option is very much like a warrant. Because options are usually written with the exercise price at the current market price of the stock, an option usually has no mathematical value at that time (that is, $V = P_c - P_o = 0$). Buyers pay positive prices for options because they believe the price of the stock optioned will rise sufficiently at some time during the option period to recover the cost of the option and provide an acceptable rate of return. On occasion, options are written at prices below the current market price of the optioned shares. In this case, the option does have a mathematical value. Such options, of course, are sold at prices above this value. The mathematical value is added to the option premium to get the market price.

Options are written for 30, 60, and 90 days and 6 months and 10 days (the last for capital gains treatment), although longer periods are sometimes contracted for. The price of an option will depend upon supply and demand factors in the market for the option. If speculators believe an upward movement in a common stock's price is imminent, they will bid up the price of options on that stock. Because the probability of an upward movement increases with time, longer options usually sell for higher prices than short-period ones (often in a relation approximating a square root function, for example, six-month options at 1.4X the cost of three-month options on the same stock).

Unfortunately, many people tend to view the option market strictly in terms of a small investor buying a call on a volatile stock in the hope of achieving a leveraged gain. Although such things do occur, they present a very limited view of the role of the market. Paper gains can be locked in by the purchase of a put if the investor has doubts about the short-term price movement of the stock. Furthermore, a portfolio that must hold a stock for tax or other reasons but has little enthusiasm for its short-run price performance can earn a tidy profit (20 percent or more) selling calls against the security. If, on the other hand, the portfolio manager is enthusiastic about a security, he can make money writing puts. Although this is hardly an area for the novice, it should be iterated that options, properly employed, can increase the return and reduce the risk of the portfolio.[11] Consider the following examples:

1. A stock sells for $40 per share. A 90-day call option can be purchased for $200 on 100 shares. What profit would be made if the stock sold for $45 within 90 days? For $42? $41? $38?

at $45: $4500 − ($4000 + 200) = $300; $\frac{300}{200}$ = 150% gain

at $42: $4200 − ($4000 + 200) =   0; $\frac{0}{200}$ = 0% (breakeven)

at $41: $4100 − ($4000 + 200) = −$100; $\frac{-100}{200}$ = 50% loss

at $38: $3800 − ($4000 + 200) = −$400; $\frac{-200}{200}$ = 100% loss (in this case,

                                                                the call would

                                                                not be

                                                                exercised)

2. Suppose a stock sells for $40 and can be straddled at a price of $400 per 100 shares for one year. What returns will be generated if the stock sells at $30 during the year, assuming the option is exercised? At $36? At $40? At $42? At $46?

at $30: ($4000 −   3000) − $400 = $600; $\frac{600}{400}$ = 150% gain

at $36: ($4000 −   3600) − $400 =   0; $\frac{0}{400}$ = 0% (breakeven)

at $40: ($4000 −   4000) − $400 = −$400; $\frac{-400}{400}$ = 100% loss (no exercise)

---

[11]See M. C. Findlay and S. Bolten, "Toward a Pareto-Optimality Justification of the Call Option Market," *Proc. Southwestern Finance Assn.*, 1973.

at $42: $4200 - ($4000 + 400) = -$200; $\dfrac{-200}{400}$ = 50% loss

at $46: $4600 - ($4000 + 400) = $200; $\dfrac{200}{400}$ = 50% gain

Until recently all options trading was done on an over-the-counter basis. In April, 1973, the first organized options exchange opened. The Chicago Board Options Exchange (CBOE) has added a degree of standardization to option trading in that all CBOE contracts expire on one of four days – the last business days of January, April, July, and October. In the over-the-counter market, an option can expire on any day; thus, an option written on one day is not interchangeable with one written the following day. The CBOE also has standardized exercise prices that are introduced at predetermined price intervals approximating the current market of the underlying stock. The premium (which is the market price of the option) is obtained through transactions on the exchange floor, where competing market-makers (specialists) are assigned to each option to help assure a fair and orderly market. Thus, an investor can obtain the most recent option prices of the almost fifty stocks on which contracts are written. Hopefully, this market will be more efficient than the rather haphazard OTC arrangement.

To illustrate an example of trading a CBOE option, assume an investor decided on May 4 to purchase the Sperry Rand October $40 option. The closing price of the option for that day was 7, while the stock closed at 41¾. Since the mathematical value of the option was $1.75 ($41.75 - $40.00), if the investor purchased at the closing price he would have paid a premium of $5.25 ($7.00 - $1.75) for the privilege of being able to buy Sperry Rand common stock at $40 per share until October 31 (179 days). If Sperry Rand advanced during that period, the investor most likely would not exercise his option. Rather, he would sell it on the exchange to another buyer. Thus, if Sperry sold at 50 on August 15, and the price of the option were 14, the investor could close out his position at a 100 percent profit. The purchaser on August 15 would have paid a premium of $4 (since the mathematical value of the option was then $10) for an option expiring in 77 days. On October 31, the option should be trading at no more than its pure mathematical value, since upon expiration that day the option would be worthless. During the final day, options would be exercised assuming the market price of the stock exceeded the option price.

Several empirical studies have been made of the profitability of trading in options, although the results are mixed. In a simulated experiment of put and call purchases, Kruizenga found that in the great bull market after the Second World War calls yielded handsome returns, but puts lost money.[12]

[12] R. J. Kruizenga, "Profit Returns from Purchasing Puts and Calls," in P. H. Cootner, *The Random Character of Stock Market Prices* (Cambridge: The M.I.T. Press, 1964), pp. 392–411.

Nevertheless, the profits that could have been made from holding common stocks *exceeded* those that purchasing options would have produced. Boness studied the period 1957–1960 and concluded that large losses (60 to 80 percent per year) would have been suffered by option purchasers.[13] He also found that individuals who wrote options (against stock they owned or promised to acquire) could have earned between 18 and 32 percent per annum if their investment commitment were sufficiently large and if they frequently revised their offerings.[14] Although these results are not terribly encouraging to the prospective options purchaser, it should be remembered that these studies were simulations of a large number of holdings. To the extent that one is very optimistic about a stock he is considering buying, or very pessimistic about a security he is considering selling (selling short), the option can be an attractive speculative vehicle.[15] The biggest danger in purchasing an option, however, is being right in the long-run but wrong in the short-run. Many speculators have bought call options on stocks that they were very bullish about, only to have the stock do nothing until their option expired and then show a remarkable advance. Since speculators have a tendency to buy heavily (holding little or no cash reserves), they are unable to purchase a second option at the expiration of their initial option. Thus, they lose all (or most) of their investment, even though their basic "hunches" were correct.[16]

WARRANTS, CONVERTIBLES, AND DILUTION

The exercise of warrants and the conversion of convertible securities result in a dilution of the short-run per share earnings of the firm. In the case of warrants,

---

[13] A. J. Boness, "Some Evidence of the Profitability of Trading in Put and Call Options," in Cootner, *op. cit.*, pp. 475–96.

[14] These simulation studies have been criticized on the grounds that transactions costs, taxes, and the thinness of the options market were ignored. The presence of the two former factors would tend to reduce returns from purchasing options, and the latter might preclude altogether the purchase of certain options that no one chose to write. See B. G. Malkiel and R. Quandt, *Strategies and Rational Decisions in the Securities Option Market* (Cambridge: The M.I.T. Press, 1969). This study also suggests that option writers who behave optimally could earn a 20 to 25 percent pretax return.

[15] Although the option is a speculative instrument, an investor need not be a risk-assumer technically speaking (as defined in Chap. 15) to purchase options. A call option that has the same return as the security optioned will have less total risk for the option seller with a long position, although more for the buyer. This risk reduction for the seller provides a rationale for a negotiated sale of options where risk averse buyers may participate. See Findlay and Bolten, "Toward a Pareto-Optimality Justification of the Call Option Market," *op. cit.*

[16] As Keynes observed, "In the long-run, we are all dead." This is particularly true for the options purchaser. Even if sufficient cash reserves are maintained to allow one to purchase another option after the expiration of the first, a stubborn stock may be an expensive one for the speculator. The costs of buying a one-year option and then replacing it for another year could run upwards of one-half the price of the stock. Thus, at least a 50 percent advance would be required just to break even!

the effect may be reduced in the long run because funds raised from the sale of additional shares to warrant holders may be used to buy assets that will generate a larger future income stream per share. In the case of convertible debentures, the issuer is relieved of making interest payments once conversion has taken place. This will increase reported earnings before taxes and will free funds for reinvestment in the firm. In both instances, the long-run effect of exercise and conversion will not be negative if the extra funds made available for reinvestment produce a large enough per share future income stream.[17] Furthermore, the current market price per share of common need not fall even if short-run dilution exceeds the extra stream generated by reinvestment. This is true because the exercise of warrants increases the firm's equity base (hence reducing its riskiness). The conversion of debentures reduces the outstanding debt of the firm and also increases the equity base (again, reducing the firm's risk position).

Because the existence of warrants and convertibles implies potential dilution of per share earnings, the accountants are now requiring that earnings per share be computed under the assumption of conversion of all securities that are common stock equivalents.[18] Such securities include all stock options issued by the firm to management and others, all outstanding warrants, and convertibles issued with a cash yield less than two-thirds of the prime rate. Statements are to be presented that also include a fully diluted EPS figure.

The dilution effect from the sale of common stock to warrant holders is similar to that of the sale of new shares (see Chapter 12) except that the price obtained is lower. The effect of a debenture conversion may be illustrated with a simple example. A firm has $100 million of 5 percent debentures outstanding that are convertible into common at $20 per share. The before and after conversion income statements are given below (assuming the issue is not considered to be a common stock equivalent by *A.P.B. Opinion 15*).

	Before Conversion	After Conversion
EBIT	$28,000,000	$28,000,000
Interest on debentures	5,000,000	—
EBT	23,000,000	28,000,000
Taxes (@50%)	11,500,000	14,000,000
Net income	11,500,000	14,000,000
Number of shares	10,000,000	15,000,000
EPS	$1.15	$.93

[17]See pages 236–37.

[18]See the A.I.C.P.A., *Accounting Principles Board Opinion 15,* May 1969. Under this opinion, dilution for warrants, stock options, and included convertibles occurs upon the sale rather than the exercise of the instrument.

PROBLEMS:

1. The Mason Company has warrants outstanding that may be used to purchase one share of common at $30. If Mason common is at $40, what is the theoretical value of the warrant? What happens if the stock rises by 25 percent to $50?

2. The Jarvis Co. has warrants outstanding to purchase 5.3 shares of common at $50 per share.

   a. If Jarvis Common is at $200, what is the theoretical value of the warrant?

   b. What happens to the theoretical value if the common rises by 20 percent to $240?

   c. What happens if it rises another 20 percent to $288?

   d. What implications can you draw from this example?

3.

   a. Warrants issued by the Racine Corp. allow the holder to buy 5 shares of Racine common for each warrant held. The stock sells for $18 per share and the option price is $15. What is the mathematical value of the warrant?

   b. Racine warrants sell at $20 each. What premium are investors paying for the warrant?

   c. Suppose Racine common advances by 50 percent. By what percentage would the warrant advance if it maintained its premium? If the premium disappeared?

   d. Let the stock fall by 50 percent. By what percentage would the warrant fall if it maintained its premium? What premium would have to develop to keep the decline in the price of the warrant to 50 percent?

4. Reconsider the Keystone Co. (see page 270) changing the exercise price from $30 to $21.50.

   a. What is the new mathematical value of the warrant?

   b. What is the premium?

   c. Given the assumptions of the problem, would it pay to exercise the warrants to buy common stock?

5.

   a. Lucerne Ltd. common sells for $49 per share. The firm has just announced a rights offering whereby its shareholders may subscribe for one new share for each eight now held. The subscription price will be $46 per share. What is the theoretical value of each right?

   b. Suppose Lucerne common advances to $52 per share. What would the new theoretical value of each right be? Compare the price increases of the common and the rights.

   c. Suppose Lucerne common fell to $46 per share. What would the theoretical value of each right be?

   d. Lucerne common has gone ex-rights. The stock is selling for $50 per share. What is the theoretical value of each right? At what price should the common have sold just before it went ex-rights?

   e. After Lucerne common went ex-rights, the stock continued to sell for $50 per share. The rights sold for $1. Can this phenomenon be explained?

6. The Continental Company, whose stock is currently selling for $30, has announced a rights offering by which its shareholders may subscribe for one new share for each ten held at $20.

    a. What is the theoretical value of each right?

    b. To what value should the price of the stock fall when it goes ex-rights?

    c. If the price stays at $30 when it goes ex-rights, what is the theoretical value of each right?

7. The Sinco Corporation, whose stock sells at $150, has announced a rights offering by which its shareholders may subscribe for one new share for each four held at $125.

    a. What is the theoretical value of the right?

    b. To what value should the price of the stock fall when it goes ex-rights?

    c. If the price in fact falls to $135 when it goes ex-rights, what is the theoretical value of the right? What is it if the price falls to $100?

8. A stock sells for $98 per share. A one-year option to buy 100 shares may be purchased for $1,000. The future price of the common stock is expected to be given by the following distribution:

Price	Probability
$ 90	.1
$ 95	.2
$100	.3
$110	.3
$120	.1

The stock will pay a dividend of $3 per share. The option contract requires that the exercise price be reduced by the amount of any dividends paid to the common shareholders during the period of the option.

    a. Compute the expected return if the common stock were purchased today and sold in one year.

    b. Compute the expected return from purchasing the call option.

9. A straddle on 100 shares of a volatile stock may be purchased at $400 for six months. The stock pays no dividend and now sells at $20 per share. Price expectations for the six-month period are:

Price	Probability
$ 25	.3
$ 20	.4
$ 15	.3

Compute the expected return from purchasing the straddle.

10. A call on the stock mentioned in number 9 above could be bought for $200. Compute the expected return and the standard deviation if the common stock were purchased today and sold in six months. Compute the expected return and standard deviation from purchasing the call option.

11. The stock of Albert, Inc., is currently selling for $50 per share. At the end of three months, there is a .5 probability that it will sell at $60, and a .5 probability it will sell for $40.

   a. What is the expected value, ignoring taxes and commissions, of buying 100 shares of Albert, Inc?

   b. What is the expected value of selling 100 shares short?

   c. What is the expected value of buying a 90-day, 100 share put on Albert at $50 for $200?

   d. What is the expected value of buying a 90-day, 100 share call on Albert at $50 for $200?

   e. Explain the above.

12. The Shumann Corp. plans to raise $50 million of debt funds either with a 5 percent bond (convertible at $100 per share) or a 6 percent issue with warrants attached to each $1,000 debenture to subscribe to six shares of common at $100 each. The present capital structure for Shumann is given below:

Debentures	$ 50,000,000
Common stock ($10 par)	100,000,000
Excess over par	100,000,000
Retained earnings	250,000,000
	$500,000,000

Construct capital structures before and after conversion, assuming the convertible bonds are issued, and before and after exercise, assuming bonds with warrants are sold. (The prime rate at the time of debenture issue is 6 percent.)

13. Shumann (above) earns $100 million before interest and taxes. The debenture issue now outstanding is a 7 percent straight-debt issue. The firm is in the 50 percent tax bracket. Prepare before and after conversion income statements assuming the convertible bonds are issued. Prepare similar statements assuming the straight bonds with warrants are sold.

REFERENCES

American Institute of Certified Public Accountants, *Accounting Principles Board Opinion 15,* May 1969.

Ayers, H. F., "Risk Aversion in the Warrants Market," *Industrial Management Review,* Fall 1963, pp. 45–53.

Boness, A. J., "Elements of a Theory of Stock-Option Value," *Journal of Political Economy*, April 1964, pp. 163-75.

——, "Some Evidence of the Profitability of Trading in Put and Call Options," in P. H. Cootner, *The Random Character of Stock Market Prices*. Cambridge: M.I.T. Press, 1964, pp. 475-96.

Bracken, J., "Models for Call Option Decisions," *Financial Analysts Journal*, September-October 1968, pp. 149-51.

Findlay, M. C., and S. Bolten, "Toward a Pareto-Optimality Justification of the Call Option Market," *Proc. Southwestern Finance Assn.*, 1973.

Giguere, G., "Warrants: A Mathematical Method of Evaluation," *The Analysts Journal*, November-December 1958, pp. 17-25.

Graham, B., D. Dodd, and S. Cottle, *Security Analysis*, 4th ed. New York: McGraw-Hill Book Company, 1962.

Kruizenga, R. J., "Profit Returns from Purchasing Puts and Calls," in Cootner, *The Random Character of Stock Market Prices*. Cambridge: M.I.T. Press, 1964, pp. 392-411.

Kassouf, S. T., *Evaluation of Convertible Securities*, New York: Analytical Publishers Co., 1966.

Malkiel, B. G., and R. Quandt, *Strategies and Rational Decisions in the Securities Option Market*. Cambridge: The M.I.T. Press, 1969.

Miller, J. D., "Effects of Longevity on Values of Stock Purchase Warrants," *Financial Analysts Journal*, November-December 1971, pp. 78-85.

Pease, F., "The Warrant: Its Powers and Its Hazards," *Financial Analysts Journal*, January-February 1963, pp. 25-32.

Samuelson, P. A., "Rational Theory of Warrant Pricing," *Industrial Management Review*, Spring 1965, pp. 13-31.

——, and R. C. Merton, "A Complete Model of Warrant Pricing that Maximizes Utility," *Industrial Management Review*, Winter 1969, pp. 17-46.

Shelton, J. P., "The Relation of the Price of a Warrant to 'the Price of Its Associated Stock," *Financial Analysts Journal*, May-June 1967, pp. 143-151; July-August 1967, pp. 88-99.

Sprenkle, C., "Warrant Prices as Indicators of Expectations," *Yale Economic Essays*, I, 1961, pp. 179-232.

Snyder, G. L., "A Look at Options," *Financial Analysts Journal*, January-February 1967, pp. 100-103.

Taylor, H. M., "Evaluating a Call Option and Optimal Timing in the Stock Market," *Management Science*, September 1967, pp. 111-20.

Van Horne, J. C., "Warrant Valuation in Relation to Volatility and Opportunity Costs," *Industrial Management Review*, Spring 1969, pp. 19-32.

Williams, E. E., and J. J. Seneca, "Dividend Policy, Growth, and Retention Rates: U.S. Public Utilities 1958-1967," *Public Utilities Fortnightly*, March 15, 1973, pp. 23-27.

III

Portfolio Analysis

15

Utility Theory

"A man who seeks advice about his actions will not be grateful
for the suggestion that he maximize expected utility."

A. D. Roy

THE PETERSBURG PARADOX

Before we can proceed with the analysis and selection of portfolios, it is
necessary to establish criteria of choice. In other words, what attribute(s) of a
particular security or portfolio of securities make(s) it more desirable than
another security or portfolio? The reader might be tempted to suggest that
return (or income or wealth – three measures that tend to move in the same
direction and are thus used somewhat interchangeably in this discussion) is the
appropriate criterion. This statement appears to be unambiguously true in at least
two cases, which we shall now consider.

All the writers we can find on the subject agree in one way or another that
more wealth is preferable to less, other things being equal. Therefore, if security
A promised a certain return of 20 percent, but security *B* promised a certain
return of only 10 percent, *A* would be unambiguously preferred to (in
terminology used later "is said to dominate") *B*, and return would be a
satisfactory criterion. The crucial point to remember, however, is that we are
discussing *certain* increments to wealth.

If we now assume that the returns on the securities discussed above are not certain but rather subject to probability distributions with the mathematical expectations of 20 percent and 10 percent, it is still possible to salvage the return criterion. To do so, we must assume it possible to engage in an infinite number of independent trials of A and B, each trial involving an infinitely small proportion of our total wealth. The law of large numbers tells us that the actual return will approach the expected return, A will be preferred to B, and the expected return will be an appropriate ranking criterion.

Unfortunately, we rarely encounter certainties or infinitely divisible and replicable events in the real world. The difficulties involved in the employment of the expected return criterion in other situations are easy to illustrate. Suppose that one were offered the following options: (1) receive $1; (2) bet $100 against $102 on the flip of a fair coin; (3) bet $100,000 against $100,002 on the same flip. The expected return of each option is $1 and, by this criterion, one would be indifferent among them. Yet it seems unlikely that any real person would be indifferent as to which option were chosen. It would appear that more refined selection criteria are required.

Perhaps the most famous illustration of the limitations of the expected return criterion is the Petersburg Paradox,[1] which is stated as follows:

> Peter tosses a coin and continues to do so until it should land "heads" when it comes to the ground. He agrees to give Paul one ducat if he gets "heads" on the very first throw, two ducats if he gets it on the second, four if on the third, eight if on the fourth, and so on, so that with each additional throw the number of ducats he must pay is doubled. Suppose we seek to determine the value of Paul's expectation.[2]

The expected return of this proposition is $[(1/2)$ (1 ducat) + $(1/4)$ (2 ducats) +

$(1/8)$ (4 ducats) + . . .] = $(1/2$ ducat + $1/2$ ducat + $1/2$ ducat + . . .) = $\displaystyle\sum_{n=1}^{\infty} \frac{2^{n-1}}{2^n}$

= ∞. Yet it was noted that no one would ever pay a very large sum, much less an infinite sum, to play the game. Therein lay the paradox.

Because it was apparent in this example and numerous others that individuals were not consistent maximizers of expected wealth, an analytical problem arose. In order to make statements and predictions about human behavior in economic decision making, it is necessary to assume some consistency in goal seeking. It is especially desirable to assume that humans act

---

[1] See Daniel Bernoulli, "Exposition of a New Theory on the Measurement of Risk," *Econometrica*, January 1954, pp. 23–36, reprinted in Archer and D'Ambrosio, *The Theory of Business Finance: A Book of Readings* (New York: The Macmillan Company, 1967), pp. 22–35. This article was a translation from Latin into English by Louise Sommer. The original article appeared in the *Papers of the Imperial Academy of Sciences in Petersburg*, 1738, pp. 175–92.

[2] *Op. cit.*, p. 31.

in order to maximize happiness, satisfaction, and so on. Expected wealth had served as a satisfactory surrogate for these goals, but its limitations became too great (as in the above case). Instead of seeking another measurable surrogate, the writers of the period simply identified an abstract concept, *utility,* as that which everyone sought to maximize. By definition, therefore, everyone is a utility maximizer, because the only meaning of utility is that bundle of happiness, satisfaction, and so on that one directs all of one's actions toward maximizing. It then follows that whichever course of action provides the greatest utility is the one to be undertaken.

Unfortunately, this analysis has solved no problems. In order to determine which course of action provides the greatest utility, it is necessary to measure the utility. This, in turn, requires identifying those measurable variables of which utility is a function and specifying the function. In view of the measurement problems, it is not surprising that early writers chose to assume that utility was simply a function of wealth (although not a linear function — which would obviate the advantages of identifying utility as a separate concept).

Daniel Bernoulli approached the problem by assuming that the same proportional additions to the initial level of wealth should have the same absolute utility. Thus, \$100,000 would have the same utility to a millionaire as \$1 to the same person when he only possessed \$10. Operationally, this approach assumes that the utility of a money gain is a log function of the size of the gain. In general, if initial wealth (α) is set at the origin on a utility scale, then the utility of an increase in wealth (Θ) can be shown[3] as a constant times $\log \dfrac{\alpha + \Theta}{\alpha}$. Specifically, Bernoulli demonstrated that the value of the Petersburg game, under these assumptions, would be $\sqrt{\alpha + 1} \cdot \sqrt[4]{\alpha + 2} \cdot \sqrt[8]{\alpha + 4} \ldots - \alpha$. If initial wealth of the player (α) were 0, this would reduce to $\sqrt{1} \cdot \sqrt[4]{2} \cdot \sqrt[8]{4} \cdots = 2$, implying that he would be indifferent between the right to play the game and a gift of two ducats.[4] Bernoulli posits the following example:

> Suppose Caius, a Petersburg merchant, has purchased commodities in Amsterdam which he could sell for ten thousand rubles if he had them in Petersburg. He therefore orders them to be shipped there by sea, but is in doubt whether or not to insure them. He is well aware of the fact that at this time of year, of one hundred ships which sail from Amsterdam to Petersburg, five are usually lost. However, there is no insurance available below the price of eight hundred rubles a cargo, an amount which he considers outrageously high. The question is, therefore, how much wealth

[3] See William Fellner, *Probability and Profit* (Homewood, Illinois: Richard D. Irwin, Inc., 1965), pp. 102–104.

[4] Bernoulli, *op. cit.*, p. 32. Other indifference points were 3 for $\alpha = 10$, 4 for $\alpha = 100$, and 6 for $\alpha = 1000$.

must Caius possess apart from the goods under consideration in order that it be sensible for him to abstain from insuring them?

If X represents his fortune, then this together with the value of the expectation of the safe arrival of his goods is given by

$$\sqrt[100]{(X + 10,000)^{95} \; X^5} = \sqrt[20]{(X + 10,000)^{19} \; X}$$

in case he abstains. With insurance he will have a certain fortune of $X + 9200$. Equating these two magnitudes we get: $(X + 10,000)^{19} \; X = (X + 9200)^{20}$ or, approximately, $X = 5043$. If, therefore, Caius, apart from the expectation of receiving his commodities, possesses an amount greater than 5043 rubles he will be right in not buying insurance. If, on the contrary, his wealth is less than this amount he should insure his cargo.[5]

ALTERNATIVE UTILITY FORMULATIONS

There have been many interesting extensions, refinements, and contradictions of the Bernoulli analysis. Professor Latané, for instance, has shown that under certain circumstances Bernoullian utility assumptions can be used to avoid utility analysis altogether. It will be recalled that Bernoulli suggested that decisions be made on the basis of the expected (arithmetic mean) utility, which was in turn based on the logs of the returns. If we assume that long-run wealth maximization is a desirable goal, then it can be shown that the arithmetic mean of the logarithms (utilities) of returns is maximized when the' geometric mean of returns is maximized.[6] Therefore, the criteria of choice may in this case revert to maximization of return, defined as the geometric mean.

Bernoulli presented the case of a poor man who came into possession of a lottery ticket promising a 50-50 chance of 20,000 ducats or nothing and asked if he would be considered unwise to sell the ticket to a rich man for 9000 ducats. Latané further assumed that the poor man possessed 1000 ducats and the rich man possessed 100,000 ducats. From these data, the following table was constructed:[7]

[5]*Ibid.*, p. 29.

[6]Henry A. Latané, "Criteria for Choice among Risky Ventures," *Journal of Political Economy*, April 1959, pp. 144–55. Reprinted in Fredrikson, *Frontiers of Investment Analysis* (Scranton: International Textbook Co., 1965) pp. 55–69.

[7]*Ibid.*, p. 62.

	Future Occurrences		Criterion	
Strategy	Ticket Wins	Ticket Loses	Arith. Mean	Geo. Mean
Poor Man				
Hold	2.1	0.1	1.1	0.46
Sell	1.0	1.0	1.0	1.0
Rich man				
Buy	1.11	0.91	1.01	1.005
Don't buy	1.00	1.00	1.00	1.00
Probability	.5	.5		

The case of the rich man is fairly simple. If he wins, his return is
$(100,000 + 20,000 - 9,000)/100,000 = 1.11$; if he loses it is $(100,000 - 9000)/100,000 = .91$. If the poor man sells the ticket, he has a 10,000 certainty; to hold the ticket then becomes a gamble which pays a $(10,000 - 9000 + 20,000)/10,000 = 2.1$ return if he wins and $(10,000 - 9,000)/10,000 = .1$ if he loses. As shown in the table, the rich man would want to buy and the poor man would want to hold the ticket on the basis of the arithmetic mean, but the transaction would be desirable for both on the basis of the geometric mean. Bernoulli would claim the latter result valid from a utility standpoint and Latané would claim the same from a long-run wealth maximization standpoint.

A solution to the paradox was also offered by Cramer and published by Bernoulli along with his own. Cramer assumed that the utility of wealth was equal to the square root of its quantity. As such, the utility of the Petersburg game was:

$$1/2 \ \sqrt{1} + 1/4 \ \sqrt{2} + 1/8 \ \sqrt{4} + \ldots = \frac{1}{2 - \sqrt{2}}$$

and its value in certain money was $[1/(2 - \sqrt{2})]^2$, or slightly less than three ducats.[8]

A second solution was also suggested by Cramer. In this case, he assumed that the utility of wealth remained constant beyond a certain point. For argument, Cramer assumed that the utility of all sums greater than 2^{24} was the same as that of 2^{24}. The value of the Petersburg game then became $1/2 + 1/2 +$ (24 times) $+ 1/2 + 1/4 + 1/8 + \ldots = 12 + 1 = 13$. The utility function implied by this solution is linear to 2^{24} and horizontal beyond; as such, it is bounded upward. This is important because Menger has shown that an unbounded function (like Bernoulli's log function) can still give an infinite value.[9] On the other hand, a bounded function is probably unrealistic and violates the

---

[8] Bernoulli, *op. cit.*, pp. 32–34.

[9] Karl Menger, quoted in Arrow, *Essays in the Theory of Risk Bearing* (Chicago: Markham, 1971), p. 23.

assumption that more wealth is always preferred to less. Menger's contention, reiterated by Fellner, "has to do with the fact that the inclinations of many people to disregard very small probabilities, very small probability differences, and also very small amounts of money cannot be fitted into an orderly axiomatic system."[10]

Finally, some authors assume that the utility function is quadratic, of the form $U_x = a + bx - cx^2$ where a, b, and c are constants and b and c are positive.[11] A limitation of quadratic utility functions is that they are not only bounded upward but, indeed, have a maximum beyond which utility declines; it is generally assumed that only the portion to the left of the maximum constitutes the relevant range. A major advantage of quadratic utility functions is that they are completely consistent with the assumption that assets are chosen on the basis of only the first two moments about the mean of the distribution of returns. We shall return to the significance of this attribute.

VON NEUMANN-MORGENSTERN UTILITY

Early writers on utility theory often claimed that it was possible to measure utility on an absolute scale, whereby the joy or pain of money gains and losses could be exactly computed and even compared among individuals. This group of writers, identified as the neoclassical cardinal utility theory school, was essentially discredited by the ordinal utility theory writers. The latter agreed that, through revealed preference, it was possible to detect which goods or combinations of goods were preferred (or were a matter of indifference) to other goods or combinations by the individual under analysis. The point of disagreement, however, was that the ordinalists contended that it was impossible to say by how much one combination of goods was preferred to another. They further insisted that interpersonal comparisons of utility gains and losses could not be made, and that all the writing about the absolute measurement of joy and pain (going back to Bentham's hedonist calculus, if not earlier) was, at best, nonoperational.

Modern cardinal utility theory, which dates from the work of von Neumann and Morgenstern,[12] contends only that, given certain assumptions and certain data about an individual's preferences, it is possible to predict his choices in certain risky situations. The method is called cardinal only because it employs

[10]Fellner, *op. cit.,* p. 107.

[11]William Sharpe, *Portfolio Theory and Capital Markets* (New York: McGraw-Hill Book Company, 1970), p. 196–201.

[12]John von Neumann and Oskar Morgenstern, *Theory of Games and Economic Behavior* (Princeton: Princeton University Press, 1944).

numbers in making these predictions; it makes no pretense of absolute measures and has essentially nothing in common with the earlier cardinal school.

In general, it is assumed that the individual is intelligent, rational, and fully understands the implications of the alternatives being presented to him. In addition, the following five axioms must be assumed for von Neumann-Morgenstern utility calculations to hold:[13]

1. *Transitivity.* If the subject is indifferent between outcomes A and B and also between B and C, he must be indifferent between A and C.

2. *Continuity of preferences.* If A is preferred to B and B is preferred to no change, there must be a probability α $(0 < \alpha < 1)$, such that the individual is indifferent between αA and B.

3. *Independence.* If A is preferred to B, then for any probability $\alpha (0 < \alpha < 1)$, $\alpha A + (1 - \alpha) B$ is preferred to B. Or, viewed another way, if one is indifferent between A and B, then one is also indifferent between αA and αB.

4. *Desire for high probability of success.* If A is preferred to no change and if $\alpha_1 > \alpha_2$, then $\alpha_1 A$ is preferred to $\alpha_2 A$.

5. *Compound probabilities.* If one is indifferent between αA and B, and if $\alpha = \alpha_1 \cdot \alpha_2$, then one is indifferent between $\alpha_1 \alpha_2 A$ and B. In sum, if the outcomes of one risky event are other risky events, the subject should act on the basis of final outcomes and their associated probabilities alone.

If these assumptions can be made, the analyst may then begin to chart the utility of wealth function of his subject. The first step is to define arbitrarily in terms of *utiles* (the cardinal utility unit of measurement) two end points of the range of wealth to be tested; it is important to use end points because the methodology is one of interpolation, but it may *not* be used for extrapolation. Suppose, for example, we defined $0 as 0 utiles and $1 million as 1000 utiles and the following conversation ensued:

Q. How much would you be willing to pay for a lottery ticket offering a 50–50 chance of $1 M or $0?
A. $250,000 [.5 (0 utiles) + .5 (1000 utiles) = 500 U]
Q. How much would you pay for a 50–50 chance of $250,000 or nothing?
A. $62,500 [.5 (0 U) + .5 (500 U) = 250 U]

We have thus assumed two points on the utility versus wealth graph (see Figure 15-1) and have been able to compute two more. In so doing, and in various applications we will make of this analysis, we have employed the expected utility maxim of von Neumann-Morgenstern analysis: *The utility of a*

---

[13]See Fellner, *op. cit.*, pp. 81ff, or William Baumol, *Economic Theory and Operations Analysis*, 2nd ed. (Englewood Cliffs, N.J.: Prentice-Hall, Inc., 1965), Chap. 22.

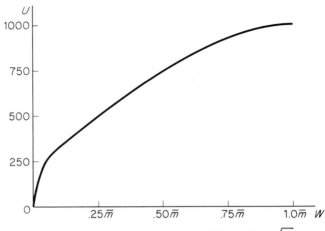

Figure 15-1   Utility as a Function of Wealth (U = √W)

game (risky event) is not the utility of the expected value of the game but rather the expected value of the utilities associated with the outcomes of the game.

To be specific, in our first question above the utility of the lottery ticket was not the utility of its expected value ($500,000) but rather the expected value of the utilities of the two outcomes ($0 and $1 M̄). If the utility of the game were the utility of its expected value, then the individual would be indifferent between the lottery and a gift of $500,000, and we would be back in the Petersburg Paradox.

It will be noted that in the numerical example the utility of wealth is a square root function. In practice, of course, it is not likely to be so well-behaved. But, by asking enough lottery-type questions it should be possible to plot a curve and from the curve to determine the utility associated with every wealth outcome within the relevant range of a risky situation.

Suppose that our subject in the above example (for whom $U = \sqrt{W}$) is faced with a risky situation with the possible outcomes enumerated below:

Outcome	Probability	EV
+ 10,000	.3	3,000
+ 90,000	.5	45,000
+490,000	.2	98,000
		μ = 146,000

The certain sum for which he would be willing to sell his interest is given by:

W	$U = \sqrt{W}$	Probability	EU
+ 10,000	100 U	.3	30
+ 90,000	300 U	.5	150
+490,000	700 U	.2	140
			320 U

$$W = U^2 = (320)^2 = \underline{\underline{\$102,400}}$$

This game possesses the same utility to the subject as a certain $102,400.

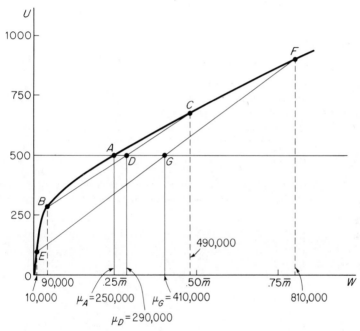

Figure 15-2   Utility as a Function of Wealth (U = $\sqrt{W}$), Specific Values

INDIFFERENCE CURVES

Let us return to our subject in the last section for whom the utility of wealth was equal to the square root of his wealth position. Again defining $0 as 0 utiles and $1 M̄ as 1000 utiles, we may conclude that having $250,000 possesses ($\sqrt{250,000}$) = 500 utiles for the subject, as shown by point *A* on Figure 15-2. A 50–50 chance, represented by point *D*, of having $90,000 ($\sqrt{90,000}$ = 300 U), point B, or $\$490,000$ ($\sqrt{490,000} = 700\ U$), point C, also provides $[(.5)\ (300\ U) + (.5)\ (700\ U)]$ 500 utiles for the subject. Furthermore, a 50–50 chance, represented by point G, of having $\$10,000$ ($\sqrt{10,000} = 100\ U$), point E, or $\$810,000$ ($\sqrt{810,000} = 900\ U$), point F, also provides $[(.5)\ (100\ U) + (.5)\ (900\ U)]$ 500 utiles. Therefore, because the opportunities represented by points A, D and G provide the same utility, the subject should be indifferent among them. Note, however, the following differences in the expected value and standard deviation of opportunities A, D, and G.

(1) μ_A = $\$250,000\ (1.0)$ = $\$250,000$

$\sigma_A = \sqrt{(250,000 - 250,000)^2\ (1.0)} = 0$

(2) μ_D = $(\$90,000)\ (.5) + (490,000)\ (.5)$ = $\$290,000$

$\sigma_D = \sqrt{(\$90,000 - 290,000)^2\ (.5) + (490,000 - 290,000)^2\ (.5)}$
$= \$200,000$

(3) μ_G = $(\$10,000)\ (.5) + (\$810,000)\ (.5)$ = $\$410,000$

$\sigma_G = \sqrt{(\$10,000 - 410,000)^2\ (.5) + (810,000 - 410,000)^2\ (.5)}$
$= \$400,000$

Because we have decided that each of these three opportunities provides equal utility let us graph them in (μ, σ) space, as shown in Figure 15-3 as curve U_2.

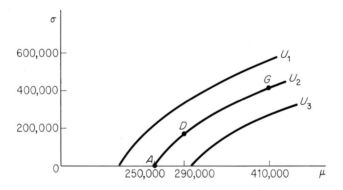

Figure 15-3   Risk Averse Indifference Curves

What we have generated, of course, is an *indifference curve,* the locus of all points on the graph providing the same utility as a $\$250,000$ certainty.[14] Because we are depicting a three-dimensional graph (μ, σ, U) in two-dimensional

[14]It is possible also to derive indifference curves from utility functions mathematically by the expansion of a Taylor series. See Fred Renwick, *Introduction to Investments and Finance* (New York: The Macmillan Company, 1971), pp. 407–8.

(μ, σ) space, there are an infinite number of indifference curves that could be drawn, one corresponding to each certain sum (U_1 and U_3 are representative examples on Figure 15-3). In dealing with indifference curves, it is important to remember that: (1) each point on a given indifference curve provides the same utility as all other points on the same curve, and (2) each point on a second given indifference curve (for the same person at the same time) provides a constant amount of greater (or less) utility than each point on the first curve.

Now observe that the indifference curves are concave and positively sloped in (μ, σ) space.[15] This implies that our subject requires a greater expected return (μ) in order to tolerate a greater dispersion of possible outcomes (σ) and be equally satisfied. Because dispersion of possible outcomes about the mean has been defined as a measure of risk, we may say, in the popular parlance, that our subject is a *risk averter.*

Suppose, instead of the above situation, that our subject had a linear total utility of wealth function; this is the same thing as assuming a constant marginal utility of wealth function or that \$200,000 is exactly twice as desirable as \$100,000. The resulting utility-of-wealth function and indifference curves are given in Figure 15-4. Because the expected utility of the outcomes equals the

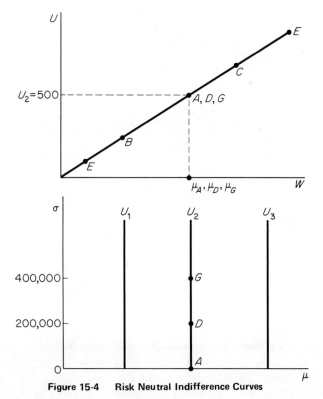

Figure 15-4   Risk Neutral Indifference Curves

[15]Since $dU/dW > 0$ and $d^2U/dW^2 < 0$, then $d\sigma/d\mu > 0$.

utility of the expected value, all opportunities having the same expected value will have the same utility, regardless of risk. The indifference curves are therefore vertical.[16] A person possessing such a function is called *risk neutral.*

   Finally, suppose our subject had an increasing marginal utility of wealth function, such that $200,000 was more than twice as desirable as $100,000. We observe, in Figure 15-5 that risky combinations D and G provide the same utility as certainty A, but with a lower expected value. The corresponding indifference curves for the subject are concave but negatively sloped.[17] Such a person is called a *risk seeker.*

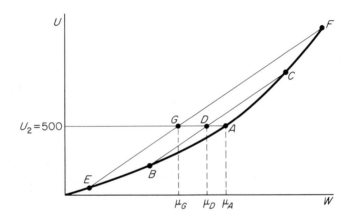

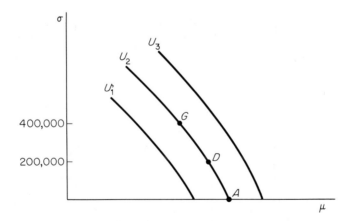

Figure 15-5   Risk-Seeking Indifference Curves

[16]Since $dU/dW > 0$ and $d^2U/dW^2 = 0$, then $d\sigma/d\mu = \infty$.
[17]Since $dU/dW > 0$ and $d^2U/dW^2 > 0$, then $d\sigma/d\mu < 0$.

Now that the indifference curves have been geometrically derived from their respective utility-of-wealth functions, it becomes convenient to switch the axes in their graphs for subsequent discussion. It will be observed that this task is accomplished in Figure 15-6, and we shall henceforth deal with the indifference curves in (σ, μ) space. Furthermore, we shall concentrate our attention upon the risk averter. Tobin has demonstrated that the risk averter's indifference curves in (σ, μ) space will be positively sloped and concave from above.[18] The actual shape of the curves, of course, depends upon the corresponding utility-of-wealth function. If the utility function happens to be quadratic $(U = a + bx - cx^2)$, Sharpe has demonstrated that the indifference curves will be concentric circles with the center at $\sigma = 0$ and $\mu =$ the value of X which maximizes the utility function $(-b/2c)$.[19] The indifference curves corresponding to other types of utility functions are not nearly so simple to specify.

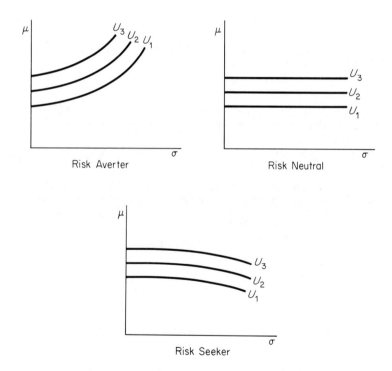

Figure 15-6   Indifference Curves in (σ, μ) Space

[18] James Tobin, "Liquidity Preference as Behavior Towards Risk," *Review of Economic Studies*, February 1958, Reprinted in Archer and D'Ambrosio, *The Theory of Business Finance: A Book of Readings* (New York: The Macmillan Co., 1967), pp. 601–25.
[19] Sharpe, *op. cit.*, pp. 196ff.

PROBLEMS

1. Bernoulli (see page 288) provided solutions to the following problems.[20] See if you can do as well.

a. What minimum fortune should be possessed by the man who offers to provide the insurance to Caius in order that he be rational in doing so? (Example on page 289)

b. Sempronius owns goods at home worth a total of 4,000 ducats and in addition possesses 8,000 ducats of commodities in foreign countries from where they can be transported only by sea. However, our daily experience teaches us that of ten ships, one perishes.

(1) What is Sempronius' expectation of the commodities?

(2) By how much would his expectation improve if he trusted them equally to two ships?

(3) What is the limit of his expectation as he trusted them to increasing numbers of ships?

2. Under the Latané-Bernoulli criteria, would a rational individual ever enter a risk venture that had any finite probability of costing all his wealth? Why? How might this result be rationalized? Why, in modern society, might it be said that it is impossible to lose all one's wealth?

3. Suppose that a man were offered either (1) a certain $230 or (2) a 50–50 chance of $400 or $100. Which option would he take if:

a. He possessed a Cramer square root of money gain utility function?

b. A Bernoulli-Latané function with initial wealth of $1,000?

c. The same as b with initial wealth of $100?

4. With regard to the material in the section on von Neumann-Morgenstern utility:

a. Determine the certain sum for which the subject in the example would relinquish the following opportunity:

W	Probability
+ 40,000	.4
+160,000	.4
+250,000	.2

b. Explain how von Neumann-Morgenstern axiom 5 treats the utility derived from gambling itself (that is, deals with the existence of Las Vegas).

c. Compute the mean and standard deviation of outcomes in the example and in a above.

(1) What is the mean and standard deviation in each case of the certain dollar value for which the subject would be indifferent?

(2) We now have two sets of (σ, μ) for each of the two opportunities. Which of the two games (example or a) would the subject prefer to play?

[20] Bernoulli, *op. cit.*, pp. 29–30.

(3) For what probability α would he be indifferent between $\alpha \cdot$ (game he prefers) and the game he does not prefer?

(4) Graph each game in (σ, μ) space under the assumption that we have enough intermediate points besides the two for each game computed above to generate two curves. What statements might be made about the curves and the points on them?

5. For this question, assume $U = \sqrt{W}$ and $\$0 = 0\ U$ and $\$1\overline{M} = 1000\ U$.

   a. For what α $(0 \leqslant \alpha \leqslant 1)$ would the subject be indifferent between α ($\$1$ million) and a certain $\$250,000$?

   b. For what α would the subject be indifferent between (α) ($\$500,000$) and (0.3) ($\$200,000$)?

   c. For what α would the subject be indifferent between (α) ($\$500,000$) and $(1 - \alpha)$ $200,000$?

6. What do you imagine it means to say that von Neumann-Morgenstern utility functions are unique up to a linear (proportionate) transformation?

7. Draw the total utility-of-wealth function and selected indifference curves for an individual for whom $U_W = -1000 + 1000W - .001W^2$.

8. Using the data in figures 15-2 and 15-3, determine which of the following risky propositions would be the most desirable:

Proposition	μ	σ
A	100,000	100,000
B	290,000	200,000
C	400,000	500,000
D	300,000	300,000
E	200,000	0

9. "Under von Neumann-Morgenstern propositions, utility is a linear function of wealth only for risk neutrals, but utility is assumed to be a linear function of probability for everybody." Discuss.

APPENDIX

More Complex Utility Constructs

In a famous article,[1] Friedman and Savage set about to rationalize the following observable phenomena:

1. People buy fire insurance, thus preferring a certain small loss to the

[1] Milton Friedman and Leonard J. Savage, "The Utility Analysis of Choices Involving Risk," *Journal of Political Economy*, August 1948. Reprinted in Archer and D'Ambrosio, *The Theory of Business Finance: A Book of Readings* (New York: The Macmillan Co., 1967), pp. 36–65.

small probability of a large loss coupled with the large probability of no loss. This game is undertaken at unfair odds (the premium pays for costs and profits of the insurance company as well as loss coverage) indicating that the individual will pay a premium to avoid risk in this range of his wealth function and is thus risk averse.

2. The same people also buy lottery tickets or engage in other forms of gambling, thus preferring a large probability of a small loss combined with the small probability of a large gain to no change in their wealth. Because such gambles are also undertaken at unfair odds (the house profit), the behavior implied is risk seeking over this range of the wealth function.

3. Finally, the lotteries considered in 2 are observed to have more than one prize, implying that people would prefer a greater probability of winning a smaller prize and thus are risk averse at wealth levels beyond some point.

The utility function implied by such behavior is shown in Figure 15A-1.

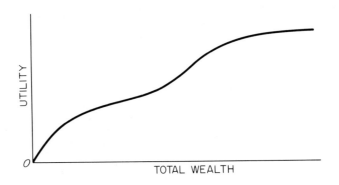

Figure 15A-1   Friedman-Savage Utility Function

The Friedman-Savage conclusions help to explain the tendency of people to risk "excess" funds at unfair odds in the hope of making a "killing." Unfortunately, however, the risk-seeking range will differ for different individuals and over time. As such, predictions about behavior are almost impossible to make under this system and few practical applications have been devised.

In another famous article, Markowitz considered some similar questions.[2] The utility function he derived is shown in Figure 15A-2. Present or accustomed wealth is placed at the origin. Small increases in wealth are shown to give increasing satisfaction (implying risk-seeking behavior), although diminishing marginal utility does eventually occur. In like manner, small losses are not too bothersome. Large losses do create large disutilities, but these tend towards a limit below some level of loss. One possible cause of the latter is that the probability of catastrophic loss is generally so low and the cost of insurance

[2]Harry Markowitz, "The Utility of Wealth," *Journal of Political Economy*, April 1952, pp. 151–58.

relatively so high that most people ignore the possibility (for example, the likelihood of being killed in an auto accident on a single trip to the grocery store). As a generalization, it may be said that an individual will ignore outcomes falling to the left of inflection point 1 in Figure 15A-2 and insure against those falling between points 1 and 2. Between points 2 and 3, the individual may gamble (or speculate at unfavorable odds); if, however, he wins or loses enough to fall outside this range, he will quit. Between points 3 and 4 (often viewed as the investment range), the individual will show increasingly risk-averse behavior. Beyond point 4, the risk aversion becomes rather severe, as there is little increase in utility associated with any gain in wealth (perhaps implying a well-diversified portfolio of treasury bills). Obviously, the Markowitz analysis is even more difficult to apply operationally than the Friedman-Savage, even though it may be more descriptive of real behavior than the simple models presented above.

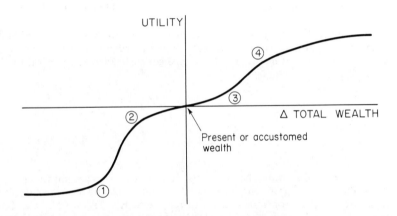

Figure 15A-2   Markowitz Utility Function

Several difficulties with utility analysis remain. Utility functions that are bounded upward (implying a zero marginal utility of wealth), as in Cramer's alternative solution to the Petersburg Paradox, not only violate the basic notion that more wealth is preferable to less, but also cause risky situations to be indeterminate. As long as all the possible outcomes of a risky event lie on the horizontal portion of the utility function, not only is the risky event as desirable as a certainty equal to the expected value of the risky event (which is true for all linear utility functions) but it is also as desirable as a certainty equal to its worst (or best!) possible outcome. Furthermore, if the slope of the utility function becomes negative at some point (implying a negative marginal utility of wealth), as in the case of the quadratic, utility can be increased by throwing money away; such pathological implications for behavior do not articulate well with the basic rationality assumptions.

The assumptions of extreme risk aversion (corresponding to very low or even negative marginal utilities of wealth) at high levels of wealth do not appear to correspond terribly well to observed individual behavior.[3] The theoretical basis of these assumptions is obscure, and empirical justification of them is virtually nonexistent. One defense often raised is that wealth exhibits diminishing marginal utility in the way any consumer good does. The point ignored, of course, is that wealth represents command over *all* goods and, although enough ice cream cones may satisfy one's craving and even cause illness beyond a point, the application of the same logic to imply total satiation of wants of all goods and services is not necessarily justified. Indeed, one of the longest standing assumptions of risk aversion seems to be in the field of public finance, where the underlying notion of a diminishing marginal utility of wealth is a necessary condition to develop a normative case for progressive income taxation.[4] Given then that the notion of risk aversion existing at all levels of wealth is open to some question, the idea of its increasing with wealth (as implied by most of the standard functions introduced in the chapter) is even more suspect. The idea of utility reaching a maximum and thereafter declining (or even remaining constant) appears even more divorced from reality. Additional measures seem required.

The implications of risk aversion varying over wealth levels and, especially, diminishing as wealth increases have been investigated by Pratt.[5] He derived a measure of local risk aversion (for small changes in wealth) $r(W)$, equal to the following:

$$r(W) = - \frac{U''(W)}{U'(W)}$$

He goes on to demonstrate that local risk aversion is a decreasing function of wealth if and only if the premium required to undertake any given risk declines as assets rise. Pratt demonstrates[6] that this requirement, $r'(W) \leqslant 0$, is equivalent to the condition $U'''(W) U'(W) \geqslant [U''(W)]^2$. A measure of proportional risk aversion, $r^*(W) = W r(W)$ is also introduced. Pratt proceeds to analyze and classify various functions in terms of constant, increasing, or decreasing proportional and absolute risk aversion. This feature alone makes his work a

[3]Many very rich individuals continue working well beyond the point when one might expect that extra contributions to wealth would produce almost no extra utility. Visions of H. L. Hunt still coming to work with his sandwich lunch in a brown paper bag and Howard Hughes still making his telephone calls in the middle of the night come immediately to mind; the entire idea that "money is merely the way you keep score" argues against the notion of zero marginal utility. In another vein, the history of families such as the Kennedys and Rockefellers may indicate that the utility derived from the power of wealth may supplant consumption requirements at high levels of wealth.

[4]Although it is not a sufficient condition under all sacrifice doctrines. See the work of Cohen-Stuart cited in Blum and Kalven, *The Uneasy Case for Progressive Taxation* (Chicago: University of Chicago Press, 1953), pp. 41ff.

[5]John Pratt, "Risk Aversion in the Small and in the Large," *Econometrica*, January–April 1964, pp. 122–36. Reprinted in Elton and Gruber, *Security Evaluation and Portfolio Analysis* (Englewood Cliffs, N.J.: Prentice-Hall, Inc., 1972), pp. 528–42.

[6]Pratt, *op. cit.*, p. 529. Note that, because the third derivative of a quadratic function is zero, quadratic utility functions cannot exhibit decreasing risk aversion.

valuable reference for a person seeking a utility function with specified properties.[7] Also important is the fact that his terminology and classification scheme is used widely elsewhere. For example, Samuelson has shown that, for utility functions possessing constant relative risk aversion at all levels of wealth, the concept of "businessman's risk" (the notion that businessmen in the peak of their earning years can take greater risks than the proverbial elderly widow) is invalid.[8] Certain of these problems relating to the realism and implications of underlying utility assumptions shall recur in subsequent chapters.

REFERENCES

Arrow, Kenneth, *Essays in the Theory of Risk Bearing.* Chicago: Markham Publishing Co., 1971.

Baumol, William, *Economic Theory and Operations Analysis,* 2nd ed., Chap. 22. Englewood Cliffs, N.J.: Prentice-Hall, Inc., 1965.

Bernoulli, Daniel, "Exposition of a New Theory on the Measurement of Risk" (Louise Sommer, trans.), *Econometrica,* January 1954, pp. 23–36 (first published 1738). Reprinted in Archer and D'Ambrosio, *The Theory of Business Finance: A Book of Readings,* New York: The Macmillan Co., 1967, pp. 22–35, and Alfred Page, ed., *Utility Theory: A Book of Readings.* New York: John Wiley and Sons, 1968, pp. 199–214.

Blum, Walter, and Harry Kalven, *The Uneasy Case for Progressive Taxation.* Chicago: University of Chicago Press, 1953.

Fellner, William. *Probability and Profit.* Homewood, Ill.: Richard D. Irwin, Inc., 1965.

Francis, Jack, and Stephen Archer, *Portfolio Analysis,* Chap. 10. Englewood Cliffs, N.J.: Prentice-Hall, Inc., 1971

Friedman, Milton, and Leonard Savage, "The Utility Analysis of Choices Involving Risk," *Journal of Political Economy,* August 1948, pp. 279–304. Reprinted in Archer and D'Ambrosio, *The Theory of Business Finance: A Book of Readings,* New York: The Macmillan Co., 1967, pp. 36–65; Fredrikson, *Frontiers of Investment Analysis,* Rev. Ed., Scranton, Pa.: International Textbook Co., 1971, pp. 13–45; Page, cited below, pp. 234–68.

Latané, Henry, "Criteria for Choice Among Risky Ventures," *Journal of Political Economy,* April 1959, pp. 144–55. Reprinted in Fredrikson, *Frontiers of Investment Analysis* (1st ed. only), Scranton, Pa.: International Textbook Co., 1965, pp. 55–69.

[7]One example of constant risk aversion (the special case of no aversion) is $U(W) = f(W)$; an example of constant proportional risk aversion is $U(W) = f(\log W)$. Pratt, *op. cit.,* pp. 536 and 540.

[8]Paul Samuelson, "Lifetime Portfolio Selection by Dynamic Stochastic Programming," *Review of Economics and Statistics,* August 1969. pp. 239–46. Reprinted in Elton and Gruber, *op. cit.,* pp. 420–33 and Fredrikson, *op. cit.,* Rev. ed. 1971, pp. 171–86.

Markowitz, Harry, "The Utility of Wealth," *Journal of Political Economy.* April 1952, pp. 151–58.

Page, Alfred, ed., *Utility Theory: A Book of Readings,* Part IV. New York: John Wiley and Sons, 1968.

Pratt, John, "Risk Aversion in the Small and in the Large." *Econometrica,* January–April 1964, pp. 122–36. Reprinted in Elton and Gruber, *Security Evaluation and Portfolio Analysis,* Englewood Cliffs, N.J.: Prentice-Hall, Inc., 1972, pp. 528–42.

Renwick, Fred, *Introduction to Investments and Finance.* New York: The Macmillan Company, 1971.

Samuelson, Paul, "Lifetime Portfolio Selection by Dynamic Stochastic Programming," *Review of Economics and Statistics,* August 1969, pp. 239–46. Reprinted in Elton and Gruber, *Security Evaluation and Portfolio Analysis,* Englewood Cliffs, N.J.: Prentice-Hall, Inc., 1972, pp. 420–33 and Fredrickson, *Frontiers of Investment Analysis,* Rev. Ed., Scranton, Pa.: International Textbook Co., 1971, pp. 171–86.

Sharpe, William, *Portfolio Theory and Capital Markets,* Chap. 9. New York: McGraw-Hill Book Company, 1970.

Smith, Keith, *Portfolio Management,* Chap. 4. New York: Holt, Rinehart, and Winston, 1971.

Tobin, James, "Liquidity Preference as Behavior Towards Risk," *Review of Economic Studies,* February 1958, pp. 65–87. Reprinted in Archer and D'Ambrosio, *The Theory of Business Finance: A Book of Readings.* New York: The Macmillan Co., 1967, pp. 601–25; Elton and Gruber, *Security Evaluation and Portfolio Analysis,* Englewood Cliffs, N.J.: Prentice-Hall, Inc., 1972, pp. 505–27.

von Neumann, John, and Oskar Morgenstern, *Theory of Games and Economic Behavior.* Princeton: Princeton University Press, 1944.

16

Portfolio Theory

"Overdiversification acts as a poor protection against lack of knowledge."

G. M. Loeb

PORTFOLIO GOALS AND OBJECTIVES

For the last 30 to 40 years, a very clear division has existed between the work of the security analyst and that of the portfolio manager. The analyst attempted to divide the universe of securities into three parts: (1) underpriced (recommended purchase); (2) fully priced (recommended long-run hold); and (3) overpriced (no longer recommended). The portfolio manager was then to determine the minimum income required by his client from the portfolio and the latter's ability to bear risk; such a determination was usually made in regard to the client's other income and assets, consumption requirements, life expectancy, and so on. With the data on client requirements and analyst recommendations in hand, the manager would proceed to build a portfolio.

The first decision to be made would usually involve the breakdown between stocks and bonds; a general heuristic was to place enough of the portfolio in bonds so that the interest payments, plus a token dividend upon the remainder in stocks, would meet the minimum income requirement of the client in all but the very worst of years. Beyond this consideration, the ratio of bonds to stocks might also be varied depending upon the manager's view of the cycle (more bonds at the peak of a boom, and so on). The bond portfolio would then be divided among governments, municipals (depending upon the client's tax status), industrials, utilities, and (in the old days) railroads according to perceived risk or the manager's tastes; diversification by maturity was also obtained (to avoid the necessity of reinvesting large sums at any future point in time). The stock portfolio would be apportioned among cyclical, defensive, and growth issues on the basis of income required, state of the market, and the client's ability to bear risk. Among the three stock categories, further allocations by industry might be made. Finally, with the bond portfolio apportioned by type and maturity range and the stock portfolio apportioned by industry, the manager would select the appropriate securities in the apportioned amounts from the analyst's list of recommendations.

Following the above sequence, the proverbial young widow (in a pre-Fem-lib era) who had just received a modest settlement from the mine owner or street traction company would generally have minimum income needs that would be quite large in relation to her principal and extend over a long time. Because a failure to earn the required income would quickly exhaust her capital and make her a public charge (in the days before the dole became fashionable), the portfolio manager would apportion most, if not all, of her portfolio to bonds (and governments at that); any equities purchased would also be of a defensive-income variety. On the other hand, the proverbial successful young businessman would generally have enough other assets and income to make no current income requirements of his portfolio and also to be able to endure a fair amount of risk. Thus, the portfolio manager would allocate most of the funds to equities and, with no income constraint, much of that to growth companies. Therefore, the resulting portfolios of government bonds for widows and of high-risk growth stocks for businessmen were derived by the systematic application of the same decision framework to differing individual circumstances.

Institutional portfolio regulations and policies were derived in a similar manner. Because banks' assets represent the funds of depositors and life insurance companies' investments represent policyholders' reserves, it was felt that little risk could be undertaken; portfolio regulation of these institutions reflects this philosophy. On the other hand, institutions like mutual funds are closer to the concept of "businessman's risk," and, consequently, they are not as severely regulated in regard to the risk of the assets they may hold.

The major difficulty with the approach outlined above is that it is based upon the assumption that portfolio risk is a weighted sum of the total risk of the component securities, considered in isolation; as demonstrated in the next section of this chapter, this is simply untrue. Another unfortunate assumption of the above methodology is that the "interior decorator" approach to security selection ("a little of this, a little of that") results in efficient diversification; as indicated in the following chapters, this contention is also incorrect.

The impact of the modern theory upon the role of security analysis has been implied by the previous chapters. It will be noted that securities have not been "priced" in this book, because securities cannot be priced upon the basis of their risk considered in isolation from other securities; furthermore, security purchasers are price takers, not price makers. The function of the security analyst has been viewed here to be the estimation of security return, risk, and covariance with the returns of other securities (perhaps employing a market index, as considered later in this chapter). Thus, the portfolio manager is no longer provided with a buy, hold, or sell recommendation, but rather an estimate of the parameters of the distribution of security returns.

The considerations of client-required return and ability to bear risk are now treated in the form of utility function determination. The goal is the same, but the use of a utility framework is more precise and also allows for trade-offs between risk and return. The proverbial widow would have a very risk-averse function (which, as demonstrated in the rest of this chapter, will cause a low-risk portfolio to be chosen), and the proverbial businessman will have a less risk-averse function (and a riskier portfolio). Under the modern theory, then, the manager takes the analyst's parameters, determines for each level of risk that portfolio with the highest attainable return (the efficiency frontier, derived in the next section), compares the market's trade-off of risk and return to his client's preferences, and selects the utility-maximizing portfolio.

The goal of portfolio management, like all other human endeavors, is thus assumed to be utility maximization. It has further been demonstrated that this goal is operationally similar to the more traditional goals (for example, income, limited income with growth, and so on), because it will have different operational implications for individuals in differing circumstances and of differing risk predilections. In addition, the goal of institutional portfolio management should be the maximization of beneficiary utility. If markets are efficient (see Chapters 17 and 19), the last goal can be achieved by an institutional portfolio policy designed to place the parameters of its own securities on the highest attainable market (risk-return trade-off) line; this policy will maximize the market value of investors' holdings, from which point they can go about the maximization of their own utility in isolation. If markets are not efficient, the institution will need to adopt a "clientele" approach, estimate a utility function representative of its beneficiaries, and work to put the parameters of its own securities on the highest attainable indifference curve of the posited utility function.

In sum, the goal of portfolio management is utility maximization, and the institutional objective is the maximization of the market value of the wealth of the portfolio beneficiary. The first step in this process is an understanding of the effects of diversification upon risk and return. The simplest way to begin is with an examination of the two-asset portfolio.

TWO-ASSET PORTFOLIOS

Suppose that we were offered the opportunity to bet $1 against $2 on a fair coin being flipped "heads," or the same odds on "tails." The expected value of such an opportunity is $[(.5)(+2) + (.5)(-1)] = 50$ cents and, because of the small sum involved, we would probably overlook the risk $[\sigma = \sqrt{(2.00 - .50)^2(.5) + (-1.00 - .50)^2(.5)} = \$1.50]$ and undertake the bet. If, however, the stakes were raised to $100,000 against $200,000, our enthusiasm for the $50,000 expected value might well be tempered by the $150,000 standard deviation; at the least, some reference to utility considerations would be required.

These difficulties could be overcome if we were allowed to subdivide our $1 (or $100,000) bet into one-half on "heads" and one-half on "tails" of the same coin. In this case we would lose $.50 on one bet and win $1.00 on the other each time. Thus, the expected value of the game would remain $.50, but the risk would be totally eliminated. The reduction in risk is effected because our winning is contingent upon the outcome of several events that do not always occur together (are not perfectly positively correlated). Indeed, we were able to eliminate risk in our example because our events (both sides of the same coin) were perfectly negatively correlated. The existence of events (that is, the return on securities) that are less than perfectly positively correlated with each other gives rise to the concept of diversification for risk reduction that underlies portfolio theory.

The expected return on a portfolio of assets is simply the weighted average of their individual expected returns, or

Let: μ = expected return on portfolio

α_i = proportion of portfolio invested in ith asset

μ_i = expected return on ith asset

n = number of assets in portfolio

Then:

$$\mu = \sum_{i=1}^{n} \alpha_i \mu_i \tag{16.1}$$

Therefore, a portfolio composed 50 percent of an asset with a 10 percent expected return and 50 percent of an asset with a 20 percent expected return would have an expected return of $[(.5)(10\%) + (.5)(20\%)] = 15\%$. It is important to note that risk does not enter the computation of expected return;

the example above has $\mu = 15\%$ regardless of the standard deviations of the two securities.

Because of the effects of correlation upon risk, the standard deviation of the portfolio is not as easily computed as the expected value.[1]

Let: C_{ij} = covariance between the returns of securities i and j = $r_{ij}\,\sigma_i\,\sigma_j$, where r_{ij} is the correlation coefficient of returns between securities i and j.[2]

$\quad\;\;\sigma$ = standard deviation of portfolio returns

Then:

$$\sigma = \sqrt{\sum_{i=1}^{n}\sum_{j=1}^{n} \alpha_i\,\alpha_j\,C_{ij}} \qquad (16.2)$$

or

$$\sigma = \sqrt{\sum_{i=1}^{n}\sum_{j=1}^{n} \alpha_i\,\alpha_j\,\sigma_i\,\sigma_j\,r_{ij}} \qquad (16.2\ \text{alt.})$$

Let us now consider the simple two-security case. The expected return will be (for $n = 2$):

$$\mu = \alpha_1\mu_1 + \alpha_2\mu_2 \qquad (16.3)$$

and the standard deviation will be:

$$\sigma = \sqrt{\alpha_1^2\,\sigma_1^2 + 2\alpha_1\alpha_2\sigma_1\sigma_2\,r_{12} + \alpha_2^2\sigma_2^2} \qquad (16.4)$$

---

[1] For a very good and extensive development of these concepts, see Harry Markowitz, *Portfolio Selection* (New York: John Wiley for the Cowles Foundation, 1959) Chaps. 3 and 4. It might be noted that Markowitz (Chap. 9) advocated the semivariance, which is computed the same way as the variance but employing only outcomes below the mean, on the grounds that the unfavorable deviations were the primary concern of risk-averse investors. The separate measure is not necessary for symmetrical distributions, but it does provide an alternative measure of skewness ($\sigma^2/2SV$). Although there appears to be growing agreement that positive skewness of returns is preferable, *ceteris paribus,* the work to incorporate such considerations is in its infancy. The semivariance, as an attempt to incorporate both dispersion and skewness considerations in a single measure, never became very popular. It seems that separate measures will be used in the future.

[2] The correlation coefficient, r, is discussed in Appendix B at the back of the book. Briefly, $r_{ij} = \dfrac{E[(I-\mu_i)(J-\mu_j)]}{\sigma_i\sigma_j}$ and, therefore, C_{ij} may be restated as $E[(I-\mu_i)(J-\mu_j)]$ or $[E(IJ) - \mu_i\mu_j]$. It should be noted that if $i = j$, then $r_{ij} = 1$ and C_{ij} is the variance ($\sigma_{i=j}^2$).

Beginning with the assumption that both securities are risky, let us examine the importance of r_{12} in determining the risk of the portfolio. Assume the following data:

Security	μ_i	σ_i
1	10%	3%
2	20%	7%

Case A: $r_{12} = +1.00$. In this instance, equation 16.4 becomes:

$$\sigma = \sqrt{(\alpha_1^2 \sigma_1^2) + 2(\alpha_1 \sigma_1)(\alpha_2 \sigma_2) + (\alpha_2^2 \sigma_2^2)}$$

which is of the general algebraic form $(a + b)^2 = a^2 + 2ab + b^2$. Thus, $\sigma = (\alpha_1 \sigma_1) + (\alpha_2 \sigma_2)$, and risk, like return, increases linearly in (σ, μ) space. Such a case is graphed as A in Figure 16-1 and illustrates that risk cannot be reduced without accepting a lower return (no gains from diversification) in the case of perfect positive correlation.

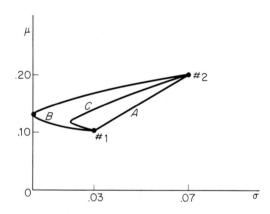

Figure 16-1   The Two-asset Portfolio (Risky Securities)

Case B: $r_{12} = -1.00$. In this instance, equation 16.4 becomes:

$$\sigma = \sqrt{(\alpha_1^2 \sigma_1^2) - 2(\alpha_1 \sigma_1)(\alpha_2 \sigma_2) + (\alpha_2^2 \sigma_2^2)}$$

which is of the algebraic form $(a-b)^2 = a^2 - 2ab + b^2$. Thus,

$$\sigma = |(\alpha_1 \ \sigma_1) - (\alpha_2 \ \sigma_2)|, \text{ and } \sigma = 0 \text{ where } \alpha_1 = \sigma_2/(\sigma_1 + \sigma_2).$$

Combinations of two securities under this assumption are graphed as *B* in Figure 16-1. Here, the gains from diversifying a portfolio composed entirely of security 1 at least to the riskless point are obvious.

Case C: $r_{12} = 0$. In this instance,[3] equation 16.4 becomes:

$$\sigma = \sqrt{(\alpha_1^2 \ \sigma_1^2) + (\alpha_2^2 \ \sigma_2^2)}$$

This combination is graphed as *C* in Figure 16-1 and exhibits gains from diversification. For the specific data given above, the curve reaches a minimum σ at $\mu = 11.55$ percent.[4] Furthermore, as the number of assets with statistically independent returns grows larger, and the proportion invested in each becomes increasingly smaller, the law of large numbers (or more precisely, the Central Limit Theorem) implies that risk can be essentially eliminated in the limit, leaving us in the simple case of dominance discussed at the beginning of Chapter 15.

If we may assume the investor to be rational and risk-averse, then certain combinations of securities 1 and 2 may be immediately eliminated. In case *B* of Figure 16-1 (where $r_{12} = -1$), for example, it will be noted that for every portfolio from the all 1 portfolio to the $\sigma = 0$ portfolio there is another portfolio, beyond the $\sigma = 0$ portfolio, which has the same σ and a larger μ. Thus, regardless of the specific shape of one's utility function, one would be foolish to invest in any of the former set of portfolios with the latter available. This notion leads directly to the concept of *efficiency.*

If a portfolio is "efficient," it is impossible to obtain a greater average return without incurring greater standard deviation; it is impossible to obtain smaller standard deviation without giving up return on the average.[5]

Therefore, all the portfolios below minimum σ on curves *B* and *C* of Figure 16-1 are inefficient. All the points on curve *A* are efficient. The points representing the coordinates of all efficient portfolios form a curve called the *efficiency frontier.* The efficiency frontier for *C* from Figure 16-1 has been graphed as *EF* in Figure 16-2. Although it cannot be known at this stage which portfolio is optimal for a given investor, it is known from the above logic that for a rational, risk-averse investor, the optimal portfolio will be on the efficiency frontier.

[3]Note that $r_{12} = 0$ is the same thing as statistical independence of returns, that is, $[(P(I|J) = P(I)]$.

[4]In general, the minimum σ point in the two-asset case is given by $d\sigma/d\alpha_1 = 0$.

$$\alpha_1 = (\sigma_2^2 - \sigma_1 \sigma_2 r_{12})/(\sigma_1^2 + \sigma_2^2 - 2\sigma_1 \sigma_2 r_{12}).$$

[5]Markowitz, *op. cit.,* p. 22.

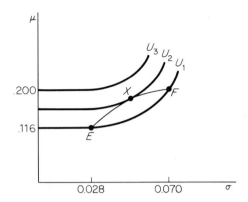

Figure 16-2   Portfolio Selection

The selection of an optimal portfolio follows in a straightforward fashion, however. Indifference curves (derived in the last chapter) are applied, and the optimal portfolio is found at the point of tangency of *EF* with the highest attainable indifference curve (point *X* in Figure 16-2). This point is preferable to any other on the curve (for example, *E* or *F*) because it provides a higher level of utility (that is, $U_2 > U_1$). A point on a higher indifference curve (for example, on U_3) would be even better, but by the definition of an efficiency frontier given above, points above *EF* do not exist.

We may consider the special case in which one of the securities (assume security 2) is riskless. Then $\sigma_2 \equiv 0$ and equation 16.4 becomes $\sigma = \alpha_1\sigma_1$, such that the risk of the portfolio is proportional to the investment in the risky asset.

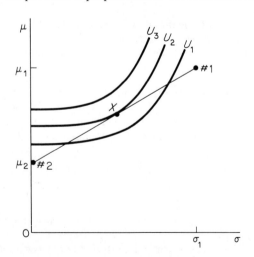

Figure 16-3   The Two-asset Portfolio
(Including a Riskless Security)

Thus, any combination of securities 1 and 2 could be drawn as a straight line in the σ, μ space, as shown in Figure 16-3. Furthermore, if 1 were a portfolio of securities with parameters (σ_1, μ_1), the same result would be obtained if a riskless security with return μ_2 were added to the portfolio. The optimal combination of the risky security or portfolio and the riskless asset may also be determined by the application of indifference curves (point X). We shall return in the next chapter to the implications of this phenomenon.

THE n-ASSET PORTFOLIO

When we move from the two-security case to the many- (or, n) security case, the theoretical problems are not very great.[6] We could merely say that the investor (1) takes all the opportunities available to him; (2) combines them in various proportions to form several (or several million) hypothetical portfolios; (3) computes the μ and σ for each of these portfolios; (4) for each level of μ, selects the portfolio with the least σ; (5) generates the efficiency frontier that is ready for application of his indifference curves; and (6) selects the optimal portfolio. This, conceptually speaking, is all there is to the n-security portfolio analysis case.

From a practical standpoint, however, the problems are enormous. Aside from computing the μ and σ for each security to be analyzed, we would also estimate the covariance for each security with every other security (a matter of $(n^2 - n)/2$ covariances, or 499,500 in the $n = 1000$ security case). Furthermore, to follow the above-suggested method, we would then compute the parameters of a very large number of portfolios; if we limited our position in a security to even multiples of 1 percent of our portfolio, in the 1000-security case there are $(100,000!)/[(99,900!)(100!)]$ possible portfolios to analyze. Even with the aid of modern computers, such a task is impossible.

A first step in the simplification of the task is to reduce the number of portfolios to be analyzed. Because we are only interested in the portfolios that form the efficiency frontier, it is only the parameters of these portfolios that should be computed. Such a problem was first approached by Markowitz.[7] His basic method, which is fairly similar conceptually to the other techniques discussed in this section, can perhaps be understood by reference to Figure 16-4; here the dots represent security parameters and the boxes represent portfolio parameters. Markowitz set about to minimize a function of the type $\sigma^2 - \theta\mu$. By initializing the procedure at $\theta = \infty$, the highest return security (F) is

---

[6] The three-security case is analyzed graphically in the appendix to this chapter.

[7] Markowitz, *op. cit.*, and "The Optimization of a Quadratic Function Subject to Linear Constraints," *Naval Research Logistics Quarterly*, March–June 1956, pp. 111–133.

obtained; note that, because diversification cannot increase return, the highest return portfolio will be composed entirely of the highest return security. From this point, Markowitz employed a quadratic programming algorithm to trace the efficiency frontier by allowing θ to decrease to 0 (at which point E, the minimum-variance portfolio, is obtained). In actuality, the iterative procedures only determine "corner" portfolios, which are those points at which a security enters or leaves the efficient portfolio; the efficiency frontier between two corner portfolios is a linear combination of the corner portfolios. Aside from the objective function, these techniques also generally involve constraints, such as the requirement that the weights assigned to securities be nonnegative and/or sum to one.

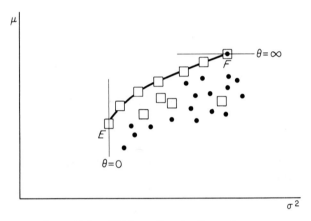

Figure 16-4   Efficiency Frontier Generation

It is also possible to generate an efficiency frontier employing calculus. The following formulation provides the minimum-risk portfolio subject to an expected return μ^* and full investment ($\Sigma\alpha=1$).

Minimize Z, where

$$Z = \sum_{i=1}^{n} \sum_{j=1}^{n} \alpha_i\alpha_j C_{ij} + \lambda_1(\sum_{i=1}^{n} \alpha_i\mu_i - \mu^*) + \lambda_2(\sum_{i=1}^{n} \alpha_i - 1) \quad (16.5)$$

and minimum Z is found where $\partial Z/\partial\alpha_i = 0$, $\partial Z/\partial\lambda_k = 0$ for all i and k, and second order conditions are met.[8]

A calculus maximization may also be employed.

_____

[8]The λ's are Lagrangian multipliers and are conceptually equivalent to a dual in programming or a shadow price (or opportunity cost) in more common parlance. See Jack Clark Francis and Stephen H. Archer, *Portfolio Analysis* (Englewood Cliffs, N.J.: Prentice-Hall, Inc., 1971), Chap. 4 for this and other applications.

Maximize Z where

$$Z = \phi \sum_{i=1}^{n} (\alpha_i \mu_i) - (\sum_{i=1}^{n} \sum_{j=1}^{n} \alpha_i \alpha_j C_{ij}) + \lambda(1 - \sum_{i=1}^{n} \alpha_i) \tag{16.6}$$

and again maximum Z is found where $\partial Z/\partial \alpha_i = \partial Z/\partial \lambda = 0$ and ϕ is an indicator of return-risk preference.[9]

To illustrate the hand solution for one point on the efficiency frontier (and also the need for access to a computer if one plans to do much work in this area), suppose that the efficient portfolio at $\mu^* = 15\%$ were desired for the two-asset case below.

Security	μ_i	σ_i	
A	10%	3%	
B	20%	7%	$r_{AB} = 0$

Although there are certainly easier solutions, employing equation 16.5 we obtain:

$$Z = \alpha_A^2 \sigma_A^2 + \alpha_B^2 \sigma_B^2 + \lambda_1(.1\alpha_A + .2\alpha_B - .15) + \lambda_2(\alpha_A + \alpha_B - 1)$$

$$Z = \alpha_A^2 \sigma_A^2 + \alpha_B^2 \sigma_B^2 + .1\alpha_A \lambda_1 + .2\alpha_B \lambda_1 - .15\lambda_1 + \alpha_A \lambda_2 + \alpha_B \lambda_2 - \lambda_2$$

Taking partial derivatives and setting them equal to zero, we obtain:

$$(1) \quad \frac{\partial Z}{\partial \alpha_A} = 2\alpha_A \sigma_A^2 + .1\lambda_1 + \lambda_2 = 0$$

$$(2) \quad \frac{\partial Z}{\partial \alpha_B} = 2\alpha_B \sigma_B^2 + .2\lambda_1 + \lambda_2 = 0$$

$$(3) \quad \frac{\partial Z}{\partial \lambda_1} = .1\alpha_A + .2\alpha_B - .15 = 0$$

$$(4) \quad \frac{\partial Z}{\partial \lambda_2} = \alpha_A + \alpha_B - 1 = 0$$

Finally, we substitute algebraically for a solution (if the problem were any larger, matrix algebra at least would be necessary).

[9]*Ibid.*

(4) $\alpha_A + \alpha_B - 1 = 0$

$\alpha_A = 1 - \alpha_B$

(3) $.1(1 - \alpha_B) + .2\alpha_B - .15 = 0$

$.1 - .1\alpha_B + .2\alpha_B - .15 = 0$

$.1\alpha_B = .05$

$\alpha_B = .5$

$\therefore$ $\alpha_A = .5$

(2) $2\,(.5)\,(.07)^2 + .2\lambda_1 + \lambda_2 = 0$

$.0049 + .2\lambda_1 + \lambda_2 = 0$

$\lambda_2 = -.0049 - .2\lambda_1$

(1) $2\,(.5)\,(.03)^2 + .1\lambda_1 + (-.0049 - .2\lambda_1) = 0$

$.0009 + .1\lambda_1 - .0049 - .2\lambda_1 = 0$

$-.1\lambda_1 - .004 = 0$

$\lambda_1 = -.04$

$\therefore \lambda_2 = -.0049 - .2(-.04) = .0031$

Therefore, the weights are 50 percent security A and 50 percent security B. The two Lagrangian multipliers are interpreted as ∂ (optimal Z satisfying other constraints)/∂ (given constraint), the denominators being .15 for λ_1 and 1 for λ_2.[10]

In general, the quadratic programming method can deal with inequalities as constraints but cannot handle negative variables, such as leverage or short sales; the opposite is true in both cases for the calculus methods. The use of artificial variables or additional Lagrangian constraints can eliminate these limitations, however. The input data (μ_i, σ_i, C_{ij}) are the same in all cases, and computer programs are available to solve problems by many of these methods. A hand solution to any but the simplest problem is very tedious and involves mathematics well beyond the scope of this book.[11]

[10]William Sharpe, *Portfolio Theory and Capital Markets* (New York: McGraw-Hill Book Company, 1970), p. 242.

[11]Several recent books that present computational methods in detail are: Markowitz, *op. cit.;* Francis and Archer, *op. cit.;* Keith V. Smith, *Portfolio Management* (New York: Holt, Rinehart and Winston, Inc., 1971); and Sharpe, *op cit.*

THE SHARPE DIAGONAL MODEL

Not only do the methods discussed thus far require that a covariance matrix (for each security with every other security) be estimated, but also the computational procedures generally require that this matrix be inverted for each portfolio to be analyzed. The inversion of large matrices (our $n = 1000$ case would provide a 1000×1000 covariance matrix), even with the aid of a computer, is extremely time consuming. To deal with both the problems of estimation and inversion, Professor Sharpe devised a simplified model of portfolio analysis that seems to provide reasonably accurate results.

The Sharpe Diagonal Model assumes that the return on a security may be related to an index (such as the Dow-Jones, S&P 500, GNP, or whatever) as follows:[12]

$$\text{Return}_i = a_i + b_i \text{ Return}_I + c_i \tag{16.7}$$

$$\mu_i = a_i + b_i\mu_I + c_i \tag{16.7 alt.}$$

Where: a_i and b_i are constants

μ_I is the return (including dividends) on the index

c_i is an error term with $\mu_{c_i} = 0$ and $\sigma_{c_i} = $ a constant.[13]

Therefore, μ_i can be estimated as $(a_i + b_i\mu_I)$. The parameters a_i and b_i can either be estimated, computed by regression analysis, or both. Furthermore, σ_{c_i} can be viewed as the variation in μ_i *not* caused by its relationship to the index, while $\sigma_i - \sigma_{c_i}$ is that portion of the total variation in μ_i caused by variation in μ_I.

The return on the portfolio becomes:

$$\mu = \sum_{i=1}^{n} \alpha_i(a_i + b_i\mu_I + c_i)$$

$$\mu = \sum_{i=1}^{n} \alpha_i(a_i + c_i) + \left(\sum_{i=1}^{n} \alpha_i b_i\right)\mu_I \tag{16.8}$$

where the first term is viewed as an investment in the essential nature of the

---

[12]Sharpe, *op. cit.*, and "A Simplified Model for Portfolio Analysis," *Management Science,* January 1963, pp. 277–93.

[13]It is further assumed that c_i is not correlated with μ_I, with itself over time, nor with any other security's c (the last implying that securities are only correlated through their common relationship to the index).

securities, and the second term is an investment in the index. The risk of the portfolio is:

$$\sigma = \sqrt{\sum_{i=1}^{n} (\alpha_i \sigma_{c_i})^2 + \left(\sum_{i=1}^{n} \alpha_i b_i\right)^2 \sigma_I^2}$$

(16.9)

where, again, the first term may be viewed as the risk of the portfolio attributable to the particular characteristics of the individual securities, and the second term as the risk attributable to the index.[14]

Thus, the Sharpe model greatly simplifies the input problem by making it directly amenable to regression analysis. In addition, by assuming that securities are only related through the index, the nonzero elements in the covariance matrix are reduced to those on the diagonal, thus easing the computational burden.

To illustrate the Sharpe approach, assume that the index currently stands at 1000 and, with reinvestment of dividends, it is expected to be at 1100 at the end of the year. Given the following data, suppose we wished to determine portfolio μ and σ for $\alpha_1 = .2$, $\alpha_2 = .5$, and $\alpha_3 = .3$.

$$\sigma_I = .10$$

$$\mu_1 = .06 + .1\mu_I, \sigma_{c_1} = .03$$

$$\mu_2 = -.03 + 2\mu_I, \sigma_{c_2} = .20$$

$$\mu_3 = .00 + \mu_I, \sigma_{c_3} = .10$$

Employing equation 16.8 we obtain:

$$\mu = (.2)(.06) + (.5)(-.03) + (.3)(.00) + [(.2)(.1) + (.5)(2) + (.3)(1)](.10)$$

$$\mu = .012 - .015 + (1.32)(.10) = 12.9\%$$

Employing equation 16.9:

$$\sigma = \sqrt{[(.2)(.03)]^2 + [(.5)(.2)]^2 + [(.3)(.1)]^2 + [(.2)(.1) + (.5)(2) + (.3)(1)]^2 (.1)^2}$$

$$\sigma = \sqrt{(.006)^2 + (.1)^2 + (.03)^2 + (1.32)^2 (.1)^2}$$

$$\sigma = \sqrt{.000036 + .01 + .0009 + .017424} = \sqrt{.02836} = 16.8\%$$

[14]Multiple index models have also been attempted. See Sharpe, *op. cit.*, and K. J. Cohen and J. A. Pogue, "An Empirical Evaluation of Alternative Selection Models," *Journal of Business,* April 1967, pp. 169–98.

PROBLEMS

1. Using the data given in the example on page 312 for securities 1 and 2, complete the following:

	α_1	α_2	r_{12}	σ	μ
(a)	.5	.5	1.0	_____	_____
(b)	.7	.3	1.0	_____	_____
(c)	.5	.5	-1.0	_____	_____
(d)	.6	.4	0.0	_____	_____
(e)	.5	.5	0.5	_____	_____

2. Using the data for α_1 given above and assuming 2 to be a riskless security with $\mu = 5\%$, compute (σ, μ) for the 5 portfolios in 1.

3. Given the data below, graph the portfolios of A and B in (σ, μ) space and determine the efficient portion:

Security	σ	μ	
A	10%	30%	$r_{12} = .4$
B	1%	5%	

4. Rework the calculus example on pages 317–18 separately for:
   a. $\mu^* = 11\%$ and
   b. Security C with $\mu_C = 15\%$, $\sigma_C = 5\%$, $r_{AC} = r_{BC} = .5$

5. Rework the Sharpe example on page 320 under each of the following assumptions separately and comment upon the effect:
   a. $\sigma_I = .2$
   b. $\sigma_{c_3} = .2$
   c. $\sigma_{c_2} = .5$

COMPREHENSIVE CASE

The Beta Fund has computed returns on three securities over the past ten years. It also has available the average annual level (including dividend reinvestment) of the Metropolis Stock Exchange:

	Return on Security			Index Level (End of Year including dividend reinvestment)
	A	B	C	
19X1	.10	.05	.15	300
19X2	.15	−.05	.25	350
19X3	.10	.10	.05	300
19X4	.20	.00	.20	400
19X5	.00	.40	−.20	250
19X6	.25	−.10	.15	500
19X7	.30	−.10	.20	550
19X8	.20	.15	.10	400
19X9	.25	.00	.15	500
19X0	.30	.00	.20	550

1. What is the arithmetic mean return on each security over the ten-year period? The geometric mean?

2. What are the slope and intercept parameters for the regression line of each security's return against the index?

3. Using Sharpe's model and an index estimate next year of 600, what are portfolio σ and μ if α_A = 50%, α_B = 30%, and α_C = 20%?

APPENDIX

Three-asset Graphical Portfolio Analysis

The three-security case of portfolio analysis has historically been analyzed graphically[1] and, because it provides some useful insights, we shall consider it briefly.

1. We initially set a conservation condition that the entire portfolio will be invested ($\alpha_1 + \alpha_2 + \alpha_3$ = 1). The amount invested in the third security (α_3), therefore, is the amount not invested in the other two ($\alpha_3 = 1 - \alpha_1 - \alpha_2$), and it is possible to conduct the analysis in two-dimensional space.

2. We then set α_1 on the abscissa and α_2 on the ordinate, as shown in Figure 16A-1. Point A represents the all 1 portfolio (α_1 = 1, $\alpha_2 = \alpha_3$ = 0), point B the all 2 portfolio (α_2 = 1, $\alpha_1 = \alpha_3$ = 0), and point C the all 3 portfolio ($\alpha_1 = \alpha_2$ = 0, α_3 = 1). If we further add nonnegativity conditions ($\alpha_1 \geqslant 0; \alpha_2 \geqslant 0; \alpha_3 \geqslant 0$), then triangle ABC becomes the attainable set of portfolios.

[1]Markowitz, op. cit., Chapter 7, and "Portfolio Selection," Journal of Finance, March 1952, pp. 77–91.

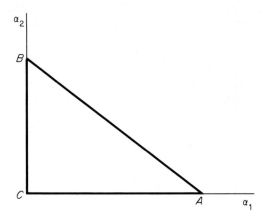

Figure 16A-1   Three Asset Portfolios

3. The mean of any portfolio in this system is thus:

$$\mu = \alpha_1\mu_1 + \alpha_2\mu_2 + \alpha_3\mu_3$$

$$\mu = \alpha_1\mu_1 + \alpha_2\mu_2 + (1 - \alpha_1 - \alpha_2)\mu_3$$

$$\mu = \mu_3 + \alpha_1(\mu_1 - \mu_3) + \alpha_2(\mu_2 - \mu_3)$$

Then, if $\mu_2 \neq \mu_3$

$$\alpha_2 = \frac{\mu - \mu_3}{\mu_2 - \mu_3} - \frac{\mu_1 - \mu_3}{\mu_2 - \mu_3}\alpha_1 \qquad (16A.1)$$

in the familiar $Y = a + bX$ form.[2]

Equation 16A.1 is significant because it provides the combinations of α_1 and α_2 (and implicitly α_3) that will return a given μ. It is also significant because it is the equation for a line with slope of $-(\mu_1 - \mu_3)/(\mu_2 - \mu_3)$ and intercept of $(\mu - \mu_3)/(\mu_2 - \mu_3)$; it will be noted that as the given return, μ, changes, the intercept of the line changes but the slope does not. From this observation is derived the concept of *isomean lines,* which are a series of parallel lines with each point on a given line promising the same return, and return increasing from one isomean line to the next in the direction of the security having the greatest expected value.[3] A system of such lines has been drawn in Figure 16A-2 under the assumption that $\mu_3 > \mu_2 > \mu_1$.

4. The variance of the three-security portfolio is:

$$\sigma^2 = \alpha_1{}^2\sigma_1{}^2 + \alpha_2{}^2\sigma_2{}^2 + \alpha_3{}^2\sigma_3{}^3 + 2\alpha_1\alpha_2C_{12} + 2\alpha_1\alpha_3C_{13} + 2\alpha_2\alpha_3C_{23}$$

[2]Markowitz, in Frederikson, *Frontiers of Investment Analysis,* Rev. Ed. (Scranton, Pa.: International Textbook Co., 1971), pp. 82ff.

[3]See Markowitz, *Portfolio Selection,* pp. 135ff.

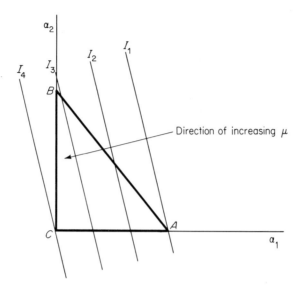

Figure 16A-2   Isomean Curves

which upon substitution and expansion is:

$$\sigma^2 = \alpha_1^2(\sigma_1^2 - 2C_{13} + \sigma_3^2) + \alpha_2^2(\sigma_2^2 - 2C_{23} + \sigma_3^2) + 2\alpha_1\alpha_2(C_{12} - $$
$$C_{13} - C_{23} + \sigma_3^2) + 2\alpha_1(C_{13} - \sigma_3^2) + 2\alpha_2(C_{23} - \sigma_3^2) + \sigma_3^2$$

which is, in turn, the equation for an ellipse. Therefore, the points representing all the portfolios having the same σ_2 will form an ellipse, a so-called *isovariance curve.*[4] Other sets of portfolios all having the same variance but larger than the first set will form a larger ellipse that has the same center. The isovariance curves are therefore said to be a series of concentric ellipses. The center of these ellipses is, of course, the minimum-variance portfolio. A series of isovariance curves is shown in Figure 16A-3.

   5. A moment's reflection should indicate that (a) the highest return to be found on any isovariance curve is at its point of tangency with the highest attainable isomean curve (the tangent on the other side of the isovariance curve will give the lowest attainable return), and (b) the lowest attainable risk on any isomean curve is at its point of tangency with an isovariance curve. The locus of these points of tangency is called the *critical line* and shown as *ll* in Figure 16A-4. The critical line is a straight line that always passes through the center of the isovariance ellipses (the minimum-variance portfolio) and is, by definition, the locus of optimal portfolios. Not all these portfolios are attainable, however. The set of efficient portfolios, therefore, tends to follow the critical line where possible and to select the minimum-variance portfolio in the direction of increasing return otherwise.

---

[4] Markowitz used σ^2 analysis rather than σ. The conclusions are similar.

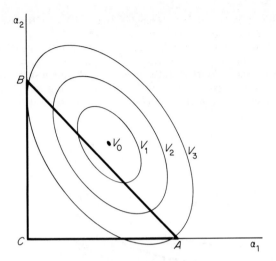

Figure 16A-3   Isovariance Curves

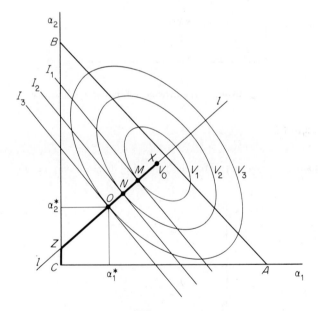

Figure 16A-4   The Efficiency Frontier in α_1 , α_2 Space

6. The set of efficient portfolios (or the efficiency frontier) can be observed in Figure 16A-4 to follow the critical line from X, the minimum-variance portfolio, to Z, the boundary of the attainable set, and then along the boundary to C. Because points on the critical line beyond Z are not attainable, those on ZC give the best available trade-off of σ^2 for μ.

7. Finally, it is possible to transfer the efficiency frontier from α_1, α_2 space of Figure 16A-4 to σ^2, μ space in Figure 16A-5.

8. The final step in portfolio selection is then to place the investor's indifference curves on the same axes and select that portfolio represented by the point on the efficiency frontier that is tangent to the highest indifference curve. In the case illustrated, this would be point O which is tangent to U_2. Referring to Figure 16A-4, it can be seen that portfolio O is composed of α_1^* of 1, α_2^* of 2, and $1 - \alpha_1^* - \alpha_2^*$ of 3.

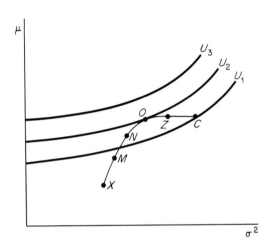

Figure 16A-5   **The Efficiency Frontier in σ^2, μ Space**

EXAMPLE

The efficiency frontier for the following diagram may be traced:

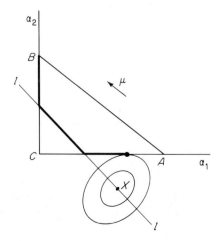

The smallest variance portfolio attainable is the point of tangency of the isovariance curves with the α_1 axis. From there, the efficiency curve moves along the boundary to the critical line, up the critical line to the α_2 boundary, and then along the α_2 boundary.

Appendix Problems

1. *Find the efficiency frontier in the following cases:*

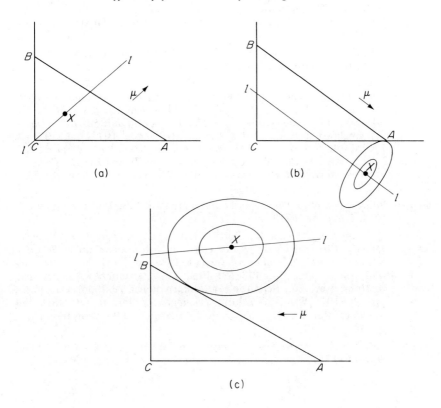

(a)

(b)

(c)

2. *If $\mu_1 = 10\%$, $\mu_2 = 5\%$, and $\mu_3 = 20\%$, what is the slope of the isomean curves? If $\mu = 15\%$, what is the intercept?*

REFERENCES

Cohen, K. J., and J. A. Pogue, "An Empirical Evaluation of Alternative Selection Models," *Journal of Business*, April 1967, pp. 169–93. Reprinted in

Elton and Gruber, *Security Evaluation and Portfolio Analysis,* Engle-wood Cliffs, N.J.: Prentice-Hall, Inc., 1972, pp. 464–95.

Findlay, M. C., and E. E. Williams, "A Portfolio Selection Algorithm for Risk Seekers," *Proceedings of the American Institute for Decision Sciences, Northeast Regional Conference,* May 1972, pp. 374–83.

Francis, Jack, and Stephen Archer, *Portfolio Analysis,* Chap. 4. Englewood Cliffs, N.J.: Prentice-Hall, Inc., 1971.

Latané, Henry, and Donald Tuttle, *Security Analysis and Portfolio Management,* Chaps. 4, 24, 25. New York: The Ronald Press, 1970.

Markowitz, Harry, "The Optimization of a Quadratic Function Subject to Linear Constraints," *Naval Research Logistics Quarterly,* March–June 1956, pp. 111–133.

———, *Portfolio Selection.* New York: John Wiley for the Cowles Foundation, 1959. Reissued in paperback by Yale University Press in 1970.

———, "Portfolio Selection," *Journal of Finance,* March 1952, pp. 77–91. Reprinted in Archer and D'Ambrosio, *The Theory of Business Finance: A Book of Readings,* New York: The Macmillan Co., 1967, pp. 588–600; Elton and Gruber, *Security Evaluation and Portfolio Analysis,* Englewood Cliffs, N.J.: Prentice-Hall, Inc., 1972, pp. 407–19; Fredrikson, *Frontiers of Investment Analysis,* Rev. Ed., Scranton, Pa.: International Textbook Co., 1971, pp. 76–89; Wu and Zakon, *Elements of Investments: Selected Readings,* Rev. Ed., New York: Holt, Rinehart and Winston, Inc., 1972, pp. 434–46.

Sharpe, William, *Portfolio Theory and Capital Markets.* New York: McGraw-Hill Book Company, 1970.

———, "A Simplified Model for Portfolio Analysis," *Management Science,* January 1963, pp. 277–93. Reprinted in Elton and Gruber, *Security Evaluation and Portfolio Analysis,* Englewood Cliffs, N.J.: Prentice-Hall, Inc., 1972, pp. 448–63; Fredrikson, *Frontiers of Investment Analysis,* Rev. Ed., Scranton, Pa.: International Textbook Co., 1971, pp. 90–107; Wu and Zakon, *Elements of Investments: Selected Readings,* Rev. Ed., New York: Holt, Rinehart and Winston, Inc., 1972, pp. 447–62.

Smith, Keith, *Portfolio Management,* Chaps. 4, 6. New York: Holt, Rinehart and Winston, 1971.

17

Capital Market Theory

"We can easily represent things as we wish them to be."

Aesop

LEVERAGED PORTFOLIOS

In the last chapter, we briefly considered the two-asset portfolio with one of the assets riskless. We concluded, designating the riskless security as 2, that:

$$\mu = \alpha_1 \mu_1 + \alpha_2 \mu_2 \qquad (17.1)$$

and

$$\sigma = \alpha_1 \sigma_1 \qquad (17.2)$$

We further decided that the same conditions would hold if 1 were a portfolio, instead of a security, and a riskless security were added to it. Figure 17-1, repeated from the last chapter, designates all combinations of portfolio 1 and riskless security 2. The combination of portfolios so depicted is called the *lending case* because in essence a portion of the funds available is being lent at the pure rate of interest, while the remainder is invested in portfolio 1.

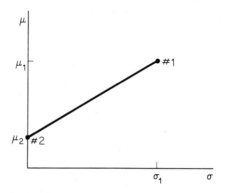

Figure 17-1   Lending Case

Using the simple construct developed above, it is also possible to consider the case of borrowing against, or leveraging, the portfolio. Because positive α_i's are used to indicate securities bought and included in the portfolio, it does not seem unreasonable to use negative α_i's to indicate liabilities sold against the portfolio.[1] In the example above, if α_2 becomes negative, then α_1 becomes > 1 and $\alpha_1\sigma_1$ also increases linearly. Making the rather unrealistic assumption that the individual can also borrow at the riskless rate, our borrowing line becomes merely an extension of the lending line beyond 1, as shown in Figure 17-2.

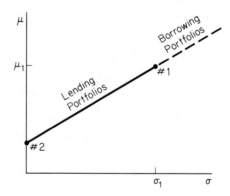

Figure 17-2   Borrowing and Lending Cases

Therefore, beginning with all our funds in portfolio 1, we can either lend some of the funds at the pure rate and move down the line in the direction of μ_2 or borrow at the pure rate to invest more funds in portfolio 1 and move up the line.

---

[1] The same result would be obtained by making the μ's negative (to indicate a cost rather than a return) but would undermine our convention that $\Sigma\,\alpha_i = 1$.

Given the effects of borrowing and lending at the riskless rate, it then becomes necessary to determine which of the available portfolios should be so employed. It would seem reasonable, as a first principle, to borrow or lend against that portfolio which provided the greatest increase in return for a given increase in risk; in other words, we should desire that borrowing-lending line with the greatest available slope. The cases are illustrated in Figure 17-3. The

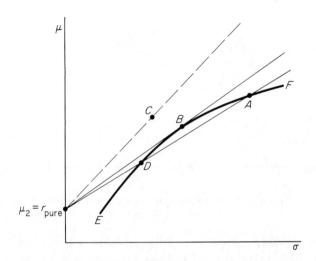

Figure 17-3   Determination of the Optimal Borrowing and Lending Portfolio ($r_L = r_B$)

efficiency frontier is shown as EF. Borrowing and lending against either portfolio A or D (which gives the same line $= \mu_2 - D - A$) is inefficient because a better risk-return trade-off is given by B. Portfolio C would appear even better, except that by definition no security or portfolio exists above EF. Therefore, the optimal attainable borrowing-lending portfolio is found by extending a straight line from the pure rate of interest tangent to the efficiency frontier.[2]

Let us take another look at such an optimal line, shown in Figure 17-4 as $r - O - Z$, through portfolio O. It will be observed that for every portfolio on the efficiency frontier between E and O, there exists some combination of portfolio O and the riskless security (given by the lending line $r - O$) that is more desirable (lower σ for the same μ, and so on). In like manner, every point on the efficiency frontier between O and F is dominated by some borrowing against O (given by the line OZ). It would therefore appear that the revised efficiency frontier is $r - O - Z$. If this were the case, then all efficient portfolios would be composed of portfolio O plus borrowing or lending. A very risk-averse person,

---

[2] The geometry of this conclusion is demonstrated more rigorously in Chapter 18 in the discussion of the excess return criterion.

such as Mr. A, might choose portfolio M (see Figure 17-4) composed of portfolio O plus riskless loans, while a less risk-averse person, such as Mr. B, might choose portfolio N, which involves leveraging portfolio O.[3]

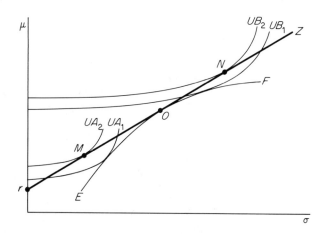

Figure 17-4   Determination of the Optimal Portfolio for Individuals with Varying Risk Preferences

Even the more realistic case of the individual who can only borrow at a higher rate than he can lend is fairly easy to handle in this framework. In this situation, we can draw lines from both the borrowing rate (r_B) and the lending rate (r_L) tangent to the efficiency frontier (see Figure 17-5) to obtain lending portfolio O and borrowing portfolio U. The revised efficiency frontier then becomes (1) lending from r_L to O; (2) movement along the efficiency frontier itself from O to U; and (3) borrowing from U on out along UZ. The indifference curves would then be applied as before.

A crucial assumption is implicitly made above, that is, that the separation theorem of Irving Fisher holds in this case.[4] The separation theorem essentially posits that the investment decision is independent of the financing decision. In our case, it would imply that investors would select portfolio O without regard to whether they would then borrow against it or buy riskless securities with

---

[3]For completeness, it is noted that a risk-neutral investor will choose that combination of securities and loans with the highest expected return, while a risk seeker will either select the same or a portfolio of even greater risk, depending upon the slope of his indifference curves. See Findlay and Williams, "A Portfolio Selection Algorithm for Risk Seekers," *Proceedings of the American Inst. for Decision Sciences, Northeast Regional Conference,* 1972, pp. 374–83.

[4]Modern interpretations of the separation theorem may be found in Tobin, "Portfolio Selection" in Hahn & Breckling, eds. *The Theory of Interest* (New York: St. Martins, 1965), and J. Hirshleifer, *Investment, Interest, and Capital* (Englewood Cliffs, N.J.: Prentice-Hall, Inc., 1970).

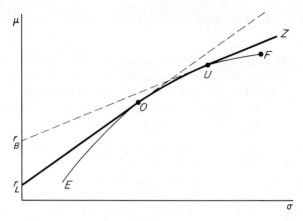

**Figure 17-5   Determination of the Optimal Borrowing and
Lending Portfolios ($r_L \neq r_B$)**

excess funds. The theorem also implies that a portfolio with a given μ and σ would possess the same utility no matter whether it were composed of (1) 100 percent securities; (2) less than 100 percent securities plus some riskless loans; or (3) more than 100 percent securities plus some borrowing. It is quite unlikely that the separation theorem holds in the real world[5] but the models in the rest of this chapter, which are based on it, provide sufficient insight that we choose to ignore temporarily this practical difficulty.

The effects of lending part of the funds in the portfolio and leveraging (borrowing against) the portfolio may be illustrated with a simple example. Suppose a risky portfolio of securities has a $\mu = 15\%$ and $\sigma = 10\%$, and the pure rate of interest = 6%. The parameters of a holding of (1) 50 percent in the portfolio and 50 percent lending, and (2) 150 percent in the portfolio and 50 percent borrowing would be determined as follows:

$$(1) \quad \mu = \alpha_1 \mu_1 + \alpha_2 \mu_2$$
$$\mu = .5\,(.15) + .5\,(.06) = 10.5\%$$
$$\sigma = \alpha_1 \sigma_1 = .5\,(.10) = 5\%$$
$$(2) \quad \mu = 1.5\,(.15) + (-.5)(.06) = 19.5\%$$
$$\sigma = 1.5\,(.10) = 15\%$$

Notice that in the case of lending both expected return and risk are reduced; conversely, in the case of borrowing each parameter is increased.

---

[5]It is for this reason that the excess return criterion discussed in Chapter 18 probably lacks universal validity as a selection criterion for risky asset portfolios.

THE CAPITAL MARKET LINE

If we may assume that investors behave in a manner consistent with the prior chapter and the first section of this chapter, then certain statements may be made about the nature of capital markets as a whole. Before a complete statement of capital market theory may be advanced, however, certain additional assumptions must be presented[6]:

1. The μ and σ of a portfolio adequately describe it for the purpose of investor decision making $[U = f(\sigma, \mu)]$.[7]
2. Investors can borrow and lend as much as they want at the pure rate of interest.
3. All investors have the same expectations regarding the future, the same portfolios available to them, and the same time horizon.[8]
4. Taxes, transactions costs, inflation, and changes in interest rates may be ignored.

Under the assumptions above, all investors will have identical efficiency frontiers (EF), borrowing and lending rates $(r_L = r_B)$ and, thus, identical optimal borrowing-lending portfolios (X). (See Figure 17-6). Because all investors will be

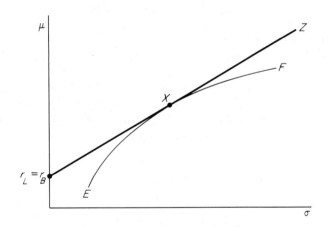

Figure 17-6   The Capital Market Line

[6] See Francis and Archer, *Portfolio Analysis* (Englewood Cliffs, N.J.: Prentice-Hall, Inc., 1971), p. 112, and Sharpe, *Portfolio Theory and Capital Markets* (New York: McGraw-Hill Book Company, 1970), pp. 77–78.

[7] Technically, this condition requires either that the distribution of security returns be normal or that the investor's utility function be quadratic.

[8] Technically, homogeneity of expectations is not required if a weighted average of divergent expectations may be employed. In the latter case, however, it is necessary that the weights be stable as well as the proportional response of each divergent expectation to new information, and so on. This condition is often referred to as "idealized uncertainty." See John Lintner, "Security Prices, Risk, and Maximal Gains from Diversification," *Journal of Finance*, December 1965, pp. 587–615.

seeking to acquire the same portfolio (X), and will then borrow or lend to move along $r - X - Z$, it must follow for equilibrium to be achieved that all existing securities be contained in the portfolio (X). In other words, all securities must be owned by somebody, and any security not initially contained in X would drop in price until it did qualify. Therefore, the portfolio held by each individual would be identical to all others and a microcosm of the market, with each security holding bearing the same proportion to the total portfolio as that security's total market value would bear to the total market value of all securities. In no other way could equilibrium be achieved in the capital market under the assumptions stated above.

The borrowing-lending line for the market as a whole ($r - X - Z$ in Figure 17-6) is called the Capital Market Line. The securities portfolio (X) employed is the total universe of available securities (called the market portfolio) by the reasoning given above. The CML is linear by the logic of the first section of this chapter because it represents the combination of a risky portfolio and a riskless security. One use made of the CML is that its slope provides the so-called market price of risk, or, that amount of increased return required by market conditions to justify the acceptance of an increment to risk, that is,

$$\frac{\mu_{Market} - r_{pure}}{\sigma_{Market}}$$

THE SECURITY MARKET LINE

A major question raised by the CML analysis of the last section involves the means by which individual securities would be priced if such a system were in equilibrium. Throughout this book, we have generally assumed that markets are not in equilibrium; therefore when we combine securities into a portfolio that has the average return of the component securities but less than the average risk, we simply ascribe this "gain from diversification" to our own shrewdness. In the type of market assumed in the last section, however, everyone will be doing the same thing, and the prices of securities will adjust to eliminate the windfall gains from diversification.

Sharpe has suggested a logical way by which such security pricing might take place.[9] If everyone were to adopt a portfolio theory approach to security analysis, then the risk of a given security might be viewed as not its risk in isolation but rather the change in the total risk of the portfolio caused by adding this security. Furthermore, because capital market theory assumes everyone to hold a perfectly diversified (that is, the market) portfolio, the addition to total

[9]Sharpe, *op. cit.*, and "Capital Asset Prices: A Theory of Market Equilibrium Under Conditions of Risk," *Journal of Finance*, September 1964, pp. 425–42.

portfolio risk caused by adding a particular security to the portfolio is that portion of the individual security's risk that cannot be eliminated through diversification with all other securities in the market. Students of statistics will recognize this concept of the nondiversifiable portion of the individual security's risk as the covariance of returns between the security and the market as a whole $(C_{iM} = \sigma_i \sigma_M r_{iM})$.

Because the concept of individual security pricing is rather elusive, let us restate it. Sharpe contends that the price (and thus return) of a given security should not be determined in relation to its total risk, because the security will be combined with other securities in a portfolio and some of the individual risk will be eliminated by diversification (unless all the securities are perfectly positively correlated). Therefore, the return of the security should only contain a risk premium to the extent of the risk that will actually be borne (that is, that portion of the total risk which cannot be eliminated by diversification – which is variously called *nondiversifiable risk* or *systematic risk*).

If this logic is accepted, it is then possible to generate a Security Market Line, as shown in Figure 17-7, where the return on individual securities is related to their covariance with the market. If capital markets are in equilibrium and all the other assumptions of this chapter hold, then the parameters of each security should lie on the SML. Furthermore, because the risk of a portfolio is the weighted sum of the nondiversifiable risk of its component securities, all portfolios should also fall on the SML in equilibrium.[10]

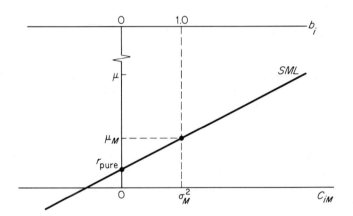

Figure 17-7   The Security Market Line

Several additional points may be made regarding the SML. In the first place, several authors differentiate between *defensive* and *aggressive* securities on the basis of whether the covariance of the security with the market is less or

[10]It should be noted that although all portfolios will fall on the SML, as a general rule no individual securities will fall on the CML (they will all lie to the right of the CML).

greater than the variance of the market return itself. If $C_{iM} < \sigma^2{}_M$, then the changes in the security's return caused by market changes are less than the market changes themselves and the security is considered defensive. If $C_{iM} > \sigma^2{}_M$, then the security responds more than proportionally to market changes and is considered aggressive.

It is also possible to discuss the SML in terms of Sharpe's index model (see pages 319-20), where[11]:

$$\mu_i = a_i + b_i \mu_I + c_i \qquad (17.3)$$

The b_i term (called Sharpe's *beta coefficient*), given μ_I, is equal to:

$$(b_i | \mu_I) = \frac{C_{iI}}{\sigma_I{}^2} = C_{iI}(1/\sigma_I{}^2) \qquad (17.4)$$

which, if the index is a valid depiction of the market:

$$(b_i | \mu_I) = \frac{C_{iM}}{\sigma_M{}^2} = C_{iM}(1/\sigma_M{}^2) \qquad (17.5)$$

Under these assumptions, the abscissa of a point on the SML expressed in terms of b_i is merely $(1/\sigma_M{}^2)$ times that of the same point expressed in terms of C_{iM} and the two are directly comparable. Viewed another way, the risk premium an individual security would exhibit in equilibrium is:

$$(\mu_i - r_{pure}) = \left[\frac{\mu_M - r_{pure}}{\sigma_M{}^2} \right] C_{iM} = (\mu_I - r_{pure}) \, b_i \qquad (17.6)$$

It is further possible to say that defensive securities would have a b_i less than, and aggressive securities greater than, unity. A major advantage of transferring the discussion into beta terminology is that the regression coefficient can be used directly to estimate the systematic risk of the asset.

Unfortunately, the beta concept also possesses serious pitfalls. In the first place, its very simplicity and popularity cause it to be used by many people who fail to understand its limitations.[12] Because the concept is subject to all the assumptions of both regression analysis and the efficient capital market

---

[11] See Francis and Archer, *op. cit.*, pp. 124 ff, for this reconciliation. The comparison was made by E. Fama, "Risk, Return, and Equilibrium: Some Clarifying Comments," *Journal of Finance*, March 1968, pp. 29-40.

[12] See Chris Wells, "The Beta Revolution: Learning to Live With Risk," *Institutional Investor*, September 1971, pp. 21-27.

hypothesis, statistical problems and economic imperfections may undermine its usefulness. Many investors are unaware of these limitations and have blithely employed the beta as a new get-rich-quick scheme. The notion that one need only fill his portfolio with securities possessing large betas and wealth shall surely follow has been adopted in many quarters by individuals who do not appreciate the fact that at best the beta is a risk-measure surrogate and *not* an indicator of future returns. The idea that the assumption of large amounts of risk will generate large returns only approaches being correct over the long run in reasonably efficient markets, and even then it ignores utility considerations. A further difficulty with the beta concept follows from empirical findings that betas for small portfolios (and, of course, individual securities) over short periods can be highly unstable,[13] although there is evidence of reasonable stability for the betas of large portfolios over long holding periods.[14] It would thus appear that one of the few valid applications of the beta concept would be as a risk-return measure for large portfolios. An example of how betas can be used in this regard is presented in the next section.

PORTFOLIO EVALUATION

Several measures directly related to capital market theory have been developed for the purpose of portfolio evaluation. The latter is essentially a retrospective view of how well a particular portfolio or portfolio manager did over a specified period in the past. Most of the published research in this area has dealt with mutual funds, seemingly because they are controversial, economically important in certain financial markets, and possessed of long life with readily available data. Much of the early work in this area (including the advertisements of the funds themselves) was of a simple time-series nature, showing how well an investor could have done over a given period in the past if he had invested then or else comparing these results to what the investor could have earned in other funds or the market as a whole. The more recent work considers both return and its variability, contending that mutual funds that invest in riskier securities should exhibit higher returns. One result of this work, considered subsequently, has been the finding that investors do as well or better on average by selecting securities at random as they could with the average mutual fund. Another implication, of more relevance here, is the growing feeling that the managers of

[13]See R. A. Levy, "Stationarity of Beta Coefficients," *Financial Analysts Journal*, November–December 1971, pp. 55–63.

[14]See N. Jacob, "The Measurement of Systematic Risk for Securities and Portfolios: Some Empirical Results," *Journal of Financial and Quantitative Analysis*, March 1971, pp. 815–34; W. F. Sharpe, "Risk, Market Sensitivity and Diversification," *Financial Analysts Journal*, January–February 1972, pp. 74–79; and M. Blume, "On the Assessment of Risk," *Journal of Finance*, March 1971, pp. 1–10.

any kind of portfolio should be rated not on the return they earn alone but rather on the return they earn adjusted for the risk to which they subject the portfolio. A very practical result is the growing pressure by the SEC for mutual-fund management performance fees to be based upon such an adjusted measure. Indeed, the measures considered below are among the SEC's leading candidates.

Before proceeding, however, a caveat is in order about the nature of *ex post* risk and return measures. As in any problem in measurement, one must delineate (1) why a measurement is being made, (2) what is to be measured, (3) which measurement technique is appropriate, and (4) the import of the results of the measurement. If one is not careful, *ex post* return measurements can easily result in the "if only I had. . ." syndrome, which is a waste of time and effort as far as making an investment in the present is concerned. For such measures to be of use, one must assume that the ability of a manager or fund to earn greater-than-average returns in the past is some indication of ability to do so in the future. As the empirical work cited below and the work discussed in Chapter 19 indicates, there is little evidence to support this contention. As far as risk is concerned, there is some doubt about what the concept of *ex post* risk means. Most of the writers in this area are careful to stress the term "return variability" instead of risk per se. Because the outcomes of all past events are currently known with certainty, the use of return variability as a measure of risk in this instance involves a different notion of risk than we have been using. Again, to make operational investment decisions, it would seem necessary to assume that past risk-return behavior of managers or portfolios either could or would be maintained in the future.[15]

Deferring judgment for the moment on the above reservations, let us consider the proposed evaluation measures. Sharpe has proposed the use of a reward-to-variability ratio related to the slope of the capital market line[16]:

$$\frac{\text{Sharpe's Measure}}{\text{for } i\text{th portfolio}} = \frac{\mu_i - r_{pure}}{\sigma_i} \qquad (17.7)$$

In effect, Sharpe is computing the slope of the borrowing-lending line going through the given portfolio and arguing that a greater slope is more desirable. In

[15]One interesting finding has been that managers appear to attempt to stay in the same risk class, earning, on average, the expected return for the target level of risk minus management costs. It has thus been suggested that an investor should buy a diversified portfolio of mutual funds that invest at a level of risk corresponding (by the CML) to the investor's desired level of return. (Cf. J. O'Brien, "How Stock Market Theory Can Help Investors Set Goals, Select Investment Managers, and Appraise Fund Performance," *Financial Analysts Journal*, July–August 1970, pp. 91–103). Although many authorities do not subscribe to this idea, the evidence offered in its support is an interesting commentary on the clientele effect discussed in the first section of Chapter 16.

[16]William Sharpe, *Portfolio Theory, op. cit.,* pp. 152–54, and "Mutual Fund Performance," *Journal of Business,* January 1966, pp. 119–38.

terms of Figure 17-8, Sharpe demonstrates that no *a priori* judgments about the performance of portfolios *J* and *K* can be made until the borrowing-lending lines are added. Subsequently, it is possible to note that a combination of the greater return to variability portfolio *J* and riskless loans dominates any combination of *K* and loans.

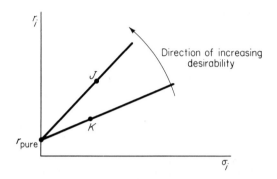

Figure 17-8   Sharpe's Return-to-Variability Criterion

A second measure based on the SML has been proposed by Treynor[17]:

$$\text{Treynor's Measure for the } i\text{th portfolio or security} = \frac{\mu_i - r_{pure}}{b_i} \qquad (17.8)$$

and the line in (beta, return) space $= r_{pure} + (\mu_i - r_{pure})/(b_i) = $ *characteristic line* of security or portfolio *i* (Figure 17-9). The implications of this analysis for the

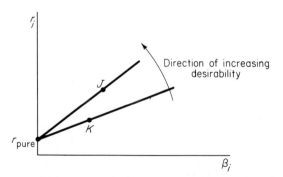

Figure 17-9   Treynor's Characteristic Line Analysis

[17]Jack L. Treynor, "How to Rate Management of Investment Funds," *Harvard Business Review*, January–February 1965, pp. 63–75, and Jack L. Treynor and Kay K. Mazuy, "Can Mutual Funds Outguess the Market?" *Harvard Business Review*, July–August 1966, pp. 131–36.

determination of the relative performance of portfolios J and K are shown in Figure 17-9. The methodology is fairly similar to that of Sharpe, except that by using the SML instead of the CML, the Treynor measure is capable of evaluating individual security holdings as well as portfolios. A disadvantage is that the accuracy of the rankings depends in part upon the assumption (implicit in the use of the SML) that the fund evaluated would have been held in an otherwise perfectly diversified portfolio.

A third measure, also based on the SML but different from Treynor's, has been proposed by Jensen[18]:

$$\text{Jensen's Measure} = (\mu_i - r_{pure}) - b_i(\mu_M - r_{pure}) \qquad (17.9)$$

This measure is expressed in units of return above or below the pure rate of a line drawn through the parameters of the security or portfolio parallel to the SML, as illustrated in Figure 17-10. This measure does allow comparisons of a portfolio to the market and is also amenable to estimation by regression; because of its treatment of differential risk, however, direct comparisons between funds or portfolios generally cannot be made. Furthermore, it has been suggested that all three of the above measures are biased against high-risk portfolios by failing to recognize the inequality of borrowing and lending rates and the resulting nonlinearity of the SML and CML.[19]

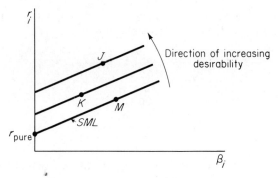

Figure 17-10   Jensen's Measure

One measure introduced earlier that seems to hold some promise as an evaluation tool is the geometric mean.[20] Over a given time period, the geometric

[18]M. C. Jensen, "The Performance of Mutual Funds in the Period 1945–1964," *Journal of Finance*, May 1968, pp. 389–416, and "Risk, the Pricing of Capital Assets, and the Evaluation of Investment Portfolios," *Journal of Business*, April 1969, pp. 167–247.

[19]See Irwin Friend and Marshall Blume, "Measurement of Portfolio Performance under Uncertainty," *American Economic Review*, September 1970, pp. 561–75.

[20]See Latané and Tuttle, *Security Analysis and Portfolio Management* (New York: The Ronald Press, 1970), Chapter 28.

mean portfolio return could be compared to that of other portfolios or some market index. There are several advantages to such a measure. Assuming that the interval considered is "sufficiently" long (and if it is not, one may doubt the validity of any evaluation technique), then undue risk taking should manifest itself in numerous low period returns and, thus, a reduced geometric mean (or terminal wealth, which is an equivalent concept in this context). If such is not the case, then the equivalence of historical variability and risk becomes increasingly dubious. The geometric mean also facilitates the use of very short investment periods (because funds value their holdings from one to four or more times a day, up to one thousand observations per year could be obtained) and provides a cumulative effect if desired (by simply including each new set of observations without discarding any of the old).[21]

Depending upon the information desired by the investor, therefore, several measures of portfolio performance are available. We must again stress, however, that the past is generally a "sunk cost" and unless certain continuity assumptions appear valid, the predictive power of these measures is seriously questionable.

PROBLEMS

1. Compute the parameters of the following holdings, given a risky portfolio (1) with $\mu = 20\%$ and $\sigma = 25\%$ and a pure rate of 5%.

	α_1	α_2
(a)	0.0	1.0
(b)	0.5	0.5
(c)	1.0	0.0
(d)	1.5	-0.5
(e)	2.0	-1.0

2. Assume an efficiency frontier composed of only the following discrete points:

Portfolio	μ	σ
A	10%	5%
B	15	10
C	20	20
D	25	30
E	30	50

[21] Which could, in turn, be used to determine a cumulative management performance fee (some of which would be withheld against poor future performance).

a. If $r_L = r_B = 6\%$, which of the above portfolios would be optimal for borrowing and lending?

b. If $r_L = 6\%$, but $r_B = 10\%$, how would your answer change?

3. What general relationship would you expect to find among r_L, r_B, and r_{pure}? Why? What are the implications of these relationships for the individual's efficiency frontier?

4.

a. Assuming that the market portfolio has $\mu = 12\%$ and $\sigma = 15\%$ and the pure rate of interest is 6 percent, draw the Capital Market Line.

b. How much expected return would be demanded under this system at a σ level of 20 percent?

c. How much would μ increase if a σ level of 25 percent were adopted?

d. State, in general terms, the relationship between $\Delta \mu$ and $\Delta \sigma$ in this system.

5. Classify the following securities as aggressive or defensive if $\sigma_M = .10$:

a. $b_1 = 1.2$

b. $C_{2M} = .02$

c. $b_3 = .7$

d. $C_{4M} = -.001$.

6.

a. Compute C_{1M} and C_{3M} from 5a and c above. What assumptions must be made?

b. If $\mu_M = .10$ and $r_{pure} = .03$, determine μ_i for the four securities in 5.

7. From the data in 5 and 6:

a. Plot the four securities on an SML using b_i.

b. Do the same thing using C_{iM}.

8. Rank the three securities described on page 320 by the Treynor and Jensen criteria, assuming a pure rate of 5 percent. Explain your results.

REFERENCES

Blume, M., "On the Assessment of Risk," *Journal of Finance*, March 1971, pp 1–10.

Fama, Eugene, "Risk, Return, and Equilibrium: Some Clarifying Comments," *Journal of Finance,* March 1968, pp. 29–40. Reprinted in Elton and Gruber, *Security Evaluation and Portfolio Analysis,* Englewood Cliffs, N.J.: Prentice-Hall, Inc., 1972, pp. 559–71; Fredrikson, *Frontiers of Investment Analysis*, Rev. Ed., Scranton, Pa.: International Textbook Co., 1971, pp. 144–58.

Findlay, M.C., and E. E. Williams, "A Portfolio Selection Algorithm for Risk Seekers," *Proceedings of the American Institute for Decision Sciences, Northeast Regional Conference*, May 1972, pp. 374–83.

Francis, Jack, and Stephen Archer, *Portfolio Analysis*, Chaps. 5 and 8. Englewood Cliffs, N.J.: Prentice-Hall, Inc., 1971.

Friend, Irwin, and Marshall Blume, "Measurement of Portfolio Performance under Uncertainty," *American Economic Review,* September 1970, pp. 561–75.

Hirshleifer, J., *Investment, Interest and Capital.* Englewood Cliffs, N.J.: Prentice-Hall, Inc., 1970.

Jacob, N., "The Measurement of Systematic Risk for Securities and Portfolios: Some Empirical Results," *Journal of Financial and Quantitative Analysis,* March 1971, pp. 815–34.

Jensen, M. C., "The Performance of Mutual Funds in the Period 1945–1964." *Journal of Finance,* May 1968, pp. 389–416. Reprinted in Wu and Zakon, *Elements of Investments: Selected Readings,* Rev. Ed., New York: Holt, Rinehart and Winston, Inc., 1972, pp. 515–40.

———, "Risk, the Pricing of Capital Assets, and the Evaluation of Investment Portfolios." *Journal of Business,* April 1969, pp. 167–247. Reprinted in Fredrikson, *Frontiers of Investment Analysis,* Rev. Ed., Scranton, Pa.: International Textbook Co., 1971, pp. 187–233.

Latané, Henry, and Donald Tuttle, *Security Analysis and Portfolio Management,* Chap. 28. New York: The Ronald Press, 1970.

Levy, R. A., "Stationarity of Beta Coefficients," *Financial Analysts Journal,* November–December 1971, pp. 55–63.

Lintner, John, "Security Prices, Risk, and Maximal Gains from Diversification," *Journal of Finance,* December 1965, pp. 587–615.

———, "The Valuation of Risk Assets and the Selection of Risky Investments in Stock Portfolios and Capital Budgets," *Review of Economics and Statistics,* February 1965, pp. 13–37. Reprinted in Archer and D'Ambrosio, *The Theory of Business Finance: A Book of Readings,* New York: The Macmillan Co., 1967, pp. 671–713.

Mossin, Jan, "Equilibrium in a Capital Asset Market," *Econometrica,* October 1966, pp. 768–83.

O'Brien, J., "How Stock Market Theory Can Help Investors Set Goals, Select Investment Managers, and Appraise Fund Performance," *Financial Analysts Journal,* July–August 1970, pp. 91–103.

Sharpe, William, "Capital Asset Prices: A Theory of Market Equilibrium under Conditions of Risk," *Journal of Finance,* September 1964, pp. 425–42. Reprinted in Archer and D'Ambrosio, *The Theory of Business Finance: A Book of Readings,* New York: The Macmillan Co., 1967, pp. 653–70; Elton and Gruber, *Security Evaluation and Portfolio Analysis,* Englewood Cliffs, N.J.: Prentice-Hall, Inc., 1972, pp. 543–58; Fredrikson, *Frontiers of Investment Analysis,* Rev. Ed., Scranton, Pa.: International Textbook Co., 1971, pp. 126–43.

———, "Mutual Fund Performance," *Journal of Business,* January 1966, pp. 119–38. Reprinted in Elton and Gruber, *Security Evaluation and Portfolio Analysis,* Englewood Cliffs, N.J.: Prentice-Hall, Inc., 1972, pp. 572–92.

———, *Portfolio Theory and Capital Markets,* Chaps. 5 and 8. New York: McGraw-Hill Book Company, 1970.

————, "Risk, Market Sensitivity and Diversification," *Financial Analysts Journal*, January–February 1972, pp. 74–79.

Smith, Keith, *Portfolio Management*, Chap. 8. New York: Holt, Rinehart, and Winston, 1971.

Tobin, James, "Portfolio Selection," in Hahn and Breckling, eds., *The Theory of Interest*. New York: St. Martins Press, 1965.

Treynor, Jack, "How to Rate Management of Investment Funds," *Harvard Business Review*, January–February 1965, pp. 63–75. Reprinted in Fredrikson, *Frontiers of Investment Analysis*, Rev. Ed., Scranton, Pa.: International Textbook Co., 1971, pp. 234–53; Wu and Zakon, *Elements of Investments: Selected Readings*, Rev. Ed., New York: Holt, Rinehart and Winston, Inc., 1972, pp. 497–514.

————, and Kay Mazuy, "Can Mutual Funds Outguess the Market?" *Harvard Business Review*, July–August 1966, p. 131–36. Reprinted in Elton and Gruber, *Security Evaluation and Portfolio Analysis*, Englewood Cliffs, N.J.: Prentice-Hall, Inc., 1972, pp. 593–601.

Welles, Chris, "The Beta Revolution: Learning to Live With Risk," *Institutional Investor*, September 1971, pp. 21–27.

18

Additional Topics in Portfolio Management

"Trust everybody, but cut the cards."

Finley Peter Dunne

TECHNIQUES FOR PORTFOLIO ELIMINATION

The portfolio selection methodology described in Chapter 16 requires a complete enumeration of the parameters of available investments and of the investor's utility function. Because of the costs of obtaining such information and the fact that some information may be unavailable at any price, any methodology that further delimits the area of investigation is of value. A major breakthrough was accomplished when Markowitz devised a quadratic programming algorithm to generate the efficiency frontier; another advance was made when Sharpe employed an index model to simplify input generation. This section considers additional techniques for reducing the number of portfolios under consideration.

Establishing Confidence Limits

Baumol has proposed a criterion that is more an addendum to the concept of efficiency than a selection criterion but nevertheless provides a good introduction to the discussion.[1] His basic point was that portfolios with low μ and σ could not be eliminated by the concept of efficiency in comparison with portfolios having much higher μ and only slightly larger σ, even though the probability that the best outcome of the former would ever exceed the worst outcome of the latter was very small. He therefore suggested that a lower *confidence limit* be set of $\mu - K\sigma$ and that low-return portfolios dominated by this rule be dropped from the efficiency frontier. The parameter K would be a function of the investor's degree of risk aversion, and if return could be assumed to be normally distributed, could be determined on a one-tail test of the percentage of the time the investor would tolerate a shortfall of actual returns (for example, 16 percent for $K = 1$, 2 percent for $K = 2$, and so on).

For example, suppose that an investor were prepared to ignore low returns that occurred no more than 2 percent of the time. This percentage would correspond to the portion remaining in the left tail of a normal distribution at a point two standard deviations below the mean; thus, $K = 2$. Now consider the following points on an efficiency frontier:

	A	B
μ	4%	10%
σ	1	3
$\mu - 2\sigma$	2	4

Neither point can be termed inefficient, as B has a higher return but at greater risk. It may be noted, however, that the investor's perceived worst outcome of B (the lower confidence limit of B) is greater than the same for A (that is, $4\% > 2\%$). Thus, portfolio A, and other portfolios in the lower range of the efficiency frontier, could be eliminated by the confidence-limit criterion.

Stochastic Dominance

A far more comprehensive concept, called *stochastic dominance,* allows for the elimination from further consideration of securities or portfolios on the basis of known characteristics of entire classes of utility functions.[2] *First-degree Stochastic Dominance* (FSD) requires only the assumption that more wealth is

[1]William Baumol, "An Expected Gain – Confidence Limit Criterion for Portfolio Selection," *Management Science,* October 1963, pp. 174–82. Reprinted in Elton and Gruber, *Security Evaluation and Portfolio Analysis,* Englewood Cliffs, N.J.: Prentice-Hall, Inc., 1972, pp. 496–504.

[2]See J. Hadar and W. R. Russell, "Rules for Ordering Uncertain Prospects," *American Economic Review,* March 1969, pp. 25–34, and R. Burr Porter and J. Gaumnitz, "Stochastic Dominance vs. Mean-Variance Portfolio Analysis: A Theoretical and Empirical Evaluation," *American Economic Review,* forthcoming. The assistance of Professor G. A. Whitmore in the preparation of this discussion is gratefully acknowledged.

preferable to less (that is, $dU/dW > 0$). It may then be said that investment B exhibits FSD over investment A if, for each possible level of return, the cumulative probability of B falling below the level of return is $\leqslant$ the same for A (and the strict inequality holds in at least one case). Consider the following example:

r_i	Prob. (A)	Prob. (B)
5%	.2	.1
10	.3	.2
15	.4	.3
20	.1	.4
	1.0	1.0
μ	12%	15%
σ	4.6	5

The cumulative probability distributions of returns for A and B are shown in Figure 18-1. The FSD decision rule is shown as follows:

r_i	Cumulative Probability $A = A(r_i)$	Cumulative Probability $B = B(r_i)$	$A(r_i) - B(r_i)$
5%	.2	.1	+ .1
10	.5	.3	+ .2
15	.9	.6	+ .3
20	1.0	1.0	0

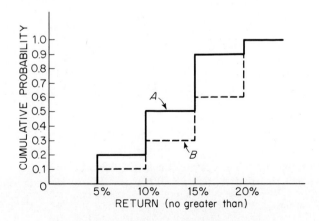

Figure 18-1   First-degree Stochastic Dominance

For investment B:

$$FSD(r_i) = A(r_i) - B(r_i) \geqslant 0 \text{ for all } r_i, \text{ and} \qquad (18.1)$$
$$> 0 \text{ for at least one } r_i$$

Thus, investment B exhibits FSD over investment A and would be preferred by anyone to whom more wealth was preferable to less (that is, all rational persons, including risk seekers and neutrals, as well as averters).

Second-degree Stochastic Dominance (SSD) requires the assumption of risk neutrality or aversion $(d^2U/dW^2 \leqslant 0)$ as well as rationality $(dU/dW > 0)$. Under these assumptions, it is possible to make selections between certain investments that do not exhibit FSD. Consider the following investment alternatives:

r_i	Prob. (A)	Prob. (B)
5%	.2	.1
10	.3	.4
15	.3	.4
20	.2	.1
	1.0	1.0
μ	12.5%	12.5%
σ	5.12	4.03

The FSD analysis would provide:

r_i	Cumulative Probability $A = A(r_i)$	Cumulative Probability $B = B(r_i)$	$A(r_i) - B(r_i)$ $= FSD(r_i)$
5%	.2	.1	+ .1
10	.5	.5	0
15	.8	.9	− .1
20	1.0	1.0	0

Thus, neither investment would exhibit FSD over the other. SSD, in effect, considers the cumulative difference between the two cumulative probability distributions employed in FSD. Again considering investment B:

$$SSD(r_i) = SSD(r_{i-1}) + (r_i - r_{i-1}) \left[A(r_{i-1}) - B(r_{i-1}) \right]$$
$$SSD(r_i) = SSD(r_{i-1}) + (r_i - r_{i-1}) FSD(r_{i-1}) \qquad (18.2)$$

(1)	(2)	(3)	(4)	(5)	(6)	(7)[3]
i	r_i	$r_i - r_{i-1}$	$FSD(r_{i-1})$	$(3) \times (4)$	$SSD(r_{i-1})$	$SSD(r_i)$
1	5%	—	—	—	—	0
2	10	.05	+.1	+.005	0	+.005
3	15	.05	0	0	+.005	+.005
4	20	.05	−.1	−.005	+.005	0

Thus, investment B is preferred by SSD if $SSD(r_i) \geqslant 0$ for all i and the strict inequality holds in at least one case.

Finally, if neither FSD nor SSD will allow a choice to be made between two investments, *Third-degree Stochastic Dominance* (TSD) may be employed.[4] In addition to the first and second order conditions for the utility of wealth function discussed above, TSD also requires that $(d^3U/dW^3 \geqslant 0)$. Following the parallelism previously established, TSD is essentially concerned with the cumulative functions employed in SSD. We present our final investment comparison with regard to showing the dominance of B:

r_i	*Prob. (A)*	*Prob. (B)*
5%	.1	0
10	0	.3
15	.9	.6
20	0	.1
	1.0	1.0
μ	14%	14%
σ	3	3

r_i	$A(r_i)$	$B(r_i)$	$FSD(r_i)$
5%	.1	.0	+ .1
10	.1	.3	− .2
15	1.0	.9	+ .1
20	1.0	1.0	0

(1)	(2)	(3)	(4)	(5)	(6)	(7)
i	r_i	$r_i - r_{i-1}$	$FSD(r_{i-1})$	$(3) \times (4)$	$SSD(r_{i-1})$	$SSD(r_i)$
1	5%	—	—	—	—	0
2	10	.05	+.1	+.005	0	+ .005
3	15	.05	−.2	−.01	+.005	− .005
4	20	.05	+.1	+.005	−.005	0

[3] By equation 18.2, col (7) = col (5) + col (6) and, in turn, becomes the entry in col (6) on the next row.

[4] See G. A. Whitmore, "Third-Degree Stochastic Dominance," *American Economic Review,* June 1970, pp. 457–59.

Because neither FSD nor SSD can be shown, the TSD for B is given by:

$$TSD(r_i) = TSD(r_{i-1}) + (r_i - r_{i-1})\,[SSD(r_i) + SSD(r_{i-1})]/2 \qquad (18.3)$$

For B to be preferred, then, $TSD(r_i) \geqslant 0$ for all i (with the strict inequality holding for at least one i) and, furthermore, $\mu_B \geqslant \mu_A$. The TSD of B over A is shown in Table 18.1.

TABLE 18.1

Worksheet for Third-Degree Stochastic Dominance

(1)	(2)	(3)	(4)	(5)	(6)
i	r_i	$r_i - r_{i-1}$	$FSD(r_{i-1})$	$(3) \times (4)$	$SSD(r_{i-1})$
1	.05	—	—	—	—
2	.10	.05	+.1	+.005	0
3	.15	.05	−.2	−.01	+.005
4	.20	.05	+.1	+.005	−.005

(7)	(8)	(9)	(10)	(11)
$SSD(r_i)$	$\dfrac{(6)+(7)}{2}$	$(8) \times (3)$	$TSD(r_{i-1})$	$TSD(r_i) = (9)+(10)$
0	—	—	—	0
+.005	+.0025	+.000125	0	+.000125
−.005	0	0	+.000125	+.000125
0	−.0025	−.000125	+.000125	0

At this writing, there exist no algorithms for the generation of stochastic dominance (SD) efficient portfolios. The work done has been of a sampling nature, primarily to demonstrate the differences between SD and (σ, μ) efficient portfolios. The Sharpe mutual fund studies (see Chapters 17 and 19) were replicated for thirty-four funds between 1954 and 1963, and it was found that no fund dominated the Dow Jones Industrial Index although the latter exhibited SSD over six funds and TSD over nine.[5] The ability to select optimal portfolios with a minimal knowledge of individual preferences provided by SD holds great promise, but many problems of implementation remain to be solved.

NONUTILITY PORTFOLIO
SELECTION TECHNIQUES

In addition to stochastic dominance, several authors have attempted to provide other portfolio selection criteria that avoid the necessity of collecting utility

[5]O. M. Joy and R. B. Porter, "Stochastic Dominance and Mutual Fund Performance," *Journal of Financial and Quantitative Analysis,* forthcoming.

data from the investor. If such techniques could prove satisfactory, numerous problems could be avoided. Among them are those cases in which an investor's risk aversion is not known, when risk aversion changes over time, or when more than one person is the beneficiary of a portfolio.

Safety-First and Excess-Return Criteria

A specific technique for portfolio selection, on the basis of minimizing the probability of the occurrence of some disastrous level of loss (D), was presented by Roy.[6] He employed Chebyschev's inequality, which does not require the assumption of a special form of probability distribution for returns. Expressed in our terminology, the relevant form of the inequality is:

$$P(X|X \leqslant D) \leqslant \frac{\sigma^2}{(\mu-D)^2} \tag{18.4}$$

which, when differentiated, set equal to zero, and solved, provides a minimum probability at $\sigma/(\mu-D)$. In Figure 18-2, it will be observed that any line connecting point D to the efficiency frontier will have slope $\sigma/(\mu-D)$ but only at the point of tangency will the point itself have the requisite slope. The point of tangency is thus the safety-first portfolio associated with a given minimum required return. Two such points are illustrated in Figure 18-2.

An approach similar in methodology has been suggested by Lintner.[7] If we let r_{pure} represent the rate to be earned on some riskless asset then Lintner defines the excess return (X) to be earned on a given risky asset as:

$$X_i = \mu_i - r_{pure} \tag{18.5}$$

It will be recalled that the parameters for the two-asset portfolio[8] when security 2 is riskless are:

$$\mu = \alpha_1 \mu_1 + \alpha_2 \mu_2, \text{ and } \sigma = \alpha_1 \sigma_1$$

thus:

$$\alpha_1 = \frac{\sigma}{\sigma_1}$$

[6] A. D. Roy, "Safety First and the Holding of Assets," *Econometrica,* July 1952, pp. 431–49.

[7] John Lintner, "Security Prices, Risk, and Maximal Gains for Diversification," *Journal of Finance,* December 1965, pp. 587–615.

[8] Bearing in mind all the while that asset 1 can be a risky portfolio as well as a security.

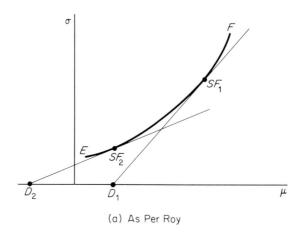

(a) As Per Roy

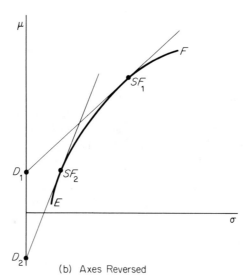

(b) Axes Reversed

Figure 18-2   Safety-first Portfolio

but:

$$\mu_2 = r_{\text{pure}} \text{ and } \alpha_2 = 1 - \alpha_1$$

therefore:

$$\mu = \alpha_1 \mu_1 + (1 - \alpha_1) r_{\text{pure}}$$

$$\mu = \alpha_1 \mu_1 + r_{\text{pure}} - \alpha_1 r_{\text{pure}}$$

$$\mu = r_{\text{pure}} + \alpha_1 (\mu_1 - r_{\text{pure}})$$

substituting the relationships defined above:

$$\mu = r_{pure} + \frac{\sigma}{\sigma_1} X_1$$

$$\mu = r_{pure} + \frac{X_1}{\sigma_1} \sigma$$

$$\mu = r_{pure} + \theta\sigma, \text{ where } \theta = \frac{\mu_1 - r_{pure}}{\sigma_1} \tag{18.6}$$

An examination of equation 18.6 will indicate that a portfolio that maximizes θ will also maximize μ for a given σ and r_{pure}. The verbal sense of this is that we are trying to maximize excess return per unit of risk. The geometric equivalence to the Roy approach is shown in Figure 18-3. Here again, any line connecting r_{pure} with a risky security or portfolio will possess the requisite slope, but a maximum slope is desired. Thus, it follows that the risk-excess return trade-off is better in the case of B than A, and further that C would be even better except that, by definition, no securities or portfolios exist above the efficiency frontier. Further reflection should indicate that the optimal portfolio by the excess-return criterion is found at the point of tangency between a ray emanating from r_{pure} and the efficiency frontier. The similarity to the Roy technique is further illustrated by the fact that, if the Roy disaster level (D) is set equal to r_{pure}, the two approaches will select the same portfolio.

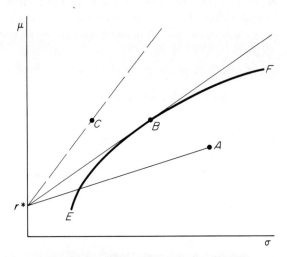

Figure 18-3   Excess-return Criterion Portfolio

In comparing the Roy and Lintner approaches, several points should be made. The safety-first model, from its basis in Chebyschev's inequality to its goal of minimization of probability of outcomes below one specific point, seems to come as close to decision making under uncertainty as any technique presented in this book; very little is assumed to be known about either the risk preferences of the investor or the distribution of returns on investment. This lack of specification is an advantage in many real-world situations, and this is one reason the model was included here. On the other hand, if more complete information is available, more precise models may be employed. Surprisingly enough, given their technical similarity, the Lintner model is on the other end of the spectrum in regard to equilibrium and perfection assumptions. To be universally applicable for risk averters, the excess-return criterion requires the separation theorem (discussed in Chapter 17) to hold, which assumes, among other things, that the portfolio can borrow or lend at the same rate (specifically, at r_{pure}). The excess-return criterion essentially involves the application of the basic capital market theory model to the selection of individual portfolios. Although this application does not require all the equilibrium assumptions of capital market theory, the likely inapplicability of the separation theorem is enough to raise doubts regarding its general adoption.

Maximization of Geometric Mean

A final criterion for portfolio selection without specific reference to utility considerations that has been suggested is the maximization of geometric mean.[9] If it may be assumed that (1) the same investment opportunities are available in each investment period; (2) the outcomes of these opportunities are independent over time; and (3) all income is reinvested, then the terminal wealth at the end of n periods associated with investment in any given portfolio is given by:

Let: $W_{i,n}$ = wealth in period n associated with investment in portfolio i

$\rho_{i,j}$ = return earned in period j on portfolio i

W_0 = initial wealth

n = number of periods

Then:

$$W_{i,n} = W_0 (1 + \rho_{i,1}) (1 + \rho_{i,2}) \ldots (1 + \rho_{i,n})$$

$$W_{i,n} = W_0 \prod_{j=1}^{n} (1 + \rho_{i,j}) \tag{18.7}$$

[9]Latané and Tuttle, *Security Analysis and Portfolio Management* (New York: The Ronald Press, 1970), Chap. 24.

$$\frac{W_{i,n}}{W_0} = \prod_{j=1}^{n} (1 + \rho_{i,j})$$

$$\left(\frac{W_{i,n}}{W_0}\right)^{\frac{1}{n}} = [\prod_{j=1}^{n} (1 + \rho_{i,j})]^{\frac{1}{n}}$$

$$E[\left(\frac{W_{i,n}}{W_0}\right)^{\frac{1}{n}} - 1] = E[(\prod_{j=1}^{n} (1 + \rho_{i,j}))^{\frac{1}{n}} - 1] \qquad (18.8)$$

The right side of equation 18.8 is the expected geometric mean return on portfolio i. The portfolio that maximizes this expectation thus will maximize the expectation of terminal wealth. It can also be shown (by the Central-Limit Theorem) that the probability of the maximum geometric mean portfolio resulting in greater terminal wealth than any other available portfolio approaches unity as n approaches infinity.

All the above, however, is simply mathematical tautology. It was shown in Chapter 15 that the maximization of the geometric mean of returns is consistent with the maximization of a log utility-of-wealth function. Thus, if the investor possesses a log utility function or, given the Central-Limit Theorem, if the number of investment periods is infinite, the geometric-mean criterion is sufficient. In some other cases, it has been found to be a reasonable approximation. However, Samuelson has shown that as long as n is finite, there exist classes of utility functions for which the proposed criterion is not even a good approximation. Indeed, he also demonstrated that there are classes of utility functions for which no uniform strategy is optimal.[10] Even without Professor Samuelson's argument, there is a good question as to whether the assumptions (1)-(3) above are very realistic. The problems of multiperiod optimization are indeed great, however, and are considered at greater length subsequently. It will soon be apparent that the other techniques are sufficiently troublesome that geometric mean maximization becomes a very attractive alternative if the assumptions are anywhere close to being fulfilled.

PROBLEMS WITH MIXED ASSET PORTFOLIOS: REAL ESTATE[11]

It should be noted from the outset that the portfolio and capital market theory outlined in the preceding chapters remains essentially unimplemented even in

[10]Paul Samuelson, "The 'Fallacy' of Maximizing the Geometric Mean in Long Sequences of Investing or Gambling." *Proc. National Acad. Sci. U.S.A.*, October 1971, pp. 2493-96.

[11]Derived from M. C. Findlay, "The Role of Real Estate in an Efficient Portfolio," a research project for the Center for Real Estate and Urban Economic Studies, University of Connecticut. Adapted by permission.

the security investment field. This result follows despite the facts that: (1) securities are homogeneous and divisible; (2) the returns from securities do not vary greatly with the holder (little management and relatively simple tax effects, at least at the margin); (3) the markets for securities are relatively efficient (in terms of transactions costs, liquidity, and so on); (4) the returns from securities appear to be independent over time (little if any serial correlation) and, thus, independent of holding period; (5) a great deal of publicly available, machine-accessible information exists on most securities; and (6) most securities of significance trade in one national market. Because none of the above analytical advantages apply as well (if at all) to real estate investments, it should not be surprising to learn that, given the current state of the art, it is impossible to integrate real estate investment into portfolio selection in a completely satisfactory manner.

In the first place, most real estate investment is not divisible; the notion of dividing a shopping center investment into fifty-dollar units is simply at odds with the facts. Thus, one is faced with an "all or none" situation. To generate a Markowitz efficiency frontier with portfolios composed partially or completely of real estate investments would thus require the solution of a quadratic integer programming problem. Unfortunately, it appears that no algorithm currently exists to solve such a problem. The lack of a quadratic integer programming algorithm does not represent a complete dead end. Reasonable approximations can often be made with "simple" quadratic programming.[12] Furthermore, reasonably small problems could be approximated exhaustively, or simulated. Finally, the lack of divisibility should be alleviated over time through improved financial intermediation (for example, the real estate investment trust).

A more serious hindrance would appear to involve input generation. The difficulties with the determination of σ, μ for a single project are considerable. For a Markowitz approach, it would be necessary to estimate the covariance of returns between each project and every other project. Obviously, an index approach would be required. The Sharpe single index is probably too broad for mixed asset (or even pure real estate) portfolios, because no single index (such as GNP or the prime rate of interest) could relate to all assets and yet not include a great deal of "noise." An intermediate approach that offers some promise is the use of a multiple index model, which comes in two basic forms: (1) a model that relates the returns on each class of asset to its appropriate index and then relates the indices by means of a Markowitz covariance approach; and (2) a model that relates index returns to another index (often GNP), in the form of one index model on top of another.[13] The latter is the easier to solve because it

[12]H. C. Friedman, *Mixed Asset Portfolio Selection* (Ann Arbor: University Microfilms, 1972), pp. 90ff.

[13]See Cohen and Pogue, "An Empirical Evaluation of Alternative Selection Models," *Journal of Business,* April 1967, pp. 169–93. Reprinted in Elton and Gruber, *Security Evaluation and Portfolio Analysis* (Englewood Cliffs, N.J.: Prentice-Hall, Inc., 1972), pp. 464–95.

essentially involves running the Sharpe model twice (first on the assets and then on the indexes); the difficulty arises because of the amount of "noise" created by such a two-level estimation procedure.

Not only is the index approach subject to these shortcomings but there is also the fact that existing indexes of real estate investment returns are not very satisfactory for portfolio analysis purposes. Friedman was forced to use:

> . . . for real estate an average of the Boeckh construction cost indexes for residences, apartments, hotels, offices, and commercial and factories and the American Appraisal Association Index . . . and for mortgages the Federal Home Loan Bank Board conventional mortgage yield. GNP was chosen as a general index.[14]

The limitations of this real estate index were so severe as to cause real estate investment to appear to be the least risky of the four media (stocks, bonds, mortgages and real estate) depicted.[15]

Finally, we are faced with the fact that prospective returns on real estate investment cannot be estimated in the same way as security returns. Because securities trade in reasonably good markets, it is possible to employ the fiction of an "annual holding period," from which holding-period returns may be computed and regressed against index (market) returns. Because of the assumption of independence of securities' returns, it then becomes possible to employ the expected value of these historical relationships as a future estimate of the risk and return of the security. The difficulty of applying this approach to real estate is illustrated by Friedman's work. His real estate sample consisted of fifty properties with estimated values in 1963 and 1968; because market data were unavailable, he was forced to assume a constant compound rate of growth from the former to the latter in order to generate annual holding-period returns. These returns were then regressed against the index discussed above. If the explained variance in the regression were simply employed as a test of the validity of the index, all might be well. The implications from portfolio theory, however, would be that the explained variance is a measure of nondiversifiable risk and that the remainder (unexplained variance) could be eliminated by diversification. In sum, total variance may be underestimated by the assumption of constant annual price growth (and thus, a fairly constant annual return), and true systematic variance could also be misestimated by the use of an index that may not be the best reflection of the market. It should also be iterated that the assumption of constant annual returns from real estate regardless of holding period does not seem to fit the facts because of transactions costs, borrowing capacity, and tax effects.

---

[14]Friedman, *op. cit.*, p. 88. None of the comments in this section are intended to detract from the monumental task undertaken by Friedman nor the significant contributions he made. Rather, we merely wish to indicate the magnitude of the problem and the compromises that must be made to obtain any solution at all.

[15]Ibid, p. 89.

In conclusion, the inclusion of real estate in a theoretically correct system of portfolio selection is hindered by:

1. The lack of a quadratic integer programming algorithm.
2. The lack of an adequate index of real estate returns.
3. The individualistic nature of real estate (with regard to taxes, holding period, and so on) that makes the estimation of returns from a general index (even a good one) difficult.
4. The lack of market data to provide even *ex post* estimations of risk and return.
5. The nonindependence of real estate returns and nonreplicability of projects.
6. Portfolio restrictions, information imperfections, and so on that preclude anyone from holding a perfectly diversified portfolio.

PORTFOLIO REVISION[16]

Over the course of time, expectations regarding the earning power and dividend-paying potential of the firm, the risk of the same, and the firm's stock's covariance with other securities will change. Furthermore, the market price of the stock and the level of interest rates will undoubtedly change. Finally, the investor's utility function itself may change or else changes in his level of wealth may cause his degree of risk aversion to change. Any of these factors will tend to cause the investor's portfolio to be suboptimal. It then becomes necessary to revise the portfolio.

Portfolio revision may be viewed as the general case of asset acquisition and disposition, with portfolio selection representing the special case of revision of the all-cash portfolio. As such, revision involves all the problems of portfolio selection and some additional difficulties as well. Any asset sold at a profit, for example, becomes subject to taxation that, in turn, reduces the amount of funds available for reinvestment; it might thus be desirable to maintain a position in a slightly inferior security if the capital gains taxes would wipe out any advantage. Also, the purchase or sale of any security will incur transactions costs, which also reduce the amount to be invested. This problem could be ignored in portfolio selection because it was assumed that the costs would be incurred no

---

[16]Much of this discussion is drawn from Andrew Chen, Frank Jen, and Stanley Zionts, "The Optimal Portfolio Revision Policy," *Journal of Business,* January 1971, pp. 51–61. Also valuable in this area are: Eugene Fama, "Multiperiod Consumption Investment Decisions," *American Economic Review,* March 1970, pp. 163–74, Jan Mossin, "Optimal Multi-Period Portfolio Policies," *Journal of Business,* April 1969, pp. 215–29, J. Pogue, "An Intertemporal Model for Investment Management," *Journal of Bank Research,* Spring 1970, pp. 17–33.

matter what was bought. A simple one-period revision model is presented below to illustrate these effects.

Let:

μ_i = expected return on ith asset

C_{ij} = covariance of return between ith and jth security

α_i = amount invested in ith security at beginning of period

β_i = amount invested in ith security at end of period before portfolio revision

γ_i = amount in ith security after portfolio revision (decision variable)

$\delta_i(\omega_i)$ = increase (decrease) in amount of ith asset held from existing to revised portfolio

$b_i(s_i)$ = buying (selling) transfer cost of ith asset ($b_0 = s_0 = 0$ for cash) and assumed proportional for convenience

r_i = realized return on ith asset, composed of cash dividend return (r_i^c) and capital gain return (r_i^g). By definition,

$$r_i = r_i^c + r_i^g$$

t_c, t_g = ordinary income and capital gain tax rates for investor

The cash account at the end of the year is equal to beginning cash plus all dividends after taxes:

$$\beta_O = \alpha_O + \left(\sum_{i=1}^{n} r_i^c \alpha_i \right) \left(1 - t_c \right) \tag{18.9}$$

and the amount invested in each risk asset is:

$$\beta_{i(i=1, \ldots , n)} = (1 + r_i^g) \alpha_i \tag{18.10}$$

From this point, short sales and borrowing are excluded:

$$\alpha_i, \beta_i, \gamma_i \geqslant 0, \text{ for all } i, 0 \text{ to } n \tag{18.11}$$

By definition, the net change in holdings of the ith asset is given by the difference between holdings in the end of period portfolio and the revised portfolio:

$$\delta_i - \omega_i = \gamma_i - \beta_i, \qquad \delta_i, \omega_i \geqslant 0$$

$$\text{and } \delta_i \text{ or } \omega_i \text{ or both} = 0$$

(18.12)

The total value of the portfolio after revision must equal the value prior to revision less any transactions costs and taxes realized:

$$\sum_{i=0}^{n} \gamma_i = \sum_{i=0}^{n} \beta_i - \sum_{i=1}^{n} \quad \{\delta_i b_i + w_i \, [s_i + (r_i^g - s_i - r_i^g s_i)t_g] \}$$

(18.13)

Subject to these constraints, the objective function then becomes:

Maximize Z,

$$Z = \sum_{i=0}^{n} (1+\mu_i)\gamma_i - \lambda \left[\sum_{i=1}^{n} \sum_{j=1}^{n} \gamma_i \gamma_j C_{ij} \right]$$

(18.14)

Multiperiod revision models generally involve dynamic programming, in which the last-period portfolio is optimized first and then the model works backward to the present. Various limitations have prevented the practical applications of such models except for very small portfolios over a limited number of periods.

Two final points should be made. One of the reasons that dynamic programming is necessary stems from Mossin's contention that one-period portfolio planning tends to be "myopic" (suboptimal) over many periods unless the underlying utility function is a log or power function.[17] Fama, however, has shown that if investors may be assumed to be risk-averse and markets perfect, one-period investment planning is consistent with long-run optimization.[18] Finally, models of the sort presented above include taxes and transactions costs, but not information costs. But for the latter, the model could be run (and revision take place) continuously. Because gathering information and running the model do require time and money, however, the question of how often to revise (or more precisely, consider revision) appears to be unanswered at this time.

[17] Mossin, *op. cit.*
[18] Fama, *op. cit.*

PROBLEMS

1. Assume that portfolios with the parameters given below lie along an efficiency frontier. Which would be eliminated if a lower confidence limit (K) of 1.0 were applied? If limits of 0.5, 2, and 3 were applied?

Security	A	B	C	D	E	F	G	H	I
μ	.30	.25	.20	.15	.13	.11	.08	.06	.03
σ	.50	.31	.19	.10	.07	.05	.03	.02	.01

2. Graph the efficiency frontier from the coordinates given in 1.

a. If the pure rate of interest were 2 percent, which portfolio would be selected by the excess-return criterion?

b. Which would be the safety-first portfolio if the disaster level (D) were set at 10 percent? At 5 percent?

3. Determine which of the following portfolios would be an optimal choice by stochastic dominance for an investor whose utility function possesses the requisite first-, second-, and third-order characteristics:

Return	Probability			
	A	B	C	D
−5%	.2	.1	0	0
0	.2	.3	.3	.4
5	.0	.0	.2	0
10	.1	.1	0	0
15	0	0	.1	.3
20	.5	.5	.4	.3
μ	.10	.105	.105	.105

4. Reconsider the four portfolios described in 3.

a. Which could be eliminated as inefficient?

b. Which would be selected by the geometric-mean criterion?

REFERENCES

Baumol, William, "An Expected Gain-Confidence Limit Criterion for Portfolio Selection," *Management Science*, October 1963, pp. 174–82. Reprinted in Elton and Gruber, *Security Evaluation and Portfolio Analysis*, Englewood Cliffs, N.J.: Prentice-Hall, Inc., 1972, pp. 496–504.

Chen, A., F. Jen, and S. Zionts, "The Optimal Portfolio Revision Policy," *Journal of Business,* January 1971, pp. 51-61.

Cohen, K. J., and J. A. Pogue, "An Empirical Evaluation of Alternative Selection Models," *Journal of Business,* April 1967, pp. 169-93. Reprinted in Elton and Gruber, *Security Evaluation and Portfolio Analysis,* Englewood Cliffs, N.J.: Prentice-Hall, Inc., 1972, pp. 464-95.

Fama, Eugene F., "Multiperiod Consumption-Investment Decisions," *American Economic Review,* March 1970, pp. 163-74.

Findlay, M. C., "The Role of Real Estate in an Efficient Portfolio," a research project for the Center for Real Estate and Urban Economic Studies, University of Connecticut, 1972.

Friedman, H. C., *Mixed Asset Portfolio Selection,* Ann Arbor: University Microfilms, 1972.

Hadar, J., and W. R. Russell, "Rules for Ordering Uncertain Prospects," *American Economic Review,* March 1969, pp. 25-34.

Joy, O. M., and R. B. Porter, "Stochastic Dominance and Mutual Fund Performance," *Journal of Financial and Quantitative Analysis,* forthcoming.

Latané, Henry and Donald Tuttle, *Security Analysis and Portfolio Management,* Chaps. 4, 24, 25. New York: The Ronald Press, 1970.

Lintner, John, "Security Prices, Risk, and Maximal Gains for Diversification," *Journal of Finance,* December 1965, pp. 587-615.

Mossin, J., "Optimal Multi-Period Portfolio Policies," *Journal of Business,* April 1969, pp. 215-29.

Pogue, J., "An Intertemporal Model for Investment Management," *Journal of Bank Research,* Spring 1970, pp. 17-33.

Porter, R. B., "A Comparison of Stochastic Dominance and Mean-Variance Portfolio Models," *Proceedings Southwestern Finance Association,* 1971, pp. 93-112.

Porter, Burr, and J. Gaumnitz, "Stochastic Dominance vs. Mean-Variance Portfolio Analysis: A Theoretical and Empirical Evaluation," *American Economic Review,* forthcoming.

Robichek, A., and S. Myers, *Optimal Financing Decisions,* Englewood Cliffs, N.J.: Prentice-Hall, Inc., 1965.

Roy, A. D., "Safety First and the Holding of Assets," *Econometrica,* July 1952, pp. 431-49.

Samuelson, Paul, "The 'Fallacy' of Maximizing the Geometric Mean in Long Sequences of Investing or Gambling," *Proc. Nat. Acad. Sci. USA,* October 1971, pp. 2493-96.

Whitmore, G. A., "Third-Degree Stochastic Dominance," *American Economic Review,* June 1970, pp. 457-59.

IV

Capital Market Efficiency

19

Capital Markets: Efficiency and Imperfections

"Interestingly, professional economists appear to think more highly of professional investors than do other professional investors."

Wm. Sharpe

CAPITAL MARKET EFFICIENCY

One of the major assumptions underlying capital market theory presented in the last two chapters was that investors possessed either homogeneous (or a stable weighted average of) expectations regarding the future. One implication of this assumption is that a change in expectations will either occur unanimously or else in some stable average way that is an operational equivalent of unanimity. Thus, if markets are in equilibrium, a change in expectations will cause them to move in a rapid and unbiased fashion to a new equilibrium. Markets that behave in this manner will always "fully reflect" available information, which is the definition of an efficient market. Various empirical tests have been made of the efficiency of the securities markets, and these form the basis of this section. A point to be borne in mind, however, is that any proof of capital market efficiency does not validate all the assumptions in Chapter 17. Efficiency is a necessary condition for equilibrium, but it is not altogether sufficient; we shall return to this point in the latter part of the chapter.

It will be recalled from Chapter 11 that, even in a world of perfect certainty, prices of securities could be expected to change over time as long as the income stream was not instantaneous and constant. Indeed, price change would be necessary in such a case to cause the expected return for each holding period to be obtained, that is,

$$P_1 + D_1 \equiv P_0 \, (1 + r_1) \qquad (19.1)$$

or

$$P_1 - P_0 \equiv r_1 \, (P_0) - D_1$$

In a world of less-than-perfect certainty, changes in expected income or the required rate of return (caused, in turn, by changes in the pure rate or the perceived risk of the issue) could also cause the prices of securities to change over time. It is argued, however, that only the availability of new information or better analysis of already available information should cause the expectations regarding income, risk, and interest rates to change and, thus, prices to change for these reasons. If it may be assumed that: (1) all relevant information is available to all market participants; (2) any new information is spread and assimilated immediately; and (3) vast numbers of market participants employ the most sophisticated analytical techniques, then the securities market may be viewed as a "fair game" where:

$$E[(\widetilde{P}_1 + \widetilde{D}_1) | I_0] = P_0 [1 + E(\widetilde{r}_1 | I_0)] \qquad (19.2)$$

The above merely states that the expected price of a security in period one given the information available in period zero (assuming all dividends or interest are reinvested) is equal to the price in period zero times one plus the expected rate of return, given available information.[1] This hypothesis also implies that (1) the excess market value of a security or (2) the excess expected return to be earned by holding the security both have, given available information, an expected value of zero.

Several points should be noted. Equation 19.2 does not imply that prices need be stable. Indeed, to the extent that $E[\widetilde{D}_1] \neq E[\widetilde{r}_1] \, (P_0)$, then $E[\widetilde{P}_1] \neq P_0$. Thus, we have a probabilistic model with implications similar to the certainty model (equation 19.1). A major difference, however, is indicated by the presence of the expectations operator and tildes for both the $(\widetilde{P}_1 + \widetilde{D}_1)$ and $\widetilde{r}_1$ terms, implying that they are random variables at time zero. Thus, although the certainty model would indicate a constant rate of price

[1]This formula and the material in this section are discussed more fully in Eugene F. Fama, "Efficient Capital Markets: A Review of Theory and Empirical Work," *Journal of Finance*, May 1970, pp. 383–417.

change over time (that is, linear on semilog graphs), the expectations model indicates that price could be expected to vary about such a line. Such a possibility is also reflected by the error term in the various capital-market estimation models.

Finally, it will be noted that both $(\widetilde{P}_1 + \widetilde{D}_1)$ and $\widetilde{r}_1$ are conditioned by available information, I_o. To the extent new information or better analysis becomes available, $E[\widetilde{P}_1 + \widetilde{D}_1]$ and $E[\widetilde{r}_1]$ can alter, and the expected rate of price change over time can shift. Adding the assumption that the timing of the arrival of new information in the market is a random variable, we see that shifts in the expected-price-change line, as well as movement about it, can be treated as random events. We shall now examine various efforts to prove or refute the efficient markets hypothesis.

Weak Tests

The earliest empirical work was produced by the "random walk" hypothesis researchers primarily to attack the "technical analysts."[2] Technical analysts have for many years contended that by analyzing only the past price movements of a security, it is possible (or, "they are able" – depending upon the size of the ego of the technical analyst involved) to predict future price movements and thus make greater-than-normal profits. The distress of the random-walk followers is perhaps best expressed by Cootner:

> If any substantial group of buyers thought prices were too low, their buy-ing would force up the prices. The reverse would be true for sellers. Except for appreciation due to earnings retention, the conditional expectation of tomorrow's price, given today's price, is today's price.
>
> In such a world, the only price changes that would occur are those that result from new information. Since there is no reason to expect that information to be nonrandom in appearance, the period-to-period price changes of a stock should be random movements, statistically independent of one another.[3]

The early random walk writers, then, concerned themselves with demon-strating that successive price changes were statistically independent of each other, that various mechanical trading rules based upon price changes did not yield profits statistically superior to a simple "buy-and-hold" strategy, and that "price changes from transaction to transaction are independent, identically distributed random variables with finite variances" (implying, by the Central-

---

[2] Technical analysis is discussed in the appendix to this chapter.

[3] Paul Cootner, ed., *The Random Character of Stock Market Prices,* (Cambridge: The MIT Press, 1964), p. 232.

Limit Theorem, that for numerous transactions price changes will be normally distributed).[4]

More recent writers have refined certain parts of the basic random-walk argument. In the first place, it is suggested that price changes do not follow a true random walk (with an expected value of zero), but rather a submartingale (with an expected value greater than zero).[5] Thus, the theory can take long-run price trends into account and accept a very modest amount of serial correlation in successive price changes.[6] The challenge to the technicians has become to demonstrate that their rules can earn greater-than-normal profits.

It has also been contended that price changes are not normally distributed about an expected trend but rather belong to the broader family of stable Paretian distributions of which the normal is only a limiting case. The implication for our purposes is that the "fat-tailed" stable distributions have an infinite variance, such that the usual portfolio approach employing σ and σ^2 cannot be used if prices (and, thus, returns) are so distributed. Fama has demonstrated, however, that a similar form of analysis, employing a different dispersion parameter, can be employed.[7]

Semistrong Tests

Although the weak tests of capital market efficiency dealt with the inability to make profitable predictions of future prices from past prices, the semistrong tests attempt to prove that prices reflect all available information. Most tests thus far have sought to demonstrate that new information results in a rapid adjustment to a new equilibrium price that, by implication, is taken to demonstrate that the price at any time must reflect available information. Specifically, the tests have taken events such as announcements of stock splits, earnings, dividends, interest-rate changes, and so on, and studied (1) how rapidly a price adjustment was made and (2) whether the price adjustment was an unbiased evaluation of the information (such that subsequent adjustments were

---

[4]Fama, *op. cit.,* p. 399. The Cootner volume contains many of the earlier studies and the Fama article has an extensive bibliography, so one is not reproduced here. Selected references are included at the end of the chapter.

[5]A martingale is a process in which the conditional expectation of the $n+1$th observation, given a set of data, is the nth observation. Rates of return are often assumed to follow a martingale, such that $E(\tilde{r}_1|I_0) = r_0$. A submartingale is a similar concept without the strict equality; stock prices are generally assumed to follow a submartingale, such that $E(\tilde{P}_1|I_0) \geqslant P_0$. A random walk is a very strict form of martingale that assumes not only the mean but the entire distribution to be the same, such that $f(r_1)|I_0 = f(r_1)$ and $f(r_1) = f(r_0) = f(r_{-1})$, and so on.

[6]In view of the general upward trend of prices over time, it was surprising to many observers that the statistical case against absolute independence of successive price changes was as weak as it was.

[7]Eugene F. Fama, "Portfolio Analysis in a Stable Paretian Market," *Management Science,* January 1965, pp. 404–19.

as likely to be in one direction as the other). The results of the tests seem to confirm that price adjustments occur rather quickly after the first public announcement of the information, implying that at least a significant portion of the market receives and interprets the information quickly. It follows, then, that the initial price adjustment has been generally found to be unbiased. A price trend caused by the slow spread and interpretation of new information could result in a profitable return for swift action; that such a trend does not occur seems affirmed.

Strong Tests

In a crude sense, it could be said that the weak tests indicate that one cannot become wealthy as a technician[8] and the semistrong tests indicate that, by the time one reads some new information, it is too late to profit from it. The theory still allows a person possessing superior information or analytical techniques to expect a better-than-normal return. The strong tests, however, go all the way to asking if there can be any information not reflected in the price of a security such that anyone can expect above-average profits. During the 1920s, it was claimed that "any day is a good day to buy a good stock." If the strong form of the efficient capital market hypothesis holds, then, "any day is as good as any other day to buy any stock (or bond, or mutual fund, and so on)."

The rationale for the strong tests lies in a combination of the semistrong tests (information assimilated in a rapid and unbiased fashion) and the fact that a great many supposedly knowledgable and trained people are engaged in the securities business. It is argued that with so many people and so much information, there should be few if any true "sleepers." Studies have indicated that corporate insiders and specialists on the floor of the exchanges (because their "book" contains unfilled orders) may have superior information and thus higher expected returns. Other investors, however, have not been shown to produce consistently higher returns. In particular, numerous studies of mutual funds have shown that their average performance is, if anything, inferior to the market as a whole.[9] It also appears that, even for individual funds, past success is an unreliable guide to future performance. In sum, it has been shown that the investor could do better picking securities at random than with the average mutual fund. And, because mutual funds are viewed as possessing as much information, analytical skill, and diversification as any investor, their inability to out-perform the market is taken as very compelling evidence in support of the strong form of the efficient markets hypothesis. It should be noted, however, that even in academic circles, the strong form has a much smaller following than the other two tests.

[8]Unless, of course, one is selling a service for $500 a year and placing the proceeds in a blind trust.

[9]The nature of these measures and the specific studies were identified on pages 339–341 and 352.

CAPITAL MARKETS AND THE REAL WORLD

In order to justify the time and money spent on the study of investments (including the purchase price of this book), it is necessary to come to terms with the strong form of the efficient capital markets hypothesis. Indeed, if the consumer groups gain additional strength, it may soon be necessary to place on the dust jacket of all investments books "Caution: Studies have shown that the contents provide no advantage over random selection." Nevertheless, it should be remembered that the strong-form tests are based almost entirely on mutual-fund performance. Some may question the use of these institutions as absolute proof that, if they cannot outperform the market, no one can. For several reasons, it may be argued that mutual funds are an unconvincing choice for a test of the strong form of the efficient capital markets hypothesis. First, *the level of training and education of a number of fund managers is not terribly high*. Although many funds are operated by competently trained managers, many more are not. Second, *the compensation scheme employed by most funds encourages suboptimal behavior*. Small funds take excessive risks in order to achieve the top of the annual performance lists. This is done in order to gain new shareholders and the subsequent profits derived from percentage-of-assets management fees. Third, *large funds cannot acquire substantial amounts of any promising issue without influencing market price unless their position is accumulated over time*. Moreover, when a fund has acquired a large holding of a thinly traded issue, the position cannot be liquidated easily without influencing price. Fourth, *even if large funds could find small companies whose stock evidenced very lucrative future potential, the shares of these firms would represent only a small percentage of a large fund's assets*. Hence, the fund could not increase its return significantly even if it did find securities that significantly out-performed the market. Fifth, *legal requirements constrain open-ended (mutual) funds to hold over-diversified portfolios*. At least 75 percent of the fund's assets must be "diversified" to qualify for special tax treatment as an investment company. To produce diversification, the law requires that no security (except government bonds) may represent over 5 percent of the investment company's total assets nor over 10 percent of the outstanding voting stock of the issuer. This means that most funds hold at least fifteen (75 ÷ 5) stocks; and, to satisfy further legal requirements (some states require 100 percent diversification), many invest in at least twenty. As a practical matter, the typical fund will hold well over one hundred securities. Nevertheless, unleveraged Markowitz efficient portfolios frequently turn out to be composed of fewer than twenty stocks; and, as additional securities are added, the portfolios become riskier without improving returns. Thus, superfluous diversification can actually *increase* risk.[10]

---

[10]Francis and Archer, *Portfolio Analysis.* (Englewood Cliffs, N.J.: Prentice-Hall, Inc., 1971), pp. 164-65.

Legal and Institutional Constraints

There are a number of legal and institutional arrangements that tend to undermine many of the assumptions required for capital market theory in addition to those that produce market inefficiency. In particular, it appears unlikely that market portfolios are (or can be) maintained by a substantial part of the investment community. In the first place, we can observe that legal and institutional arrangements eliminate some securities from consideration, much less selection, by certain investors. Banks and savings and loan associations (SLAs), for example, are effectively prohibited from owning any stock (with a few insignificant exceptions). Banks, mutual savings banks, and some other institutional investors are also effectively precluded from owning low-grade (Ba or lower) bonds. Thus, whole classes of securities do not appear in the investment universe for the affected institutions.

More pervasive still than the outright prohibitions of securities are the various limitations on holdings. Thus, although most life insurance companies and mutual savings banks may legally purchase stock, they may only do so to a very small extent (5–10 percent of total portfolio). The legally required "crude" diversification also applies to banks (no more than 1 percent of total assets in the securities of one issuer) and mutual funds (discussed above). In the case of savings banks and life companies, there are also maximum allowable proportions of mortgages in the portfolio as well as loan-to-value limits on the mortgages themselves. Finally, SLAs and savings banks are also constrained in their non-VA or FHA mortgage lending to the geographically proximate area.

Many of the above restrictions, and others, reflect a rather curious legal philosophy that completely ignores portfolio concepts. It is generally agreed that most financial institutions serve a public purpose that requires that they continue to exist and avoid insolvency. It is then contended that this goal is best served by requiring the institutions to have a low-risk portfolio (this assertion alone is questionable). Moreover, it is felt that a low-risk portfolio is composed of a large number of low-risk securities. Hence, some institutions are provided with a "legal list" of high-rated, low-risk securities from which to select their portfolios. Others, especially trust departments, operate under the "prudent man rule" (requiring them to exhibit the care a prudent man would in managing his own affairs). Unfortunately, the courts seem to feel that the philosophy of this paragraph represents prudence. Thus, the investment manager must be concerned not only that the portfolio succeed but also that no individual security fail lest he be sued. "Prudence" usually prevails. It is an unfortunate truism that no trustee has been successfully sued for portfolio dissipation because he invested in government bonds.[11]

---

[11] Some recent court actions indicate that the prudent man rule may eventually be abandoned. However, the growing demand that funds be channeled to "socially desirable" investments (which can include mortgages, municipals, minority loans, pollution control equipment loans, or loans to whatever other powerful special-interest group desires cheap money) is causing an entirely new set of constraints to arise to take its place.

A second set of legal and institutional constraints also mitigates against the validity of some necessary assumptions of capital market theory. It appears very likely that the separation theorem probably does not apply in the real world. In addition to all the investment constraints already considered, it should be noted that many institutions are prohibited from selling short, while individuals are limited in this regard. (See the discussion of short selling in Chapter 2). Both institutions and individuals are also quite restricted in borrowing against their portfolios. Some institutions can have only a limited (or no) debt outstanding, and individuals are subject to Federal Reserve margin requirements (see Chapter 2). It thus cannot even be pretended that the crucial assumption that the investment decision is independent of the financing decision holds.

It seems clear that many investors cannot hold the market portfolio. It is also clear that the separation theorem does not apply. Can it be argued, consequently, that capital market theory (and efficiency implying equilibrium) is invalid? Economists would say no. As long as some participants can borrow and others can lend and every security can be held by at least some participants, the efficiency proponents can bring forth their stable weighted average arguments. The latter then becomes an argument in positive economics: markets behave *as though* they were in static equilibrium with all participants having free access and homogeneous expectations, even though this is not indeed the case. This argument will fail to hold to the extent that changes in the distribution of wealth alter the weights or different participants do not revise their expectations proportionately to new information.

EXPECTATIONS, CONVERGENCE, AND THE EFFICIENT MARKET HYPOTHESIS[12]

In most areas of economics, dynamic theory is the most complicated form of analysis. This is true because expectations, rather than existing conditions, are the main determinants. Equilibrium is based on a given state of expectations, and any changes in those expectations will force a movement to a new equilibrium. Unfortunately, "the adjustments needed to bring about equilibrium take time."[13] When markets are inefficient, time becomes the most important variable to the analysis. But when markets are efficient, the adjustments occur rather quickly and time is not terribly important. A perfectly efficient market will return to equilibrium immediately. Proponents of the efficient-capital-market hypothesis maintain that timing is not important in analyzing invest-

---

[12]This section draws heavily from E. E. Williams and M. C. Findlay, "Expectations, Convergence, and the Efficient Market Hypothesis," *Faculty of Management Working Paper,* McGill University, 1973.

[13]J. R. Hicks, *Value and Capital,* 2nd ed., (London: Oxford University Press, 1946), pp. 116.

ments because the market digests new information instantaneously, redetermines expectations, and recalculates prices accordingly.

A condition of static equilibrium can cease to exist if new information concerning systematic risk, expected dollar returns, or the market price of systematic risk (that is, the slope of the SML) is perceived. For example, let us assume a market in which all dividends are reinvested so that returns over the next period ($t = 1$) are given by:

$$\tilde{r}_1 = \frac{\tilde{P}_1 - P_0}{P_0} \qquad (19.3)$$

where: $\tilde{r}_1$ = the expected return one period hence

$\tilde{P}_1$ = the expected market price of the stock one period hence (with dividends reinvested)

P_0 = the current market price ($t=0$)

We further assume that time periods are very short (that is, they are too short to act between $t = 0$ and $t = 1$). Finally, we assume that R is the appropriate return for a given level of systematic risk (taken from the SML). In equilibrium,

$$E(\tilde{r}_1 \mid I_0) = R = r_0 \qquad (19.4)$$

If R changes either because of a shift in the *SML* or a change in the systematic risk of a stock, there exists a new $R^*(R^* \neq R)$ which will produce the potential for a windfall gain between $t = 0$ and $t = 1$ of ω.

$$E(\tilde{r}_1 \mid I^*) = R + \lambda\omega$$

$$= R + \lambda(\frac{\tilde{P}_1{}^* - \tilde{P}_1}{P_0}) \qquad (19.5)$$

$$E(\tilde{r}_2 \mid I^*, \lambda=1) = R^* \qquad (19.6)$$

where: I_0 = available information at period $t=0$

I^* = new information becoming available between $t=0$ and $t=1$

R^* = the new equilibrium return, given new information about either the level of risk evidenced by the shares or the position of the *SML*

P_0 = the share price at $t=0$

$\tilde{P}_1$ = the share price at $t=1$ (corresponding to information I_0)

$\tilde{P}_1{}^*$ = the share price at $t=1$ (corresponding to information I^*)

λ = a one-period price adjustment coefficient

ω = the potential windfall gain which would occur between
$t=0$ and $t=1$ assuming complete adjustment (that is,
where $\lambda=1$).

If markets are efficient, $\lambda = 1$ and adjustment takes place immediately. Because time periods are assumed to be short, only those holding the security when new information reaches the market will receive the windfall (that is, ω will result too quickly for anyone to act on the information profitably). Beyond period $t = 1$, the only return expected would be the new equilibrium rate R^*. If markets are inefficient, $\lambda \neq 1$ and adjustment will not take place immediately. In the case $0 < \lambda < 1$, the entire windfall gain will not be allocated before profitable action can be taken. Indeed, if $\lambda < 0$ (which corresponds to a complete misinterpretation of the new information), then a potential windfall even greater than ω could be possible to the extent that the market eventually interprets the information correctly. If $\lambda > 1$, the market overreacts, and a windfall in the opposite direction is possible.

We have considered two of the conditions that will produce a disturbance in the static equilibrium of stock prices. The third condition (a change in expected dollar returns) will initially manifest itself as $\tilde{P}_1^* \neq \tilde{P}_1$ whereas, in the former conditions, the disturbance was introduced by $R^* \neq R$. The analysis proceeds along similar lines, with equation 19.5 remaining intact. The expected return for $t = 2$, however, becomes:

$$E(\tilde{r}_2 \mid I^*, \lambda=1) = R \qquad\qquad (19.7)$$

rather than equation 19.6.

In all three instances, empirical evidence suggests that λ is close to 1. Nevertheless, all the semistrong studies have examined I^* of a fairly obvious sort (earnings announcements, stock splits, and so on). They do not address themselves to the fact that analysts may obtain other kinds of I^* that cannot be neatly measured. The analyst who has a better forecasting method, for example, may be able to discern information that no simple sort of empirical investigation could detect, and his long-run returns could be expected to surpass the market return.

Of course, determining better I^* is what security analysis is all about. The analyst should be cautioned, however, that his returns will be above the market's only if what he knows eventually becomes known by the market (hence, producing a new equilibrium). If he envisages a disequilibrium that will produce a windfall gain (ω) and the market never "learns" ($\lambda = 0$ in all future periods), he is better off only to the extent that his superior insight allows him to earn higher returns for a given level of risk than would be provided by the market's perception of equilibrium risk-return relationships. He does not earn the windfall adjustment return, however, that would follow if the market eventually came to agree with his superior insight. On the other hand, if the market received and correctly interpreted new information at the same time as the analyst ($\lambda = 1$), no above-normal returns would be expected. Thus, the analyst must be rather sure that his insight is indeed superior, and that the market will eventually agree with him, in order to derive the most benefit from his prognostications.

Expectations about future dollar returns (and estimated risk) may be even more important than expectations about future rates of return for making above-average profits. If an analyst foresees better prospects for a security than the market, he may get even greater returns if the market eventually comes around to his view. Suppose an analyst expects security C (Figure 19-1) to

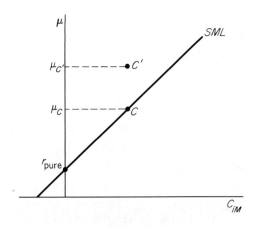

Figure 19-1   Differences in Expected Rates of Returns

produce a future stream that will yield 12 percent, given the current market price ($100), but the market only forecasts a 10 percent return, which is the equilibrium yield. The analyst expects a perpetual earnings stream (perhaps in the form of dividend payments) of $12, whereas the market only expects $10. If the analyst turns out to be correct, the price of the security will rise to ($12/.1) = $120, assuming the stock is still in the 10 percent risk class. If the market moves toward the analyst's position within one year, his return would not only be better than the equilibrium 10 percent, but it would also exceed his expected 12 percent. His yield, in fact, would be:

$$\frac{120 + 12 - 100}{100} = 32\%$$

This result can be found by using equation 19.5. Assuming the reinvestment of dividends, the stock price at $t = 1$ would be $120 + $12 = $132. The price that would prevail without market recognition would be expected to be $110 (the market anticipates $10 in dividends, rather than $12, for reinvestment). Hence, when recognition occurs $\lambda = 1$ and:

$$E(\tilde{r}_1 \mid I^*) = R + \lambda \left(\frac{\tilde{P}_1{}^* - \tilde{P}_1}{P_0} \right)$$

$$= 10\% + (1) \left(\frac{132 - 110}{100} \right)$$

$$= 32\%$$

Again, the time required for convergence is seen to be very important. If it took the market three years to converge (suppose the stock paid $12 in years one and two, but the market only became convinced that this dividend could hold in the long run in period $t = 3$), his return would be:

at 18 percent,

$$t = 0 \quad - \$100 \ (1.000) = - \$100.00$$
$$t = 1\text{-}3 + \quad 12 \ (2.174) = + \quad 26.09$$
$$t = 3 \quad + \quad 120 \ (\ .609) = + \quad \underline{73.08}$$
$$- \$ \quad .83$$

or just under 18 percent. If the market never came to accept the analyst's judgment (and the yield, in fact, was 12 percent), he would still earn a larger return than that expected by the market. On the other hand, if the analyst's view were adopted by the market, his return would be far greater still. Thus, having better insight than the market would have given the analyst a 2 percent higher return in our example (12 percent - 10 percent), whereas having insight about patterns of market expectations could produce a 20 percent additional return (that is, 32 percent - 12 percent).

The movement of stock prices from expected levels $(\tilde{P}_1)$ to those that the analyst thinks are justifiable $(\tilde{P}_1{}^*)$ is called *convergence*. The principle of convergence has been recognized by conventional authorities for years,[14] and the importance of timing in convergence has been given renewed consideration.[15] It is clear that rapidity of convergence will greatly influence returns, and the longer the time required for the market to recognize the superior insight of the analyst, the lower will be his annual rate of return. In terms of the Security Market Line,

[14] See Graham, Dodd, and Cottle, *Security Analysis,* 4th ed. (New York: McGraw-Hill Book Company, 1962).

[15] See Latané and Tuttle, *Security Analysis and Portfolio Management* (New York: The Ronald Press, 1970).

convergence takes place as the market realizes that a security is under- (or over-) priced and that the security moves toward the line. In Figure 19-2, two securities are shown. The first, A, is seen to be "under"-priced. That is, the return from $A(\mu_A)$ is greater than it should be given A's risk characteristic. Once the market agrees that A is underpriced, demanders will bid up prices until the security reaches the SML at A'. At this point, the rate of return will be $\mu_A{}'$, which, of course, is lower than μ_A. In the process of reaching equilibrium, the security rises in price, and investors who bought A when its yield was μ_A receive a windfall gain. Similarly, security B is overpriced, given its risk characteristic. Its price will be bid down (expected returns rising from B to B') until it reaches the SML, if the analyst is correct in his appraisal. Investors who sold B short would reap a windfall gain as the price of B falls to yield $\mu_B{}'$.

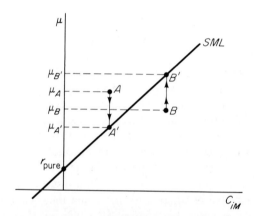

Figure 19-2   Convergence and the Security Market Line

The investor who wishes to achieve returns above the market must consistently find securities that are under- (over-) priced, buy (sell-short), and hope that the market soon agrees with him. Efficient-market proponents would argue that no one could repeatedly find securities off the SML, and even if he could, this would not constitute "beating the market." It is suggested that "even if a true disequilibrium security is found and a capital gain is obtained, the market hasn't been 'beaten.' The equilibrating mechanism of the market is what allowed the capital gain."[16] Notwithstanding the semantics of the argument, it seems only logical that one who could find securities off the SML frequently would enjoy above-average returns.

Expectations play a major role in convergence. Furthermore, it is *changes in expectations,* rather than simply new information, that influence returns.

---

[16]Francis and Archer, *op. cit.,* p. 193.

This distinction is important because all new information does not change expectations. A stock split, for example, does not change the fundamental position of the firm, and it should not be surprising that the long-run effect of a split on investor returns is nil. On the other hand, expectations can change *even though new information does not develop.*

Although all three conditions producing disequilibrium can affect future expectations, we will focus our attention on the market price of risk (that is, shifts in the SML) and not the parameters of an individual security. Examination of market factors, rather than unique security characteristics, is more conducive to generalization and comparison to prior theoretical work. Extending a Hicksian scheme over the entire SML,[17] it could be argued that there exists an elasticity of expectations about equilibrium rates of return at a given level of systematic risk that may be defined as:

$$\epsilon_x = \frac{E[\tilde{R}_{t+1} - R_t]}{(R_t - R_{t-1})} \qquad (19.8)$$

for the simple one-period forecasting model. ϵ_x may be negative, zero, positive, positive and unity, or positive and greater than unity. If $\epsilon_x = 0$, we have the case of rigidly inelastic expectations, where changes in historical returns do not cause changes in expected future returns. This case would most closely correspond to the efficient market hypothesis.[18] If $\epsilon_x = 1$, expectations about changes in future returns do depend on changes in historical returns, and patterns of historical changes will alter expected future returns in the same direction and in the same proportion. If $\epsilon_x > 1$, this historical pattern will "make people feel that they can recognise a trend, so that they try to extrapolate."[19] Finally, if $\epsilon_x < 0$, people make "the opposite kind of guess, interpreting the change as the culmination point of fluctuation."[20] Although a reasonably strong *a priori* case can be made for $\epsilon_x = 0$,[21] empirical tests using expectations are very difficult to construct. It may be that other elasticities do exist at times (when interest rates have been advancing or declining very rapidly),[22] and the analyst

[17]Hicks, *op. cit.,* p. 205.

[18]Properly defined, R_t is the cost of equity capital to a firm in the given systematic risk class. Thus, when firms apply a given discount rate (that is, cost of capital) to all future flows generated by a capital budgeting proposal, they are implicitly assuming $\epsilon_x = 0$.

[19]*Ibid.* Hicks outlined his elasticities in terms of commodity prices initially, but they are later applied to his discussion of interest rates (pp. 260–62, 281–82).

[20]*Ibid.*

[21]Hicks felt that the interest elasticity of expectations was small if not zero. *Ibid.* p. 282.

[22]Because nominal rates of return depend on the price level, various elasticities (positive and negative) might prevail depending upon inflationary expectations. See Milton Friedman, "Factors Affecting the Level of Interest Rates," in *Conference on Savings and Residential Financing,* (Chicago: U.S. Savings and Loan League, 1968).

who can properly judge expectations about future rates will earn superior returns.[23] We shall consider the implications of this phenomenon on market equilibrating behavior, as forcefully identified by Lord Keynes, in the next chapter.

PROBLEMS

1. Review the graphical presentation of the three-security portfolio on pages 322–27. For this question, security A should be graphed on the abscissa, B on the ordinate, and C equal to the remainder by convention. Begin with the simple triangular attainable set. Demonstrate the effects upon the attainable set as the following constraints are added:

    a. Debt may be incurred up to 10 percent of the total investment.

    b. $\alpha_A \leqslant .25$ (total investment).

    c. $.3$ (total investment) $\leqslant \alpha_C \leqslant .7$ (total investment).

2.

    a. The shares of the Serita Corporation are expected to pay a dividend of $1 per year forever and possess a degree of systematic risk corresponding to a return of 10 percent on the SML. At what price should Serita shares sell?

    b. Suppose that markets are not in equilibrium and the data in part a only refer to the expectations of a particular group of investors, while another group of investors expects a dividend of $1.50 per year forever and has a SML indicating an 8 percent return for Serita shares. What may now be said about the price of Serita shares? What would you expect to happen to the price of Serita if the first group of investors became more wealthy while the second group became poorer, *ceteris paribus*? What do you imagine to be the impact of a new issue of shares by Serita?

3. In his review of Jensen's work on mutual fund evaluation, Fama states: "...regardless of how mutual fund returns are measured (i.e., net or gross of loading charges and other expenses), the number of funds with large positive deviations of returns from the market line...is *less than* the number that would be expected by chance with 115 funds under the assumption that fund managements have no special talents in predicting returns."[24] (Emphasis added.) Comment on the implications of the above for the evaluation of strong form tests.

---

[23]Whether one could (or could not) make superior predictions about future interest rates depends upon the theory of term structure one accepts (see Appendix to Chapter 4). Under the unbiased expectations theory, this prediction would be made in the form of existing forward rates by current market forces. In this case one would have to outguess everyone else consistently about the trend of forward rates to make above average profits. (That anyone, except perhaps a member of the Federal Reserve Board, could do this seems unlikely.) Under liquidity preference theories, however, prospects for superior predictions are improved, because forward rates would not give a clear (unbiased) estimate of the future. Error-learning model explanations would or would not allow consistently superior predictions, depending on the nature of the learning curve.

[24]Fama, "Efficient Capital Markets," *op. cit.,* p. 413.

4. Obtain biographical data on well-known mutual-fund managers. A collection of biographical sketches from the *Institutional Investor* has been published under the title *The Money Managers,* and several managers have been the subjects of entire books (for example, Bernard Cornfeld in *Do You Sincerely Want to Be Rich?*). Study especially the education and training of these managers in line with the ability of their rapier-like minds to assimilate and analyze all available information. Also check to see if investment decisions by one manager may be viewed as independent of decisions made by others. Can you then find any other interpretation of mutual-fund performance than capital market efficiency?

APPENDIX

Technical Analysis and Investment Timing

Although technical analysis has been brought into serious question by research into the weak form of the efficient markets hypothesis, it is felt that some insight into the behavior of imperfect markets (and into the imperfect nature of the techniques themselves) may still be gained by examination of the tools associated with it. The techniques discussed in this section, drawn from a much larger body of technical indicators, generally deal with the projected behavior of the market as a whole. Since the King study indicated that an average of 50 percent of the return of securities was related to market movements,[1] information about such movements is obviously of interest. Furthermore, supply, demand, and information factors may have a more predictable impact upon the market as a whole than upon individual securities. The indicators are presented merely as factors to consider rather than absolute guides. If nothing else, a sufficiently widespread belief in technical analysis may create a certain amount of self-verification. Furthermore, the use of technical indicators for timing decisions (assuming information and waiting costs are not great) is not refuted by the efficient markets hypothesis.[2] The first group of indicators attempts to take a broad view of the market.

A.

High-grade versus All Securities

If we accept the notion that the risk structure of yields tends to narrow during boom markets (when investor expectations regarding all securities are

[1] See Benjamin F. King, "Market and Industry Factors in Stock Price Behavior," *Journal of Business,* Special Supplement, January 1966, pp. 139–90.

[2] The same statement could be made, of course, about the use of the mean high tide at Brooklyn Bridge for timing decisions.

good) and widen during recessions (when risk is, if anything, exaggerated), then evidence of a changing spread in the risk structure may provide some clue to the current state of the market. One popular method is to compare an *advance-decline line* (number of stocks declining in a day are subtracted from the number advancing and net advances are cumulated over time) with the Dow Jones Average. The former is a broad indicator of the number of stocks advancing (presumably some broad index like the S&P 500 or the NYSE index could also be used); the latter only reflects thirty blue-chip stocks. A divergence of the two, then, might indicate a change in the risk structure; the stronger case is supposedly made when the broad index declines while the DJ continues to rise, implying potential weakness in the market. The arguments regarding the interpretation of the Confidence Index (a ratio of high-grade bond yields to lower-grade yields) are similar.

Volume

The general argument related to volume is that any price movement accompanied by large volume should be considered more representative of the market's "thinking" than if volume is light. If nothing else, high volume implies a broader market with more individual transactors involved. This further implies that any price change occurred with the knowledge and consent of more people and that any reversal in a broad market would also require more people to change their evaluation.

B.

Another school of thought would argue that there are certain "professional" investors who are smarter, have better information, and so on, and further that the actual state of the market can be detected from observing these "professionals."

Broker Debit Balances

Debit balances at brokers represent borrowings from brokers to purchase stocks on margin. It is argued by proponents of this line of reasoning that only the more experienced investors buy on margin, such that an increase in debit balances indicates that the "smart money" thinks the market will rise.

Short Sales

The example of short sales illustrates a major problem involved in the analysis discussed in this section. On the one hand, short sales are generally undertaken by professional investors, such that an increase would be bearish. On the other hand, short sales must be covered by a purchase at some subsequent point; therefore an increase in short sales represents an increase in latent demand and could be viewed as bullish. At the least, an increase in short sales represents a growing divergence of opinion and an increase in market uncertainty.[3]

---

[3]Empirical evidence suggests that the bearish view is the correct one. See J. J. Seneca, "Short Interest: Bearish or Bullish," *Journal of Finance,* March 1967, pp. 67–70.

Mutual-Fund Cash Position

Because mutual funds generally try to stay invested, a large cash position will probably be invested in the near future and is interpreted as bullish. On the other hand, a small mutual-fund cash position (especially if accompanied by net share redemptions) implies that not only will more cash not be funneled into the market but also some sales of securities by the funds may be necessary; such a condition is almost universally viewed as bearish.

Secondaries and "Hot" Issues

A secondary offering is the sale of a block of stock by a large holder. As such, it is often viewed as a "bail out" by the "smart money," much as large sales of the holdings of corporate officers and insiders would also be taken as a bearish sign. A large rash of new issues of small and speculative companies is also typical of the last speculative flurry before a market break.

C.

If it can be argued that "professionals" exist who can expect to earn greater-than-normal profits, then some investors must earn less-than-normal profits. The conventional wisdom of the market generally assigns this role to the small individual investor. Indeed, it can almost be said that a caricature exists of the small investor who sells when the "smart money" is buying, finally becomes convinced that the boom is real at the peak and buys, watches the prices fall to the trough, and then becomes disheartened and sells, and so on. The theory of "contrary opinion" therefore posits that if one can merely discover what the small investor is doing, and do the opposite, riches shall follow.

Odd Lot Transactions

Because odd-lot purchasers are almost by definition small investors, net purchases (especially if odd-lot volume is large) are taken to indicate that a market peak is imminent. A large odd-lot sell-out is also taken to indicate that the trough has been reached in a market decline.

Credit Balances

Credit balances at brokers represent cash left on deposit at no interest. It is felt that such balances represent latent demand for shares. It is also felt that such balances are held by small investors (large sums would be put at interest if no immediate stock purchase were planned), such that balances are expected to rise during bull markets and peak at the boom phase.

Trading Rules and Formula Plans

Another set of heuristics has been developed over time in an attempt to profit from market cycles without the necessity of any predictions. The mechanical trading rules or formula plans discussed below assume that the investor has the capital and faith to follow the rules in good times and bad.

Filters

A typical filter rule can be expressed as: "If the price of a security rises $M\%$, buy and hold until it declines $N\%$ from a previous high, at which time sell and go short until it rises $M\%$ from a previous low, etc." If stock prices actually did form nice, steep trends up or down, then a fairly good profit could be earned from the use of filters. The careful reader will note that profitable use of filters would refute the random-walk hypothesis. Indeed, much work has been done with filters in establishing the weak form of the efficient capital markets hypothesis.[4] It has been found that large filters (say, $M = N = 30\%$) are unprofitable; a stock would rise 30 percent before it would be bought and would rise another 30 percent + before it could be sold at a profit after a 30 percent decline. Small filters ($M = N = 1\%$) did create a small gross profit, but so many transactions were involved that brokerage fees would drive the entire operation into a loss.

Dollar Cost Averaging

The dollar-averaging method, advanced as a long-run investment policy, can be expressed as: "Buy $\$M$ worth of security N every period (where a period is no more than a year)." By expressing the rule in terms of a constant dollar amount, more shares will be purchased when the price is low, and the average cost of the shares will be less than the average price at which they were bought. A variant of this method would invest a larger proportion each period in those securities in the portfolio that seemed relatively "cheaper." Like many methods, this one works fine in rising markets and even does well in a market cycling around no trend; unfortunately, it merely averages down losses in a declining market. It is generally advanced as a long-run technique under the assumption that the market is in a long-run uptrend and any decline will be temporary. The key to success of the method lies in the purchases of larger numbers of shares in depressed markets; unfortunately, this is also the time that people are least able or disposed to invest.

Ratio or Formula Plans

A constant ratio investment plan could be expressed as "keep $M\%$ of the portfolio in stocks and $(1-M)\%$ of the portfolio in bonds at all times." The basic assumption is that stock and bond prices move inversely (as noted on page 68, this is theoretically questionable). At any rate, granting the assumption, stock prices would rise in a boom and bonds would fall, unbalancing the portfolio; stock would be sold and bonds bought to bring the proportions back into line.

---

[4]See Sidney S. Alexander, "Price Movements in Speculative Markets: Trends or Random Walks," *Industrial Management Review,* (May 1961), pp. 7–26; and "Price Movements in Speculative Markets: Trends or Random Walks, No. 2," pp. 338–72 in Paul Cootner, ed., *The Random Character of Stock Market Prices,* (Cambridge: The MIT Press, 1964).

As a stock price decline set in, more and more stock would be bought as prices fell and bond prices rose. Thus, the portfolio would profit from both sides of the cycle. The variable ratio plan would attempt to increase profit by not only selling stock during booms but also cutting its proportion of the portfolio. The major difficulty of such an approach lies in the assumption that stock and bond prices not only cycle, but do so inversely with each other.

Appendix Problems

1.

a. Assume that we undertake a $3,000 per year dollar cost-averaging program. Determine average cost, average price, and profit for each of the following sequences of stock prices:

Year	A	B	C
1	25	25	25
2	30	30	20
3	35	25	15
4	40	20	10
5	45	25	5

b. Suppose instead that A, B, and C are three securities, and we invested $1,000 per year in each. Evaluate the portfolio at the end of year five.

2.

a. Assume that the data in problem 1a refers to end-of-year prices on three stocks and that prices move linearly during the year. Starting with $10,000 in cash at the end of year one and employing a 10 percent (M = N = 10%) filter rule on investments in A, how much would you have at the end of year 5 (ignoring taxes and brokerage)?

b. Rework part a for B and then for C.

c. How would your answers to a and b change if you used a 30 percent filter? a 1 percent filter?

d. Comment upon your analysis.

3. Assuming the price sequence of stock B in 1a above, the sequence of bond prices given below, a linear movement of prices during the years, and a 50–50 constant ratio plan beginning with $100,000 at the end of year one, determine the sequence of transactions and the final value of the portfolio at the end of year five (assume readjustment will not occur until the portfolio reaches 45–55 balance and will only be considered every six months).

Year	Bonds
1	1000
2	800
3	1000
4	1200
5	1000

REFERENCES

Alexander, Sidney S., "Price Movements in Speculative Markets: Trends or Random Walks," *Industrial Management Review,* May 1961, pp. 7–26.

————, "Price Movements in Speculative Markets: Trends or Random Walks, No. 2," in Cootner, *The Random Character of Stock Market Prices.* Cambridge: The MIT Press, 1964, pp. 338–72.

Ball, Ray, and Philip Brown, "An Empirical Evaluation of Accounting Income Numbers," *Journal of Accounting Research,* Autumn 1968, pp. 159–78.

Beaver, William, "The Information Content of Annual Earnings Announcements," *Empirical Research in Accounting: Selected Studies, 1968,* Supplement to Vol. 7 of the *Journal of Accounting Research,* pp. 67–92.

Cootner, Paul, ed., *The Random Character of Stock Market Prices.* Cambridge: The MIT Press, 1964.

Fama, Eugene F., Lawrence Fisher, Michael Jensen, and Richard Roll, "The Adjustment of Stock Prices to New Information," *International Economic Review,* February 1969, pp. 1–21.

————, "Efficient Capital Markets: A Review of Theory and Empirical Work," *Journal of Finance,* May 1970, pp. 383–417.

————, and Marshall Blume, "Filter Rules and Stock Market Trading Profits," *Journal of Business,* Special Supplement, January 1966, pp. 226–41.

————, "Portfolio Analysis in a Stable Paretian Market," *Management Science,* January 1965, pp. 404–19.

Francis, Jack, and Stephen Archer, *Portfolio Analysis,* Chap. 4. Englewood Cliffs, N.J.: Prentice-Hall, Inc., 1971.

Friedman, M., "Factors Affecting the Level of Interest Rates," in *Conference on Savings and Residential Financing.* Chicago: U.S. Savings and Loan League, 1968.

Godfrey, Michael D., C. W. J. Granger, and O. Morgenstern, "The Random Walk Hypothesis of Stock Market Behavior," *Kyklos,* 1964, pp. 1–30.

Graham, B., D. Dodd, and S. Cottle, *Security Analysis,* 4th ed. New York: McGraw-Hill Book Company, 1962.

Hicks, J. R., *Value and Capital,* 2nd ed., London: Oxford University Press, 1946.

King, Benjamin F., "Market and Industry Factors in Stock Price Behavior," *Journal of Business*, Special Supplement, January 1966, pp. 139-90.

Latané, Henry, and Donald Tuttle, *Security Analysis and Portfolio Management*, Chaps. 4, 24, 25. New York: The Ronald Press, 1970.

Mandelbrot, Benoit, "Forecasts of Future Prices, Unbiased Markets and Martingale Models," *Journal of Business*, Special Supplement, January 1966, pp. 242-55.

Niederhoffer, Victor, and M. F. M. Osborne, "Market Making and Reversal on the Stock Exchange," *Journal of the American Statistical Assoc.*, December 1966, pp. 897-916.

Samuelson, Paul A., "Proof That Properly Anticipated Prices Fluctuate Randomly," *Industrial Management Review*, Spring 1965, pp. 41-49.

Seneca, J. J., "Short Interest: Bearish or Bullish," *Journal of Finance*, March 1967, pp. 67-70.

Williams, E. E. and M. C. Findlay, "Expectations, Convergence, and the Efficient Market Hypothesis," *Faculty of Management Working Paper*, McGill University, 1973.

20

Do You Sincerely Want to be Rich?

"Who shall decide when doctors disagree?"

A. Pope

A RAISON D'ÊTRE

The discussion of the previous chapters may well leave the reader under the impression that it is virtually impossible to attain great wealth from investing in the stock market. At best, it may appear that investors should be able to earn no more than average returns. This conclusion is not unwarranted, although the reader should bear in mind that all the evidence is not yet in. Our understanding of investments as an economic phenomenon is still limited, and only recently have scientific tools been employed to analyze the process. Furthermore, the discipline of investment analysis and its underlying theoretical constructs are being reconsidered in the light of an ever-expanding body of literature. The learned opinions of many leading scholars in the area differ widely even after surveying similar documentation. On the one hand, there are those who reject much of the evidence and argue that superior returns are possible for the investor who acquires sufficient expertise. A leading professor goes so far as to argue that it is not even necessary to forecast to achieve above-average returns:

> One can conclude, therefore, that the job of asset management, though interdisciplinary and frustrating, can be performed. It appears that through the use of a judicious combination of expert judgment and objective analysis, one can achieve superior returns consistently, without forecasting, and with small probability of incorrect classification.[1]

At the other end of the spectrum, a professor who is convinced by the efficient market evidence maintains:

> Some investors think that fundamental analysis may hold the key to beating the market, but if stock markets are intrinsic-value, random-walk markets as the evidence reviewed. . .suggests, then most fundamental analysts will not be able to beat the market. Only a very few expert fundamental analysts who discover news will enjoy large profits. It takes, years of hard work to become an expert. It is doubtful, moreover, that any particular person will be able to consistently discover important financial news. Thus, any higher-than-average returns earned by using fundamental analysis were probably preceded by years of training and some losses while learning. Fundamental analysis offers no key to getting something for nothing.[2]

In light of the strong efficient market evidence, two other scholars reflect upon the work required to analyze and select securities and ask:

> Why bother? The answer should be clear. If the investor sees no need to insure that potential risk is balanced by potential return, then perhaps there is no need to bother. But many elements relevant to the behavior of companies, industries and markets can be quantified. Probabilities about the future behavior of those elements can also be quantified. Inputs quantitatively determined by security analysis and quantitatively manipulated by the portfolio manager should lead to an optimum balance between risk and return, and to maximization of long-run portfolio wealth. To us, these means and ends seem the only rational ones worthy of consideration.[3]

Where do Williams and Findlay stand? We feel some obligation to apprise the reader of our views since we have asked him to patiently traverse many pages of somewhat difficult (and perhaps even occasionally tedious) material. Al-

[1] Fred Renwick, *Introduction to Investments and Finance: Theory and Analysis* (New York: The Macmillan Company, 1971), p. 493. Cited by H. A. Latané in his review of Professor Renwick's book, *Journal of Business,* January 1973, p. 115.

[2] Jack Clark Francis, *Investments: Analysis and Management* (New York: McGraw-Hill Book Company, 1972), pp. 588–89.

[3] H. A. Latané and D. L. Tuttle, *Security Analysis and Portfolio Management* (New York: The Ronald Press, 1970), p. 730.

though we have tried to make our work as entertaining as possible, diversion is certainly no justification for spending the money required to buy this book. First, we do believe that security analysis is a necessary task for every investor. There is no other way that one can make determinations of risk and return. Even if it is impossible to gain above-average rewards (a point on which we shall reserve judgment for the time being), forecasts of expected risk-return relationships are required for all but the most simple-minded decision algorithms. Second, we would argue that portfolio analysis is also a required activity if one is to decide in a rational framework which securities should be purchased in order to maximize utility. Although some aspects of portfolio analysis in the current state of the art are rather abstract, we maintain that operational decisions can be made using the tools we have suggested. Utility analysis is an important aspect of portfolio construction. The investor must be able to determine his personal risk preferences in order to make optimal selections. Finally, an understanding of the constructs of capital market theory is essential if one is to grasp clearly the significance of many of the issues that we have raised above. Although capital market theory may not be as yet a completely accurate description of the operations of the capital markets, as markets become more efficient the theory becomes a better depiction of reality.

A Revised Individual CML

Notwithstanding the existing pitfalls of capital market theory, we would argue that it is still possible for the investor to generate an efficiency frontier, drawn with no more than the constrained proportions of securities in which he may legally invest (*EF* in Figure 20-1). Because virtually anyone can buy

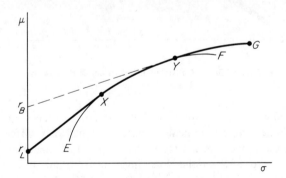

Figure 20-1   Constrained Individual CML

Treasury bills (or, failing that, put money in a savings deposit), the lending line (r_L-*X*) can be determined. To the extent the investor may also borrow, a borrowing line may also be determined (r_B-*Y*-*G*). Borrowing is generally more expensive than lending. Also, costs tend to rise with the amount borrowed, and total borrowing is subject to some limit. Thus, Y-G is a curve, and r_B-Y-G becomes discontinuous at G. The rather cumbersome looking r_L-X-Y-G is the individual's revised CML. Further refinements could be made to illustrate the effects of transactions costs (which, unfortunately, exist in the real world). These costs are small when the portfolio is entirely held in risk-free assets (Treasury bills) but increase as the investor buys risky assets. Commission rates on Treasury bills are low (or nonexistent when purchase is made at original issue), rise for bonds, and reach higher limits for equities. A further revised individual CML is indicated in Figure 20-2. Here, the CML is shown to display bands around the original CML as transactions costs are included. The bands would tend to widen as the investor included more risky assets in his portfolio, would remain constant as the investor held only risky assets but did not borrow (bands between X and Y), and would again widen as the investor levered his portfolio. Within these bands, it would not be profitable for investors to buy and sell securities and thus effect the portfolio revisions required to achieve equilibrium. Hence, transactions costs would tend to make it possible for some investors to gain above-average returns.

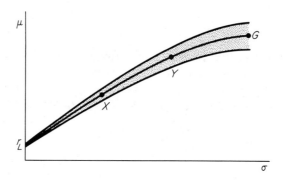

Figure 20-2   Constrained Individual CML (with Transactions Costs)

Other real-world constraints would also prevent markets from clearing and equilibrium from being established. Because individuals pay different tax rates on varying levels of income, investors do not pay the same average tax rate. Thus, after-tax returns from the same investment would differ among individuals, and each would have a slightly different CML. Although it is assumed that a pure rate of interest exists, the rate on Treasury bills varies over time. Hence, even these securities will evidence systematic variability of return.[4] Finally, and most importantly, the assumption of equilibrium requires that

---

[4]See Chapter 7 appendix.

investor expectations be homogeneous and change in unison or that there exists a stable weighted average of opinion. In actuality, information comes to various investors at different times, and expectations may neither be homogeneous nor change in unison (see Chapter 19). Although a stable weighted average of expectations may prevail, this may only make markets behave *as though* they were in static equilibrium. For the social scientist observing markets as a phenomenon, this may be a satisfactory equivalence, but for the investor operating in the microcosm it is not. Professor Sharpe has warned:

> In sum, the economist interested in the behavior of the capital market may prefer the model based on an assumption of complete agreement. The investor hoping to profit from superior predictive ability may reject the model.[5]

Thus, we are left with a Capital Market Line for each individual that reflects: (1) whatever institutional or legal constraints the investor faces; (2) different borrowing and lending rates; (3) the presence of transactions costs; (4) the investor's peculiar tax position; (5) the lack of existence of a pure rate of interest; and (6) the investor's individual expectations. Such a function is shown in Figure 20-3. Notice that the curve no longer emanates from the ordinate (because there is no riskless lending rate). Line segment *WX* would be the new efficiency frontier resulting from assuming that all securities are risky. Segment *XY* would not change. And segment *YG* still reflects the borrowing rate r_B. Curve *WXYG* is the individual's unique CML now ready for the application of indifference curves.

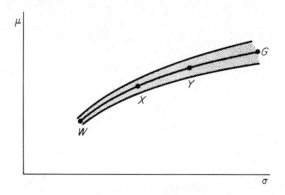

Figure 20-3   A Real-world Individual CML

[5]William F. Sharpe, *Portfolio Theory and Capital Markets* (New York: McGraw-Hill Book Company, 1970), p. 113.

DISEQUILIBRIUM AND THE REAL WORLD

In the previous section, we presented our views on why security analysis and portfolio, utility, and capital market theory must be studied by the investor. We also constructed an individual Capital Market Line that reflects real-world conditions. We have yet to present our conclusions about market efficiency, although the reader may have gotten glimpses of our views as the book developed:

1. We would argue that *"average" returns may in fact be better than average*. To the extent that institutional portfolio constraints cause superfluous diversification and suboptimal investment policies (see Chapter 19), the Capital Market Line may tend to become steeper. Thus, when institutions are confined to purchasing an inordinate amount of low-yield-low-absolute-risk securities, bargains may develop in the range just above the constrained cutoff. (Consider the yield differences on BB versus BBB bonds, for example.[6]) This will make it possible for individuals to get even greater returns at higher levels of risk than they otherwise would be able to obtain. Thus, even though apparent average returns would accrue to investors (differing only according to risk-class preferences), these average returns would tend to be higher than those that would prevail if institutional investors were not constrained. This phenomenon would not be evidenced in the numerous efficient market studies because a constrained equilibrium could still be stable.

[6]In an empirical study of corporate bond returns, Hickman found that lower quality (BB, Ba, and below) bonds yielded substantially more than the "investment grade" issues (BBB, Baa and above) even after default experience. In the twentieth century, the yield pattern has been:

Rating	Realized Yield
AAA	5.1%
AA	5.0
A	5.0
BBB	5.7
BB and below	8.6

See W. B. Hickman, *Corporate Bond Quality and Investor Experience* (Princeton: N.B.E.R., Princeton University Press, 1958). It appears likely that the 290-basis point yield difference between the minimum investment grade issues (BBB) and the speculative bonds is not solely due to the lower risk of the higher-rated bonds. Institutional constraints probably account for much of the spread.

It should be noted, however, that the analysis is very sensitive to the terminal date of the study (Hickman used 1944, when bond prices of all rating classes were quite high). A subsequent study with a later cut-off date found much less spectacular results. See H. Fraine and R. Mills, "Effect of Defaults and Credit Deterioration on Yields of Corporate Bonds," *Journal of Finance,* September 1961, pp. 423–34.

2. It may be observed that some *institutional investors pursue suboptimal investment policies by choice and thus create continuing opportunities for individual investors who do have optimal policies.* Institutions are not motivated by the same goals as the individual entrepreneur seeking his own profit. Hence, the "invisible hand" cannot be counted on to clear the capital markets any more than the goods or factor markets. In order to demonstrate that they are working for their stockholders, mutual fund managers try to maintain fully invested positions. Although short-run bearishness may develop from time to time, long-run periods of being completely liquid (holding only cash or Treasury bills) would invite large-scale share redemption. Because management fees are based on the size of the fund, there is a definite reluctance to follow any consistent strategy that would reduce the volume of the fund's assets (even though long-run performance might be significantly better). Individual investors are not constrained to an effective fully invested position, and it would seem logical that one could outperform most of the funds simply by acting rationally. Thus, if an individual who had superior predictive insight foresaw bearish conditions, he could profit by maintaining a bearish position (being out of the market) until his opinion changed.

3. We would suggest that *the risk-return measures used in most of the efficient market studies (and in capital market theory) are not necessarily the same measures as those used by investors in ex ante decision making.* These measures are essentially *ex post* approximations of what investors may (or may not) have expected. Furthermore, the usual risk-return measures are based on annual holding-period returns and may in fact overstate the true risk borne by the investor's portfolio if his holding period is longer.

4. We have shown (see Chapter 19) that *the efficient market assumption of homogeneous expectations may not hold*; and we have seen that even though a stable weighted average of opinion may still allow capital market theory to be an adequate explanation of a social phenomenon, this does not preclude some investors from having superior predictive abilities. It can even be argued that there are strong reasons for believing that the activities of expert participants tend to perpetuate (or even encourage) disequilibrium in the market. Thus, even the assumption of stable weighted average expectations may be invalid. In this regard, some of the astute observations of John Maynard Keynes are applicable:

> It might have been supposed that competition between expert professionals, possessing judgment and knowledge beyond that of the average private investor, would correct the vagaries of the ignorant individual left to himself. It happens, however, that the energies and skill of the professional investor and speculator are mainly occupied otherwise. For most of these persons are, in fact, largely concerned, not with making superior long-term forecasts of the probable yield of an investment over its whole life, but with foreseeing changes in the conventional basis of

valuation a short time ahead of the general public. They are concerned, not with what an investment is really worth to a man who buys it "for keeps," but with what the market will value it at, under the influence of mass psychology, three months or a year hence. Moreover, this behaviour is not the outcome of a wrongheaded propensity. It is an inevitable result of an investment market organised along the lines described. For it is not sensible to pay 25 for an investment of which you believe the prospective yield to justify a value of 30, if you also believe that the market will value it at 20 three months hence.[7]

The lessons that Keynes drew from his study of security markets do not make pleasant reading for proponents of efficient market hypotheses. Particularly, those who believe that well-informed professional investors make use of all available data to select securities and thereby eliminate the possibility of above-average returns (the strong-test argument) are ill at ease with Keynesian conclusions. And yet, the Cambridge professor's arguments even today are convincing to many.

5. It must follow that *above-average return opportunities can be created if the capital markets are not in equilibrium.* Any of the forces that can prevent equilibrium (legal and institutional constraints, transactions costs, differing expectations, imperfect information, and so on) may make possible above-average returns for some investors.

CONCLUSIONS

We might conclude from the above that it is indeed possible for the investor to obtain better-than-average profits. Although institutional investors may not be able to achieve these results, others can. Of course, we must assume that an individual has sufficient funds for investment to justify the costs (in terms of time and money) of doing adequate research and to obtain adequate diversification. There are many investors who do have the sums required, and those who do not probably should not be investing in the first place. Individuals who have mastered the material in this book should be well prepared to begin the task of obtaining better-than-average profits, although the authors tend to accept part of the conventional wisdom that luck may play an important role. Furthermore, we would emphasize the importance of being willing to take a bearish stand when conditions warrant. There is compelling evidence that many investors are unwilling to get out of the "game" (to borrow a phrase from "Adam Smith"). This undoubtedly accounts for the poor performance of many individuals in the market.

In this book, we have argued that the major goal of investment activity is not to become rich quickly but rather to avoid becoming poor quickly ("hot" issues

---

[7]J. M. Keynes, *The General Theory of Employment, Interest, and Money* (New York: Harcourt, Brace, and World, 1936), pp. 154–55.

that turn cold) or slowly (government bonds). The principles espoused may not cause you to uncover the new Xerox, but we hope that you will at least know an obvious "loser" (we omit examples to avoid lawsuits) when you see one. Principles of economic valuation may on occasion be suspended by an euphoric market, but they are never repealed. The mere avoidance of very bad investments or impropitious market conditions is sufficient for an expectation of above-average returns.

PROBLEM

Go forth and seek thy treasure!

REFERENCES

Fraine, H. and R. Mills, "Effect of Defaults and Credit Deterioration on Yields of Corporate Bonds," *Journal of Finance,* September 1961, pp. 423–34.

Francis, J. C., *Investments: Analysis and Management.* New York: McGraw-Hill Book Company, 1972.

Hickman, W. B., *Corporate Bond Quality and Investor Experience.* Princeton: N.B.E.R., Princeton University Press, 1958.

Keynes, J. M., *The General Theory of Employment, Interest, and Money.* New York: Harcourt, Brace, and World, 1936.

Latané, H., and D. Tuttle, *Security Analysis and Portfolio Management.* New York: The Ronald Press, 1970.

Renwick, F., *Introduction to Investments and Finance: Theory and Analysis.* New York: Macmillan Company, 1971.

Sharpe, W. F., *Portfolio Theory and Capital Markets.* New York: McGraw-Hill Book Company, 1970.

A

Financial Mathematics: Compound Interest, Present Values and Yields

A.1 SIMPLE AND COMPOUND INTEREST

A good part of financial analysis depends upon calculations of compound interest. This is because the time horizon in finance is usually long, and some method must be obtained to compare financial flows over time. Because financial flows may be "invested" at some positive rate of interest, a flow received today is worth more than an equal flow received in the future. This idea may be expressed as a very simple equation:

$$D_n = D_0 (1 + i)^n \qquad (A.1)$$

Where:

D_0 is a financial flow (number of dollars) invested today

D_n is the value n periods from now of the invested flow D_0

i is the rate of interest by which D_0 will grow for n periods.

Thus, if $1,000 is put into a savings account today and is left there for one year at a rate of interest of 5 percent compounded and paid annually, that sum will be worth $1,050 after one year. If the $1,000 is left on deposit for two years, at the end of the second year it would be worth:

$$D_n = \$1,000 \, (1.05)^2$$
$$D_n = \$1,102.50$$

The factor $(1 + i)^n$ may be obtained immediately from compound interest tables such as those that appear in Appendix C.1. Thus, if $1,000 is left on deposit for twenty years (assuming annual compounding), at the end of that period it would be worth:

$$\$1,000 \, (2.653) = \$2,653.00$$

The factor was obtained by looking in the row for year 20 under the column for 5 percent.

For rates of interest that are not covered by the tables, interpolation may be necessary. If the rate of interest one wished to compound by were 4.5 percent, and one had tabular values for 4 and 5 percent only, the following computation could be made:

Factor 4.0 percent @ 20 years = 2.191

Factor 5.0 percent @ 20 years = 2.653

Factor 4.5 percent @ 20 years = 2.422

Thus, $1,000 invested at 4.5 percent compounded annually for 20 years would be worth $2,422.00 at the end of that period. The factor 2.422 is only an approximation, however, because compound interest functions are not linear.

Readers who wish to be precise about calculations may employ a table of common logarithms to solve for values not given in compound interest tables. In fact, the tables themselves are constructed in this manner. In our example above, where $D_0 = \$1,000$; $i = 5$ percent; and $n = 20$, we would find:

$$\log D_n = \log D_0 + n \log (1 + i)$$
$$= 3 + 20 \, (.0212)$$
$$= 3.4240$$

The antilog of 3.4240 is 2,653.00 or $2,653.00. In the case of $i = 4.5$ percent, we find:

$$\log D_n = \log D_0 + n \log (1 + i)$$
$$= 3 + 20 \, (.0191)$$
$$= 3.3820$$

The antilog of 3.3820 is 2,410.00 or $2,410.00. Tables of common logarithms are found in Appendix C.6.

PROBLEMS

1. How much will $5,000 be worth in ten years if the rate of interest is 10 percent under conditions of annual compounding?

2. Let $250 be placed in a savings account that pays interest of 1 percent per quarter compounded quarterly. How much will it be worth after one year (four compounding periods)?

3. A savings account in Mexico pays interest of 12.5 percent compounded annually. If $100,000 is put into this account today, how much will be on deposit twenty years from now? (Solve through interpolation and the use of common logarithms. Account for the rather large difference in your results.)

A.2 CONTINUOUS COMPOUNDING

Interest may be compounded more often than once per year. When interest is compounded several times during the year, equation A.1 may be substituted by:

$$D_n = D_0 (1 + \frac{i}{c})^{nc} \qquad (A.2)$$

This equation simply adjusts the annual percentage rate by the number of compounding periods per year (c), and multiplies the number of years of compounding by the number of compounding periods. In equation A.2 i is assumed to be an annual rate and n the number of years of compounding. In equation A.1, i was simply an interest rate *per period* and n was the number of compounding periods. Thus, using equation A.1, if $100 were placed in a bank account that paid interest of 1 percent per quarter, we would find that after one year our balance would be: $100 (1.041) = $104.10. We can get the same result from equation A.2:

$$D_n = \$100 (1 + \frac{.04}{4})^4$$

$$D_n = \$100 (1.01)^4$$

$$D_n = \$104.10$$

In this instance, the annual percentage rate is assumed to be 4 percent.

If c becomes very large, we say that compounding takes place continuously. A convenient compounding equation may be devised for this case. Let $x = c/i$. Then we may rewrite equation A.2 as:

$$D_n = D_0 \left(1 + \frac{1}{x}\right)^{xni}$$

Now, if we let $c \to \infty$, we know that $x \to \infty$. Recalling that $e = \operatorname*{Lim}_{x \to \infty} (1 + 1/x)^x$, we find that as $c \to \infty$,

$$D_n = D_0 e^{ni} \tag{A.3}$$

This equation allows us to compute immediately sums that are compounded many times during the year (savings accounts that are compounded daily, for example, may be approximated by this equation).

EXAMPLES

1. The sum of $1,000 is placed in a savings account that pays 5 percent annual interest compounded quarterly. If the funds are left on deposit, how much will be in the account after five years?

$$D_n = \$1,000 \, (1.0125)^{20}$$
$$D_n = \$1,000 \, (1.286)$$
$$D_n = \$1,286.00$$

The factor 1.286 was taken by interpolation between the factor for 1 percent for twenty periods and 2 percent for twenty periods.

2. How much will $1,000 be worth after twenty years if the rate of interest is 5 percent compounded continuously?

$$D_n = \$1,000 \, e^{ni}$$
$$= \$1,000 \, (2.71828)^{20 \times .05}$$
$$= \$2,718.28$$

Compare this with the value of $2,653.00 when compounding was done annually.

PROBLEMS

1. The sum of $5,000 is placed in a savings account that pays interest of 4 percent compounded annually. How much will be in the account after twenty-five years?

2. What would your result be in the problem above if interest were compounded quarterly (at the same 4 percent annual rate)?

3. Suppose the savings account mentioned above paid interest of 4 percent (annually) compounded daily. What would be the approximate amount in the account after twenty-five years?

A.3 ANNUITY VALUES

When funds are deposited periodically to an account, the terminal or annuity value of the payments is given by a series of the following type:

$$V_n = D_0 (1 + i)^n +$$
$$D_1 (1 + i)^{n-1} +$$
$$D_2 (1 + i)^{n-2} +$$
$$\ldots\ldots +$$
$$D_n (1 + i)^{n-n}$$

This series may be rewritten as:

$$V_n = \sum_{t=0}^{n} D_t (1 + i)^{n-t} \qquad\qquad (A.4)$$

V_n is the annuity value of funds put on deposit over n periods. Thus, if D_0 is put on deposit today, it will be worth $D_0(1 + i)^n$ after n periods. If D_1 is added one period from now, it will be worth $D_1(1 + i)^{n-1}$ at the end of the nth period, and so on. The total terminal value of all deposits made over the n periods is the sum V_n.

In equation A.4, it should be noted that a final payment is made at period $t = n$. Because that payment has no chance to earn interest, its value at the terminal date is simply $D_n(1 + i)^0 = D_n$. It is unlikely that a deposit would be made to an account just before the withdrawal date, and we may wish to eliminate this final payment from the annuity value. In this case, equation A.4 becomes:

$$V_n = \sum_{t=0}^{n} D_t(1 + i)^{n-t} - D_n$$

$$V_n = \sum_{t=0}^{n-1} D_t(1 + i)^{n-t}$$

If it is further assumed that all deposits are equal (that is, $D_0 = D_1 = \ldots D_{n-1} = D$), then we obtain:

$$V_n = D \sum_{t=0}^{n-1} (1 + i)^{n-t} \tag{A.5}$$

$$\frac{V_n}{D} = \sum_{t=0}^{n-1} (1 + i)^{n-t} \tag{A.5 alt.}$$

Appendix C.2 provides the factors for the right-hand side of equation A.5 alt.

In the case of continuous compounding, equation A.4 becomes:

$$V_n = \int_{0}^{n} D(t) (1 + \frac{i}{c})^{(n-t)c} dt$$

Letting c become very large, we find:

$$V_n = \int_{0}^{n} D(t) e^{i(n-t)} dt$$

If we assume $D(t)$ and i are constants, we may integrate to produce:

$$V_n = \frac{D}{i}(e^{in} - 1) \tag{A.6}$$

EXAMPLE

Schmidt places $50 in the bank each quarter. His bank pays interest quarterly at an annual rate of 4 percent. How much will Schmidt have on deposit after three years? The quarterly interest payment is i/c or $4/4 = 1$ percent. The number of compounding periods is $n \cdot c$ or $3 \cdot 4 = 12$. Thus, the factor is the same as 1 percent compounded for twelve years. Hence,

$$(\$50)(12.809) = \$640.45$$

PROBLEMS

1. What is the annuity value of twenty-five payments of $100 at a rate of 10 percent per period?

2. Gormann puts $600 in a savings account each year. He is paid interest of 6 percent per annum compounded annually. How much will he have after five years?

3. A special depository account requires annual payments of $1,000. After eight years, the account matures and pays to the holder $10,000. At what annual rate of interest do funds grow in this account?

A.4 PRESENT VALUES

A *present value* is the value today of funds received in the future. It is, in effect, the reverse operation of a compounded sum. Thus, if we know D_n dollars will be received n periods from now, and if we know the rate of interest, we can determine the present value, D_o, of that future sum. This process is described simply by rewriting equation A.1 in the following form:

$$D_0 = D_n (1 + i)^{-n} \qquad (A.7)$$

Because $(1 + i)^{-n}$ is merely the reciprocal of $(1 + i)^n$, the first section of Appendix C could be used to determine present values by dividing each factor into one. This process is done for the reader in the third section of Appendix C, which indicates the present value of $1.00 received n years in the future.

In the case of continuous compounding, equation A.3 may be rewritten as:

$$D_0 = D_n e^{-ni} \qquad (A.8)$$

This equation indicates the present value of funds received n years from now when it is assumed that interest is compounded continuously.

EXAMPLES

1. If interest is compounded annually at a rate of 3 percent, the present value of $1,000 received twenty years from now would be:

$$(\$1,000)(.554) = \$554.00$$

2. If interest is compounded continuously at a rate of 6 percent, the present value of $1,000 received ten years from now could be computed with the use of logarithms:

$$\log D_0 = \log D_n - ni \log e$$

Hence,

$$\log D_0 = 3 - (10)(.06)(.4343)$$

$$\log D_0 = 2.74$$

The antilog of 2.74 is 549.50. Thus, the present value is $549.50.

PROBLEMS

1. What is the present value of $1,000 received ten years from now if interest is compounded annually at a rate of 6 percent? Compare your result with that obtained in the example above.

2. What is the present value of $250 received in nine years if interest is compounded annually at a rate of 8.5 percent?

3. Determine the present value of $10,000 received in twenty years when interest is compounded continuously at 5 percent. (Hint: $1/e \cong .368$)

A.5 PRESENT VALUE OF ANNUITIES

The present value of a series of payments received over n periods is the summation of the separate present values of each payment. Expressed in equation form, the present value (PV) of a stream of payments is:

$$PV = D_0 (1 + i)^{-0} + D_1 (1 + i)^{-1} + D_2 (1 + i)^{-2} + \ldots + D_n (1 + i)^{-n}$$

or more simply,

$$PV = \sum_{t=0}^{n} D_t (1 + i)^{-t} \tag{A.9}$$

When the payments D_t vary from year to year, the present value may be determined by adding the appropriate products obtained by multiplying the factors in the third section of Appendix C times their respective D_t's. If the payments are constant over time, however, equation A.9 may be simplified to:

$$PV = D \sum_{t=0}^{n} (1 + i)^{-t} \qquad (A.10)$$

Furthermore, if it assumed that the first payment is received one year from now, then the equation becomes:

$$PV = D \sum_{t=1}^{n} (1 + i)^{-t} \qquad (A.11)$$

The factors in the fourth part of Appendix C are based on this equation.

EXAMPLES

1. Mrs. Robinson bought a bond that will mature in two years. She expects payments of $50 interest in one year plus $1,050 in interest and principal in two years. If she wishes to earn 10 percent on her investment, how much would she pay for the bond? The answer may be computed immediately with the use of Appendix C, section three. The present value of $50 received one year hence at 10 percent is (.909)($50.00) = $45.45. The present value of $1,050 received two years hence at 10 percent is (.826)($1,050.00) = $867.30. Thus, the present value of the bond is $45.45 + $867.30 = $912.75. If Mrs. Robinson wished to earn 10 percent on her bond, she would pay approximately 91¼ (that is, $912.50) for it. (Note: bond prices are quoted in percentages of par. Thus, a $1,000 bond is selling at 100 when it is at par.)

2. A bond is expected to pay interest of $40 for ten years. At the end of ten years, it will return $1,000 in principal. If an investor wishes to earn 8 percent on his bond, how much would he pay for it? The solution is most easily obtained by using both sections three and four of Appendix C. From the fourth section, we find the present value of a stream of $40 for ten years at 8 percent: (6.710)($40.00) = $268.40. From the third section, we find the present value of a payment of $1,000 received in ten years: (.386)($1,000.00) = $386.00. Thus, the present value of the bond is $654.40. The investor would pay about 65½ for the bond if he desired a return of 8 percent.

PROBLEMS

1. The Atlantic Share Corp. has purchased stock in the Lambert Co. It is expected that Lambert shares will be selling for about $100 in ten years and that Lambert will pay a dividend of about two dollars per share over the next ten years. If Atlantic wished to earn 20 percent on its investment, how much should it have paid for the Lambert shares?

2. The Ludmilla Corp. pays a dividend of one dollar per share and expects to increase the dividend by ten cents per year for the next five years. Ludmilla now sells for $20 per share. If an investor wished to earn 10 percent on Ludmilla shares, at what price would the stock have to sell in five years?

A.6 CAPITALIZATION OF AN INCOME STREAM

Under continuous compounding assumptions, the basic present value equation A.9 becomes:

$$PV = \int_0^n D(t) \, e^{-it} \, dt \qquad\qquad \text{(A.12)}$$

If $D(t)$ and i are constant, equation A.12 can be integrated to produce:

$$PV = \frac{D}{i} (1 - e^{-in}) \qquad\qquad \text{(A.13)}$$

In the case when n becomes very large (that is, payments are received forever), $n \to \infty$, and the equation reduces to:

$$PV = \frac{D}{i} \qquad\qquad \text{(A.14)}$$

This last equation is a very important one, and the process underlying the equation is frequently referred to as *capitalization*. A number of financial instruments have very long (or infinite) lives. A perpetual bond, for example, promises to pay a coupon of a constant amount forever. Such an instrument may be evaluated very quickly with equation A.14. Common stocks may also be valued with this equation, but one must be careful about growth assumptions in this case. For a firm that pays a reasonably constant dividend, the equation is adequate. For a growth stock where D is increased over time, the assumption of a constant $D(t)$ is violated, and the equation is inappropriate.

EXAMPLES

1. A mortgage pays the mortgagee a sum of $500 annually for twenty years. If it is assumed that interest is compounded continuously on the mortgage at 5 percent, the value of the mortgage would be:

$$PV = \frac{D}{i}(1-e^{-in})$$

$$= \frac{\$500}{.05}(1-e^{-1})$$

$$= \$10,000 \ (1-.368)$$

$$= \$6,320.00$$

2. The Canadian Perpetual 3 percent bond pays interest of $30 annually. If the market rate of interest for bonds in this risk class is 6 percent, the Canadian Perpetual will sell for:

$$PV = \frac{D}{i}$$

$$= \frac{\$30}{.06}$$

$$= \$500.00$$

PROBLEMS

1. The Daland Shipping Corp. has paid a dividend of three dollars per share to its common stockholders for the past twenty years and plans to continue doing so in the future. Prospects for growth in the firm are negligible because the firm merely reinvests annual depreciation flows and does not retain earnings or seek external financing. If investors believe Daland should yield 6 percent, determine the market price of the shares.

2. A mortgage has a term of twenty-five years. The face value of the mortgage is $30,000, and it has a yield to maturity of 4 percent. Assuming continuous compounding, what annual payment should be made on the mortgage?

B

Financial Statistics: Probability, Variance, and Correlation Analysis

B.1 PROBABILITY DISTRIBUTIONS

A variable that eludes predictability but that has a specific range or set of possible values and a definite probability associated with each value is called a *random variable*. In finance, one makes use of random variables frequently because many of the values determined are based on future events. These are rarely known with certainty, but with effort it is usually possible to attach probabilities to each possible outcome of a given future event. The assignment of probabilities is generally a subjective matter, although the use of statistical methods may reduce the uncertainty associated with obtaining relative likelihoods.

An exhaustive set of probabilities attaching to all possible outcomes of a given future event is called a *probability distribution*. Suppose x_i is the ith outcome of event X; then $p(x_i)$ is the probability that X will take on the value x_i. The probability distribution for event X is given by $p(x)$. For example, let event X be the price of a stock in ten years. If we can make educated guesses about the range of prices at which the stock may sell and the relative likelihood for each price, this range and the attaching probabilities constitute a probability distribution.

One may generate several important statistics from a probability distribution. Perhaps the most important is the mean or *expected value,* which is defined as:

$$E(X) = \sum_i x_i p(X_i) \tag{B.1}$$

For an exhaustive distribution (where all possible values are specified), $\sum_i p(x_i) = I$.

The expected value is a measure of *central tendency* and is frequently the best value to assume for X for decision-making purposes. There are other measures of central tendency, however, that may be useful for specific types of decisions. The *mode* of a distribution is that value of X with the largest $p(x_i)$. The *median* is the value that is the midpoint in the distribution; that is, it is the value that divides the distribution in half.

A second important statistic that may be generated from a probability distribution is the *variance.* The variance is defined as:

$$V(X) = \sum_i [x_i - E(X)]^2 p(x_i) \tag{B.2}$$

The variance is a least-squares measure of the degree of deviation about the mean. Hence, it is often used as an indicator of the "riskiness" of a distribution. The square root of the variance, the *standard deviation,* is sometimes used in place of the variance as a measure of deviation.[1]

Dispersion and risk are frequently used interchangeably in finance. More concretely, however, three states of future events should be delineated. In the first state, that of *certainty,* we know which value X will take. In this instance, $[x_i - E(X)] = 0$, because $x_i = E(X)$. When $[x_i - E(X)] = 0$, $V(X)$ also equals zero. This is the best of all possible worlds, but it rarely prevails in the real world. The second state is that of *uncertainty.* This state exists when $\sum p(x_i) < 1$ or when probabilities cannot be assigned to given values. When $\sum p(x_i) < 1$, all possible outcomes are not known; the distribution is not exhaustive; and $V(X)$ is undefined. This is an intolerable state that must be altered if decisions are to be made. The final state, *risk,* obtains when $p(x_i) \neq 1$, but $\sum p(x_i) = 1$. In this case, we do not know which value X will take on, but we can specify probabilities that $(X = x_i)$, and all possible outcomes are known (the distribution is exhaustive). Under conditions of risk, it is clear that the greater $V(X)$ becomes, the poorer estimate of the ultimate outcome will be $E(X)$, or any x_i. Therefore, the greater the dispersion of the distribution, the riskier the distribution becomes.

The variance and standard deviation are absolute measures of dispersion. As such, they do not always provide a basis for good comparisons. For example,

---

[1]The symbols μ and σ are used to indicate mean and standard deviation in many finance texts, although for samples the symbols $\bar{x}$ and s are more appropriate.

suppose two stocks had expected prices of $10 and $100 respectively and standard deviations of $1 and $5. If we examined only the standard deviation, the second stock might appear riskier than the first. On the other hand, the expected value of the second is much greater than that of the first. The relative dispersion, hence, is actually larger for the first stock. A good measure of relative dispersion is the *coefficient of variation,* which is given by:

$$CV(X) = \frac{\sqrt{V(X)}}{E(X)}$$

(B.3)

or σ/μ in terms of other frequently employed symbols. When we compute the coefficient of variation, we find that for the first stock $\sigma/\mu = 1/10$; whereas for the second, $\sigma/\mu = 5/100$. Using this relative measure of dispersion, the first stock is clearly the riskier.

Another type of relative measure of dispersion is the *semivariance.* This statistic indicates only the variability in the negative direction and places the following constraint on equation B.2:

$$[x_i - E(X)] < 0$$

(B.4)

As a measure of risk, the semivariance has the advantage of not penalizing values that are better than expected.

The variance is known technically as the second moment about the mean. There are higher-degree moments that may also be significant in financial analysis. Associated with the third moment is the notion of *skewness.* Skewness is a measure of the *symmetry* of a distribution about its mean. A distribution that is not skewed is said to be symmetrical. A distribution with a long left tail is said to be negatively skewed. One with a long right tail is said to be positively skewed (see Figure B-1). A measure of skewness is provided by computing the third moment about the mean and dividing it by the cube of the standard deviation:

$$SK = \frac{\sum_i [x_i - E(X)]^3 \, p(x_i)}{(\sqrt{V(X)})^3}$$

(B.5)

In general, positive values for SK are preferred to negative ones.[2]

A final statistic that may be important is associated with the fourth moment about the mean. *Kurtosis* measures the peakedness of a distribution. A

[2]Specifically, positive skewness has been shown to be a necessary but not sufficient condition for preference, *ceteris paribus,* for all families of utility functions that meet the requirements for third-degree stochastic dominance (defined in Chapter 18). See G. A. Whitmore, "Some Theoretical Results about Skewness Preference," McGill University Working Paper, Montreal, 1973.

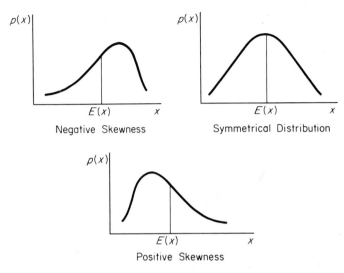

Figure B-1   Skewness Illustration

normal, bell-shaped distribution is said to be *mesokurtic.* One that is flatter than the bell-shaped curve is said to be *platykurtic,* and one that is steeper is said to be *leptokurtic* (see Figure B-2). A common measure of kurtosis is computed by

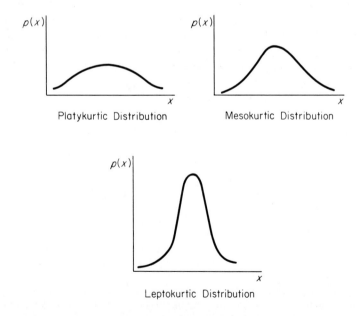

Figure B-2   Kurtosis Illustration

dividing the fourth power of the standard deviation (square of the variance) into the fourth moment about the mean:

$$KU = \frac{\sum_i [x_i - E(X)]^4\, p(x_i)}{[V(X)]^2}$$

(B.6)

Larger values for KU indicate a more peaked distribution. KU for a mesokurtic distribution is +3. Lower values indicate a platykurtic distribution, and higher ones suggest a leptokurtic distribution. There seems to be no general agreement on the relative desirability of the degree of kurtosis.

EXAMPLES

An analyst is attempting to forecast the earnings per share of Dynamo Quebec Power Ltd. for next year. He believes that four values are possible and that the relative likelihood of each is described as follows:

$$x_1 = \$2.50 \quad p(x) = .3$$
$$x_2 = \$2.00 \quad p(x) = .4$$
$$x_3 = \$1.70 \quad p(x) = .2$$
$$x_4 = \$1.10 \quad p(x) = .1$$

1. What is the expected value of earnings for next year?

$$(\$2.50) \times (.3) = \$0.75$$
$$(\$2.00) \times (.4) = \$0.80$$
$$(\$1.70) \times (.2) = \$0.34$$
$$(\$1.10) \times (.1) = \underline{\$0.11}$$
$$E(X) = \$2.00$$

2. What are the mode and median values of the distribution? The mode is the most likely value. At $x_i = \$2.00$, $p(x_i)$ is greatest. The median divides the distribution in half. This occurs at $x_i = \$2.00$.
3. What is the standard deviation of the distribution?

$2.50 - $2.00 = $0.50; ($0.50)^2 = ($0.250) \times (.3) = $0.075

$2.00 - $2.00 = $0.00; ($0.00)^2 = ($0.000) \times (.4) = $0.000

$1.70 - $2.00 = -0.30; (-0.30)^2 = ($0.090) \times (.2) = $0.018

$1.10 - $2.00 = -0.90; (-0.90)^2 = ($0.810) \times (.1) = \underline{$0.081}

$$V(X) = $0.174$$

$$\sigma = \sqrt{$0.174} = $0.42$$

4. What is the coefficient of variation of Dynamo Quebec earnings?

$$CV(X) = \frac{$.42}{$2.00} = .21$$

5. What is the semivariance of earnings?

$$x_i - E(X) < 0$$

$$$0.018 + $0.081 = $0.099$$

6. Determine the symmetry of the distribution.

$$($0.50)^3 = ($0.125) \times (.3) = $0.0375$$
$$(\quad 0)^3 = (\quad 0) \times (.4) = \quad 0$$
$$(-0.30)^3 = (-0.027) \times (.2) = -0.0054$$
$$(-0.90)^3 = (-0.729) \times (.1) = \underline{-0.0729}$$

$$$-0.0408$$

$$SK = \frac{-0.0408}{0.0730} = -.56$$

The distribution is negatively skewed.

7. Compute the kurtosis of the distribution.

$$($0.50)^4 = ($0.0625) \times (.3) = $0.01875$$
$$(\quad 0)^4 = (\quad 0) \times (.4) = \quad 0$$
$$(-.30)^4 = ($0.0081) \times (.2) = $0.00162$$
$$(-.90)^4 = ($0.6561) \times (.1) = \underline{$0.06561}$$

$$$0.08598$$

$$KU = \frac{0.08598}{0.03066} = 2.80$$

The distribution is slightly platykurtic.

PROBLEMS

An analyst is attempting to predict the price of a bond next year. The bond currently sells at 90, has six years to maturity, and has a 6 percent coupon. The analyst has obtained predictions from the economics department of his firm about the prime rate of interest for next year. They feel the chances are about .5 that the prime rate will be 6 percent, about .3 that it will be 5 percent, and about .2 that it will be 4 percent. The analyst believes that the bond he is analyzing should yield about 200 basis points (a basis point equals .01 percent) more than the prime rate.

    1. Formulate a probability distribution for the price of the bond next year. (Use the short-cut yield formula given in Chapter 3 and compute the price to the nearest dollar.)

    2. Determine the expected value of the price.

    3. Compute the mode and median prices.

    4. What is the standard deviation of the distribution? The coefficient of variation?

    5. Determine the semivariance of the distribution. Comment on the efficacy of this statistic as a measure of risk in this instance.

    6. Describe the symmetry and kurtosis of the distribution.

B.2 THE NORMAL DISTRIBUTION

A very important distribution for decision-making purposes is the *normal* distribution. This distribution has the characteristics of being perfectly symmetrical and mesokurtic. The mean, median, and mode for this distribution are identical, because it is not skewed. Probability calculations involving the normal distribution are easily made with tables such as the one provided in the fifth section of Appendix C.

    One convenient feature of the normal distribution is that about 68 percent of the distribution lies within one standard deviation of the mean. Within two standard deviations is about 96 percent of the distribution, and all but a fraction of 1 percent of the distribution lies within three standard deviations of the mean (see Figure B-3).

EXAMPLES

    1. It is believed that interest rates on high-grade utility bonds are normally distributed. It is felt that the mean value for the first quarter of next year will be 8 percent with a standard deviation of 1 percent. What is

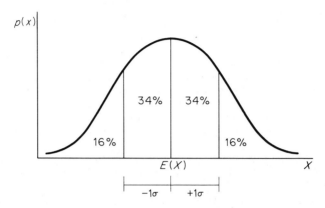

Figure B-3   The Normal Distribution

the probability that the rate on these bonds will be no lower than 7 percent?

$$P(x_i \geqslant .07) = .84$$

This may be taken directly from Appendix C, fifth section. The value 7 percent is exactly one standard deviation from the mean. Hence, values less than 7 percent will occur with a probability of about .16, and values 7 percent or greater will occur with a probability of $1.00 - .16 = .84$.

    2. The short-run price (over the next month) of a stock is assumed to be normally distributed with a mean of $20 and a standard deviation of $3. The current price of the stock is $15. What is the probability that the purchase of the stock will result in a loss by next month?

$$P(x_i < 15) = \text{about } .05$$

$15 is $1.67\,\sigma$ from the mean. Values below $15 will occur with a probability of .0475.

PROBLEMS

    1. The dividend payment for next year of the Elsa Savings and Loan Association is expected to be one dollar per share with a standard deviation of ten cents. What is the probability that the dividend will be greater than one dollar? What is the probability that no dividend will be paid? What is the minimum dividend that one might reasonably expect? Assume that dividend payments by Elsa are normally distributed.

    2. Jones bought a call on one hundred shares of Ionocon Corp. this week. His call entitles him to buy the shares at a price of $10 per share for the next six

months. The shares are now $10.50 per share, and Jones' call cost him a total of $150. He believes the price of Ionocon shares for the near future is normally distributed with a mean of $15 and a standard deviation of $5. What is the probability that Jones will lose money?

B.3 REGRESSION AND CORRELATION ANALYSIS

The relationship between two or more random variables may be described through the use of a technique called *regression* analysis. When only two variables are involved, the analysis is referred to as *simple* regression. When more than two variables are involved, the term *multiple* regression is applied. In order to determine the closeness of the relationship between variables, one variable must be selected as the *dependent* variable. This choice is important and will depend on the nature of the variables. The other variables are said to be *independent.* With the establishment of the dependent and independent variables, a least-squares trend line may be computed. This line may take the form of a linear equation, if it is believed that the relationship between the variables is linear, or it may take the form of a non-linear equation.

Suppose we wish to establish the relationship between two variables, Y and X. Suppose further that we believe X to be the independent variable and Y to be the dependent one. We may establish a general equation of the form $Y = f(X)$. Now, let us try to decide what form the equation should take. One method of doing this would be to prepare a simple *scatter diagram* plotting pairs of points representing Y and X values (see Figure B-4). In the case of our general equation above, we shall assume that the relationship appears to be more or less linear. Thus, we shall be fitting a linear least-squares trend line when we *regress* Y against X.

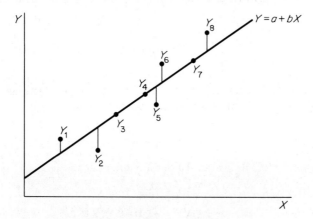

Figure B-4   A Least-squares Trend Line

The properties of the least-squares trend line may be described by two equations:

$$\Sigma\,(Y-Y_c) = 0 \tag{B.7}$$

$$\Sigma\,(Y-Y_c)^2 = \text{minimum} \tag{B.8}$$

where:

Y are original observations

Y_c are trend-line computed values

Equation B.7 assures that the positive and negative deviations of observed values Y from trend values Y_c exactly balance out. Equation B.8 guarantees a "best fit" in that the sum of the squares of the deviations about this line is smaller than for any other line. It should be noted that the properties of the least-squares trend line are the same as those of the arithmetic average (mean) for a probability distribution.

The equation for a straight line (linear relationship) is of the form $Y = a + bX$. Hence, we need to find values for a and b that will satisfy the properties detailed in equations B.7 and B.8. This may be done by solving two additional equations called *normal* equations. The first normal equation is obtained by multiplying the general equation through by the coefficient of the first constant and summing (note that the coefficient of a is one):

$$Y = a + bX$$

$$\Sigma Y = \Sigma a + \Sigma bX$$

Because a is a constant, $\Sigma\,a = na$. Also, because b is a constant, $\Sigma\,bX = b\Sigma X$. Thus,

$$\Sigma Y = na + b\Sigma X \tag{B.9}$$

The second normal equation may be found by multiplying the general equation through by the coefficient of the second constant and summing:

$$Y = a + bX$$

$$XY = aX + bX^2$$

$$\Sigma XY = \Sigma aX + \Sigma bX^2$$

$$\Sigma XY = a\Sigma X + b\Sigma X^2 \tag{B.10}$$

Suppose the Alberich Mining Corp. wished to regress its sales activity and the net income it earns. Data for the past five years are given below:

Year	Sales (millions)	Net Income (millions)
1968	10	0
1969	12	1
1970	13	2
1971	11	3
1972	14	4

A least-square regression equation for Alberich could be determined by using the normal equations:

$$Y = f(X), \text{ where } Y \text{ is net income and } X \text{ is sales.}$$

$$\Sigma Y = 10$$

$$\Sigma X = 60$$

$$\Sigma XY = 127$$

$$\Sigma X^2 = 730$$

$$\Sigma Y = na + b\Sigma X$$

$$10 = 5a + 60b$$

$$\Sigma XY = a\Sigma X + b\Sigma X^2$$

$$127 = 60a + 730b$$

Solving simultaneously, we find:

$$127 = 60a + 730b$$
$$\underline{120 = 60a + 720b}$$
$$7 = 10b \qquad\qquad b = .7$$
$$10 = 5a + 60(.7) \qquad\qquad a = -6.4$$

Thus, the least-squares regression equation is:

$$Y_c = -6.4 + .7X$$

The computation of least-squares trend lines may be done more efficiently than through the use of equations B.9 and B.10. The intercept a may be computed by:

$$a = \frac{\Sigma Y - b\Sigma X}{n} \tag{B.11}$$

and the slope b by:

$$b = \frac{(\Sigma XY) - (\Sigma X \Sigma Y)/n}{\Sigma X^2 - (\Sigma X)^2/n} \tag{B.12}$$

The solution to the problem posed above would be (solving for b first because it is required to compute a):

$$b = \frac{[127] - [(60)(10)]/5}{(730) - (60)^2/5} = .7$$

$$a = \frac{10 - (.7)(60)}{5} = -6.4$$

The simplest method of computing least-squares equations is by use of the computer. Programs exist that can handle large amounts of correlated data. Computations involving more than twenty or so inputs become onerous when calculations are made manually, and few analysts rely on calculators any longer to fit least-squares trend lines. Computers can also perform the more complicated computations associated with multiple regression analysis and nonlinear least-squares equations. Because few analysts use hand methods anymore, the calculations presented above should serve as an explication of the mathematical process underlying regression and correlation analysis rather than as a tool to provide solutions.

Once the least-squares trend line is established, the analyst may wish to know just how good the fit is between the variables. Thus, a measure of the closeness of the relationship between the variables must be sought. The first step in this process requires the determination of the *standard error of the estimate,* which is a measure of the deviation of actual values around the estimated trend line. The standard error of the estimate is given by the following equation:

$$s_{y \cdot x} = \sqrt{\frac{\Sigma (Y - Y_c)^2}{n}} \tag{B.13}$$

If $s_{y \cdot x} = 0$, we know that all actual values lie on the trend line, and there is a clear linear relationship between Y and X. On the other hand, if there were no linear relationship between the variables, the standard error of the estimate would equal the standard deviation of the dependent variable, or $s_{y \cdot x} = s_y$.

Determination of the standard error of the estimate allows us to compute an index of the closeness of the relationship between the variables. This index, called the *coefficient of correlation,* is given by:

$$r_{y \cdot x} = \sqrt{1 - \frac{s^2_{y.x}}{s_y{}^2}} \qquad \text{(B.14)}$$

The square of the coefficient of correlation, r^2, is called the *coefficient of determination.* Values for r^2 may be between 0 and 1. If two variables are perfectly correlated, $s^2_{y \cdot x} = 0$. Hence, $r^2 = 1 - \frac{0}{s_y{}^2} = 1$. If two variables are completely uncorrelated, $s^2_{y \cdot x} = s_y{}^2$. In this case, $r^2 = 1 - \frac{s^2_{y \cdot x}}{s_y{}^2} = 0$. Thus, when two variables are highly correlated, r^2 will be a large decimal. When they are poorly correlated, r^2 will be a small decimal.

The equation for multiple regression is one of the form:

$$Y = a \pm bX_1 \pm cX_2 \pm dX_3 \qquad \text{(B.15)}$$

In this instance, several independent variables are correlated with the dependent variable, and a general measure of the closeness of the relationship between the dependent variable and the joint simultaneous configuration of the independent variables is required. This measure, designated the *coefficient of multiple determination,* or R^2, is complicated to compute by hand. Although a number of basic statistics books present short-cut equations for the calculation, the statistic is always provided by computer programs that compute multiple-regression equations. Because the analyst will rarely perform these calculations, we shall omit a detailed listing of the equations required to determine R^2.

Coefficients of partial determination measure the relationship between the dependent variable and any one of the independent variables, while the other independent variables are *held constant.* These coefficients are distinct from the separate coefficients of determination of each independent variable with the dependent variable. An interpretation of a coefficient of partial determination may be made by considering an example multiple-regression equation with partial coefficients given under the independent variables:

$$Y = a + bX_1 + cX_2 + dX_3 \qquad \text{(B.16)}$$

$$(.82) \quad (.91) \quad (.41)$$

$$R^2 = .86$$

In this example, 82 percent of the variation in Y that is not associated with X_2 or X_3 is incrementally associated with X_1.

There are several problems that develop in interpreting regression results. High R^2 values may occur when n is very small simply because too few inputs are included to demonstrate variability. Also, it should be remembered that R^2 measures covariation, *not* causality. If green lights are highly associated with moving automobiles, this does not mean that green lights *cause* automobiles to move. There are further problems of inference from sample data to populations. It may be necessary to test the hypothesis that the R^2 determined is significantly different from zero. The F test may be used for this purpose, and its application is discussed in most statistics texts. Other problems develop when serial correlation is suspected among the disturbance terms. This phenomenon is particularly associated with the use of time-series data, and the analyst should be aware of the fact that the presence of serial correlation reduces the efficiency of his estimators. Tests such as that developed by Durbin-Watson may be used to discern serial correlation, although the problem is beyond the scope of this book.

PROBLEMS

1. Compute the standard error of the estimate, the coefficient of correlation, and the coefficient of determination for the Alberich Mining Corp. (See discussion above.) Interpret your results.

2. The Rheingold Jewelry Co. is attempting to correlate its sales (Y) with several independent variables. It is felt that such variables as national income (X_1), the retail price level (X_2), and the level of interest rates (X_3) might influence sales. After gathering data for twenty years, the firm has determined the following equation:

$$Y = 186 + .038\ (X_1) - .124\ (X_2) - 1.81\ (X_3)$$
$$(.84) \qquad\quad (.22) \qquad\quad (.45)$$
$$R^2 = .64$$

a. If sales are in thousands, what are the likely units for national income, the retail price level, and the level of interest rates?

b. Let

$$X_1 = 1,000$$
$$X_2 = 126$$
$$X_3 = 7$$

Determine the trend value of sales.

c. Interpret the R^2 value and the coefficients of partial determination.

d. Suppose data had been gathered for only five years. What would you expect to happen to R^2? Why?

B.4 COVARIANCE

The *covariance* of two random variables Y and X is defined as:

$$\text{Cov}(Y,X) = E[(X-\bar{X})(Y-\bar{Y})] \tag{B.17}$$

Expanding, we find:

$$\begin{aligned}
\text{Cov}(Y,X) &= E[(XY - Y\bar{X} - X\bar{Y} + \bar{X}\bar{Y})] \\
&= E(XY) - \bar{X}\bar{Y} - \bar{X}\bar{Y} + \bar{X}\bar{Y} \\
&= E(XY) - \bar{X}\bar{Y} \tag{B.18}
\end{aligned}$$

The covariance gives some indication of how two random variables will vary together.

The correlation coefficient and the covariance of two random variables are related in the following way:

$$r_{y \cdot x} = \frac{\text{Cov}(Y,X)}{\sigma_y \sigma_x} \tag{B.19}$$

which may be rewritten as:

$$\text{Cov}(Y,X) = r_{y \cdot x}\, \sigma_y \sigma_x \tag{B.20}$$

Suppose the future performance of two stocks, X and Y, is being considered. Stock X is believed to perform quite favorably under bull market conditions, and an investment in it should produce a handsome profit. Under bear market conditions, however, this stock should do very badly, and the investment would show a sizeable loss in this case. Stock Y, on the other hand, will do moderately well in a bull market, but will remain at current levels even if the market in general does rather poorly. A return matrix under the two possible market conditions is given below:

Market Condition	Probability	Profit Stock X	Profit Stock Y
Bull Market	.5	$4,000	$1,000
Bear Market	.5	−2,000	—0—

The independent expected value and variance for each stock would be:

$$\begin{aligned}
\text{Stock } X: \quad (.5)(4{,}000) &= 2{,}000 \\
(.5)(-2{,}000) &= \underline{-1{,}000} \\
E(X) &= 1{,}000
\end{aligned}$$

$$(\ 4{,}000) - (1{,}000) = (\ 3{,}000)^2 = 9{,}000{,}000 \ (.5) = 4{,}500{,}000$$
$$(-2{,}000) - (1{,}000) = (-3{,}000)^2 = 9{,}000{,}000 \ (.5) = \underline{4{,}500{,}000}$$
$$V(X) = 9{,}000{,}000$$

$$\text{Stock } Y: \ (.5) \ (1{,}000) = 500$$
$$(.5) \ (\quad 0) = \underline{\quad 0 \quad}$$
$$E(X) = 500$$

$$(1{,}000) - (500) = (\ 500)^2 = 250{,}000 \ (.5) = 125{,}000$$
$$(0) - (500) = (-500)^2 = 250{,}000 \ (.5) = \underline{125{,}000}$$
$$V(X) = 250{,}000$$

The covariance between the two investments would be:

$$\text{Cov } (X,Y) = E(XY) - \bar{X}\bar{Y}$$
$$E(XY) = (4{,}000) \ (1{,}000) \ (.5) + (-2{,}000) \ (0) \ (.5) = 2{,}000{,}000$$
$$\bar{X}\bar{Y} = (1{,}000) \ (500) = 500{,}000$$
$$\text{Cov } (X,Y) = 2{,}000{,}000 - 500{,}000 = 1{,}500{,}000$$

The correlation coefficient between the investments is given by:

$$r_{x \cdot y} = \frac{\text{Cov } (X,Y)}{\sigma_x, \sigma_y} = \frac{1{,}500{,}000}{(3{,}000) \ (500)} = \frac{1{,}500{,}000}{1{,}500{,}000} = 1.00$$

Notice that when the two variables are correlated using only two values for each variable, the loss of degrees of freedom forces a correlation coefficient of unity.

PROBLEM

Glamour Glow, Ltd., is a growth stock. The price of its shares moves with the market. When stock prices are up, Glamour Glow generally outperforms the averages. Alchemy Mining is a contracyclical stock. When the market is up, Alchemy does not do very well because investment dollars are chasing up stocks like Glamour Glow. When the market is down, particularly if the negative movement is the result of an international money panic, Alchemy does extremely well. A return matrix for investment in Glamour Glow and Alchemy under three market conditions is given below:

Market Condition	Probability	Profit–Glamour	Profit–Alchemy
Prosperity	.6	$3,000	-$1,000
Recession	.3	-1,000	0
Money panic	.1	-2,000	5,000

1. Calculate the independent expected value and variance for each stock.
2. What is the covariance between the two? The correlation coefficient?

B.5 CONDITIONAL PROBABILITY DISTRIBUTIONS

Two random variables are said to be *independent* if and only if:

$$P(X,Y) = P(X) \cdot P(Y) \tag{B.21}$$

In this case, the probability of X assuming any value is not affected by any value Y might take on, and vice versa.

Statistical independence may be illustrated with a set of *conditional* probabilities. Consider the following *joint* probability distribution:

TABLE B-1

A Joint Probability Distribution

Possible Outcomes for X	Possible Outcomes for Y		Total Probability
	$Y_1 = \$10$	$Y_2 = \$500$	
$X_1 = \$100$	.30	.10	.40
$X_2 = \$200$	.20	.40	.60
Total Probability	.50	.50	1.00

There are two possible outcomes for X (that is, X_1 and X_2) and two for Y (Y_1 and Y_2). Variable X may take on either of its values without being influenced by or influencing Y. Thus, given the fact that $X=X_1$, we may observe that $P(Y=Y_1) = .30/.40 = .75$. Given the fact that $X=X_1$, it is also clear that $P(Y=Y_2) = .10/.40 = .25$. Because Y can only be Y_1 or Y_2, the sum of the probabilities $(.75 + .25)$ must equal 1.00. Similarly, given the fact that $X=X_2$, $P(Y=Y_1) = .20/.60$ and $P(Y=Y_2) = .40/.60$, and $1/3 + 2/3 = 1.00$. The mathematical relationship of the variables is described by:

$$P(Y|X) = \frac{P(Y,X)}{P(X)} \tag{B.22}$$

Where:

$P(Y|X)$ is the conditional probability of event Y, given that event X has occured

$P(X)$ is the probability of event X occuring

$P(Y,X)$ is the joint probability of Y and X both occuring

In Table B-1, the probability that X will take on value X_1 [that is, $P(X=X_1)$] is simply .4. The probability that $X=X_1$, *given that* $Y=Y_2$, however, is:

$$P(X_1|Y_2) = .10/.50 = .20$$

The probability that $X=X_1$ *and* $Y=Y_1$ would be:

$$P(X_1, Y_1) = P(Y_1) \cdot P(X_1|Y_1)$$
$$= (.50)(.30/.50)$$
$$= .30$$

If we assume that X will occur before Y (that is, X is assumed to be given before Y takes on values), a tree diagram may be drawn to indicate all possible outcomes:

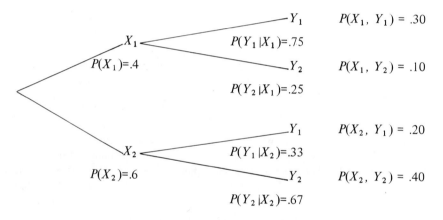

Figure B-1   A Tree Diagram

PROBLEMS

1. In Table B-1, assume that Y will occur before X. Draw a tree diagram indicating all possible outcomes.
2. Let the outcomes in Table B-1 take on the numerical values given (that is, $X_1 = \$100$, and so on). Calculate the following:
   a. The independent expected value and variance for X and Y.
   b. The covariance between them.
   c. The correlation coefficient between them.

d. The expected return and variance of the combination.

3. Two investments have the following characteristics:

$$\bar{X} = \$30,000 \qquad \sigma_X = \$10,000$$

$$\bar{Y} = \$20,000 \qquad \sigma_Y = \quad 0$$

What are the covariance and correlation coefficient between the investments?

B.6 EXPECTED VALUES AND VARIANCES OF TWO OR MORE RANDOM VARIABLES

The expected value of two (or more) random variables is simply the sum of the respective expected values, or:

$$E(Y + X) = E(Y) + E(X) \tag{B.23}$$

The variance of two or more random variables is given by:

$$V = \sum_{i=y}^{N} \sum_{j=y}^{N} r_{ij}\sigma_i\sigma_j \tag{B.24}$$

For two random variables, we find:

$$V = r_{y \cdot y}\sigma_y\sigma_y + r_{y \cdot x}\sigma_y\sigma_x + r_{x \cdot y}\sigma_x\sigma_y + r_{x \cdot x}\sigma_x\sigma_x \tag{B.25}$$

Now, we know $r_{y \cdot y} = 1$ and $r_{x \cdot x} = 1$. We also know that $r_{y \cdot x} = r_{x \cdot y}$. Hence, we may simplify equation B.25:

$$V = \sigma_y^2 + \sigma_x^2 + 2\sigma_y\sigma_x r_{y \cdot x} \tag{B.26}$$

In covariance form, we have:

$$V = V(Y) + V(X) + 2\text{Cov}\,(Y,X) \tag{B.27}$$

When random variables are percentages (such as in the case of rates of return), the expected value of two or more random variables is the weighted average of the respective expected returns:

$$E = \sum_{i=y}^{N} \alpha_i E_i \tag{B.28}$$

where α_i is the proportion of the total placed in the ith investment. In this case, the variance becomes:

$$V = \sum_{i=y}^{N} \sum_{j=y}^{N} \alpha_i \alpha_j r_{ij} \sigma_i \sigma_j \tag{B.29}$$

For two random variables,

$$V = \alpha_y^2 \sigma_y^2 + \alpha_x^2 \sigma_x^2 + 2\alpha_y \alpha_x r_{y \cdot x} \sigma_y \sigma_x \tag{B.30}$$

which, in covariance form, is:

$$V = \alpha_y^2 V(Y) + \alpha_x^2 V(X) + 2\alpha_y \alpha_x \text{Cov}(Y,X) \tag{B.31}$$

Reconsider the two stocks X and Y that were examined in the section on Covariance. There, we found Stock X had an expected profit of $1,000 and a variance of $9 million. Stock Y had an expected profit of $500 and a variance of $250,000. The covariance between the two investments was $1,500,000. Suppose an investor purchased *both* stocks. His expected return from the portfolio would be:

$$E(X + Y) = 1,000 + 500 = 1,500$$

The variance of the total portfolio would be:

$$V(X + Y) = 9,000,000 + 250,000 + 2(1,500,000) = 12,250,000$$

In the above case, we may assume that an equal investment of $10,000 had been made in each stock (total investment of $20,000). If all the dollars had been put into Stock X, the expected return and variance would be:

$$E(X) = (2)\,(1,000) = 2,000$$

$$V(X) = \quad 8,000 - 2,000 = (\ 6,000)^2 = 36,000,000\ (.5) = 18,000,000$$
$$-4,000 - 2,000 = (-6,000)^2 = 36,000,000\ (.5) = \underline{18,000,000}$$
$$V(X) = 36,000,000$$

A comparison of the return-variance pattern from each portfolio would show:

$E(X + Y) = \$1,500$	$E(X) = \$2,000$
$V(X + Y) = \$12,250,000$	$V(X) = \$36,000,000$

Thus, the diversified portfolio would provide a lower expected return and a lower risk.

PROBLEMS

1. Reconsider the prospective prices of Glamour Glow, Ltd., and Alchemy Mining (problem on page 426).

    a. Determine the expected return and variance if both stocks are bought.

    b. Given the miserable expected performance of Alchemy, is there any argument for including it in the portfolio?

2. A portfolio contains two stocks, A and B. The expected yield from A is 10 percent, with a variance of 25 percent. The expected yield from B is 8 percent, with a variance of 9 percent. The correlation between returns from A and B is zero. If 1/5 of the portfolio is in A and 4/5 in B, what is the expected return and variance from the portfolio?

Tables

Table C.1
COMPOUND VALUE OF $1

PERIOD	C.01	C.02	0.03
1	1.0100	1.0200	1.0300
2	1.0201	1.0404	1.0609
3	1.C303	1.C612	1.C927
4	1.C4C6	1.C824	1.1255
5	1.C510	1.1040	1.1592
6	1.C615	1.1261	1.1940
7	1.C721	1.1486	1.2298
8	1.C828	1.1716	1.2667
9	1.C936	1.1950	1.3047
10	1.1C46	1.2189	1.3439
11	1.1156	1.2433	1.3842
12	1.1268	1.2682	1.4257
13	1.1380	1.2936	1.4685
14	1.1494	1.3194	1.5125
15	1.1609	1.3458	1.5579
16	1.1725	1.3727	1.6047
17	1.1843	1.4C02	1.6528
18	1.1961	1.4282	1.7024
19	1.2C81	1.4568	1.7535
20	1.2201	1.4855	1.8C61
21	1.2323	1.5156	1.8602
22	1.2447	1.5459	1.9161
23	1.2571	1.5768	1.9735
24	1.2697	1.6084	2.0327
25	1.2824	1.6406	2.0937
26	1.2952	1.6734	2.1565
27	1.3C82	1.7C68	2.2212
28	1.3212	1.7410	2.2879
29	1.3345	1.7758	2.3565
30	1.3478	1.8113	2.4272
31	1.3613	1.8475	2.5CCC
32	1.3749	1.8845	2.5750
33	1.3886	1.9222	2.6523
34	1.4025	1.9606	2.7319
35	1.4166	1.9998	2.8138
36	1.43C7	2.C398	2.8982
37	1.4450	2.0806	2.9852
38	1.4595	2.1222	3.C747
39	1.4741	2.1647	3.1670
40	1.4888	2.2C8C	3.2620
41	1.5C37	2.2522	3.3598
42	1.5187	2.2972	3.4606
43	1.5339	2.3431	3.5645
44	1.5493	2.3900	3.6714
45	1.5648	2.4378	3.7815
46	1.5804	2.4866	3.8950
47	1.5962	2.5363	4.0118
48	1.6122	2.587C	4.1322
49	1.6283	2.6388	4.2562
50	1.6446	2.6915	4.3839

0.04	0.05	0.06	0.07
1.0400	1.0500	1.0600	1.0700
1.0816	1.1025	1.1236	1.1449
1.1248	1.1576	1.1910	1.2250
1.1698	1.2155	1.2624	1.3107
1.2166	1.2762	1.3382	1.4025
1.2653	1.3400	1.4185	1.5007
1.3159	1.4071	1.5036	1.6057
1.3685	1.4774	1.5938	1.7181
1.4233	1.5513	1.6894	1.8384
1.4802	1.6288	1.7908	1.9671
1.5394	1.7103	1.8982	2.1048
1.6010	1.7958	2.0121	2.2521
1.6650	1.8856	2.1329	2.4098
1.7316	1.9799	2.2609	2.5785
1.8009	2.0789	2.3965	2.7590
1.8729	2.1828	2.5403	2.9521
1.9479	2.2920	2.6927	3.1588
2.0258	2.4066	2.8543	3.3799
2.1068	2.5269	3.0255	3.6165
2.1911	2.6532	3.2071	3.8696
2.2787	2.7859	3.3995	4.1405
2.3699	2.9252	3.6035	4.4304
2.4647	3.0715	3.8197	4.7405
2.5633	3.2250	4.0489	5.0723
2.6658	3.3863	4.2918	5.4274
2.7724	3.5556	4.5493	5.8073
2.8833	3.7334	4.8223	6.2138
2.9987	3.9201	5.1116	6.6488
3.1186	4.1161	5.4183	7.1142
3.2433	4.3219	5.7434	7.6122
3.3731	4.5380	6.0881	8.1451
3.5080	4.7649	6.4533	8.7152
3.6483	5.0031	6.8405	9.3253
3.7943	5.2533	7.2510	9.9781
3.9460	5.5160	7.6860	10.6765
4.1039	5.7918	8.1472	11.4239
4.2680	6.0814	8.6360	12.2236
4.4388	6.3854	9.1542	13.0792
4.6163	6.7047	9.7035	13.9948
4.8010	7.0399	10.2857	14.9744
4.9930	7.3919	10.9028	16.0226
5.1927	7.7615	11.5570	17.1442
5.4004	8.1496	12.2504	18.3443
5.6165	8.5571	12.9854	19.6284
5.8411	8.9850	13.7646	21.0024
6.0748	9.4342	14.5904	22.4726
6.3178	9.9059	15.4659	24.0457
6.5705	10.4012	16.3938	25.7289
6.8333	10.9213	17.3775	27.5299
7.1066	11.4673	18.4201	29.4570

CCMPOUND VALUE CF $1

PERICD	C.08	0.09	0.10
1	1. 08 0(	1. 0900	1. 1000
2	1. 166.	1. 1881	1. 2100
3	1.2597	1.2950	1. 3310
4	1.36C4	1.4115	1. 4641
5	1.4653	1.5386	1.6105
6	1.5868	1.6771	1.7715
7	1.7138	1.8280	1.9487
8	1.85C9	1.9925	2.1435
9	1.9990	2.1718	2.3579
10	2.1589	2.3673	2.5937
11	2.3316	2.5EC4	2.8531
12	2.5181	2.8126	3.1384
13	2.7156	3.0658	3.4522
14	2.9371	3.3417	3.7974
15	3.1721	3.6424	4.1772
16	3.4259	3.9703	4.5949
17	3.7000	4.3276	5.0544
18	3.9960	4.7171	5.5599
19	4.3157	5.1416	6.1159
20	4.6609	5.6044	6.7274
21	5.C338	6.1C88	7.4002
22	5.4365	6.6586	8.1402
23	5.8714	7.2578	8.9543
24	6.3411	7.9110	9.8497
25	6.8484	8.6230	1C.8347
26	7.3963	9.3991	11.9181
27	7.9880	10.2450	13.1C99
28	8.6271	11.1671	14.4209
29	9.3172	12.1721	15.8630
30	1C.C626	13.2676	17.4494
31	1C.8676	14.4617	19.1943
32	11.7370	15.7633	21.1137
33	12.6760	17.1820	23.2251
34	13.6901	18.7284	25.5476
35	14.7853	20.4139	28.1024
36	15.9681	22.2512	30.9126
37	17.2456	24.2538	34.0039
38	18.6252	26.4366	37.4043
39	20.1152	28.8159	41.1447
40	21.7245	31.4C94	45.2592
41	23.4624	34.2362	49.7851
42	25.3394	37.3175	54.7636
43	27.3666	40.6761	60.2400
44	29.5559	44.3369	66.2640
45	31.9204	48.3272	72.8904
46	34.4740	52.6767	80.1795
47	37.2320	57.4176	88.1974
48	40.2105	62.5852	97.0172
49	43.4274	68.2179	106.7189
50	46.9C16	74.3575	117.39C8

C.11	C.12	0.13	0.14
1.1100	1.1200	1.1300	1.1400
1.2321	1.2544	1.2769	1.2996
1.3676	1.4049	1.4428	1.4815
1.5180	1.5735	1.6304	1.6889
1.6850	1.7623	1.8424	1.9254
1.8704	1.9738	2.0819	2.1949
2.0761	2.2106	2.3526	2.5022
2.3045	2.4759	2.6584	2.8525
2.5580	2.7730	3.0040	3.2519
2.8394	3.1058	3.3945	3.7072
3.1517	3.4785	3.8358	4.2262
3.4984	3.8959	4.3345	4.8179
3.8832	4.3634	4.8980	5.4924
4.3104	4.8871	5.5347	6.2613
4.7845	5.4735	6.2542	7.1379
5.3108	6.1303	7.0673	8.1372
5.8950	6.8660	7.9860	9.2764
6.5435	7.6899	9.0242	10.5751
7.2633	8.6127	10.1974	12.0556
8.0623	9.6462	11.5230	13.7434
8.9491	10.8038	13.0210	15.6675
9.9335	12.1003	14.7138	17.8610
11.0262	13.5523	16.6266	20.3615
12.2391	15.1786	18.7880	23.2122
13.5854	17.0000	21.2305	26.4619
15.0798	19.0400	23.9905	30.1665
16.7386	21.3248	27.1092	34.3899
18.5799	23.8838	30.6334	39.2044
20.6236	26.7499	34.6158	44.6931
22.8922	29.9599	39.1158	50.9501
25.4104	33.5551	44.2009	58.0831
28.2055	37.5817	49.9470	66.2148
31.3082	42.0915	56.4402	75.4849
34.7521	47.1425	63.7774	86.0527
38.5748	52.7996	72.0685	98.1001
42.8180	59.1355	81.4374	111.8342
47.5280	66.2318	92.0242	127.4909
52.7561	74.1796	103.9874	145.3397
58.5593	83.0812	117.5057	165.6872
65.0008	93.0509	132.7815	188.8835
72.1509	104.2170	150.0431	215.3272
80.0875	116.7231	169.5487	245.4730
88.8972	130.7299	191.5901	279.8392
98.6758	146.4175	216.4968	319.0167
109.5302	163.9876	244.6414	363.6790
121.5785	183.6661	276.4447	414.5941
134.9522	205.7060	312.3826	472.6373
149.7969	230.3907	352.9923	538.8065
166.2746	258.0376	398.8813	614.2394
184.5648	289.0021	450.7359	700.2329

CCMPOUND VALLE CF $1

PERIOD	C.15	0.16	0.17
1	1.1500	1.1600	1.1700
2	1.3225	1.3456	1.3689
3	1.52C8	1.5608	1.6016
4	1.7490	1.8106	1.8738
5	2.0113	2.1C03	2.1924
6	2.3130	2.4363	2.5651
7	2.66C0	2.8262	3.0012
8	3.C590	3.2784	3.5114
9	3.5178	3.8029	4.1C84
10	4.C455	4.4114	4.8C68
11	4.6523	5.1172	5.6239
12	5.35C2	5.9360	6.5800
13	6.1527	6.8857	7.6986
14	7.C757	7.9875	9.0074
15	8.1370	5.2655	10.5387
16	9.3576	10.748C	12.3303
17	10.7612	12.4676	14.4264
18	12.3754	14.4625	16.8789
19	14.2317	16.7765	19.7483
20	16.3665	19.4607	23.1055
21	18.8215	22.5144	27.0335
22	21.6447	26.1863	31.6292
23	24.8914	30.3762	37.0062
24	28.6251	35.2364	43.2972
25	32.9189	40.8742	5C.6578
26	37.8567	47.4141	59.2696
27	43.5353	55.C0C3	69.3454
28	5C.C656	63.8004	81.1342
29	57.5754	74.C085	54.9270
30	66.2117	85.8498	111.C646
31	76.1435	55.5858	129.9456
32	87.5650	115.5195	152.0363
33	100.6598	134.C027	177.8825
34	115.8C48	155.4431	208.1226
35	133.1755	180.3140	243.5034
36	153.1518	209.1643	284.8990
37	176.1246	242.6306	333.3319
38	202.5433	281.4515	389.5583
39	232.9248	326.4837	456.2980
40	267.8635	378.7211	533.8687
41	3C8.C430	439.3165	624.6263
42	354.2495	5C9.6C71	730.8128
43	4C7.3869	551.1443	855.0510
44	468.4950	685.7274	1CCC.4C97
45	538.7652	755.4438	1170.4794
46	619.5846	922.7148	1369.46C9
47	712.5223	1070.3492	1602.2692
48	819.4CC7	1241.6C50	1874.6550
49	942.3108	1440.2618	2193.3463
50	1C83.6574	1670.7C38	2566.2152

0.18	0.19	0.20	0.21
1.1800	1.1900	1.2000	1.2100
1.3924	1.4161	1.4400	1.4641
1.6430	1.6851	1.7279	1.7715
1.9387	2.0053	2.0735	2.1435
2.2877	2.3863	2.4883	2.5937
2.6955	2.8397	2.9859	3.1384
3.1854	3.3793	3.5831	3.7974
3.7588	4.0213	4.2998	4.5949
4.4354	4.7854	5.1597	5.5599
5.2338	5.6946	6.1917	6.7274
6.1759	6.7766	7.4300	8.1402
7.2875	8.0642	8.9161	9.8497
8.5993	9.5964	10.6993	11.9181
10.1472	11.4197	12.8391	14.4209
11.9737	13.5895	15.4070	17.4494
14.1290	16.1715	18.4884	21.1137
16.6722	19.2441	22.1861	25.5476
19.6732	22.9005	26.6233	30.9126
23.2144	27.2516	31.9479	37.4043
27.3930	32.4294	38.3375	45.2592
32.3237	38.5910	46.0051	54.7636
38.1420	45.9233	55.2061	66.2640
45.0076	54.6487	66.2473	80.1795
53.1090	65.0319	79.4968	97.0172
62.6686	77.3880	95.3962	117.3908
73.9489	92.0918	114.4754	142.0429
87.2597	109.5892	137.3705	171.8719
102.9665	130.4112	164.8446	207.9650
121.5005	155.1893	197.8135	251.6377
143.3706	184.6753	237.3763	304.4816
169.1773	219.7636	284.8515	368.4227
199.6292	261.5187	341.8218	445.7915
235.5625	311.2072	410.1862	539.4077
277.9638	370.3366	492.2235	652.6834
327.9972	440.7006	590.6682	789.7469
387.0368	524.4337	708.8018	955.5938
456.7034	624.0761	850.5622	1156.2685
538.9100	742.6505	1020.6746	1399.0849
635.9138	883.7542	1224.8096	1692.8927
750.3783	1051.6675	1469.7715	2048.4002
885.4464	1251.4843	1763.7258	2478.5642
1044.8268	1489.2663	2116.4710	2999.0627
1232.8956	1772.2269	2539.7652	3628.8659
1454.8168	2108.9500	3047.7183	4390.9277
1716.6838	2509.6506	3657.2619	5313.0226
2025.6869	2986.4842	4388.7143	6428.7573
2390.3106	3553.9162	5266.4572	7778.7964
2820.5665	4229.1603	6319.7487	9412.3436
3328.2685	5032.7007	7583.6984	11388.9358
3927.3568	5988.9139	9100.4381	13780.6123

CCMPOUND VALUE CF $1

PERIOD	C.22	0.23	0.24
1	1. 2200	1. 2300	1. 2400
2	1. 4884	1. 5129	1.5376
3	1.8158	1.8608	1.9066
4	2.2153	2.2888	2.3642
5	2.7027	2.8153	2.9316
6	3.2973	3.4628	3.6352
7	4.0227	4.2592	4.5076
8	4.5077	5.2389	5.5895
9	5.9874	6.4438	6.9309
10	7.3046	7.9259	8.5944
11	8.9116	9.7489	10.6570
12	10.8722	11.9911	13.2147
13	13.2641	14.7491	16.3863
14	16.1822	18.1414	20.3190
15	19.7422	22.3139	25.1956
16	24.0855	27.4461	31.2425
17	29.3844	33.7587	38.7408
18	35.8489	41.5233	48.0385
19	43.7357	51.0736	59.5678
20	53.3576	62.8206	73.8641
21	65.0963	77.2693	91.5915
22	79.4175	95.0413	113.5735
23	96.8893	116.9008	140.8311
24	118.2050	143.7880	174.6306
25	144.2101	176.8592	216.5419
26	175.9363	217.5368	268.5120
27	214.6423	267.5703	332.9549
28	261.8636	329.1115	412.8641
29	319.4736	404.8072	511.9515
30	389.7578	497.9128	634.8159
31	475.5046	612.4328	787.1767
32	580.1156	753.2923	976.0991
33	707.7410	926.5496	1210.3629
34	863.4441	1139.6560	1500.8500
35	1053.4018	1401.7769	1861.0540
36	1285.1502	1724.1855	2307.7069
37	1567.8833	2120.7482	2861.5566
38	1912.8176	2608.5203	3548.3302
39	2333.6375	3208.4800	4399.9295
40	2847.0377	3946.4304	5455.9126
41	3473.3860	4854.1095	6765.3316
42	4237.5310	5970.5546	8389.0112
43	5169.7878	7343.7822	10402.3739
44	6307.1411	9032.8521	12898.9436
45	7694.7121	11110.4081	15994.6901
46	9387.5488	13665.8020	19833.4158
47	11452.8096	16808.9365	24593.4356
48	13972.4277	20674.9919	30495.8601
49	17046.3618	25430.2400	37814.8666
50	20796.5614	31279.1953	46890.4346

0.25	0.26	0.27	0.28
1.2500	1.2600	1.2700	1.2800
1.5625	1.5876	1.6129	1.6384
1.9531	2.0003	2.0483	2.0971
2.4414	2.5204	2.6014	2.6843
3.0517	3.1757	3.3038	3.4359
3.8146	4.0015	4.1958	4.3980
4.7683	5.0418	5.3287	5.6294
5.9604	6.3527	6.7675	7.2057
7.4505	8.0045	8.5947	9.2233
9.3132	10.0856	10.9153	11.8059
11.6415	12.7079	13.8624	15.1115
14.5519	16.0120	17.6053	19.3428
18.1898	20.1751	22.3587	24.7588
22.7373	25.4207	28.3956	31.6912
28.4217	32.0300	36.0624	40.5648
35.5271	40.3579	45.7993	51.9229
44.4089	50.8509	58.1652	66.4613
55.5111	64.0722	73.8698	85.0705
69.3889	80.7310	93.8146	108.8903
86.7361	101.7210	119.1446	139.3796
108.4202	128.1685	151.3136	178.4059
135.5252	161.4923	192.1683	228.3596
169.4065	203.4803	244.0538	292.3003
211.7582	256.3852	309.9483	374.1444
264.6977	323.0454	393.6343	478.9048
330.8722	407.0372	499.9156	612.9982
413.5903	512.8669	634.8928	784.6377
516.9878	646.2123	806.3139	1004.3362
646.2348	814.2275	1024.0187	1285.5504
807.7935	1025.9267	1300.5038	1645.5045
1009.7419	1292.6677	1651.6398	2106.2458
1262.1774	1628.7613	2097.5825	2695.9946
1577.7218	2052.2392	2663.9298	3450.8731
1972.1522	2585.8214	3383.1909	4417.1176
2465.1903	3258.1350	4296.6525	5653.9106
3081.4879	4105.2501	5456.7487	7237.0055
3851.8598	5172.6151	6930.0708	9263.3671
4814.8248	6517.4951	8801.1899	11857.1099
6018.5310	8212.0438	11177.5112	15177.1007
7523.1638	10347.1752	14195.4393	19426.6889
9403.9548	13037.4408	18028.2079	24866.1518
11754.9435	16427.1754	22895.8241	31828.6871
14693.6793	20698.2410	29077.6966	40740.7195
18367.0992	26079.7837	36928.6747	52148.1209
22958.8740	32860.5274	46899.4168	66749.5948
28698.5925	41404.2646	59562.2594	85439.4814
35873.2406	52169.3734	75644.0694	109362.5362
44841.5508	65733.4104	96067.9682	139984.0463
56051.9385	82824.0972	122006.3196	179179.5793
70064.9232	104358.3624	154948.0259	229349.8615

CCMPOUND VALUE CF $1

PERIOD	C.29	0.30	0.35
1	1.2900	1.3000	1.3500
2	1.6641	1.6900	1.8225
3	2.1466	2.1970	2.4603
4	2.7692	2.8561	3.3215
5	3.5723	3.7129	4.4840
6	4.6082	4.8268	6.0534
7	5.9446	6.2748	8.1721
8	7.6686	8.1573	11.0324
9	9.8925	10.6044	14.8937
10	12.7613	13.7858	20.1065
11	16.4621	17.9216	27.1438
12	21.2361	23.2980	36.6441
13	27.3946	30.2875	49.4696
14	35.3391	39.3737	66.7840
15	45.5874	51.1858	90.1584
16	58.8078	66.5416	121.7139
17	75.8621	86.5041	164.3138
18	97.8621	112.4554	221.8236
19	126.2421	146.1920	299.4619
20	162.8524	190.0496	404.2735
21	210.0796	247.0645	545.7693
22	271.0027	321.1838	736.7886
23	349.5934	417.5390	994.6646
24	450.9756	542.8007	1342.7972
25	581.7585	705.6410	1812.7762
26	750.4684	917.3333	2447.2479
27	968.1043	1192.5332	3303.7847
28	1248.8546	1550.2932	4460.1094
29	1611.0224	2015.3812	6021.1477
30	2078.2189	2619.9956	8128.5495
31	2680.9024	3405.9943	10973.5418
32	3458.3642	4427.7926	14814.2814
33	4461.2898	5756.1304	19999.2799
34	5755.0639	7482.9695	26999.0279
35	7424.0324	9727.8604	36448.6877
36	9577.0018	12646.2185	49205.7284
37	12354.3323	16440.0841	66427.7334
38	15937.0887	21372.1093	89677.4401
39	20558.8444	27783.7421	121064.5442
40	26520.9094	36118.8648	163437.1346
41	34211.9731	46954.5242	220640.1318
42	44133.4453	61040.8815	297864.1779
43	56932.1444	79353.1459	402116.6402
44	73442.4663	103159.0897	542857.4643
45	94740.7816	134106.8167	732857.5768
46	122215.6083	174338.8617	989357.7287
47	157658.1347	226640.5202	1335632.9337
48	203378.9937	294632.6763	1803104.4606
49	262358.9019	383022.4792	2434191.0218
50	338442.9835	497929.2229	3286157.8794

0.40	0.45	0.50	0.60
1.4000	1.4500	1.5000	1.6000
1.9600	2.1025	2.2500	2.5600
2.7440	3.0486	3.3750	4.0960
3.8416	4.4205	5.0625	6.5536
5.3782	6.4097	7.5937	10.4857
7.5295	9.2941	11.3906	16.7772
10.5413	13.4764	17.0859	26.8435
14.7578	19.5408	25.6289	42.9496
20.6610	28.3342	38.4433	68.7194
28.9254	41.0846	57.6650	109.9511
40.4956	59.5728	86.4975	175.9218
56.6939	86.3805	129.7463	281.4749
79.3714	125.2518	194.6195	450.3599
111.1200	181.6151	291.9292	720.5759
155.5680	263.3419	437.8938	1152.9215
217.7953	381.8458	656.8408	1844.6744
304.9134	553.6764	985.2612	2951.4790
426.8788	802.8308	1477.8918	4722.3664
597.6303	1164.1046	2216.8378	7555.7863
836.6825	1687.9518	3325.2567	12089.2581
1171.3555	2447.5301	4987.8850	19342.8131
1639.8978	3548.9186	7481.8276	30948.5009
2295.8569	5145.9320	11222.7414	49517.6015
3214.1997	7461.6015	16834.1121	79228.1625
4499.8795	10819.3222	25251.1682	126765.0600
6299.8314	15688.0172	37876.7524	202824.0960
8819.7639	22747.6250	56815.1286	324518.5536
12347.6695	32984.0562	85222.6929	519229.6358
17286.7373	47826.8815	127834.0394	830767.4973
24201.4323	69348.9782	191751.0592	1329227.9957
33882.0052	100556.0185	287626.5888	2126764.7932
47434.8074	145806.2268	431439.8832	3402823.6692
66408.7303	211419.0289	647159.8249	5444517.8707
92972.2225	306557.5919	970739.7373	8711228.5931
130161.1115	444508.5083	1456109.6060	13937965.7490
182225.5561	644537.3371	2184164.4090	22300745.1985
255115.7786	934579.1387	3276246.6136	35681192.3176
357162.0900	1355139.7512	4914369.9204	57089907.7082
500026.9261	1964952.6393	7371554.8806	91343852.3331
700037.6965	2849181.3270	11057332.3209	146150163.7330
980052.7752	4131312.9241	16585998.4814	233840261.9729
1372073.8853	5990403.7400	24878997.7221	374144419.1567
1920903.4394	8686085.4230	37318496.5831	598631070.6507
2689264.8152	12594823.8634	55977744.8747	957809713.0411
3764970.7413	18262494.6019	83966617.3121	1532495540.8658
5270959.0378	26480617.1728	125949925.9682	2451992865.3854
7379342.6529	38396894.9006	188924888.9523	3923188584.6166
10331079.7141	55675497.6059	283387333.4284	6277101735.3866
14463511.5998	80729471.5286	425081000.1426	10043362776.6186
20248916.2397	117057733.7165	637621500.2140	16069380442.5897

Table C.2
COMPOUND VALUE OF ANNUITY (FIRST RECEIVED IN PERIOD ZERO)

PERIOD	C.01	0.02	0.03
1	1.0100	1.0200	1.0300
2	2.0300	2.0603	2.0908
3	3.0604	3.1216	3.1836
4	4.1010	4.2040	4.3091
5	5.1520	5.3081	5.4684
6	6.2135	6.4342	6.6624
7	7.2856	7.5829	7.8923
8	8.3685	8.7546	9.1591
9	9.4622	9.9497	10.4638
10	10.5668	11.1687	11.8077
11	11.8825	12.4120	13.1920
12	12.8093	13.6803	14.6177
13	13.9474	14.9739	16.0863
14	15.0968	16.2934	17.5989
15	16.2578	17.6392	19.1568
16	17.4304	19.0120	20.7615
17	18.6147	20.4123	22.4144
18	19.8108	21.8405	24.1168
19	21.0190	23.2973	25.8703
20	22.2391	24.7833	27.6764
21	23.4715	26.2989	29.5367
22	24.7163	27.8449	31.4528
23	25.9734	29.4218	33.4264
24	27.2431	31.0302	35.4592
25	28.5256	32.6709	37.5530
26	29.8208	34.3443	39.7096
27	31.1290	36.0512	41.9309
28	32.4503	37.7922	44.2188
29	33.7848	39.5680	46.5754
30	35.1327	41.3794	49.0026
31	36.4940	43.2270	51.5027
32	37.8690	45.1115	54.0778
33	39.2576	47.0338	56.7301
34	40.6602	48.9944	59.4620
35	42.0768	50.9943	62.2759
36	43.5076	53.0342	65.1742
37	44.9527	55.1149	68.1594
38	46.4122	57.2372	71.2342
39	47.8863	59.4019	74.4012
40	49.3752	61.6100	77.6632
41	50.8789	63.8622	81.0231
42	52.3977	66.1594	84.4838
43	53.9317	68.5026	88.0484
44	55.4810	70.8927	91.7198
45	57.0458	73.3305	95.5014
46	58.6263	75.8171	99.3965
47	60.2226	78.3535	103.4083
48	61.8348	80.9405	107.5406
49	63.4631	83.5794	111.7968
50	65.1078	86.2709	116.1807

0.04	0.05	0.06	0.07
1.0400	1.0500	1.0600	1.0700
2.1215	2.1524	2.1835	2.2148
3.2464	3.3101	3.3746	3.4400
4.4163	4.5256	4.6370	4.7507
5.6329	5.8019	5.9753	6.1532
6.8982	7.1420	7.3938	7.6540
8.2142	8.5491	8.8974	9.2598
9.5827	10.0265	10.4913	10.9779
11.0061	11.5778	12.1807	12.8164
12.4863	13.2067	13.9716	14.7835
14.0258	14.9171	15.8699	16.8884
15.6268	16.7129	17.8821	19.1406
17.2919	18.5986	20.0150	21.5504
19.0235	20.5785	22.2759	24.1290
20.8245	22.6574	24.6725	26.8880
22.6975	24.8403	27.2128	29.8402
24.6454	27.1323	29.9056	32.9990
26.6712	29.5390	32.7599	36.3789
28.7780	32.0659	35.7855	39.9954
30.9692	34.7192	38.9927	43.8651
33.2479	37.5052	42.3922	48.0057
35.6178	40.4304	45.9958	52.4361
38.0826	43.5019	49.8155	57.1766
40.6459	46.7270	53.8645	62.2490
43.3117	50.1134	58.1563	67.6764
46.0842	53.6691	62.7057	73.4838
48.9675	57.4025	67.5281	79.6976
51.9662	61.3227	72.6397	86.3465
55.0849	65.4388	78.0581	93.4607
58.3283	69.7607	83.8016	101.0730
61.7014	74.2938	89.8897	109.2181
65.2095	79.0637	96.3431	117.9334
68.8579	84.0669	103.1837	127.2587
72.6522	89.3203	110.4347	137.2368
76.5983	94.8363	118.1208	147.9134
80.7022	100.6281	126.2681	159.3374
84.9703	106.7095	134.9042	171.5610
89.4091	113.0950	144.0584	184.6402
94.0255	119.7997	153.7619	198.6351
98.8265	126.8397	164.0476	213.6095
103.8195	134.2317	174.9505	229.6322
109.0123	141.9933	186.5075	246.7764
114.4128	150.1430	198.7580	265.1208
120.0293	158.7001	211.7435	284.7493
125.8705	167.6851	225.5081	305.7517
131.9453	177.1194	240.0986	328.2243
138.2632	187.0253	255.5645	352.2700
144.8337	197.4266	271.9584	377.9989
151.6670	208.3479	289.3359	405.5289
158.7737	219.8153	307.7560	434.9859

COMPOUND VALUE OF ANNUITY

PERIOD	0.08	0.09	0.10
1	1.0800	1.0900	1.1000
2	2.2463	2.2780	2.3100
3	3.5061	3.5731	3.6409
4	4.8666	4.9847	5.1050
5	6.3359	6.5233	6.7156
6	7.9228	8.2004	8.4871
7	9.6366	10.0284	10.4358
8	11.4875	12.0210	12.5794
9	13.4865	14.1929	14.9374
10	15.6454	16.5602	17.5311
11	17.9771	19.1407	20.3842
12	20.4952	21.9533	23.5227
13	23.2149	25.0191	26.9749
14	26.1521	28.3609	30.7724
15	29.3242	32.0033	34.9497
16	32.7502	35.9737	39.5447
17	36.4502	40.3013	44.5991
18	40.4462	45.0184	50.1590
19	44.7619	50.1601	56.2749
20	49.4229	55.7645	63.0024
21	54.4567	61.8733	70.4027
22	59.8932	68.5319	78.5430
23	65.7647	75.7898	87.4973
24	72.1059	83.7008	97.3470
25	78.9544	92.3239	108.1817
26	86.3507	101.7231	120.0999
27	94.3388	111.9682	133.2099
28	102.9659	123.1353	147.6309
29	112.2832	135.3075	163.4940
30	122.3458	148.5752	180.9434
31	133.2135	163.0369	200.1377
32	144.9506	178.8003	221.2515
33	157.6266	195.9823	244.4766
34	171.3168	214.7107	270.0243
35	186.1021	235.1247	298.1268
36	202.0703	257.3759	329.0394
37	219.3159	281.6297	363.0434
38	237.9412	308.0664	400.4477
39	258.0565	336.8824	441.5925
40	279.7810	368.2918	486.8518
41	303.2435	402.5281	536.6369
42	328.5830	439.8456	591.4006
43	355.9496	480.5217	651.6407
44	385.5056	524.8587	717.9048
45	417.4260	573.1860	790.7953
46	451.9001	625.8627	870.9748
47	489.1321	683.2804	959.1723
48	529.3427	745.8656	1056.1895
49	572.7701	814.0835	1162.9085
50	619.6717	888.4410	1280.2993

C.11	C.12	0.13	0.14
1. 1100	1.1200	1. 1300	1.1400
2. 3420	2.3743	2.4068	2.4395
3. 7097	3.7793	3.8497	3.9211
5. 2278	5.3528	5. 4802	5.6101
6.9128	7.1151	7.3227	7.5355
8. 7832	9.C890	9.4046	9.7304
10. 8594	11.2996	11. 7572	12.2327
13.1639	13.7756	14.4157	15.0853
15. 7220	16.5487	17.4197	18.3372
18.5614	19.6545	20.8143	22.0445
21. 7131	23.1331	24.6501	26.2707
25.2116	27.0291	28.9847	31.0886
29.C949	31.3926	33.8827	36.5810
33.4C53	36.2797	39.4174	42.8424
38.1899	41.7532	45.6717	49.9803
43.5008	47.8836	52.7390	58.1176
49.3559	54.7497	60.7251	67.3940
55.9394	62.4396	69.7494	77.9692
63.2C28	71.0524	79.9468	90.0249
71.2651	8C.6987	91.4699	103.7684
80.2143	91.5025	104.4910	119.4359
90.1478	103.6C28	119.2048	137.2970
101.1741	117.1552	135.8314	157.6586
113.4133	132.3338	154.6195	180.8708
126.9987	149.3339	175.8500	207.3327
142.C786	168.3740	199.8406	237.4993
158.8172	189.6988	226.9498	271.8892
177.3971	213.5827	257.5833	311.0937
198.02C8	240.3326	292.1992	355.7868
220.9131	27C.2926	331.3151	406.7370
246.3236	303.8477	375.5160	464.8201
274.5292	341.4294	425.4631	531.0350
305.8374	383.5209	481.9033	606.5199
340.5895	430.6634	545.68C8	692.5727
379.1644	483.4631	617.7493	790.6728
421.9824	542.5986	699.1867	902.5070
469.5105	608.8305	791.2110	1029.9980
522.2667	683.0101	895.1984	1175.3378
580.8260	766.0914	1012.7042	1341.0250
645.8269	859.1423	1145.4857	1529.9086
717.9778	963.3594	1295.5289	1745.2358
798.C654	1C80.0826	1465.C777	1990.7088
886.9626	1210.8125	1656.6678	2270.5480
985.6385	1357.2300	1873.1646	2589.5647
1095.1688	1521.2176	2117.8060	2953.2438
1216.7473	1704.8837	2394.2508	3367.8380
1351.6995	1910.5898	2706.6334	3840.4753
1501.4965	2140.9805	3059.6257	4379.2818
1667.7711	2399.0182	3458.5071	4993.5213
1852.3359	2688.0204	3909.2430	5693.7543

COMPOUND VALUE OF ANNUITY

PERIOD	C.15	0.16	0.17
1	1.1500	1.1600	1.1700
2	2.4724	2.5C55	2.5388
3	3.9933	4.0664	4.1405
4	5.7423	5.8771	6.0144
5	7.7537	7.9774	8.2C68
6	10.C667	10.4138	1C.7720
7	12.7268	13.2400	13.7732
8	15.7E58	16.5185	17.2E47
9	19.3037	20.3214	21.3931
10	23.3492	24.7329	26.1999
11	28.C016	29.8501	31.8239
12	33.3519	35.7861	38.4039
13	39.5C47	42.6719	46.1026
14	46.5804	50.6595	55.1101
15	54.7174	59.9250	65.6488
16	64.C750	70.6730	77.9791
17	74.E363	83.1407	92.4056
18	87.2118	97.6C32	1C9.2845
19	101.4435	114.3797	129.0329
20	117.E1C1	133.8405	152.1385
21	136.6316	156.4149	179.1720
22	158.2763	182.6013	210.8013
23	183.1678	212.9776	247.8C75
24	211.7930	248.2140	291.1C48
25	244.7119	289.C882	341.7626
26	2E2.5687	336.5C23	401.0323
27	326.1040	391.5027	470.3778
28	376.1696	455.3032	551.5120
29	433.7451	529.3117	646.4391
30	499.9569	615.1616	757.5C37
31	576.1004	714.7474	887.4494
32	663.6655	830.2670	1039.4E58
33	764.3653	964.2697	1217.3683
34	880.1701	1119.7129	1425.4910
35	1013.3456	1300.027C	1668.9944
36	1166.4975	1509.1913	1953.8935
37	1342.6221	1751.8219	2287.2254
38	1545.1654	2033.2734	2677.2237
39	1778.C9C3	2359.7572	3133.5218
40	2045.9538	2738.4783	3667.39C5
41	2353.9969	3177.7949	4292.0169
42	27C8.2464	36E7.4021	5022.8298
43	3115.6334	4278.5464	5877.8808
44	3584.1284	4964.2739	6878.2906
45	4122.8977	5759.7177	EC48.7700
46	4742.4823	6682.4325	9418.2309
47	5455.CC47	7752.7817	1102C.5002
48	6274.4054	8994.3E68	12895.1552
49	7216.7162	10434.6487	15088.5016
50	830C.3737	12105.3525	17654.7169

0.18	0.19	0.20	0.21
1.1800	1.1900	1.2000	1.2100
2.5723	2.6060	2.6400	2.6740
4.2154	4.2912	4.3679	4.4456
6.1542	6.2965	6.4415	6.5892
8.4419	8.6829	8.9299	9.1829
11.1415	11.5227	11.9159	12.3214
14.3269	14.9020	15.4990	16.1189
18.0858	18.9234	19.7989	20.7138
22.5213	23.7088	24.9586	26.2738
27.7551	29.4035	31.1504	33.0013
33.9310	36.1802	38.5805	41.1415
41.2186	44.2444	47.4966	50.9913
49.8180	53.8409	58.1959	62.9094
59.9652	65.2606	71.0351	77.3304
71.9390	78.8502	86.4421	94.7798
86.0680	95.0217	104.9305	115.8936
102.7402	114.2658	127.1166	141.4413
122.4135	137.1664	153.7399	172.3540
145.6279	164.4180	185.6879	209.7583
173.0210	196.8474	224.0255	255.0176
205.3447	235.4384	270.0307	309.7813
243.4868	281.3617	325.2368	376.0453
288.4944	336.0104	391.4842	456.2249
341.6034	401.0424	470.9810	553.2421
404.2721	478.4305	566.3772	670.6330
478.2210	570.5223	680.8527	812.6759
565.4808	680.1116	818.2233	984.5478
668.4474	810.5228	983.0679	1192.5129
789.9479	965.7121	1180.8815	1444.1506
933.3186	1150.3874	1418.2578	1748.6323
1102.4959	1370.1511	1703.1094	2117.0550
1302.1252	1631.6698	2044.9313	2562.8466
1537.6878	1942.8770	2455.1176	3102.2544
1815.6516	2313.2137	2947.3411	3754.9378
2143.6489	2753.9143	3538.0093	4544.6848
2530.6857	3278.3480	4246.8112	5500.2786
2987.3891	3902.4241	5097.3734	6656.5471
3526.2991	4645.0747	6118.0481	8055.6320
4162.2130	5528.8289	7342.8578	9748.5248
4912.5913	6580.4964	8812.6294	11796.9250
5798.0378	7831.9808	10576.3552	14275.4893
6842.8646	9321.2471	12692.8263	17274.5520
8075.7602	11093.4741	15232.5916	20903.4179
9530.5771	13202.4242	18280.3099	25294.3457
11247.2609	15712.0748	21937.5719	30607.3683
13272.9479	18698.5590	26326.2863	37036.1257
15663.2585	22252.4752	31592.7435	44814.9221
18483.8251	26481.6355	37912.4922	54227.2658
21812.0936	31514.3363	45496.1907	65616.2016
25739.4505	37503.2502	54596.6289	79396.8139

COMPOUND VALUE OF ANNUITY

PERIOD	C.22	0.23	0.24
1	1.2200	1.2300	1.2400
2	2.7083	2.7428	2.7775
3	4.5242	4.6037	4.6842
4	6.7395	6.8926	7.0484
5	9.4422	9.7079	9.9800
6	12.7395	13.1707	13.6152
7	16.7623	17.4300	18.1229
8	21.6700	22.6689	23.7124
9	27.6574	29.1128	30.6434
10	34.9620	37.0387	39.2378
11	43.8736	46.7876	49.8949
12	54.7459	58.7788	63.1097
13	68.0100	73.5279	79.4960
14	84.1922	91.6693	99.8151
15	103.9345	113.9833	125.0107
16	128.0200	141.4295	156.2533
17	157.4045	175.1883	194.9941
18	193.2535	216.7116	243.0327
19	236.9892	267.7853	302.6006
20	290.3469	330.6059	376.4647
21	355.4432	407.8752	468.0563
22	434.8607	502.9166	581.6298
23	531.7501	619.8174	722.4609
24	649.9551	763.6054	897.0916
25	794.1652	940.4647	1113.6336
26	970.1016	1158.0015	1382.1457
27	1184.7439	1425.5719	1715.1006
28	1446.6076	1754.6834	2127.9648
29	1766.0813	2159.4906	2639.9163
30	2155.8392	2657.4035	3274.7363
31	2631.3438	3269.8363	4061.9130
32	3211.4595	4023.1287	5038.0121
33	3919.2006	4949.6783	6248.3750
34	4782.6447	6089.3343	7749.2251
35	5836.0465	7491.1112	9610.2791
36	7121.1568	9215.2968	11917.9861
37	8689.0801	11336.0451	14779.5427
38	10601.8977	13944.5655	18327.8730
39	12935.5352	17153.0455	22727.8025
40	15782.5730	21099.4760	28183.7152
41	19255.9590	25953.5855	34949.0468
42	23493.4900	31924.1402	43338.0581
43	28663.2779	39267.9225	53740.4320
44	34970.4190	48300.7747	66639.3757
45	42665.1312	59411.1829	82634.0659
46	52052.6801	73076.9849	102467.4817
47	63505.4897	89885.9215	127060.9174
48	77477.9174	110560.9134	157556.7776
49	94524.2793	135991.1535	195371.6442
50	115320.8407	167270.3488	242262.0788

0.25	0.26	C.27	0.28
1.2500	1.2600	1.2700	1.2800
2.8125	2.8475	2.8828	2.9183
4.7656	4.8479	4.9312	5.0155
7.2070	7.3684	7.5327	7.6999
1C.2587	10.5442	10.8365	11.1358
14.C734	14.5457	15.0324	15.5339
18.8418	19.5876	20.3611	21.1634
24.8C23	25.9404	27.1287	28.3691
32.2529	33.9449	35.7234	37.5925
41.5661	44.0306	46.6388	49.3984
53.2C76	56.7385	60.5012	64.5100
67.7595	72.7506	78.1066	83.8528
85.9494	92.9257	100.4654	108.6116
1C8.6868	118.3465	128.8611	140.3029
137.1085	150.3765	164.9236	180.8677
172.6356	190.7345	210.7229	232.7907
217.C446	241.5854	268.8881	299.2521
272.5557	305.6577	342.7579	384.3227
341.9446	386.3887	436.5726	493.2130
428.68C8	488.1097	555.7172	632.5927
537.101)	616.2783	707.0309	810.9986
672.6263	777.7706	899.1992	1039.3583
842.0329	981.2510	1143.2530	1331.6586
1C53.7911	1237.6363	1453.2014	1705.8)30
1318.4889	1560.6817	1846.8357	2184.7079
1649.3612	1967.719)	2346.7514	2797.7C61
2062.5515	2480.5860	2981.6443	3582.3438
2579.9394	3126.7983	3787.9583	4586.6801
3226.1742	3941.0259	4811.9770	5872.2305
4033.9678	4966.9527	6112.4808	7517.7351
5043.7097	6259.62)4	7764.1207	9623.9809
63C5.8872	7888.3817	9861.7033	12319.9756
7883.6090	9940.6209	12525.6332	15770.8487
5855.7613	12526.4424	15908.8241	2C187.9664
12320.9516	15784.5774	20205.4767	25841.8770
15402.4395	19889.8275	25662.2254	33078.8826
19254.2994	25062.4427	32592.2962	42342.2497
24069.1243	31579.9378	41393.4862	54199.3597
30087.6553	39791.9817	52570.9975	69376.4604
3761C.8192	5C139.1569	66766.4368	88803.1493
47014.7740	63176.5977	84794.6448	113669.3111
58769.7175	79603.7732	107690.4689	145497.9983
734€3.3969	10C302.0142	136768.1655	186238.7178
91830.4961	126381.7979	173596.8403	238386.8388
114789.3701	159242.3254	220596.2571	305136.4337
143487.9627	20C646.5900	280158.5166	390575.9151
179361.2034	252815.9634	355802.5861	499938.4513
224202.7542	318549.3739	451870.5543	639922.4)77
280254.6928	401373.4711	573876.8740	819102.C771
350319.6160	505731.8336	728824.9000	1048451.9387

CCMPOUND VALLE CF ANNLITY

PERIOD	C.29	0.30	0.35
1	1.2900	1.3000	1.3500
2	2.9540	2.9900	3.1724
3	5.1CC7	5.1869	5.6328
4	7.87C0	8.0430	8.9543
5	11.4423	11.7560	13.4384
6	16.C5C5	16.5828	19.4918
7	21.9552	22.8576	27.6640
8	29.6638	31.0149	38.6964
9	39.5564	41.6194	53.5901
10	52.3177	55.4C53	73.6567
11	68.7799	73.3269	100.8405
12	90.C161	96.6250	137.4847
13	117.4108	126.9125	186.9544
14	152.7499	166.2863	253.7384
15	198.3374	217.4722	343.8969
16	257.1453	284.0138	465.61C8
17	333.CC74	370.5180	629.9246
18	430.8655	482.9734	851.7483
19	557.1117	629.1654	1151.2102
20	719.9641	819.2150	1555.4838
21	930.C438	1066.2796	21C1.2531
22	1201.0465	1387.4635	2838.0418
23	1550.6400	18C5.CC25	3832.7C64
24	2001.6156	2347.8033	5175.5036
25	2583.3741	3053.4443	6988.2799
26	3333.8426	3970.7776	9435.5279
27	4301.9470	5163.3109	12739.3127
28	5550.8C16	6713.6042	17199.4222
29	7161.8241	8728.9854	23220.5700
30	9240.0430	11348.9811	31349.1195
31	11920.9455	14754.9754	42322.6613
32	15379.3098	19182.7680	57136.9427
33	19840.5996	24938.8985	77136.2227
34	25595.6635	32421.8680	104135.2507
35	33019.6959	42149.7285	140583.9385
36	42596.6978	54795.9470	189789.6669
37	54951.C302	71236.0311	256217.40C4
38	7C888.1189	92608.1405	345894.8405
39	91446.9634	120351.8826	466959.3848
40	117967.8728	156510.7475	630356.5194
41	152179.8459	203465.2717	851036.6512
42	196313.2913	264506.1532	1148900.8292
43	253245.4358	343859.2992	1551017.4694
44	326687.9C22	447C18.3890	2093874.9338
45	421428.6838	581125.2057	2826732.51C6
46	543644.2921	755464.0674	3816090.2393
47	701302.4268	982104.5877	5151723.1731
48	904681.4206	1276737.2640	6954827.6337
49	1167040.3226	1659759.7432	9389C18.6555
50	1505483.3C62	2157688.9662	12675176.5350

0.40	0.45	0.50	0.60
1.4000	1.4500	1.5000	1.6000
3.3600	3.5524	3.7500	4.1600
6.1039	6.6011	7.1250	8.2560
9.9455	11.0216	12.1875	14.8095
15.3238	17.4313	19.7812	25.2953
22.8533	26.7254	31.1718	42.0725
33.3947	40.2019	48.2578	68.9161
48.1526	59.7428	73.8867	111.8657
68.8136	88.0770	112.3300	180.5852
97.7391	129.1617	169.9951	290.5364
138.2347	188.7345	256.4926	466.4582
194.9286	275.1151	386.2390	747.9332
274.3001	400.3669	580.8585	1198.2932
385.4202	581.9820	872.7877	1918.8691
540.9883	845.3240	1310.6816	3071.7906
758.7836	1227.1698	1967.5225	4916.4650
1063.6971	1780.8462	2952.7837	7867.9441
1490.5759	2583.6771	4430.6756	12590.3106
2088.2063	3747.7818	6647.5134	20146.0969
2924.8389	5435.7336	9972.7701	32235.3551
4096.2445	7883.2637	14960.6552	51578.1583
5736.1423	11432.1824	22442.4829	82526.6692
8031.9992	16578.1145	33665.2243	132044.2708
11246.1989	24039.7160	50499.3365	211272.4333
15746.0785	34859.0383	75750.5048	338037.4933
22045.9099	50547.0555	113627.2573	540861.5894
30865.6739	73294.6805	170442.3859	865380.1430
43213.3434	106278.7368	255665.0789	1384609.8289
60500.0808	154105.6184	383499.1184	2215377.3263
84701.5132	223454.5967	575250.1776	3544605.3220
118583.5185	324010.6152	862876.7665	5671370.1153
166018.3259	469816.8420	1294316.6498	9074193.7845
232427.0563	681235.8710	1941476.4747	14518711.6552
325359.2788	987793.4629	2912216.2120	23229940.2484
455560.3904	1432301.9713	4368325.8181	37167905.9975
637785.9466	2076839.3084	6552490.2272	59468651.1560
892901.7252	3011418.4472	9828736.8408	95149843.5137
1250063.8153	4366558.1984	14743106.7612	152239751.2219
1750090.7414	6331510.8378	22114661.6418	243583603.5551
2450128.4380	9180692.1648	33171993.9628	389733767.2882
3430181.2132	13312005.0889	49757992.4442	623574029.2611
4802255.0986	19302408.8290	74636990.1663	997718448.4178
6723158.5380	27988494.2520	111955486.7495	1596349519.0686
9412423.3532	40583318.1155	167933231.6242	2554159232.1098
13177394.0949	58845812.7175	251899848.9364	4086654772.9756
18448353.1324	85326429.8903	377849774.9046	6538647638.3610
25827695.7854	123723324.7910	566774663.8569	10461836222.9777
36158775.4999	179398822.3970	850161997.2853	16738937958.3643
50622287.0994	260128293.9256	1275242997.4280	26782300734.9829
70871203.3391	377186027.6422	1912864497.6421	42851681177.5727

Table C.3
PRESENT VALUE OF $1 RECEIVED N PERIODS HENCE

PERIOD	0.01	0.02	0.03	0.04	0.05	0.0€
1	0.990099	C.980392	0.970873	0.961538	0.952380	0.94339€
2	0.980296	C.961168	0.942595	0.924556	0.907029	0.88999€
3	C.970590	0.942322	0.915141	C.888996	C.863837	0.83961˙
4	C.960980	0.923845	0.888487	0.854804	C.822702	C.792C9.
5	0.951465	0.905730	0.862608	0.821927	0.783526	0.74725█
6	0.942045	0.887971	0.837484	C.790314	C.746215	C.7C496˙
7	0.932718	C.870560	0.813091	0.759917	0.710681	0.665C5
8	0.923483	0.853490	0.789409	C.730650	C.676839	0.62741.
9	0.914339	0.836755	0.766416	0.702586	C.644608	0.559189█
10	C.905286	C.820348	0.744093	C.675564	C.613913	0.55839█
11	C.896323	0.804263	0.722421	0.649580	0.584679	0.52678
12	C.887449	0.788493	0.701379	0.624597	0.556837	0.49696
13	0.878662	C.773032	0.680951	0.600574	0.530321	0.46883˙
14	0.869962	0.757875	0.661117	0.577475	C.505067	C.44230█
15	C.861349	0.743014	0.641861	0.555264	0.481017	0.41726
16	0.852821	C.728445	0.623166	C.533908	C.458111	0.39364
17	0.844377	C.714162	0.605016	C.513373	0.436296	0.37136
18	C.836017	C.700159	0.587394	C.493628	0.415520	0.35034
19	0.827739	C.686430	0.570286	0.474642	C.395733	C.33051
20	0.819544	C.672971	0.553675	0.456386	0.376889	0.31180
21	C.811430	C.659775	0.537549	0.438833	0.358942	0.29415
22	0.803396	0.646839	0.521892	0.421955	C.341849	C.27750
23	0.795441	C.634155	0.506691	0.405726	C.325571	0.26179
24	0.787566	C.621721	0.491933	C.390121	C.310067	0.24697
25	C.779768	0.609530	0.477605	0.375116	C.295302	0.23299
26	C.772047	0.597579	0.463694	0.360689	0.281240	0.21981
27	C.764403	0.585862	0.450189	0.346816	C.267848	0.20736
28	C.756835	0.574374	0.437076	0.333477	0.255093	0.19563█
29	0.749342	0.563112	0.424346	0.320651	0.242946	0.18455█
30	0.741922	0.552070	0.411986	0.308318	0.231377	0.17411
31	0.734577	C.541245	0.399987	C.296460	0.220359	0.16425█
32	0.727304	C.530633	0.388337	0.285057	C.209866	0.15495
33	0.720103	C.520228	0.377026	C.274094	0.199872	0.14618
34	0.712973	C.510028	0.366044	0.263552	C.190354	0.13791
35	0.705914	C.500027	0.355383	0.253415	0.181290	C.13010
36	0.698924	0.490223	0.345032	0.243668	0.172657	0.12274
37	C.692004	C.480610	0.334982	C.234296	0.164435	0.11579
38	0.685153	0.471187	0.325226	0.225285	0.156605	0.10923
39	C.678369	0.461948	0.315753	C.216620	0.149147	0.10305
40	0.671653	0.452890	0.306556	C.208289	C.142045	0.09722
41	0.665003	C.444010	0.297628	C.200277	0.135281	0.09171
42	C.658418	C.435304	0.288959	0.192574	0.128839	0.08652
43	C.651899	C.426768	0.280542	C.185168	C.122704	0.08162
44	0.645445	C.418400	0.272371	0.178046	0.116861	0.07700
45	0.639054	C.410196	0.264438	C.171198	C.111296	0.07265
46	0.632727	C.402153	0.256736	0.164613	0.105996	0.06853
47	C.626463	0.394268	0.249258	0.158282	0.100949	0.06465
48	0.620260	0.386537	0.241998	0.152194	C.096142	0.06099
49	0.614119	0.378958	0.234950	0.146341	0.091563	0.05754
50	0.608038	C.371527	0.228107	0.140712	0.087203	0.05428

0.07	0.08	0.09	0.10	0.11	0.12
0.934579	0.925925	0.917431	0.909090	0.900900	0.892857
0.873438	0.857338	0.841679	0.826446	0.811622	0.797193
0.816297	0.793832	0.772183	0.751314	0.731191	0.711780
0.762895	0.735029	0.708425	0.683013	0.658730	0.635518
0.712986	0.680583	0.649931	0.620921	0.593451	0.567426
0.666342	0.630169	0.596267	0.564473	0.534640	0.506631
0.622749	0.583490	0.547034	0.513158	0.481658	0.452349
0.582009	0.540268	0.501866	0.466507	0.433926	0.403883
0.543933	0.500248	0.460427	0.424097	0.390924	0.360610
0.508349	0.463193	0.422410	0.385543	0.352184	0.321973
0.475092	0.428882	0.387532	0.350493	0.317283	0.287476
0.444011	0.397113	0.355534	0.318630	0.285840	0.256675
0.414964	0.367697	0.326178	0.289664	0.257514	0.229174
0.387817	0.340461	0.299246	0.263331	0.231994	0.204619
0.362446	0.315241	0.274538	0.239392	0.209004	0.182696
0.338734	0.291890	0.251869	0.217629	0.188292	0.163121
0.316574	0.270268	0.231073	0.197844	0.169632	0.145644
0.295863	0.250249	0.211993	0.179858	0.152822	0.130039
0.276508	0.231712	0.194489	0.163507	0.137677	0.116106
0.258419	0.214548	0.178430	0.148643	0.124033	0.103666
0.241513	0.198655	0.163698	0.135130	0.111742	0.092559
0.225713	0.183940	0.150181	0.122845	0.100668	0.082642
0.210946	0.170315	0.137781	0.111678	0.090692	0.073787
0.197146	0.157699	0.126404	0.101525	0.081704	0.065882
0.184249	0.146017	0.115967	0.092295	0.073608	0.058823
0.172195	0.135201	0.106392	0.083905	0.066313	0.052520
0.160930	0.125186	0.097607	0.076277	0.059741	0.046893
0.150402	0.115913	0.089548	0.069343	0.053821	0.041869
0.140562	0.107327	0.082154	0.063039	0.048487	0.037383
0.131367	0.099377	0.075371	0.057308	0.043682	0.033377
0.122773	0.092016	0.069147	0.052098	0.039353	0.029801
0.114741	0.085200	0.063438	0.047362	0.035453	0.026608
0.107234	0.078888	0.058200	0.043056	0.031940	0.023757
0.100219	0.073045	0.053394	0.039142	0.028775	0.021212
0.093662	0.067634	0.048986	0.035584	0.025923	0.018939
0.087535	0.062624	0.044941	0.032349	0.023354	0.016910
0.081808	0.057985	0.041230	0.029408	0.021040	0.015098
0.076456	0.053690	0.037826	0.026734	0.018955	0.013480
0.071455	0.049713	0.034702	0.024304	0.017076	0.012036
0.066780	0.046030	0.031837	0.022094	0.015384	0.010746
0.062411	0.042621	0.029208	0.020086	0.013859	0.009595
0.058328	0.039464	0.026797	0.018260	0.012486	0.008567
0.054512	0.036540	0.024584	0.016600	0.011248	0.007649
0.050946	0.033834	0.022554	0.015091	0.010134	0.006829
0.047613	0.031327	0.020692	0.013719	0.009129	0.006098
0.044498	0.029007	0.018983	0.012472	0.008225	0.005444
0.041587	0.026858	0.017416	0.011338	0.007410	0.004861
0.038866	0.024869	0.015978	0.010307	0.006675	0.004340
0.036324	0.023026	0.014658	0.009370	0.006014	0.003875
0.033947	0.021321	0.013448	0.008518	0.005418	0.003460

PRESENT VALUE OF $1

PERIOD	0.13	0.14	0.15	0.16	0.17	0.18
1	0.8E4955	C.E77192	0.869565	0.862C68	C.854700	0.847457
2	C.783146	C.769467	0.756143	0.743162	0.730513	C.718184
3	0.693050	C.674971	0.657516	C.640657	C.624370	0.6C663C
4	C.613318	C.592C80	0.571753	0.552291	0.533650	0.515788
5	0.542759	C.519368	0.497176	C.476113	C.456111	0.437109
6	C.480318	0.455586	0.432327	0.410442	C.389838	C.37043
7	0.42506C	C.399637	0.375937	C.353829	C.333195	0.313925
8	0.376159	C.350559	0.326901	C.305025	0.284782	C.266038
9	C.332884	0.3C7507	0.284262	0.262992	0.243403	0.225456
10	0.294588	C.269743	0.247184	0.226683	0.2C8037	0.191C64
11	0.26C697	0.236617	0.214943	0.195416	C.177809	C.161919
12	C.230705	C.2C7559	0.186907	0.168462	0.151974	0.137219
13	0.204164	0.182069	0.162527	C.145226	C.129892	0.116287
14	C.18C676	0.159709	0.141328	0.125195	0.111019	0.098548
15	C.159890	C.14CC96	0.122894	0.1C7927	0.C94888	0.C8351C
16	0.141496	0.122891	0.1C6864	C.C9304C	C.081101	C.C7C776
17	C.125217	C.1C7799	0.092925	0.0802C7	C.069317	C.C5997*
18	C.110812	C.C94561	0.C8C8C5	0.069144	0.C59245	0.C5C839
19	C.C98C63	0.C82948	0.C7C265	0.C556C7	C.C5C637	C.C4307*
20	C.C86782	0.C72761	0.061100	0.051385	0.043279	0.03650!
21	0.C76798	0.C63826	0.053130	0.044297	C.C36991	0.C3C936
22	0.C67963	0.055987	0.046200	0.038187	0.031616	0.C2621
23	C.C6C144	C.C49112	0.04C174	0.032920	0.027022	0.02221!
24	0.053225	C.C43080	0.034934	0.028379	0.023096	C.C1882
25	0.C47101	0.C37790	0.03C377	0.024465	0.019740	C.C1599
26	0.C41683	0.C33149	0.C26415	0.021090	0.016872	0.01352;
27	0.C36887	C.C29C78	0.022969	0.C18181	0.014420	0.01146*
28	C.032644	0.C2550C	0.C19973	0.015673	0.012325	0.0C971
29	0.028888	C.022374	0.C17368	C.013911	0.01C534	C.0C823*
30	0.025565	0.C19627	0.015103	0.011648	C.CC9C03	C.0C697*
31	C.022623	0.C17216	0.013133	0.01C041	0.CC7695	0.0C591*
32	C.020021	0.C15102	0.011420	0.0C8656	0.006577	C.CC5CC
33	0.017717	0.C13247	0.CC9930	0.007462	0.005621	0.00424
34	0.C15679	0.C11620	0.0C8635	0.006433	0.004804	0.00359
35	0.C13875	C.010193	0.CC75C8	0.005545	C.004106	0.CC3C4
36	0.012279	C.CC8941	0.006529	0.004780	0.003510	0.0C258
37	0.01C866	C.CC7843	0.CC5677	0.0C4121	C.CC3C00	0.00218
38	0.CC9616	0.0C6880	0.C4937	0.003553	0.002564	0.00185
39	0.008510	C.CC6C35	0.CC4293	0.003C62	0.002191	0.00157
40	0.0C7531	C.CC5294	0.0C3733	0.CC264C	0.CC1873	0.00133
41	C.CC6664	0.CC4644	0.0C3246	0.002276	0.0C1600	0.00112
42	C.CC5898	C.CC4C73	0.CC2822	0.0C1962	0.001368	0.CCC95
43	0.005219	0.C03573	0.002454	0.0C1691	0.001169	0.CCC81
44	0.CC4619	0.CC3134	0.002134	0.0C1458	0.000999	0.0CC68
45	0.C04087	0.002749	0.0C1856	0.001257	C.CCC854	0.0CC58
46	C.0C3617	0.C02411	0.CC1613	0.001C83	C.CCC730	0.0CC49
47	C.CC3201	C.C02115	0.CC1403	C.CCC934	0.000624	0.0CC41
48	0.002832	0.CC1855	0.001220	0.0C0805	0.0CC533	C.0CC35
49	0.CC25C7	C.CC1628	0.001061	0.0CC694	0.000455	0.0CC30
50	0.002218	C.CC1428	0.CCC922	0.0CC598	0.000389	0.00C25

0.19	0.20	0.21	0.22	0.23	0.24
0.840336	0.833333	0.826446	0.819672	0.813008	0.806451
0.706164	0.694444	0.683013	0.671862	0.660982	0.650364
0.593415	0.578703	0.564473	0.550706	0.537383	0.524487
0.498668	0.482253	0.466507	0.451399	0.436897	0.422973
0.419049	0.401877	0.385543	0.369999	0.355201	0.341107
0.352142	0.334897	0.318630	0.303278	0.288781	0.275086
0.295917	0.279081	0.263331	0.248588	0.234781	0.221844
0.248670	0.232568	0.217629	0.203761	0.190879	0.178906
0.208966	0.193806	0.179858	0.167017	0.155186	0.144279
0.175602	0.161505	0.148643	0.136899	0.126167	0.116354
0.147565	0.134587	0.122845	0.112212	0.102575	0.093834
0.124004	0.112156	0.101525	0.091977	0.083394	0.075672
0.104205	0.093463	0.083905	0.075391	0.067800	0.061026
0.087567	0.077886	0.069343	0.061796	0.055122	0.049214
0.073586	0.064905	0.057308	0.050652	0.044814	0.039689
0.061837	0.054087	0.047362	0.041518	0.036434	0.032007
0.051963	0.045073	0.039142	0.034031	0.029621	0.025812
0.043667	0.037561	0.032349	0.027894	0.024082	0.020816
0.036695	0.031300	0.026734	0.022864	0.019579	0.016787
0.030836	0.026084	0.022094	0.018741	0.015918	0.013538
0.025912	0.021736	0.018260	0.015361	0.012941	0.010918
0.021775	0.018113	0.015091	0.012591	0.010521	0.008804
0.018298	0.015094	0.012472	0.010321	0.008554	0.007100
0.015377	0.012579	0.010307	0.008459	0.006954	0.005726
0.012921	0.010482	0.008518	0.006934	0.005654	0.004618
0.010858	0.008735	0.007040	0.005683	0.004596	0.003724
0.009124	0.007279	0.005818	0.004658	0.003737	0.003003
0.007668	0.006066	0.004808	0.003813	0.003038	0.002422
0.006443	0.005055	0.003973	0.003130	0.002470	0.001953
0.005414	0.004212	0.003284	0.002565	0.002008	0.001575
0.004550	0.003510	0.002714	0.002103	0.001632	0.001270
0.003823	0.002925	0.002243	0.001723	0.001327	0.001024
0.003213	0.002437	0.001853	0.001412	0.001079	0.000826
0.002700	0.002031	0.001532	0.001158	0.000877	0.000666
0.002269	0.001692	0.001266	0.000949	0.000713	0.000537
0.001906	0.001410	0.001046	0.000778	0.000579	0.000433
0.001602	0.001175	0.000864	0.000637	0.000471	0.000349
0.001346	0.000979	0.000714	0.000522	0.000383	0.000281
0.001131	0.000816	0.000590	0.000428	0.000311	0.000227
0.000950	0.000680	0.000488	0.000351	0.000253	0.000183
0.000799	0.000566	0.000403	0.000287	0.000206	0.000147
0.000671	0.000472	0.000333	0.000235	0.000167	0.000119
0.000564	0.000393	0.000275	0.000193	0.000136	0.000096
0.000474	0.000328	0.000227	0.000158	0.000110	0.000077
0.000398	0.000273	0.000188	0.000129	0.000090	0.000062
0.000334	0.000227	0.000155	0.000106	0.000073	0.000050
0.000281	0.000189	0.000128	0.000087	0.000059	0.000040
0.000236	0.000158	0.000106	0.000071	0.000048	0.000032
0.000198	0.000131	0.000087	0.000058	0.000039	0.000026
0.000166	0.000109	0.000072	0.000048	0.000031	0.000021

PRESENT VALUE OF $1

PERIOD	C.25	C.26	C.27	0.28	0.29
1	0.800000	C.793650	0.787401	0.781250	0.775193
2	0.640000	C.629881	0.620001	0.610351	0.600925
3	0.512000	C.499906	0.488189	0.476837	C.465833
4	0.409600	C.396750	0.384401	0.372529	C.361111
5	0.327680	0.314881	0.302678	0.291038	C.279931
6	0.262144	C.249906	0.238329	0.227373	0.217001
7	0.209715	C.198338	0.187660	0.177635	0.168217
8	0.167772	0.157411	0.147764	0.138777	C.130401
9	C.134217	0.124929	0.116350	0.108420	C.101086
10	0.107374	0.099150	0.091614	0.084703	C.078361
11	0.085899	C.078690	0.072137	0.066174	C.060745
12	C.068719	C.062453	0.056800	0.051658	0.047089
13	0.054975	0.049565	0.044725	C.040389	C.036503
14	0.043980	0.039338	0.035216	0.031554	0.028297
15	C.035184	0.031220	0.027729	0.024651	0.021935
16	0.028147	0.024778	0.021834	0.019259	0.017004
17	0.022517	0.019665	0.017192	0.015046	0.013181
18	0.018014	C.015607	0.013537	0.011754	0.010218
19	0.014411	0.012386	0.010659	0.009183	0.007921
20	0.011529	C.009830	0.008393	0.007174	0.006140
21	0.009223	0.007802	0.006608	0.005605	0.004760
22	0.007378	0.006192	0.005203	0.004379	0.003690
23	0.005902	C.004914	0.004097	0.003421	0.002860
24	0.004722	0.003900	0.003226	0.002672	0.002217
25	0.003777	C.003095	0.002540	0.002088	0.001718
26	0.003022	0.002456	0.002000	0.001631	0.001332
27	0.002417	0.001949	0.001575	0.001274	0.001032
28	0.001934	0.001547	0.001240	0.000995	0.000800
29	0.001547	0.001228	0.000976	0.000777	0.000620
30	0.001237	C.000974	0.000768	0.000607	0.000481
31	C.000990	C.000773	0.000605	0.000474	0.000373
32	0.000792	C.000613	0.000476	0.000370	0.000289
33	C.000633	0.000487	0.000375	0.000289	0.000224
34	0.000507	C.000386	0.000295	0.000226	C.000173
35	0.000405	0.000306	0.000232	0.000176	C.000134
36	0.000324	0.000243	0.000183	0.000138	0.000104
37	0.000259	C.000193	0.000144	0.000107	0.000080
38	0.000207	C.000153	0.000113	0.000084	0.000062
39	C.000166	C.000121	0.000089	0.000065	0.000048
40	0.000132	0.000096	0.000070	0.000051	0.000037
41	0.000106	C.000076	0.000055	0.000040	0.000029
42	0.000085	C.000060	0.000043	0.000031	0.000022
43	0.000068	C.000048	0.000034	0.000024	0.000017
44	C.000054	C.000038	0.000027	0.000019	0.000013
45	0.000043	0.000030	0.000021	0.000014	0.000010
46	0.000034	C.000024	0.000016	0.000011	0.000008
47	0.000027	C.000019	0.000013	0.000009	0.000006
48	0.000022	0.000015	0.000010	0.000007	0.000004
49	0.000017	0.000012	0.000008	0.000005	0.000003
50	0.000014	C.000009	0.000006	0.000004	0.000002

0.30	0.35	0.40	0.45	0.50	0.60
0.769230	0.740740	0.714285	0.689655	0.666666	0.625000
0.591715	0.548696	0.510204	0.475624	0.444444	0.390625
0.455166	0.406442	0.364431	0.328016	0.296296	0.244140
0.350127	0.301068	0.260308	0.226218	0.197530	0.152587
0.269329	0.223013	0.185934	0.156012	0.131687	0.095367
0.207176	0.165195	0.132810	0.107594	0.087791	0.059604
0.159366	0.122366	0.094864	0.074203	0.058527	0.037252
0.122589	0.090642	0.067760	0.051174	0.039018	0.023283
0.094299	0.067142	0.048400	0.035292	0.026012	0.014551
0.072538	0.049735	0.034571	0.024339	0.017341	0.009094
0.055798	0.036840	0.024694	0.016786	0.011561	0.005684
0.042921	0.027289	0.017638	0.011576	0.007707	0.003552
0.033016	0.020214	0.012598	0.007983	0.005138	0.002220
0.025397	0.014973	0.008999	0.005506	0.003425	0.001387
0.019536	0.011091	0.006428	0.003797	0.002283	0.000867
0.015028	0.008215	0.004591	0.002618	0.001522	0.000542
0.011560	0.006085	0.003279	0.001806	0.001014	0.000338
0.008892	0.004508	0.002342	0.001245	0.000676	0.000211
0.006840	0.003339	0.001673	0.000859	0.000451	0.000132
0.005261	0.002473	0.001195	0.000592	0.000300	0.000082
0.004047	0.001832	0.000853	0.000408	0.000200	0.000051
0.003113	0.001357	0.000609	0.000281	0.000133	0.000032
0.002394	0.001005	0.000435	0.000194	0.000089	0.000020
0.001842	0.000744	0.000311	0.000134	0.000059	0.000012
0.001417	0.000551	0.000222	0.000092	0.000039	0.000007
0.001090	0.000408	0.000158	0.000063	0.000026	0.000004
0.000838	0.000302	0.000113	0.000043	0.000017	0.000003
0.000645	0.000224	0.000080	0.000030	0.000011	0.000001
0.000496	0.000166	0.000057	0.000020	0.000007	0.000001
0.000381	0.000123	0.000041	0.000014	0.000005	0.000000
0.000293	0.000091	0.000029	0.000009	0.000003	0.000000
0.000225	0.000067	0.000021	0.000006	0.000002	0.000000
0.000173	0.000050	0.000015	0.000004	0.000001	0.000000
0.000133	0.000037	0.000010	0.000003	0.000001	0.000000
0.000102	0.000027	0.000007	0.000002	0.000000	0.000000
0.000079	0.000020	0.000005	0.000001	0.000000	0.000000
0.000060	0.000015	0.000003	0.000001	0.000000	0.000000
0.000046	0.000011	0.000002	0.000000	0.000000	0.000000
0.000035	0.000008	0.000001	0.000000	0.000000	0.000000
0.000027	0.000006	0.000001	0.000000	0.000000	0.000000
0.000021	0.000004	0.000001	0.000000	0.000000	0.000000
0.000016	0.000003	0.000000	0.000000	0.000000	0.000000
0.000012	0.000002	0.000000	0.000000	0.000000	0.000000
0.000009	0.000001	0.000000	0.000000	0.000000	0.000000
0.000007	0.000001	0.000000	0.000000	0.000000	0.000000
0.000005	0.000001	0.000000	0.000000	0.000000	0.000000
0.000004	0.000000	0.000000	0.000000	0.000000	0.000000
0.000003	0.000000	0.000000	0.000000	0.000000	0.000000
0.000002	0.000000	0.000000	0.000000	0.000000	0.000000
0.000002	0.000000	0.000000	0.000000	0.000000	0.000000

Table C.4
PRESENT VALUE OF ANNUITY

PERIOD	0.01	C.02	C.C3	C.C4	0.05	C.06
1	C.99CC	C.9803	C.97C8	C.9615	0.9523	0.9433
2	1.9703	1.9415	1.9134	1.8860	1.8594	1.8333
3	2.94C9	2.8838	2.8286	2.7750	2.7232	2.6730
4	3.9C19	3.8C77	3.717C	3.6298	3.5459	3.4651
5	4.8534	4.7134	4.5797	4.4518	4.3294	4.2123
6	5.7954	5.6014	5.4171	5.2421	5.0756	4.9173
7	6.7281	6.4719	6.2302	6.CC2C	5.7863	5.5823
8	7.6516	7.3254	7.C199	6.7327	6.4632	6.2C97
9	8.5660	8.1622	7.7861	7.4353	7.1C78	6.8016
10	9.4713	8.9825	8.5302	8.11C8	7.7217	7.3600
11	10.3676	9.7868	9.2526	8.76C4	8.3064	7.8868
12	11.2550	1C.5753	9.9540	9.3850	8.8632	8.3838
13	12.1337	11.3483	10.6349	9.9856	9.3935	8.8526
14	13.C037	12.1C62	11.2960	10.5631	9.8586	9.2949
15	13.8650	12.8492	11.9379	11.1183	1C.3796	9.7122
16	14.7178	13.5777	12.5611	11.6522	1C.8377	1C.1C58
17	15.5622	14.2918	13.1661	12.1656	11.2740	10.4772
18	16.3982	14.9920	13.7535	12.6592	11.6895	1C.8276
19	17.2260	15.6784	14.3237	13.1339	12.0853	11.1581
20	18.C455	16.3514	14.8774	13.59C3	12.4622	11.4699
21	18.8569	17.0112	15.4150	14.0291	12.8211	11.764C
22	19.66C3	17.6580	15.9369	14.4511	13.1630	12.0415
23	2C.4558	18.2922	16.4436	14.8568	13.4885	12.3C33
24	21.2433	18.9139	16.9355	15.2469	13.7986	12.5503
25	22.0231	19.5234	17.4131	15.6220	14.C939	12.7833
26	22.7952	20.1210	17.8768	15.9827	14.3751	13.CC31
27	23.5596	20.7C68	18.3270	16.3255	14.6430	13.2105
28	24.3164	21.2812	18.7641	16.6630	14.8981	13.4C61
29	25.0657	21.8443	19.1864	16.9837	15.1410	13.59C7
30	25.8077	22.3964	19.6004	17.2920	15.3724	13.7648
31	26.5422	22.9377	2C.CCC4	17.5884	15.5928	13.929C
32	27.2695	23.4683	20.3887	17.8735	15.8C26	14.C84C
33	27.9896	23.9885	2C.7657	18.1476	16.0C25	14.2302
34	28.7026	24.4985	21.1318	18.4111	16.1929	14.3681
35	29.4C85	24.9986	21.4872	18.6646	16.3741	14.4982
36	30.1075	25.4888	21.8322	18.9C82	16.5468	14.620S
37	30.7995	25.9694	22.1672	19.1425	16.7112	14.7367
38	31.4846	26.4406	22.4924	19.3678	16.8678	14.846C
39	32.1630	26.9C25	22.8C82	19.5844	17.0170	14.949C
40	32.8346	27.3554	23.1147	19.7927	17.1590	15.C46.
41	33.4996	27.7994	23.4123	19.9930	17.2943	15.138C
42	34.1581	28.2347	23.7013	20.1856	17.4232	15.2245
43	34.8100	28.6615	23.9819	20.37C7	17.5459	15.306
44	35.4554	29.C799	24.2542	20.5488	17.6627	15.3831
45	36.0945	29.4901	24.5187	20.72CC	17.7740	15.455∎
46	36.7272	29.8923	24.7754	20.8846	17.8800	15.524
47	37.3536	3C.2865	25.C247	21.C429	17.9810	15.589(
48	37.9739	30.6731	25.2667	21.1951	18.C771	15.650
49	38.5880	31.0520	25.5C16	21.3414	18.1687	15.7C7∎
50	39.1961	31.4236	25.7297	21.4821	18.2559	15.761.

0.07	0.08	0.09	0.10	0.11	0.12
0.9345	0.9259	0.9174	0.9090	0.9009	0.8928
1.8080	1.7832	1.7591	1.7355	1.7125	1.6900
2.6243	2.5770	2.5312	2.4868	2.4437	2.4018
3.3872	3.3121	3.2397	3.1698	3.1024	3.0373
4.1001	3.9927	3.8896	3.7907	3.6958	3.6047
4.7665	4.6228	4.4859	4.3552	4.2305	4.1114
5.3892	5.2063	5.0329	4.8684	4.7121	4.5637
5.9712	5.7466	5.5348	5.3349	5.1461	4.9676
6.5152	6.2468	5.9952	5.7590	5.5370	5.3282
7.0235	6.7100	6.4176	6.1445	5.8892	5.6502
7.4986	7.1389	6.8051	6.4950	6.2065	5.9376
7.9426	7.5360	7.1607	6.8136	6.4923	6.1943
8.3576	7.9037	7.4869	7.1033	6.7498	6.4235
8.7454	8.2442	7.7861	7.3666	6.9818	6.6281
9.1079	8.5594	8.0606	7.6060	7.1908	6.8108
9.4466	8.8513	8.3125	7.8237	7.3791	6.9739
9.7632	9.1216	8.5436	8.0215	7.5487	7.1196
10.0590	9.3718	8.7556	8.2014	7.7016	7.2496
10.3355	9.6035	8.9501	8.3649	7.8392	7.3657
10.5940	9.8181	9.1285	8.5135	7.9633	7.4694
10.8355	10.0168	9.2922	8.6486	8.0750	7.5620
11.0612	10.2007	9.4424	8.7715	8.1757	7.6446
11.2721	10.3710	9.5802	8.8832	8.2664	7.7184
11.4693	10.5287	9.7066	8.9847	8.3481	7.7843
11.6535	10.6747	9.8225	9.0770	8.4217	7.8431
11.8257	10.8099	9.9289	9.1609	8.4880	7.8956
11.9867	10.9351	10.0265	9.2372	8.5478	7.9425
12.1371	11.0510	10.1161	9.3065	8.6016	7.9844
12.2776	11.1584	10.1982	9.3696	8.6501	8.0218
12.4090	11.2577	10.2736	9.4269	8.6937	8.0551
12.5318	11.3497	10.3428	9.4790	8.7331	8.0849
12.6465	11.4349	10.4062	9.5263	8.7686	8.1115
12.7537	11.5138	10.4644	9.5694	8.8005	8.1353
12.8540	11.5869	10.5178	9.6085	8.8293	8.1565
12.9476	11.6545	10.5668	9.6441	8.8552	8.1755
13.0352	11.7171	10.6117	9.6765	8.8785	8.1924
13.1170	11.7751	10.6529	9.7059	8.8996	8.2075
13.1934	11.8288	10.6908	9.7326	8.9185	8.2209
13.2649	11.8785	10.7255	9.7569	8.9356	8.2330
13.3317	11.9246	10.7573	9.7790	8.9510	8.2437
13.3941	11.9672	10.7865	9.7991	8.9649	8.2533
13.4524	12.0066	10.8133	9.8173	8.9773	8.2619
13.5069	12.0432	10.8379	9.8339	8.9886	8.2695
13.5579	12.0770	10.8605	9.8490	8.9987	8.2764
13.6055	12.1084	10.8811	9.8628	9.0079	8.2825
13.6500	12.1374	10.9001	9.8752	9.0161	8.2879
13.6916	12.1642	10.9175	9.8866	9.0235	8.2928
13.7304	12.1891	10.9335	9.8969	9.0302	8.2971
13.7667	12.2121	10.9482	9.9062	9.0362	8.3010
13.8007	12.2334	10.9616	9.9148	9.0416	8.3044

PRESENT VALUE OF ANNUITY

PERIOD	0.13	C.14	C.15	0.16	0.17
1	C.8849	C.8771	0.8695	0.8620	0.8547
2	1.6681	1.6466	1.6257	1.6052	1.5852
3	2.3611	2.3216	2.2832	2.2458	2.2095
4	2.9744	2.9137	2.8549	2.7981	2.7432
5	3.5172	3.4330	3.3521	3.2742	3.1993
6	3.9975	3.8886	3.7844	3.6847	3.5891
7	4.4226	4.2883	4.1604	4.0385	3.9223
8	4.7987	4.6388	4.4873	4.3435	4.2071
9	5.1316	4.9463	4.7715	4.6065	4.4505
10	5.4262	5.2161	5.0187	4.8332	4.6586
11	5.6869	5.4527	5.2337	5.0286	4.8364
12	5.9176	5.6602	5.4206	5.1971	4.9883
13	6.1218	5.8423	5.5831	5.3423	5.1182
14	6.3024	6.0020	5.7244	5.4675	5.2292
15	6.4623	6.1421	5.8473	5.5754	5.3241
16	6.6038	6.2650	5.9542	5.6684	5.4052
17	6.7290	6.3728	6.0471	5.7487	5.4746
18	6.8399	6.4674	6.1279	5.8178	5.5338
19	6.9379	6.5503	6.1982	5.8774	5.5844
20	7.0247	6.6231	6.2593	5.9288	5.6277
21	7.1015	6.6869	6.3124	5.9731	5.6647
22	7.1695	6.7429	6.3586	6.0113	5.6963
23	7.2296	6.7920	6.3988	6.0442	5.7233
24	7.2828	6.8351	6.4337	6.0726	5.7464
25	7.3299	6.8729	6.4641	6.0970	5.7662
26	7.3716	6.9060	6.4905	6.1181	5.7831
27	7.4085	6.9351	6.5135	6.1363	5.7975
28	7.4411	6.9606	6.5335	6.1520	5.8098
29	7.4700	6.9830	6.5508	6.1655	5.8203
30	7.4956	7.0026	6.5659	6.1771	5.8293
31	7.5182	7.0198	6.5791	6.1872	5.8370
32	7.5382	7.0349	6.5905	6.1958	5.8436
33	7.5560	7.0482	6.6004	6.2033	5.8492
34	7.5716	7.0598	6.6090	6.2097	5.8540
35	7.5855	7.0700	6.6166	6.2153	5.8581
36	7.5978	7.0789	6.6231	6.2201	5.8617
37	7.6087	7.0868	6.6288	6.2242	5.8647
38	7.6183	7.0937	6.6337	6.2277	5.8672
39	7.6268	7.0997	6.6380	6.2308	5.8694
40	7.6343	7.1050	6.6417	6.2334	5.8713
41	7.6410	7.1096	6.6450	6.2357	5.8729
42	7.6469	7.1137	6.6478	6.2377	5.8743
43	7.6521	7.1173	6.6503	6.2394	5.8754
44	7.6567	7.1204	6.6524	6.2408	5.8764
45	7.6608	7.1232	6.6542	6.2421	5.8773
46	7.6644	7.1256	6.6559	6.2432	5.8780
47	7.6676	7.1277	6.6573	6.2441	5.8786
48	7.6705	7.1296	6.6585	6.2449	5.8792
49	7.6730	7.1312	6.6595	6.2456	5.8796
50	7.6752	7.1326	6.6605	6.2462	5.8800

0.18	0.19	0.20	0.21	0.22	0.23	0.24
0.8474	0.8403	0.8333	0.8264	0.8196	0.8130	0.8064
1.5656	1.5465	1.5277	1.5094	1.4915	1.4739	1.4568
2.1742	2.1399	2.1064	2.0739	2.0422	2.0113	1.9813
2.6900	2.6385	2.5887	2.5404	2.4936	2.4482	2.4042
3.1271	3.0576	2.9906	2.9259	2.8636	2.8034	2.7453
3.4576	3.4097	3.3255	3.2446	3.1669	3.0922	3.0204
3.8115	3.7056	3.6045	3.5079	3.4155	3.3270	3.2423
4.0775	3.9543	3.8371	3.7255	3.6192	3.5179	3.4212
4.3030	4.1633	4.0309	3.9054	3.7862	3.6731	3.5655
4.4940	4.3389	4.1924	4.0540	3.9231	3.7992	3.6818
4.6560	4.4864	4.3270	4.1769	4.0353	3.9018	3.7756
4.7932	4.6105	4.4392	4.2784	4.1273	3.9852	3.8513
4.9095	4.7147	4.5326	4.3623	4.2027	4.0530	3.9123
5.0080	4.8022	4.6105	4.4316	4.2645	4.1081	3.9616
5.0915	4.8758	4.6754	4.4890	4.3152	4.1529	4.0012
5.1623	4.9376	4.7295	4.5363	4.3567	4.1894	4.0333
5.2223	4.9896	4.7746	4.5755	4.3907	4.2190	4.0591
5.2731	5.0333	4.8121	4.6078	4.4186	4.2431	4.0799
5.3162	5.0700	4.8434	4.6345	4.4415	4.2626	4.0967
5.3527	5.1008	4.8695	4.6566	4.4602	4.2786	4.1102
5.3836	5.1267	4.8913	4.6749	4.4756	4.2915	4.1211
5.4099	5.1485	4.9094	4.6900	4.4882	4.3020	4.1299
5.4321	5.1668	4.9245	4.7025	4.4985	4.3106	4.1370
5.4509	5.1822	4.9371	4.7128	4.5070	4.3175	4.1428
5.4669	5.1951	4.9475	4.7213	4.5139	4.3232	4.1474
5.4804	5.2060	4.9563	4.7283	4.5196	4.3278	4.1511
5.4918	5.2151	4.9636	4.7341	4.5242	4.3315	4.1541
5.5016	5.2227	4.9696	4.7390	4.5280	4.3346	4.1565
5.5098	5.2292	4.9747	4.7429	4.5312	4.3370	4.1585
5.5168	5.2346	4.9789	4.7462	4.5337	4.3390	4.1601
5.5227	5.2392	4.9824	4.7489	4.5358	4.3407	4.1613
5.5277	5.2430	4.9853	4.7512	4.5376	4.3420	4.1623
5.5319	5.2462	4.9878	4.7530	4.5390	4.3431	4.1632
5.5355	5.2489	4.9898	4.7546	4.5401	4.3440	4.1638
5.5386	5.2512	4.9915	4.7558	4.5411	4.3447	4.1644
5.5412	5.2531	4.9929	4.7569	4.5419	4.3453	4.1648
5.5433	5.2547	4.9941	4.7577	4.5425	4.3457	4.1652
5.5452	5.2560	4.9951	4.7585	4.5430	4.3461	4.1654
5.5468	5.2572	4.9959	4.7590	4.5435	4.3464	4.1657
5.5481	5.2581	4.9965	4.7595	4.5438	4.3467	4.1659
5.5492	5.2589	4.9971	4.7599	4.5441	4.3469	4.1660
5.5502	5.2596	4.9976	4.7603	4.5443	4.3470	4.1661
5.5510	5.2601	4.9980	4.7605	4.5445	4.3472	4.1662
5.5517	5.2606	4.9983	4.7608	4.5447	4.3473	4.1663
5.5523	5.2610	4.9986	4.7610	4.5448	4.3474	4.1664
5.5528	5.2613	4.9988	4.7611	4.5449	4.3475	4.1664
5.5532	5.2616	4.9990	4.7612	4.5450	4.3475	4.1664
5.5535	5.2619	4.9992	4.7613	4.5451	4.3476	4.1665
5.5538	5.2621	4.9993	4.7614	4.5451	4.3476	4.1665
5.5541	5.2622	4.9994	4.7615	4.5452	4.3476	4.1665

PRESENT VALUE OF ANNUITY

PERIOD	0.25	0.26	0.27	0.28	0.29
1	0.8000	0.7936	0.7874	0.7812	0.7751
2	1.4400	1.4235	1.4074	1.3916	1.3761
3	1.9520	1.9234	1.8955	1.8684	1.8419
4	2.3616	2.3201	2.2799	2.2409	2.2030
5	2.6892	2.6350	2.5826	2.5320	2.4829
6	2.9514	2.8849	2.8210	2.7593	2.6999
7	3.1611	3.0833	3.0086	2.9370	2.8682
8	3.3289	3.2407	3.1564	3.0757	2.9986
9	3.4631	3.3656	3.2727	3.1842	3.0997
10	3.5705	3.4648	3.3643	3.2689	3.1780
11	3.6564	3.5434	3.4365	3.3350	3.2388
12	3.7251	3.6059	3.4933	3.3867	3.2858
13	3.7800	3.6555	3.5380	3.4271	3.3224
14	3.8240	3.6948	3.5732	3.4587	3.3506
15	3.8592	3.7260	3.6010	3.4833	3.3726
16	3.8874	3.7508	3.6228	3.5026	3.3896
17	3.9099	3.7705	3.6400	3.5176	3.4028
18	3.9279	3.7861	3.6535	3.5294	3.4130
19	3.9423	3.7985	3.6642	3.5386	3.4209
20	3.9538	3.8083	3.6726	3.5458	3.4271
21	3.9631	3.8161	3.6792	3.5514	3.4318
22	3.9704	3.8223	3.6844	3.5557	3.4355
23	3.9763	3.8272	3.6885	3.5592	3.4384
24	3.9811	3.8311	3.6917	3.5618	3.4406
25	3.9848	3.8342	3.6942	3.5639	3.4423
26	3.9879	3.8367	3.6962	3.5656	3.4436
27	3.9903	3.8386	3.6978	3.5668	3.4447
28	3.9922	3.8402	3.6991	3.5678	3.4455
29	3.9938	3.8414	3.7000	3.5686	3.4461
30	3.9950	3.8424	3.7008	3.5692	3.4466
31	3.9960	3.8431	3.7014	3.5697	3.4469
32	3.9968	3.8437	3.7019	3.5701	3.4472
33	3.9974	3.8442	3.7023	3.5703	3.4475
34	3.9979	3.8446	3.7026	3.5706	3.4476
35	3.9983	3.8449	3.7028	3.5707	3.4478
36	3.9987	3.8452	3.7030	3.5709	3.4479
37	3.9989	3.8454	3.7031	3.5710	3.4479
38	3.9991	3.8455	3.7032	3.5711	3.4480
39	3.9993	3.8456	3.7033	3.5711	3.4481
40	3.9994	3.8457	3.7034	3.5712	3.4481
41	3.9995	3.8458	3.7034	3.5712	3.4481
42	3.9996	3.8459	3.7035	3.5713	3.4481
43	3.9997	3.8459	3.7035	3.5713	3.4482
44	3.9997	3.8460	3.7036	3.5713	3.4482
45	3.9998	3.8460	3.7036	3.5713	3.4482
46	3.9998	3.8460	3.7036	3.5713	3.4482
47	3.9998	3.8460	3.7036	3.5713	3.4482
48	3.9999	3.8460	3.7036	3.5714	3.4482
49	3.9999	3.8461	3.7036	3.5714	3.4482
50	3.9999	3.8461	3.7036	3.5714	3.4482

0.30	0.35	0.40	0.45	0.50	0.60
0.7692	0.7407	0.7142	0.6896	0.6666	0.6249
1.3609	1.2894	1.2244	1.1652	1.1111	1.0156
1.8161	1.6958	1.5889	1.4932	1.4074	1.2597
2.1662	1.9969	1.8492	1.7195	1.6049	1.4123
2.4355	2.2199	2.0351	1.8755	1.7366	1.5077
2.6427	2.3851	2.1679	1.9831	1.8244	1.5673
2.8021	2.5075	2.2628	2.0573	1.8829	1.6045
2.9247	2.5981	2.3305	2.1085	1.9219	1.6278
3.0190	2.6653	2.3789	2.1437	1.9479	1.6424
3.0915	2.7150	2.4135	2.1681	1.9653	1.6515
3.1473	2.7518	2.4382	2.1849	1.9768	1.6571
3.1902	2.7791	2.4559	2.1964	1.9845	1.6607
3.2232	2.7993	2.4685	2.2044	1.9897	1.6629
3.2486	2.8143	2.4775	2.2099	1.9931	1.6643
3.2682	2.8254	2.4839	2.2137	1.9954	1.6652
3.2832	2.8336	2.4885	2.2164	1.9969	1.6657
3.2947	2.8397	2.4918	2.2182	1.9979	1.6661
3.3036	2.8442	2.4941	2.2194	1.9986	1.6663
3.3105	2.8476	2.4958	2.2203	1.9990	1.6664
3.3157	2.8500	2.4970	2.2209	1.9993	1.6665
3.3198	2.8519	2.4978	2.2213	1.9995	1.6665
3.3229	2.8532	2.4984	2.2215	1.9997	1.6666
3.3253	2.8542	2.4989	2.2217	1.9998	1.6666
3.3271	2.8550	2.4992	2.2219	1.9998	1.6666
3.3286	2.8555	2.4994	2.2220	1.9999	1.6666
3.3296	2.8559	2.4996	2.2220	1.9999	1.6666
3.3305	2.8562	2.4997	2.2221	1.9999	1.6666
3.3311	2.8565	2.4997	2.2221	1.9999	1.6666
3.3316	2.8566	2.4998	2.2221	1.9999	1.6666
3.3320	2.8567	2.4998	2.2221	1.9999	1.6666
3.3323	2.8568	2.4999	2.2222	1.9999	1.6666
3.3325	2.8569	2.4999	2.2222	1.9999	1.6666
3.3327	2.8569	2.4999	2.2222	1.9999	1.6666
3.3328	2.8570	2.4999	2.2222	1.9999	1.6666
3.3329	2.8570	2.4999	2.2222	1.9999	1.6666
3.3330	2.8570	2.4999	2.2222	1.9999	1.6666
3.3331	2.8570	2.4999	2.2222	1.9999	1.6666
3.3331	2.8571	2.4999	2.2222	1.9999	1.6666
3.3332	2.8571	2.4999	2.2222	1.9999	1.6666
3.3332	2.8571	2.4999	2.2222	1.9999	1.6666
3.3332	2.8571	2.4999	2.2222	1.9999	1.6666
3.3332	2.8571	2.4999	2.2222	1.9999	1.6666
3.3332	2.8571	2.4999	2.2222	1.9999	1.6666
3.3333	2.8571	2.4999	2.2222	1.9999	1.6666
3.3333	2.8571	2.4999	2.2222	1.9999	1.6666
3.3333	2.8571	2.4999	2.2222	1.9999	1.6666
3.3333	2.8571	2.4999	2.2222	1.9999	1.6666
3.3333	2.8571	2.4999	2.2222	1.9999	1.6666
3.3333	2.8571	2.4999	2.2222	1.9999	1.6666
3.3333	2.8571	2.4999	2.2222	1.9999	1.6666

TABLE C.5
AREAS UNDER THE NORMAL CURVE

Example

$$Z = \frac{X - \mu}{\sigma}$$

$P[Z > 1] = .1587$

$P[Z > 1.96] = .0250$

Normal Deviate Z	.00	.01	.02	.03	.04	.05	.06	.07	.08	.09
0.0	.5000	.4960	.4920	.4880	.4840	.4801	.4761	.4721	.4681	.4641
0.1	.4602	.4562	.4522	.4483	.4443	.4404	.4364	.4325	.4286	.4247
0.2	.4207	.4168	.4129	.4090	.4052	.4013	.3974	.3936	.3897	.3859
0.3	.3821	.3783	.3745	.3707	.3669	.3632	.3594	.3557	.3520	.3483
0.4	.3446	.3409	.3372	.3336	.3300	.3264	.3228	.3192	.3156	.3121
0.5	.3085	.3050	.3015	.2981	.2946	.2912	.2877	.2843	.2810	.2776
0.6	.2743	.2709	.2676	.2643	.2611	.2578	.2546	.2514	.2483	.2451
0.7	.2420	.2389	.2358	.2327	.2296	.2266	.2236	.2206	.2177	.2148
0.8	.2119	.2090	.2061	.2033	.2005	.1977	.1949	.1922	.1894	.1867
0.9	.1841	.1814	.1788	.1762	.1736	.1711	.1685	.1660	.1635	.1611
1.0	.1587	.1562	.1539	.1515	.1492	.1469	.1446	.1423	.1401	.1379
1.1	.1357	.1335	.1314	.1292	.1271	.1251	.1230	.1210	.1190	.1170
1.2	.1151	.1131	.1112	.1093	.1075	.1056	.1038	.1020	.1003	.0985
1.3	.0968	.0951	.0934	.0918	.0901	.0885	.0869	.0853	.0838	.0823
1.4	.0808	.0793	.0778	.0764	.0749	.0735	.0721	.0708	.0694	.0681
1.5	.0668	.0655	.0643	.0630	.0618	.0606	.0594	.0582	.0571	.0559
1.6	.0548	.0537	.0526	.0516	.0505	.0495	.0485	.0475	.0465	.0455
1.7	.0446	.0436	.0427	.0418	.0409	.0401	.0392	.0384	.0375	.0367
1.8	.0359	.0351	.0344	.0336	.0329	.0322	.0314	.0307	.0301	.0294
1.9	.0287	.0281	.0274	.0268	.0262	.0256	.0250	.0244	.0239	.0233
2.0	.0228	.0222	.0217	.0212	.0207	.0202	.0197	.0192	.0188	.0183
2.1	.0179	.0174	.0170	.0166	.0162	.0158	.0154	.0150	.0146	.0143
2.2	.0139	.0136	.0132	.0129	.0125	.0122	.0119	.0116	.0113	.0110
2.3	.0107	.0104	.0102	.0099	.0096	.0094	.0091	.0089	.0087	.0084
2.4	.0082	.0080	.0078	.0075	.0073	.0071	.0069	.0068	.0066	.0064
2.5	.0062	.0060	.0059	.0057	.0055	.0054	.0997	.0051	.0049	.0048
2.6	.0047	.0045	.0044	.0043	.0041	.0040	.0039	.0038	.0037	.0036
2.7	.0035	.0034	.0033	.0032	.0031	.0030	.0029	.0028	.0027	.0026
2.8	.0026	.0025	.0024	.0023	.0023	.0022	.0021	.0021	.0020	.0019
2.9	.0019	.0018	.0018	.0017	.0016	.0016	.0015	.0015	.0014	.0014
3.0	.0013	.0013	.0013	.0012	.0012	.0011	.0011	.0011	.0010	.0010

Source: "Areas Under the Normal Curve" in STATISTICS: AN INTRO-
DUCTORY ANALYSIS, 2nd Edition by Taro Yamane. (Harper & Row, 1967).
Reprinted by permission of the publishers.

TABLE C.6

TABLE OF LOGARITHMS TO BASE 10

N	0	1	2	3	4	5	6	7	8	9	1	2	3	4	5
												P. P.			
10	0000	0043	0086	0128	0170	0212	0253	0294	0334	0374	4	8	12	17	21
11	0414	0453	0492	0531	0569	0607	0645	0682	0719	0755	4	8	11	15	19
12	0792	0828	0864	0899	0934	0969	1004	1038	1072	1106	3	7	10	14	17
13	1139	1173	1206	1239	1271	1303	1335	1367	1399	1430	3	6	10	13	16
14	1461	1492	1523	1553	1584	1614	1644	1673	1703	1732	3	6	9	12	15
15	1761	1790	1818	1847	1875	1903	1931	1959	1987	2014	3	6	8	11	14
16	2041	2068	2095	2122	2148	2175	2201	2227	2253	2279	3	5	8	11	13
17	2304	2330	2355	2380	2405	2430	2455	2480	2504	2529	2	5	7	10	12
18	2553	2577	2601	2625	2648	2672	2695	2718	2742	2765	2	5	7	9	12
19	2788	2810	2833	2856	2878	2900	2923	2945	2967	2989	2	4	7	9	11
20	3010	3032	3054	3075	3096	3118	3139	3160	3181	3201	2	4	6	8	11
21	3222	3243	3263	3284	3304	3324	3345	3365	3385	3404	2	4	6	8	10
22	3424	3444	3464	3483	3502	3522	3541	3560	3579	3598	2	4	6	8	10
23	3617	3636	3655	3674	3692	3711	3729	3747	3766	3784	2	4	5	7	9
24	3802	3820	3838	3856	3874	3892	3909	3927	3945	3962	2	4	5	7	9
25	3979	3997	4014	4031	4048	4065	4082	4099	4116	4133	2	3	5	7	9
26	4150	4166	4183	4200	4216	4232	4249	4265	4281	4298	2	3	5	7	8
27	4314	4330	4346	4362	4378	4393	4409	4425	4440	4456	2	3	5	6	8
28	4472	4487	4502	4518	4533	4548	4564	4579	4594	4609	2	3	5	6	8
29	4624	4639	4654	4669	4683	4698	4713	4728	4742	4757	1	3	4	6	7
30	4771	4786	4800	4814	4829	4843	4857	4871	4886	4900	1	3	4	6	7
31	4914	4928	4942	4955	4969	4983	4997	5011	5024	5038	1	3	4	6	7
32	5051	5065	5079	5092	5105	5119	5132	5145	5159	5172	1	3	4	5	7
33	5185	5198	5211	5224	5237	5250	5263	5276	5289	5302	1	3	4	5	6
34	5315	5328	5340	5353	5366	5378	5391	5403	5416	5428	1	3	4	5	6
35	5441	5453	5465	5478	5490	5502	5514	5527	5539	5551	1	2	4	5	6
36	5563	5575	5587	5599	5611	5623	5635	5647	5658	5670	1	2	4	5	6
37	5682	5694	5705	5717	5729	5740	5752	5763	5775	5786	1	2	3	5	6
38	5798	5809	5821	5832	5843	5855	5866	5877	5888	5899	1	2	3	5	6
39	5911	5922	5933	5944	5955	5966	5977	5988	5999	6010	1	2	3	4	6
40	6021	6031	6042	6053	6064	6075	6085	6096	6107	6117	1	2	3	4	5
41	6128	6138	6149	6160	6170	6180	6191	6201	6212	6222	1	2	3	4	5
42	6232	6243	6253	6263	6274	6284	6294	6304	6314	6325	1	2	3	4	5
43	6335	6345	6355	6365	6375	6385	6395	6405	6415	6425	1	2	3	4	5
44	6435	6444	6454	6464	6474	6484	6493	6503	6513	6522	1	2	3	4	5
45	6532	6542	6551	6561	6571	6580	6590	6599	6609	6618	1	2	3	4	5
46	6628	6637	6646	6656	6665	6675	6684	6693	6702	6712	1	2	3	4	5
47	6721	6730	6739	6749	6758	6767	6776	6785	6794	6803	1	2	3	4	5
48	6812	6821	6830	6839	6848	6857	6866	6875	6884	6893	1	2	3	4	4
49	6902	6911	6920	6928	6937	6946	6955	6964	6972	6981	1	2	3	4	4
50	6990	6998	7007	7016	7024	7033	7042	7050	7059	7067	1	2	3	3	4
51	7076	7084	7093	7101	7110	7118	7126	7135	7143	7152	1	2	3	3	4
52	7160	7168	7177	7185	7193	7202	7210	7218	7226	7235	1	2	2	3	4
53	7243	7251	7259	7267	7275	7284	7292	7300	7308·	7316	1	2	2	3	4
54	7324	7332	7340	7348	7356	7364	7372	7380	7388	7396	1	2	2	3	4

NOTE: $\log_e N = \log_e 10 \log_{10} N = 2.3026 \log_{10} N$

$\log_{10} e^x = x \log_{10} e = 0.43429x$

N	0	1	2	3	4	5	6	7	8	9	P. P. 1	2	3	4	5
55	7404	7412	7419	7427	7435	7443	7451	7459	7466	7474	1	2	2	3	4
56	7482	7490	7497	7505	7513	7520	7528	7536	7543	7551	1	2	2	3	4
57	7559	7566	7574	7582	7589	7597	7604	7612	7619	7627	1	2	2	3	4
58	7634	7642	7649	7657	7664	7672	7679	7686	7694	7701	1	1	2	3	4
59	7709	7716	7723	7731	7738	7745	7752	7760	7767	7774	1	1	2	3	4
60	7782	7789	7796	7803	7810	7818	7825	7832	7839	7846	1	1	2	3	4
61	7853	7860	7868	7875	7882	7889	7896	7903	7910	7917	1	1	2	3	4
62	7924	7931	7938	7945	7952	7959	7966	7973	7980	7987	1	1	2	3	3
63	7993	8000	8007	8014	8021	8028	8035	8041	8048	8055	1	1	2	3	3
64	8062	8069	8075	8082	8089	8096	8102	8109	8116	8122	1	1	2	3	3
65	8129	8136	8142	8149	8156	8162	8169	8176	8182	8189	1	1	2	3	3
66	8195	8202	8209	8215	8222	8228	8235	8241	8248	8254	1	1	2	3	3
67	8261	8267	8274	8280	8287	8293	8299	8306	8312	8319	1	1	2	3	3
68	8325	8331	8338	8344	8351	8357	8363	8370	8376	8382	1	1	2	3	3
69	8388	8395	8401	8407	8414	8420	8426	8432	8439	8445	1	1	2	3	3
70	8451	8457	8463	8470	8476	8482	8488	8494	8500	8506	1	1	2	2	3
71	8513	8519	8525	8531	8537	8543	8549	8555	8561	8567	1	1	2	2	3
72	8573	8579	8585	8591	8597	8603	8609	8615	8621	8627	1	1	2	2	3
73	8633	8639	8645	8651	8657	8663	8669	8675	8681	8686	1	1	2	2	3
74	8692	8698	8704	8710	8716	8722	8727	8733	8739	8745	1	1	2	2	3
75	8751	8756	8762	8768	8774	8779	8785	8791	8797	8802	1	1	2	2	3
76	8808	8814	8820	8825	8831	8837	8842	8848	8854	8859	1	1	2	2	3
77	8865	8871	8876	8882	8887	8893	8899	8904	8910	8915	1	1	2	2	3
78	8921	8927	8932	8938	8943	8949	8954	8960	8965	8971	1	1	2	2	3
79	8976	8982	8987	8993	8998	9004	9009	9015	9020	9025	1	1	2	2	3
80	9031	9036	9042	9047	9053	9058	9063	9069	9074	9079	1	1	2	2	3
81	9085	9090	9096	9101	9106	9112	9117	9122	9128	9133	1	1	2	2	3
82	9138	9143	9149	9154	9159	9165	9170	9175	9180	9186	1	1	2	2	3
83	9191	9196	9201	9206	9212	9217	9222	9227	9232	9238	1	1	2	2	3
84	9243	9248	9253	9258	9263	9269	9274	9279	9284	9289	1	1	2	2	3
85	9294	9299	9304	9309	9315	9320	9325	9330	9335	9340	1	1	2	2	3
86	9345	9350	9355	9360	9365	9370	9375	9380	9385	9390	1	1	2	2	3
87	9395	9400	9405	9410	9415	9420	9425	9430	9435	9440	0	1	1	2	2
88	9445	9450	9455	9460	9465	9469	9474	9479	9484	9489	0	1	1	2	2
89	9494	9499	9504	9509	9513	9518	9523	9528	9533	9538	0	1	1	2	2
90	9542	9547	9552	9557	9562	9566	9571	9576	9581	9586	0	1	1	2	2
91	9590	9595	9600	9605	9609	9614	9619	9624	9628	9633	0	1	1	2	2
92	9638	9643	9647	9652	9657	9661	9666	9671	9675	9680	0	1	1	2	2
93	9685	9689	9694	9699	9703	9708	9713	9717	9722	9727	0	1	1	2	2
94	9731	9736	9741	9745	9750	9754	9759	9763	9768	9773	0	1	1	2	2
95	9777	9782	9786	9791	9795	9800	9805	9809	9814	9818	0	1	1	2	2
96	9823	9827	9832	9836	9841	9845	9850	9854	9859	9863	0	1	1	2	2
97	9868	9872	9877	9881	9886	9890	9894	9899	9903	9908	0	1	1	2	2
98	9912	9917	9921	9926	9930	9934	9939	9943	9948	9952	0	1	1	2	2
99	9956	9961	9965	9969	9974	9978	9983	9987	9991	9996	0	1	1	2	2

Index